The Meaning of Democracy
and the
Vulnerability of Democracies

The Meaning of Democracy and the Vulnerability of Democracies

A Response to Tocqueville's Challenge

Vincent Ostrom

Ann Arbor

THE UNIVERSITY OF MICHIGAN PRESS

Copyright © by the University of Michigan 1997
All rights reserved
Published in the United States of America by
The University of Michigan Press
Manufactured in the United States of America
⊗ Printed on acid-free paper

2009   2008   2007   2006   6   5   4   3

A CIP catalog record for this book is available from the British Library.

Library of Congress Cataloging-in-Publication Data

Ostrom, Vincent, 1919–
      The meaning of democracy and the vulnerability of democracies : a
   response to Tocqueville's challenge / Vincent Ostrom.
         p.   cm.
      Includes bibliographical references and index.
      ISBN 0-472-10797-6 (cloth : acid-free paper). — ISBN
   0-472-08456-9 (pbk. : acid-free paper)
      1. Democracy.   I. Title.
   JC423.O8   1997
   321.8—dc21   96-51299
                                                                          CIP

   ISBN 978-0-472-10797-1 (cloth : acid-free paper)
   ISBN 978-0-472-08456-2 (pbk. : acid-free paper)

*To students, colleagues, and fellow citizens
with whom I have been privileged to work
and who have contributed so much to
my own search for understanding*

The universal creative rondo revolves on people and stories. *People create stories create people;* or rather, *stories create people create stories.* Was it stories first and then people, or the other way round? Most creation myths would seem to suggest the antecedence of stories—a scenario in which the story was already unfolding in the cosmos before, and even as a result of which, man came into being.

—Chinua Achebe 1988

If language is incorrect, then what is said does not concord with what was meant; and if what is said does not concord with what was meant, what is to be done cannot be effected.

—Confucius

The twentieth century will open the age of federalism, or else humanity will undergo another purgatory of a thousand years.

—Pierre-Joseph Proudhon 1863

It is odd indeed to see that twentieth-century American even more than European learned opinion is often inclined to interpret the American Revolution in the light of the French Revolution, or to criticize it because it so obviously did not conform to lessons learned from the latter. The sad truth of the matter is that the French Revolution, which ended in disaster, has made world history, while the American Revolution, so triumphantly successful, has remained an event of little more than local importance.

What the men of the Russian Revolution had learned from the French Revolution—and this learning constituted almost their entire preparation—was history and not action.

. . . they were fooled by history, and they have become the fools of history.

—Hannah Arendt 1965

Democratization is a colossal restructuring of the mentality.

—Alexander Lebed, *Wall Street Journal,* November 20, 1996

Preface

Orientation

This inquiry is concerned with a puzzle that has persisted throughout my politically aware lifetime: What does it mean to live in a democratic society? Unfortunately, that puzzle is bound up with questions that are not easily resolved and that ultimately turn on mysteries about the nature of life and existence that cannot be resolved in a definitive way. As a result, what it means to live in a democratic society accrues as much from coping with threats to democratic ways of life as it does by being intentionally concerned about the constitution and viability of democratic societies. Understanding the vulnerability of democracies is necessary to realizing democratic potentials.

My own experience with what it means to live in a democratic society was first stirred by the Great Depression in the United States and by events in Europe concerning Germany and Spain, Italy and Ethiopia, developments in the Soviet Union, events in Asia with regard to Japan and China, and the cataclysm of World War II. Those concerns were sharpened as fundamental intellectual issues by a challenge from a teacher who, as a devoted student of Machiavelli's *Prince,* conceptualized "politics" as "getting what you want and making other people like it." William Riker in *The Art of Manipulation* later expressed the same idea: "Structuring the world so you can win" (1986, ix). Politics from that perspective is an art of manipulation devoted to making a political system work to one's advantage.

I could not accept the moral connotations of Machiavelli's *Prince* set against the background of disputation about ideas associated with systems of government then called communism, fascism, imperialism, socialism, capitalism, and democracy. All of this was too much for me to comprehend with a deep and abiding commitment, which I drew from John Dewey, that a "political science" should relate theory to practice, hypotheses to consequences, or, equivalently, ideas to deeds. Success in the art of manipulation posed a potential threat to the viability of democracies.

My effort to engage that struggle has proceeded over a period of some sixty years, since my adolescence. I have learned to appreciate that a focus on problems of public administration is an essential way to tie theory to practice. I have only gradually become aware that what I viewed as a basic paradigm problem in *The Intellectual Crisis in American Public Administration* ([1973] 1989) reached more deeply into the constitution of order in democratic societies than what applies to public affairs narrowly construed. This awareness was deepened as I slowly learned how to read not just the words but the larger message in the second volume of Alexis de Tocqueville's *Democracy in America* and to appreciate more fully its concern about the vulnerability of democracies. It is within families and other institutional arrangements characteristic of neighborhood, village, and community life that citizenship is learned and practiced for most people most of the time. The first order of priority in learning the craft of citizenship as applied to public affairs needs to focus on how to cope with problems in the context of family, neighborhood, village, and community. This is where people acquire the rudiments for becoming self-governing, by learning how to live and work with others.

Patterns of interaction in the modern world reach to global proportions and get bound up with Nation-States and State-to-State relationships. A theory of sovereignty is presumed to prevail in which each State is governed by some single center of Supreme Authority, autonomous with regard to its own internal affairs and independent of each other State. Such conceptions leave open opportunities for States to war on one another. Those vested with Supreme Authority are also able to use their control over instruments of violence to exploit and war on their own subjects. The ruler-ruled relationship implies dominance, if rulers cannot be effectively challenged, and obedience. Such ways of conceptualizing order in human societies are, in my judgment, clearly inadequate for developing democratic ways of life consistent with a lawful existence. Democracies are rendered vulnerable by theories of sovereign Nation-States.

Coming to terms with what it means to live in democratic societies requires one who has been devoted to a study of political science to reflect critically on a lifetime of inquiry. Such an inquiry is as much a memoir bearing witness to the place of fundamental beliefs as it is a theoretical inquiry. I hope that the unfolding chapters in this intellectual journey are a helpful way to clarify basic theoretical problems about the relationship of the cultural and social sciences and humanities to what it means to live in democratic societies and to resolve Tocqueville's puzzle about whether democratic societies are viable forms of civilization.

A Note on My Own Use of Language

I am a dweller in Plato's Cave who cannot see the direct light of Truth. I must rely on the ambiguities of language—that "cloudy medium" through which we must communicate. Every word is an abstraction that stands for some set of referents. There are, moreover, tendencies to rely on language conventions that are necessarily inaccurate. The concept *mankind* refers not to male-kind or to female-kind but to both. Every language has these problems. The German language uses the term *Mädchen* to refer to a young woman, but it is expressed in the neuter gender and applies to a period of life that is highly sensitive to distinctions of gender. I do not follow the conventions of some scholars in which all actors are associated with pronouns of the feminine gender. This I view as no improvement over using the standard convention of the English language, even though I regret the difficulty in making accurate distinctions. We inevitably must assume the burden of compensating for regrettable inadequacies that are built into the conventions of language.

When I use brackets within sentences or quotations, I am supplying information or suggesting a connotation that applies to the way a term is being used in a particular context. Such usages are especially important in the treatment of Harold Lasswell's terminology in chapter 2. Lasswell introduced a technical language of discourse that he used with great care in his own work as a political scientist and with colleagues with whom he worked. I learned to appreciate the importance of the careful use of language in political discourse from Robert Agger and Dwaine Marvick, who were careful and devoted students of Lasswell.

I have some reservations about current tendencies to reduce the capitalization of nouns to a very minimum, largely confined to proper names. There are circumstances where, for example, the term *federal* is applied to the American national government, which is no more "federal" than the fifty states, some eighty thousand units of local government, and multitudes of other federated associations. This has become a source of conceptual confusion. Whenever I use the term *federal* to apply to the American national government, I assume that designation is an alternative proper name where capitalization is appropriate—the Federal government.

The term *state* may refer to any state of being, e.g., "state of affairs." The term as used in political discourse might be applied to any system of governance in a context of nation-states. There is, however, a critical issue with regard to a theory of sovereignty where systems of governance based on principles of self-governance are radically different than ones based on a single center of supreme authority. To keep these distinctions clearly as a focus of attention, I capitalize Supreme Authority and State when the referent is to a theory of sovereignty, the authority to make law, presuming a single center of Supreme Authority. When concepts like *gridlock* are articulated, such concepts are likely to be associated with a theory of "the State" rather than to be posed as a problem of conflict and conflict resolution in a federal system of governance requiring further inquiries, deliber-ations, and innovations in efforts to reach resolutions.

Similar ambiguities exist with regard to the term *society.* If the term applies generally to patterns of relationships among human beings, I do not capitalize it. If the term is associated with those social relationships confined to the boundaries of nation-states, I capitalize it, as in "State-governed Societies." This issue is important in determining the standing of relationships among individuals and collectivities that transcend national boundaries.

I extend this principle of capitalizing terms when giving a special meaning associated with a specialized use of language. That pattern is especially strong in chapter 3, "Newspeak and Doublethink," because spe-cialized languages of political discourse place a strong emphasis on reify-ing concepts and giving them a meaning that is more closely associated with a proper name for a concept rather than using the term in a more gen-eral context. I rely on this usage in assigning capital letters to such terms to call your attention to a specialized use of the term.

This usage is important for our purposes because the use of language always carries multiple meanings. All of us learn to read "between the lines," so to speak. In reading literature, reports, proceedings, and archival materials, Alexis de Tocqueville, for example, indicated to a friend and colleague: "What I am looking for is less the facts than the signs of the movements of ideas and feelings" (Palmer 1987, 241). If we focus on the relationship of "ideas" to "deeds," we must be concerned with the multiple meanings to be assigned to the uses of language in com-munication. When I rely on capitalizations, I am trying to tell you the reader that terms require special attention not associated with the more generalized use of a word.

While I give serious attention to the place of language and culture in human affairs, I am not a linguist or an anthropologist. I have great respect for the work of many linguists and anthropologists. Problems of symbolization and signification seem to have no limits in semiotics; and I have not found a way through what seems to be a jumble of discourse. Tzvetan Todorov's *Theories of the Symbol* (1982) suggests to me that there are serious inconsistencies in the meaning of such terms as *symbol* and *sign,* but these inconsistencies may reflect ambiguities about stories and people/people and stories. I address issues of symbolization and signification as these pertain to political discourse. Yet I hope that my use of language does no violence to the diverse specialized languages in the cultural and social sciences and in related fields of professional discourse. I am more concerned with enlightenment than with rhetorical success in winning elections, forming dominant coalitions, and using legal mandates to command others. Rhetoric pursued as an art of manipulation can be a trap contributing to the vulnerability of democratic societies.

I presume that the term *culture* tends to emphasize the ideational character of language and its meaning, while the terms *social* and *society* tend to emphasize the interpersonal character of human relationships. The distinction is a matter of emphasis. The essential feature is the complementarity of ideas to what is achieved. My point of emphasis is on the knowledge, skill, and intelligibility of human beings, who embody much of what is constitutive of human societies. I do not presume that social "reality" is something out there in the "real world" without references to how human beings think. Language enables us to learn how patterns of meaning and order hang together. Language makes possible democratic societies in which each person is presumed to have acquired the capabilities for first being one's own governor and then working out arrangements with others for the governance of their common affairs. The shift in the meaning of language in coming to an understanding of the meaning of democracy is of radical proportions.

I presume that you as a person and as a citizen function as a sovereign representative if you aspire to being a citizen in a democratic society. I address you as a sovereign representative with whom I seek to associate as we perform rulership prerogatives in ordering our lives. We rely on diverse agents to perform essential functions, but they are our agents, to be held accountable to the performance of limited functions. They are to be regarded not as our rulers—our masters—but as fellow citizens and colleagues. I only hope that this beginning opens a world of diversity and opportunity for you the reader, so that you become motivated to extend your own horizons of inquiry in what can become a most rewarding and enlightening adventure about what it means to live in democratic societies.

If the essential core of my analysis is correct, we are in rather deep trouble. We have developed a language of discourse that has become an obstacle to resolving problems in constructive ways. To understand the character of the problem and to come to terms with the conditions necessary for constructive resolutions requires us to rethink the place of the cultural and social sciences and humanities in human affairs. We have a great deal of serious work to do, but work that offers immense potentials for reward.

Acknowledgments

To acknowledge all of those who have been of essential help would require an autobiography. Scholarship is both an individual endeavor and a social enterprise. I can only dedicate this volume to my colleagues in and out of academia and to the students with whom I have worked, in appreciation for the contributions they have made to whatever I have been able to accomplish. There are even those whose names I can no longer recall but of whom I have vivid memories about questions posed to which I could not then respond. Those challenges stimulated me to take intellectual excursions and to engage many minds whom I have never known as mortal human beings. The bibliography contains only a small portion of those scholars from whom I have benefited. My sense of gratitude is commensurate with my own sense of humility about what any one person can hope to achieve given the fragile and transitory character of life.

In the preparation of this book, I have been stimulated by and have drawn on the work of many colleagues at the Workshop in Political Theory and Policy Analysis over the course of the last twenty years or so. Many of these works are available to you. These include Bish 1971; O'Brien 1975; Loveman 1976; Sabetti 1984; Advisory Commission on Intergovernmental Relations [Ronald J. Oakerson] 1987; Advisory Commission on Intergovernmental Relations [Ronald J. Oakerson, Roger B. Parks, and Henry A. Bell] 1988; E. Ostrom 1990; Stein 1990; Advisory Commission on Intergovernmental Relations [Roger B. Parks and Ronald J. Oakerson] 1992; Blomquist 1992; Kaminski 1992; E. Ostrom 1992; Sawyer 1992; Tang 1992; Thomson 1992; Keohane, McGinnis, and E. Ostrom 1993; Loveman 1993; Netting 1993; Sproule-Jones 1993; Jillson and Wilson 1994; Landa 1994; E. Ostrom, Gardner, and Walker 1994; Keohane and E. Ostrom 1995; and Wunsch and Olowu [1990] 1995.

In addition to the discussions that have occurred as chapters of this book were presented as papers at conferences, symposia, and colloquia, I have benefited from a detailed discussion of this particular manuscript at an extended review session held at the Workshop in Political Theory and Policy Analysis on March 13, 1995, chaired by Elinor Ostrom and attended by Barbara Allen, Arun Agrawal, Jamal Choudhry, Yuzhuang Deng, Wal Duany, Ray Eliason, Clark Gibson, Robert Hawkins, Wai-Fung Lam, Michael McGinnis, Anas Bin Malik, Charles Myers, Alexander Obolonsky, Mary Beth Wertime, and John Williams. Robert Agger, William Ascher, Dustin Becker, Piotr Chmielewski, David Darland, J. M. B. Edwards, Heinz Eulau, Iliya Harik, Janet Landa, Eliza Lee, Michael Libonati, Hamidou Magassa, Peter Örebech, Jan Aage Riseth, Filippo Sabetti, Branko Smerdel, Mark Sproule-Jones, Jeffrey Steele, Bert Swanson, and James Thomson offered written comments on one or another draft. I also had the benefit of comments from Jos Raadschelders, J. J. A. Thomassen, Herman von Gunsteren, Gary Wamsley, and several of the participants in a summer school at Leiden University; several days of intensive discussions with Piotr Chmielewski in Warsaw and Robert Agger in Rome; and many, many occasions for continuing, almost daily, discussions with Elinor Ostrom. Members of a seminar on Institutional Analysis and Development during the 1995 fall semester have been especially helpful in contributing to the farther revision of this inquiry. The members of this seminar have included Toh-Kyeong Ahn, Nathan Basik, Peter Beck, Lars Carlsson, Bradley Carso, Fabio de Castro, Yuzhuang Deng, Lars Engberg, Małgorzata Korzycka-Iwanow, Margaret Polski, James Prichard, Shamsa Rana-Sinclair, Maria Clara da Silva-Forsberg, Branko Smerdel, James Thomson, Robert Wehnke, and Xin Zhang. I hope that my response has been commensurate with the helpfulness of their comments. Other colleagues on the staff of the Workshop have been essential to my work. Gayle Higgins keeps my working life in order, and I am especially indebted to her and Patty Dalecki for putting this book together.

Chapters 4 and 10 draw on materials previously published in the *International Journal of Public Administration* and *Public Choice.* The earlier version of "Epistemic Choice and Public Choice" was published in an article by that name in *Public Choice* (77, no. 1 [September 1993]: 163–76). An earlier version of "East and West" appeared as "The Challenge of the Quest for Excellence," which appeared in the *International Journal of Public Administration* (19, no. 2 [1996]: 125–49). I appreciate the extension of permission to use these essays extended by Kluwer Academic Publishers and Marcel Dekker, Inc., the copyright holders.

The chapter "East and West" is being translated into Chinese by Mao Shoulong for publication in *Public Review* published by the Research Center for Public Policy in Beijing, China.

Chapter 3 was originally prepared for presentation at a conference on "The World in Transition. Transformation in the System of Political and Economic Institutions," held in Moscow on May 25–29, 1992. Chapter 6 was originally prepared as a research memorandum addressed to Piotr Chmielewski and Hamidou Magassa when the three of us were concerned with the place of language in the constitution of human societies.

My own measure of success is whether you the reader find the discussion that follows worthy of continuing study and reflection after an initial reading. I look on this effort as a sequel to my book *The Meaning of American Federalism: Constituting a Self-Governing Society* (1991) and as further response to Tocqueville's challenge about the vulnerability of democracies.

Contents

Tables

Figure

PART 1

Introduction

Great ambiguities exist about the relationship of ideas to structures, processes, and achievements in the constitution of order in human societies. This problem is especially critical with regard to societies that presume to be democratic. If citizens are to be first their own governors and active participants in the governance of their affairs as they relate to one another in diverse communities of relationships, can such societies be constituted by some single center of Supreme Authority exercising governmental prerogatives for Societies as a Whole? Or do democratic societies get constituted by using ideas to pool, rearrange, and compromise existing interests in relevant communities of relationships applicable to the scope and domain of activities that take account of what needs to be accomplished?

The language of political discourse is of fundamental importance. Are ideas to be treated as ideologies reflecting the rhetoric of politicians in building winning coalitions? Are democracies to be associated with factions engaged in wars of words with one another? Are error-correcting potentials abandoned to patterns of deception and self-deception to such a degree that democratic societies run the risk of trampling civilization underfoot?

CHAPTER 1

Are Democratic Societies Viable?

My response to the question "Are democratic societies viable?" is: Only under limited conditions. "One person, one vote, majority rule" is an inadequate and superficial formulation for constituting viable democratic societies. The condition of popular election of officials who form governments is necessary but is far from the more fundamental conditions for establishing and maintaining the viability of democratic societies. It is possible to have elections, political parties, and governing coalitions that, under some conditions, tear societies apart and, under other conditions, contribute to the breakdown and collapse of essential institutions. What it means to live in a democratic society is much more demanding than electing representatives who form governments. Not only are democratic societies constructed around the essential place of citizens in those societies, but they cannot be maintained without the knowledge, moral integrity, skill, and intelligibility of citizens in the cultivation of those societies. Calling all persons in all States "citizens" and all States "republics" is a misleading use of language and an erroneous way of conceptualizing political "realities."

At a superficial level, I believe that it has become apparent to many Americans that the institution called "family" is in serious trouble. Similar problems exist in speaking of "neighborhoods" and "communities." Large expanses of central cities have been reduced to rubble, with numerous homeless people wandering in city streets while economic indicators suggest high levels of prosperity. At the same time, it is all too apparent that financial obligations associated with social entitlements intended to solve welfare problems and advance public welfare threaten the viability of basic monetary and financial institutions. In my judgment, American democracy is at risk. Why has a flood of crises inundated the United States of America and other democracies in the contemporary world?

Perhaps the answer is to be found in the superficial way we think about citizenship in democratic societies. How people conduct themselves as they directly relate to one another in the ordinary exigencies of life is much more fundamental to a democratic way of life than the principle of "one person, one vote, majority rule." Person-to-person, citizen-to-citizen relationships are what life in democratic societies is all about. Democratic ways of life turn on self-organizing and self-governing capabilities rather than presuming that something called "the Government" governs.

My conclusion is that we in the United States and peoples in other areas of the world confront serious intellectual and cultural crises that place the future of human civilization at risk. My search is an attempt to understand these problems at their most basic levels rather than to address the great multitude of specific problems in their symptomatic manifestations. The challenge that I believe everyone confronts everywhere is how to achieve greater self-governing capabilities in confronting problems and realizing opportunities in light of the diverse contexts in which people live. How to achieve such capabilities requires the use of general knowledge in particular situations among numerous individuals functioning in more general communities of relationships. A critical issue, then, is how human beings constitute their relationships with one another in the patterns of order that prevail in human societies. Are systems of order constituted by reference to entities called "States," with closed boundaries and a system of command and control emanating from a single center of Supreme Authority within each State? Or, by contrast, are democratic systems of order open to workable relationships that can be achieved within and among diverse entities reaching out to global proportions?

Either possibility turns on how participants conceive of their relationships with one another. Is the world constituted by patterns of dominance in which some exercise power over others, or is it possible to conceive of binding and workable relationships being achieved by mutual agreement among colleagues working with one another? Perhaps both forces need to be at work. I have come to the conclusion, however, that democratic societies are necessarily placed at risk when people conceive of their relationships as being grounded on principles of command and control rather than on principles of self-responsibility in self-governing communities of relationships. How are these tensions to be resolved? If they cannot be, democracies are not viable over successive generations that reach across centuries. Neither are autocratic systems of governance, which rely on the dominance of single centers of Supreme Authority, so far as discrete individuals and regimes are concerned. Emperors come and go; empires rise and fall. Yet autocracies as systems of rule relying on some single center of Supreme Authority show surprising endurance. In such circumstances, the most that can be hoped for is some sequence of coups d'état, revolutionary struggles, and short-lived democratic regimes amid persistent autocracies.

How you and I conceptualize our relationships with one another and to the world in which we live is, in my judgment, the foundation on which systems of order are constituted in human societies. How ideas get articulated in words and expressed in language is critical to what we might hope to achieve. My Chinese colleagues tell me that the term *party,* meaning political party, is composed of two characters in the Chinese language translated as "still" and "dark." This compound term applies alike to "party," "gang," and "faction." Who can deny that "still" and "dark" are important attributes of political parties, factions, and gangs? With some amplification, meaning "continuing darkness," such attributes might apply alike to parties, gangs, factions, coalitions, business firms, labor unions, and bureaucracies. The term *republic,* as I understand that term, derives from the Latin term *res publica,* meaning the "public thing," to be construed as an open public realm. "Still dark" has quite different implications for enlightenment than the "public thing." How words, ideas, and deeds get related to one another in patterns of communication is fundamental to human experience.

In this introductory chapter, I am first concerned with puzzles and anomalies about the relationship of words, ideas, and deeds. I then turn my attention to the design and interpretation of what might be called "the American experiment." This was a puzzle addressed more than a century and a half ago by Alexis de Tocqueville in his two-volume work *Democracy in America.* He too was addressing the question of whether democracies were viable systems of order. I then consider the new image of American democracy introduced by Woodrow Wilson at the turn of the nineteenth century, focusing, as he did, on Congressional and Presidential Government. Due to the strong influence of Wilson's approach on contemporary political science, serious ambiguities are raised about the meaning of democracy. These ambiguities require a major rethinking of what it means to govern and to function as citizens in democratic republics. Rethinking the meaning and viability of democracy is the central task of this inquiry. This is a task that each of us who aspire to living in a democratic society must face. In the last section of this chapter, I lay out the way I intend to proceed with this inquiry.

Words, Ideas, and Deeds

In the realm of political discourse, it is much too easy to talk about abstract ideas as though the world of ideas pertained to something called "ideologies" without bearing on success or failure in addressing practical problems in human affairs. From such a perspective, being pragmatic implies doing whatever works to achieve success. The difficulty is how to distinguish between successes and failures and to whom those successes and failures apply.

In democratic societies, success in the political realm is usually determined by winning elections, creating winning coalitions, claiming popular mandates, and enjoying the fruits of victory. Such circumstances pose basic questions about the relationship of ideas to deeds, as Milovan Djilas has emphasized. This is the key to understanding the relationship between conceptions being acted on and the consequences that follow. In his basic critique of the Communist system, Djilas asserted:

> Everything happened differently in the U.S.S.R. and other Communist countries from what the leaders—even such prominent ones as Lenin, Stalin, Trotsky, and Bukharin—anticipated. They expected that the *state* would rapidly *wither away,* that *democracy* would be *strengthened.* The reverse happened. (1957, 37, my emphasis)

When a concept is used to inform action and the reverse happens, serious problems about the relationship of ideas to deeds exist.

Presumably, adopting a policy involves choices about ways to conceptualize a problem and then about how to deal with that problem. For John Dewey (1938), a policy was a hypothesis. The test of the hypothesis was whether the expected consequences flowed from the concepts being acted on. In a similar vein, Donald Campbell (1969) viewed reforms as experiments. When everything happens differently than key leaders anticipated—when the reverse happens—serious questions prevail. Leaders may succeed while their policies fail. Stalin achieved outstanding success as a widely recognized historical figure, but his regime failed. Such discrepancies are generally associated with repressive and despotic regimes. But democracies may also be vulnerable to comparable problems if ideas are ambiguously referred to as "ideologies" and if success is measured by winning elections, forming winning coalitions, and enjoying the fruits of victory.

As a first step in this inquiry, we need to recognize that ideas used to characterize problems may be unrelated to deeds. Such a possible mismatch between ideas and deeds expressed in actions places human rationality at risk. Those who seek election have incentives to appeal to voters. Abstract slogans have their appeals. Politicians seek to create favorable images. Once elected, however, decisions are made in closed circles among those who form winning coalitions. Public discourse can take on the character of double-talk, with glittering generalities being offered for public consumption while confidential decisions are made by members of winning coalitions. When that happens, there are serious risks. The connections between ideas and deeds may lose their essential coherence. Languages may lose meaning; ambiguities and confusion may come to prevail. Normal patterns of partisan politics can yield corruption in the use of language and the way we live our lives.

Fed 'Beige Book' Sees Indications of Weakness in the Economy

His carefully calibrated ambiguity included enough hints and caveats to leave room for the Fed to make almost any decision. And that seemed to be exactly what Mr. [Alan] Greenspan intended. "I worry incessantly that I might be too clear," he said in a question-and-answer session after the speech. To gales of laughter from the audience of economists and financial experts, Mr. Greenspan said he had mastered "Fed-speak" in which the goal is to "mumble with great incoherence."

(Keith Bradsher, *New York Times,* June 22, 1995)

Hidden agendas and the actions of winning coalitions create differential opportunities and burdens that radically diverge from public discourse and the expectations of public opinion. These circumstances contain potentials for surprise, disappointment, disillusionment, alienation, and distrust. When people are being played for suckers by those engaged in the "art of manipulation," the basic elements of trust and candor necessary in considering the relationship of ideas to deeds and the viability of democratic societies and civilizations are placed at risk. These are the circumstances in which Alexis de Tocqueville presumed that democratic peoples become vulnerable to trampling civilizations underfoot ([1835–40] 1945, 2:47).

The circumstances provoked by deception, strategic opportunism, and distrust may, in turn, evoke revolutionary potentials. A shift of paradigm—the framework for constituting systems of thought and ways of life—can occur. The significance of such paradigmatic shifts for human civilizations is always problematic. Paradigmatic shifts can be the occasion for a new burst of productive potential or another quest for utopian illusions. The line of succession to those who promise "liberation" and "salvation" is inevitably plagued by the fragile character of human mortality. Promises are rationalized as leaders succeed one another, inevitably giving way to temptations to win and to enjoy the fruits of victory. The world of politics is likely to attract both those who presume to know the Truth and seek to lead others to Salvation and those who are attracted by the fruits of victory like bees to a pot of honey on a warm summer day. Human beings cannot know the Truth in any conclusive way. The most they can do is subject assertions to critical scrutiny. The fate of humanity is, in my judgment, confined to learning how to read the shadows on the walls of the Cave, to use Plato's metaphor. The shadows in Plato's Cave are the words we use to stand for, symbolize, or represent "reality" and to relate thinking and acting to whatever it is that human beings achieve. The ultimate conceit and massive source of deception and self-deception is to presume that one can see the direct light of Truth and explain the way to Salvation to others through the use of words.

The words we use and the ideas with which we work are the most fundamental part of human reality. How we communicate with one another, think, act, and do whatever we seek to achieve is shaped by the ambiguities of language. What we presume to be true is expressed and mediated through the conventions of language and the experiences that human beings share in talking with, relating to, and working with one another. The exigencies of language and culture apply to what people profess as knowledge, what they do, and how they relate to one another in whatever they manage to achieve.

The centrality of language in the constitution of life in human societies and the ambiguities associated with the use of words in the articulation of language present us with a most fundamental anomaly. In addressing this problem, Tocqueville alleged that the Deity discerns everything without "the necessity of collecting a considerable number of analogous objects under the same form for greater convenience in thinking." As a result, "General ideas are no proof of the strength, but rather of the insufficiency of the human intellect. . . . The chief merit of general ideas is that they enable the human mind to pass a rapid judgment on a great many objects at once; but, on the other hand, the notions they convey are never other than incomplete, and they always cause the mind to lose as much in accuracy as it gains in comprehensiveness" (ibid., 2:13).

The centrality of language and ambiguities of language can be ameliorated by working with ideas and with one another in the material conditions of the world in which we live. What we are able to accomplish by communicating and working with others implies that deeds are essential complements to ideas. Shared knowledge and understanding come not from ideas alone but from the way that ideas and deeds complement each other in what gets accomplished. The centrality and ambiguities of language can only be resolved through the common experiences of relating ideas to deeds and reflecting on what is accomplished in the realm of knowledgeable and intelligible activities.

The context in which ideas are put to use and people act in relation to one another is a critical factor in determining the warrantability of knowledge. No experiment ever conducts itself. No product ever produces itself. Knowledgeable and intelligible action is always mediated by skill in taking appropriate actions in a context in which anticipated states of affairs can be brought to realization. One cannot make bread or bricks—similar processes are used in both—without careful attention to appropriate conditions (Fathy 1973). Can we expect democracies to be created and maintained by muddling through devoid of knowledge, skill, and intelligibility? Everything we attempt to do requires knowledge, skill, and intelligibility in *the use of present means to achieve some future apparent good*—what Thomas Hobbes meant by the term *power.* Those conditions always apply in context. There is no universal contextless realm of human *activities.*

The basic ambiguities inherent in all languages are radically increased when incentives exist to obfuscate meaning. Such incentives exist in all political systems as well as in the purely personal aspects of human existence. Personal fantasies need not have public significance. How individuals in public life cope with personal fantasies, including the intoxication of ideas, may have profound significance. The character of political discourse in democratic societies directly affects the character of public life shared by multitudes of people. The relationship of ideas and deeds is of crucial importance if people are to be informed about public affairs and to act intelligibly based on trust and reciprocity, rather than on deception and collusion, in strategic pursuits. Working out the connection between ideas and deeds with regard to the American "experiment" has been an essential part of my own effort to explore the place of a political science in the constitution of democratic societies.

Exploring the Meaning of the American Experiment

Design Concepts

The approach taken by the authors of *The Federalist* (Hamilton, Jay, and Madison [1788] n.d.) and the participants in the Philadelphia Convention presumed an essential connection between ideas and deeds. A diagnostic assessment was offered for the failure of confederation. Alexander Hamilton argued that justice cannot be done when governments govern governments and rely on sanctions imposed on collectivities to maintain order. Imposing sanctions on collectivities places the burden for remedies on innocent bystanders rather than on those directly responsible for wrongdoing. To correct that flaw, the basic "fabric"—the configurations of relationships—had to be reworked to relate each unit of government to the persons of individuals. Both the *Constitution of the United States* and the constitutions of the states were viewed by James Madison as great experiments to establish "the fabrics of governments which have no model on the face of the globe" (ibid., 85). Note the plural in "fabrics of governments."

The design and conduct of such experiments were plagued by difficulties, including the veil of ambiguities inherent in language.

> . . . the medium through which the conceptions of men are conveyed to each other adds a fresh embarrassment. The use of words is to express ideas. Perspicuity, therefore, requires not only that the ideas

should be distinctly formed, but that they should be expressed by words distinctly and exclusively appropriate to them. But no language is so copious as to supply words and phrases for every complex idea, or so correct as not to include many equivocally denoting different ideas. . . . And this unavoidable inaccuracy must be greater or less, according to the complexity and novelty of the objects defined. When the Almighty himself condescends to address mankind in their own language, his meaning, luminous as it must be, is rendered dim and doubtful by the cloudy medium through which it is communicated. (Ibid., 229–30)

As a result, "decent regard" needed to be given to the opinions and arguments of others, including those of "former times and other nations," without suffering "a blind veneration for antiquity, for custom, or for *names,* to overrule the *suggestions of their own good sense,* the *knowledge of their own situation,* and the *lessons of their own experience*" (ibid., 85, my emphasis). A willingness to engage in experiments to establish the merit of ideas occurs only in light of experience. This relationship of ideas to deeds was the foundation for a philosophy that John Dewey called "pragmatism": Will the conjecture, the hypothesis, the conception work?

The analyses offered by the authors of *The Federalist* were posed against a background that has reference to human societies—to all mankind—even though the particulars were being related to the situation facing the American people. A fundamental issue with regard to the American experiment was posed by Alexander Hamilton in the opening paragraph of the first essay in *The Federalist.*

It has been frequently remarked that it seems to have been reserved to the people of this country, by their conduct and example, to decide the important question, whether societies of men are really capable or not of establishing good government from reflection and choice, or whether they are forever destined to depend for their political constitutions on accident and force. If there be any truth in the remark, the crisis at which we are arrived may with propriety be regarded as the era in which that decision is to be made; and a wrong election of the part we shall act may, in this view, deserve to be considered as the general misfortune of mankind. (Ibid., 3)

A series of essays explaining the design for an experiment worthy of deciding the question of whether societies of men could establish systems of governance from reflection and choice was addressed to the people of New York, not to the philosophers of the world. Yet the issues addressed were treated with a critical awareness of key problems in political philosophy; and philosophers of the world could scrutinize those essays for their merit. If societies of men are to constitute systems of governance from reflection and choice, those societies are required to establish a culture of inquiry rather than a culture of command and control dominated by those engaged in the art of manipulation. A due process of inquiry, under these circumstances, is necessary to a due process of law.

Human societies under such constitutions are not determinate systems. They are created by drawing on ideas to come to terms with problems of change in moving from what has been to what is to be in the course of future efforts. Creative efforts require a positive knowledge of prevailing conditions and how those might be transformed by intelligible actions. For the people of New York, the process of change was concerned with crafting a body of common knowledge and shared community of understanding about patterns of social accountability in what would become a limited national government, to be identified as the Government of the United States of America.

Rather than relying on a system of command and control associated with exigencies of accident and force, the basic principle used in conceptualizing the design of the American system of governance drew on Montesquieu's concept of "using power to check power" ([1748] 1966, 200) as a fundamental constitutive principle. That principle, however, was extended by Madison in the following formulation.

In framing a government which is to be administered by men over men, the great difficulty lies in this: you must first enable the government to control the governed; and in the next place oblige it to control itself. A dependence on the people is, no doubt, the primary control on the government; but *experience* has taught mankind the necessity of auxiliary precautions.

This policy of supplying, by opposite and rival interests, the defect of better motives, might be traced through the whole system of human affairs, private as well as public. We see it particularly displayed in all the subordinate distributions of power, where the constant aim is to divide and arrange the several offices in such a manner as that each may be a check on the other—that the private interest of every individual may be a sentinel over the public rights. These inventions of prudence cannot be less requisite in the distribution of the supreme powers of the State. (Hamilton, Jay, and Madison [1788] n.d., 337–38, my emphasis)

In summation, such a system would use power to check power, through opposite and rival interests that extended to the whole system of human affairs. The defect of better motives implies that varying degrees and types of opportunism prevail in public affairs. Such a system is obviously vulnerable to stalemate unless conflicts are mediated by processes of conflict resolution in a culture of inquiry using ideas to give expression to possibilities in shaping and reshaping emergent patterns of order. *The Political Theory of a Compound Republic* ([1971] 1987) was my effort to reconstruct the theory that was being used by Alexander Hamilton and James Madison as the principal authors of *The Federalist,* based on the analyses and arguments that they offered in explaining the design of the *Constitution of the United States*—the design for one and only one of the experiments in the more general constitution of the American political system.

An Account of the Experiment

Two French observers, Gustave de Beaumont and Alexis de Tocqueville, provide us with excellent accounts of the American experiment as it had developed by the 1830s. In this discussion, I shall refer exclusively to Tocqueville's *Democracy in America* ([1835–40] 1945), even though Beaumont's novel *Marie, or Slavery in the United States* ([1835] 1958b) is an insightful account of American culture, and though his essay entitled "Note on the Social and Political Conditions of the Negro Slaves and of Free People of Color" ([1835] 1958a) is a perceptive commentary on the institution of slavery and on racial prejudice in the United States.

In a transitional paragraph at the end of the first chapter, "Exterior Form of North America," Tocqueville gave the reader a clue about the essential thrust of what was to follow.

> In that land the great experiment of the attempt to construct society upon a new basis was to be made by civilized man; and it was there, for the first time, that theories hitherto unknown, or deemed impracticable, were to exhibit a spectacle for which the world had not been prepared by the history of the past. ([1835–40] 1945, 1:25)

The basic idea that Tocqueville identified in chapter 2 as "the key to almost the whole work" (ibid., 1:28) was found in the covenantal theology of the Puritans. That key idea was expressed in the *Mayflower Compact,* in which the participants undertook a commitment "in the presence of God and one another" to "covenant and combine ourselves together into a civil body politick" (ibid., 1:35). The term *foedus* in Latin means "to covenant." A covenantal theology was also referred to as a "federal theology." A federal system of governance is, then, a covenantal system of governance. In a biography entitled *Tocqueville,* Larry Siedentop asserts that "By writing

Democracy in America [1835] Tocqueville attempted something extraordinary—the overturn of the established European idea of the state" (1994, 41).

In distinguishing "the great experiment of the attempt to construct society upon a new basis," Tocqueville identified its basic principle with "the doctrine of the sovereignty of the people" ([1835–40] 1945, 1:55). He defined sovereignty as the right to make laws (ibid., 1:123). The right to make the "political laws" (ibid., 1:55), applicable to the structure and conduct of government, resided in the people through processes of constitutional choice. The net result was a system of governance where "society governs itself for itself," in contrast to circumstances where a State, external to society, or where the "ruling force . . . being partly within and partly without the ranks of the people" (ibid., 1:57), rules over Society. This was the character of the challenge to overturn the idea of the State.

Making law, especially political laws, applicable to the conduct of governments requires a critical reflective awareness of what it means to represent others while realizing one's own place in associating with others as one's equals. Methods of normative inquiry for making interpersonal comparisons can only be realized by drawing on the resources of language and culture that have become a part of human existence in a world of human creativity. Tocqueville's analytics turned on the deepest levels of human consciousness about creative potentials.

Volume 1 of *Democracy in America* is an analysis of the American system of government as that system had evolved in the 1830s. In assessing the relationship of the basic ideas used to design the American experiment, I note here only key observations in the concluding chapters. The relevance of Tocqueville's analysis of the American federal system is addressed in more depth in *The Meaning of American Federalism* (V. Ostrom 1991). In identifying the factors that led to the maintenance of democracy in America, Tocqueville gave primacy to religion, which he identified as "the first of their political institutions" even though it takes "no direct part in the government of society" ([1835–40] 1945, 1:305). Succeeding generations of Americans learned the foundations for a covenantal way of life in religious congregations and the practice of religious precepts in the social circles of family, neighborhood, community, and society. Tocqueville warned of the dangers of a "tyranny of the majority," which he identified with the structure of governments within the states (ibid., 1:269 n. 6). This had been a critical concern in Madison's commentaries. Tyranny of the majority in a system of government that relies on majority vote was for Madison the most serious of republican diseases. How to preserve the spirit and form of "popular [democratic] government" and secure "the public good and private rights" against the danger of majority faction was for Madison "the great object to which our inquiries are directed" (Hamilton, Jay, and Madison [1788] n.d., 57–58). For Tocqueville, that danger was worthy of two chapters of analysis and commentary even though that potential had not yet come to its fuller realization by the 1830s.

In his concluding commentary on democracy in America, Tocqueville identified three "causes," or factors, which had contributed to the maintenance of democracy. First in order of importance were "the manners and customs of the people" ([1835–40] 1945, 1:288). These he identified with the Latin term *mores,* which he applied not only to *"the habits of the heart*—but to the various notions and opinions current among men and to the mass of those ideas which constitute their character of mind." "I comprise under this term, therefore," he continued, "the whole moral and intellectual condition of a people" (ibid., 1:299, Tocqueville's emphasis). In light of the meaning to be assigned to the manner and customs of the people, we can understand why Tocqueville identified religion as the first of their political institutions even though religion took no direct part in the government of society. The place of religion was important to the whole moral and intellectual tradition of a people when complemented by the place of families, friends, neighbors, and schooling in the shaping of what might be called "habits of the heart and mind." The place of habits of the heart and mind is critical to the possibility that societies of men might establish systems of governance appropriate to the exercise of reflection and choice as ways of coping with problems of conflict and conflict resolution.

Tocqueville assigned the place of second importance in the maintenance of democracy in America to "the laws" (ibid., 1:288). Here, Tocqueville was somewhat more concerned with "political laws," the laws that applied to patterns of governance. He identified three features of "the law" as being more important than others to the maintenance of democracy: first, "that federal form of government" that enabled "the Union to combine the power of a great republic with the security of a small one"; second, "those township institutions which limit the despotism of the majority and at the same time impart to the people a taste for freedom and the art of being free"; and third, "the constitution of the judicial power" in which citizens as jurors directly participate in the application and enforcement of law (ibid., 1:299). Tocqueville maintained that acting as jurors "teaches men to practice equity; every man learns to judge his neighbor as he would himself be judged" (ibid., 1:284). The idea that the federal union combined the power of a great republic with numerous smaller republics was the idea that Montesquieu had proposed as a way for popular governments to overcome the dual threat of foreign aggression and internal imperfections.

Montesquieu's formulation pertained to confederation, and the design of the American federal system was conceptualized as a way to resolve the basic conceptual problem associated with governments governing governments.

The least important, but not insignificant, factor in the maintenance of American democracy was "the peculiar and accidental situation in which Providence has placed the Americans" (ibid., 1:288). These circumstances did not exist in a Europe plagued by warfare and quests for imperial dominance: "In order that one such state should exist in the European world, it would be necessary that similar institutions should be simultaneously introduced into all the other nations" (ibid., 1:229).

Every institutional arrangement has limits and is the source of potential failure. A serious difficulty of a fundamental cultural character plagued American democracy because two races other than the Anglo-Americans constituted its population. Native Americans faced flight, decimation by infectious diseases, and destruction of their aboriginal ways of life. Tocqueville could see no resolution to that problem or to the problem engendered by the institution of slavery as it was applied to Africans imported as slaves and held in servitude. A society of two radically different cultures existed: one of masters; the other of slaves. Slavery was demeaning for labor among both slaves and their masters. Such circumstances could not be reconciled with the constitution of a self-governing society.

The potential for Majority Tyranny and the anomaly of societies composed of masters and slaves left the viability of democracy in America in doubt. For such a society to survive required a critical analysis to determine whether successive generations into the indefinite future could reproduce appropriate habits of the heart and mind and could sustain a culture of inquiry. Because of the problem of mortality and the loss of memory with death, subsequent generations experience a loss of consciousness about the conditions necessary to the viability of American democracy.

Tocqueville's conclusion was that if people act on the basis of *natural inclinations,* democratic societies will yield a new form of "democratic despotism" quite different than the "tyranny of the majority." A culture of inquiry grounded in reflection and choice will give way to "simple and general notions" presuming "a great nation" in which "a single and central power . . . governs the whole community by its direct influence" and that is "composed of citizens all formed upon one pattern and all governed by a single power." Since each citizen sees others as like oneself, "he cannot understand why a rule that is applicable to one man should not be equally applicable to all others," and "uniformity of legislation appears to him to be the first condition of good government" (ibid., 2:289). Under these circumstances, "the notion they all form of government is that of a sole, simple, providential, and creative power" (ibid., 2:291). This is the antithesis of the principles articulated by James Madison about the problem of "framing a government which is to be administered by men over men." It is as though men could choose to be governed by angels. Such circumstances are especially vulnerable to the art of manipulation.

Tocqueville, in a chapter entitled "What Sort of Despotism Democratic Nations Have to Fear," presents the following pictographic characterization.

The first thing that strikes the observation is an innumerable multitude of men, all equal and alike, incessantly endeavoring to procure the petty and paltry pleasures with which they glut their lives. Each of them, living apart, is as a stranger to the fate of all the rest; his children and his private friends constitute to him the whole of mankind. As for the rest of his fellow citizens, he is close to them, but he does not see them; he touches them, but he does not feel them; he exists only in himself and for himself alone; and if his kindred still remain to him, he may be said at any rate to have lost his country.

Above this race of men stands an immense and tutelary power, which takes upon itself alone to secure their gratifications and to watch over their fate. That power is absolute, minute, regular, provident, and mild. It would be like the authority of a parent if, like that authority, its object was to prepare men for manhood; but it seeks, on the contrary, to keep them in perpetual childhood: it is well content that the people should rejoice, provided they think of nothing but rejoicing. For their happiness such a government willingly labors, but it chooses to be the sole agent and the only arbiter of that happiness; it provides for their security, foresees and supplies their necessities, facilitates their pleasures, manages their principal concerns, directs their industry, regulates the descent of property, and subdivides their inheritances: what remains, but to spare them all the care of thinking and all the trouble of living?

Thus it every day renders the exercise of the free agency of man less useful and less frequent; it circumscribes the will within a narrower range and gradually robs a man of all the uses of himself. The principle of equality has prepared men for these things; it has predisposed men to endure them and often to look on them as benefits.

After having thus successively taken each member of the community in its powerful grasp and fashioned him at will, the supreme power then extends its arm over the whole community. It covers the surface of society with a network of small complicated rules, minute and uniform, through which the most original minds and the most energetic characters cannot penetrate, to rise above the crowd. The will of man is not shattered, but softened, bent, and guided; men are seldom forced by it to act, but they are constantly restrained from acting. Such a power does not destroy, but it prevents existence; it does not tyrannize, but it compresses, enervates, extinguishes, and stupefies a people, till each nation is reduced to nothing better than a flock of timid and industrious animals, of which the government is the shepherd. (Ibid., 2:318–19)

In such circumstances, Tocqueville concluded that "the vices of rulers and the ineptitude of the people would speedily bring about its ruin; and the nation, weary of its representatives and of itself, would create freer institutions or soon return to stretch itself at the feet of a single master" (ibid., 2:321). Tocqueville had diagnosed a republican disease of even more serious proportion than Madison's tyranny of the majority.

Using Madison's metaphor of republican diseases, the Tyranny of the Majority might be viewed as a sickness of governments. Partisan coalitions would pursue narrow partisan advantages to the detriment of the more general public good, minority interests, and private rights. What Tocqueville is referring to as Democratic Despotism is by contrast a sickness of the people. Sicknesses of a people can be characterized by such vices as greed, envy, and a sense of helplessness. Perhaps the most fatal affliction of a people is a combination of helplessness, envy, and greed. These characteristics can be gradually created by the appeals of politicians in seeking to win elections and form winning coalitions. Democracies are in serious difficulties when a sickness of the people creates a dependency, a form of servitude, in which the people no longer possess the autonomous capabilities to modify their constitutional arrangements and reform their system of government in appropriate ways. When republican diseases afflict both the Government and the people, it is not at all clear how democratic societies can maintain error-correcting potentials and self-governing capabilities.

Tocqueville's *Democracy in America* was not preoccupied with an exotic experiment on the North American continent. Rather, he was concerned with the viability of democratic societies under circumstances of increasing conditions of equality among mankind. His prognosis turned on the development of "a new science of politics . . . for a new world" (ibid., 1:7). That new science of politics presumably would enable individuals to adapt the doctrine of self-interest to systems of rule-ordered relationships that would take account of the interest of others (ibid., 1:11). "Self-interest rightly understood" depended on a right understanding to be achieved by the development of a science and art of association that would enable citizens to act in such ways that individual interests would become associated in patterns of reciprocal and complementary interests. The constitution of democratic societies is a product of human artisanship in which "freedom, public peace, and social order itself will not be able to exist without education" (ibid., 2:124)—presumably an education appropriate to citizenship in self-governing societies.

How to cope with the affliction of Democratic Despotism is Tocqueville's challenge not only to Americans but to all people who aspire to freedom in democratic societies. Tocqueville's analysis poses a profound anomaly. A democratic people in a self-governing society can, by acting on "natural" inclinations, be led to commit themselves to a form of servitude—a gentle form of slavery. The road to serfdom, as Friedrich von Hayek (1944) identified the phenomenon, will be marked by the way that ideas and deeds are related to one another to achieve a transformation in which the domestication of the human animal, as "a flock of timid and industrious animals," is viewed as beneficial in a quest for happiness.

That a gentle form of slavery can be indefinitely maintained is doubtful. Can servitude be reconciled with happiness? Perhaps Robert Michels's closing paragraph in his sociological study of oligarchical tendencies in modern societies, entitled *Political Parties,* reflects the struggle between freer institutions and servitude.

> The democratic currents of history resemble successive waves. They break ever on the same shoal. They are ever renewed. This enduring spectacle is simultaneously encouraging and depressing. When democracies have gained a certain stage of development, they undergo a gradual transformation, adopting the aristocratic spirit, and in many cases also the aristocratic forms, against which at the outset they struggled so fiercely. Now new accusers arise to denounce the traitors; after an era of glorious combats and of inglorious power, they end by fusing with the old dominant class; whereupon once more they are in their turn attacked by fresh opponents who appeal to the name of democracy. It is probable that this cruel game will continue without end. ([1911] 1966, 371)

Why should these patterns marked by striving and betrayal occur? Do these patterns reflect problems of deception, self-deception, and diverse opportunistic strategies that inevitably get built into the way that democratic processes are organized and subjected to manipulation? Are democracies destined to oscillate between struggles for freedom and servitude? These factors make democracies vulnerable to destruction. Or is it possible to use problem-solving modes of inquiry to achieve a more steady course, by using political processes to craft common knowledge and shared communities of understanding, establish patterns of social accountability, and maintain mutual trust?

The odyssey of American history saw the threat of the Tyranny of the Majority come to dominance in the era of "machine politics and boss rule" in the closing decades of the nineteenth century (following the Civil War), at which time great utility enterprises associated with railroads, electricity, telecommunication, and gas emerged and came to span the continent (V. Ostrom [1971] 1987, chap. 8). Moisei Ostrogorski carefully examined the problem of machine politics and boss rule in the second volume of his *Democracy and the Organization of Political Parties* ([1902] 1964). His study was based on extended inquiries in Great Britain and the United States during the 1880s and 1890s.

A New Image: Congressional Government and Presidential Government

During the last two decades in the nineteenth century, Woodrow Wilson and many others engaged in critical assessments of the American experiment. Wilson's doctoral dissertation, published as *Congressional Government* ([1885] 1956), and his essay "The Study of Administration" (1887) evoked a paradigmatic challenge in the use of ideas to conceptualize the nature of the American political system. The explanations offered by the authors of *The Federalist* and by John Adams were explicitly rejected as "literary theory" ([1885] 1956, 37) and "paper pictures" (ibid., 31). Wilson saw an irreconcilable conflict between "the Constitution of the books" and "the Constitution in operation" (ibid., 30). His quest, then, was to study the living reality—the living constitution. In considering the task of the analyst, Wilson offered the following commentary.

> It is, therefore, the difficult task of one who would now write at once practically and critically of our national government to escape from theories and attach himself to facts, not allowing himself to be confused by a knowledge of what that government was intended to be, or led away into conjectures as to what it may one day become, but striving to catch its present phases and to photograph the delicate organism in all its characteristic parts exactly as it is today; an undertaking all the more arduous and doubtful of issue because it has to be entered upon without guidance from writers of acknowledged authority. (Ibid.)

Here we have the seeds for the behavioral revolution in the political and social sciences. The *idea* that human beings use *ideas* to shape their thinking, planning, and what gets accomplished is missing. The possibility that societies might use reflection and choice to construct systems of governance is obscured. The very nature of vision to a political observer must be conveyed through Madison's reference to the cloudy medium of language. Wilson's living constitution was presumably left to the accidents of history associated with winning elections, putting together dominant coalitions, and enjoying the fruits of victory. The place of reflection and choice in processes of constitutional deliberations did not penetrate Wilson's consciousness. Instead, he ridiculed the efforts of his contemporaries for "the tinkering of constitutions" (1887, 205) rather than creating what he presumed to be an efficient system of bureaucratic administration. Governments could presumably govern in democratic societies without regard for the processes of crafting and recrafting the common knowledge, shared communities of understanding, patterns of social accountability, and mutual trust necessary for self-governing societies.

Wilson's vision was profoundly influenced by the conceptions advanced in Walter Bagehot's *The English Constitution* ([1865] 1964) and by his own familiarity, as a student who had studied in Europe, with the French and Prussian systems of public administration, which he presumed to be applicable to all Governments alike. His conception of a democratic system of government merged Parliamentary Government and Bureaucratic Administration. Wilson presumed that "there is always a centre of power." The burden of the analyst is to determine "the real depositaries and the essential machinery of power": "where in this system is that centre? in whose hands is self-sufficient authority lodged and through what agencies does that authority speak and act?" ([1885] 1956, 30). Government is a process of command and control exercised from some supreme and self-sufficient center of authority. The State is an autonomous entity that rules over Society. Wilson's vision is articulated in the following pictographic description.

> ... the predominant and controlling force, the centre and source of all motive and of all regulative power, is Congress. All niceties of constitutional restriction and even many broad principles of constitutional limitation have been overridden, and a thoroughly organized system of congressional control set up which gives a very rude negative to some theories of balance and some schemes for distributed powers. (Ibid., 31)

Wilson's observations about Congress were reasonably accurate in light of Ostrogorski's *Democracy and the Organization of Political Parties.* In an era of machine politics and boss rule, the Senate had become a club of bosses. The House of Representatives had become a machine dominated by the Speaker, who controlled its proceedings and its agenda. The problem is whether that "reality" was to be construed as a manifestation of the true character of democratic government or as a manifestation of institutional failures and needs for reform.

Wilson's close tie to the conceptual formulation of Walter Bagehot's *The English Constitution* demonstrates an affinity to traditions of thought associated with the "liberalism" reflected in the works of Jeremy Bentham, James Mill, and John Stuart Mill, traditions more compatible with the concepts of the French revolution than with those of the American experiments. The core concept for Bagehot was the unitary character of Cabinet Government in a Parliamentary system of government. The mainstreams of American and European political science were to emphasize the place of Parliamentary Government and Bureaucratic Administration with regard to what was presumed to be Responsible Party Government. The boss, as head of Government, could presumably be made politically responsible to the legislature, but the boss dominates the electoral processes for selecting legislators.

Bagehot's introduction to the second edition of *The English Constitution* dwelled on the dangers of machine politics and boss rule that he expected to follow from reform efforts to achieve universal manhood suffrage. Those anchoring their concept of democracy on Parliamentary Government presumed that Parliament was competent to make constitutional decisions without reference to constitutional law. Federal democracy, by contrast, placed its emphasis on the covenantal character of constitutional law, presuming a broad sharing and distribution of authority consistent with a self-governing society. Bagehot impatiently dismissed Tocqueville's concern about local government in the following way.

> . . . we need not care about how much power is delegated to outlying bodies, and how much is kept for the central body. We have had the instruction municipalities could give us; we have been through all of that. Now we are quite grown up, and can put away childish things. ([1865] 1964, 265)

The American Progressive Reform movement included contradictory tendencies. Some involved widespread changes in state constitutions reaching to local systems of government, and others involved centralizing administrative authority in chief executives. In the fifteenth printing of *Congressional Government,* Wilson, in a new preface dated August 15, 1900, anticipated that "the new leadership of the Executive" might "substitute statesmanship for government by mass meeting" and "put this whole volume hopelessly out of date" ([1885] 1956, 23). I presume that government by "statesmanship" referred to Presidential Government and that government by "mass meeting" referred to Congressional Government. And so we have the seeds being sown for "the notion" that "government is . . . a sole, simple, providential, and creative power," as Tocqueville had written some forty-five years before the publication of *Congressional Government* and some sixty years before Wilson's new prefatory observations.

The beginning of the second century of the American experiment brought a fundamental paradigmatic shift in thinking about the American system of government. The American experiments were to be interpreted in light of ideas associated with Parliamentary Government and Bureaucratic Administration. The basic presupposition that Wilson had made was that the more authority is divided, the more irresponsible it becomes. The corollary of this proposition is, of course, that the more authority is unified, the more responsible it becomes. This notion is in direct contrast to Madison's presupposition that vesting authority in a single center of Supreme Authority is the very definition of tyranny. In the course of his own presidency, Woodrow Wilson faced the challenge and tragedy of taking a leading role in the constitution of the League of Nations. A choice to ignore the "knowledge of what that government was intended to be" and to reject "guidance from writers of acknowledged authority" became a new way of conceptualizing "pragmatism"—as anything that works. The place of ideas as conceptions, conjectures, and hypotheses was eclipsed. Such different personalities as Franklin Roosevelt and Richard Nixon conceived their own vision of American government from what they presumed to have learned from Woodrow Wilson.

The "living constitution" took on a fundamentally different character than "the Constitution of the books," meaning words on paper and the conceptualization that lay behind words on paper. What Hamilton had conceptualized as "a general theory of limited constitutions" (Hamilton, Jay, and Madison [1788] n.d., 524) gave way to the new "pragmatism" of living constitutions as anything that works. Lyndon Johnson's War on Poverty elicited a commentary from James Sundquist, in his book *Making Federalism Work,* that the coordination of the whole system of administration had to be "induced, overseen, managed, and directed from . . . the Executive Office of the President" (1969, 244). The term *federalism* took on a new meaning, associated with the dominant authority of the Federal Government as it is subject to a unified command from the Executive Offices of the President.

Conceptual Ambiguities

Ironically, two economists, James Buchanan and Gordon Tullock in *The Calculus of Consent* (1962), revived the conceptualization of a constitutional level of analysis as having an important place in establishing the terms and conditions of governance in contrast to the collective-choice level of analysis. It is possible for those who play games characterized by winning and losing to establish the rules of a fair game with unanimity even though each round in the play of the game would involve winning and losing. At the constitutional level of analysis, we might view unanimity, rather than majority rule, as the base rule in constituting the games people play in governing democratic societies. Majority rule might be used in making collective decisions, so long as basic constitutional rules were respected.

A serious dilemma arises when we recognize that the constitutional provisions for collective choice refer to plurality or majority vote rules, or, in the case of emergencies, to the decisions of a single official such as the mayor of a city, the governor of a state, or the president of the United States. The patterns of normal partisan politics involve incentives to diverge from constitutional requirements. Confronting new problems or pursuing a reform agenda in a highly fragmented federal system of government creates incentives to explore diverse alternatives of a constitutional character allowing for innovative potentials. The crafting of institutional arrangements for water resource development in the Los Angeles metropolitan region, which I had previously explored in *Water and Politics* (1953), placed much greater emphasis on political agendas involving both constitutional and collective choice considerations in public entrepreneurial efforts to build a "great metropolis" in a desert region on the periphery of the North American continent (see also Blomquist 1992).

Public administration as practiced by those engaged in water resource development in the southern California metropolitan region did not adhere to principles of bureaucratic administration relying on concepts of unity of command, a limited span of control, and a hierarchy of superior-subordinate relationships reaching from a single chief executive to the most subordinate functionaries in a system of command and control. Instead, the relationships among the diverse instrumentalities of local, state, and national governments adhered much more closely to that of independent public enterprises pursuing contractual relationships in a system that could be considered to be a "water industry" (Bain, Caves, and Margolis 1966; V. Ostrom 1971). The thrust was one of complementary forms of public entrepreneurship in building features of life in a metropolis.

The modes of analysis used by those engaged in public entrepreneurship drew on the analytical capabilities of engineers, lawyers, accountants, economists, and those knowledgeable about public affairs. An engineering report entitled *Santa Ana Investigation, Flood Control and Conservation* indicated how these diverse modes of analysis were put together in establishing and maintaining productive working relationships among those concerned with water problems.

> Control of water to secure maximum supply at costs determined by the economic situation is the engineering problem, and that problem is solvable.
>
> Ahead of the engineering accomplishment is the engineering of men. The decision of the community at large must be made. For accomplishment, its public body, its semipublic water organizations, and its individuals must unite in team work to pool, rearrange and compromise existing interests, to legislate and to create a competent organization to carry out the engineering solution. (California Department of Public Works 1928, 32)

Engineering had to do with water supply; and water supply affected economic potentials. The key features of entrepreneurship—the engineering of men—involved, first, the use of ideas in pooling, rearranging, and compromising existing interests through the consent of the community at large as expressed in legislation and, second, the creation of a competent organization to carry out the engineering solution. The planning and preparation of that "legislation" was being viewed as constitutional in character for establishing a competent organization capable of making collective decisions to bring the engineering solution to an operational reality.

The phrase, "the engineering of men," was used as a figure of speech—a metaphor—to refer to the place of political processes in constituting patterns of relationships to both alleviate dangers [e.g., floods] and realize opportunities [e.g., irrigation]. The engineering of men was to engage in a problem-solving mode to transform the prior state of affairs into an emergent state of affairs to shape a new reality. Politics was conceived as a problem-solving process using ideas drawn from diverse modes of analysis to accomplish deeds.

The water industry in the southern California metropolitan region, composed of hundreds, if not thousands, of public and semipublic agencies, represented only one facet in the public economy of life in that region. Patterns of organization marked by overlapping jurisdictions and fragmentation of authority constituted a public economy that had some of the characteristics of a competitive market economy when complemented with an array of institutional arrangements for processing conflicts, achieving conflict resolutions, and monitoring performance. Radically different approaches to the "engineering of men" in the constitution of order appeared to be possible. How well such systems performed was an empirical question determined by reference to standards of performance. Different conceptions needed to be related to deeds in an effort to establish a comparative assessment of alternatives. Patterns of organization in the California water industry were in marked contrast, for example, to the TVA [Tennessee Valley Authority] idea that captivated public attention in the late 1930s and 1940s (Lilienthal 1945).

Presumably, systems of government can be conceptualized, can be constructed, and can function in different ways that have radically different implications for ways of life and for the potentials that people might realize. Systems of governance might hypothetically be as different from each other as are different types of ball games played in human societies, which depend on variable sets of rules, use variously shaped and sized balls, and are played on differently arranged "fields" and "courts." The logic for choosing strategies in playing baseball is quite different from the logic of choosing strategies in playing American football. There is no need to create a single, universal ball game that applies to all mankind. Seeking to understand different ball games by following Woodrow Wilson's suggestion "to escape from theories and attach [oneself] to facts, not allowing [oneself] to be confused by a knowledge of what that [game] was intended to be," would not be very good advice. The problem is especially critical in a democracy, in which people are presumed to exercise fundamental authority to make "law," especially such "political laws" as those having to do with the exercise of the prerogatives of governments.

John Searle, a philosopher concerned with the study of language, posed a serious challenge to Wilson's presumption about escaping from theory and attaching oneself to facts. In *Speech Acts,* Searle distinguishes between "brute facts" and "institutional facts." "Brute facts" might presumably exist in nature. Searle suggests how "a group of highly trained observers" might observe a game of American football as "brute facts" and discover patterns of regularity that could be formulated as "the law of periodical clustering."

> . . . at statistically regular intervals organisms in like colored shirts cluster together in a roughly circular fashion (the huddle). Furthermore, at equally regular intervals, circular clustering is followed by linear clustering (the teams line up for the play), and linear clustering is followed by the phenomenon of linear interpenetration. (1969, 52)

Observing "brute facts" and discovering a law of periodic clustering would not contribute to an understanding of American football. Searle argues that football can only be understood by the way that the rules of the game are constitutive of the game. "Institutional facts" can only be understood by the constitutive character of institutional arrangements in human society. Our effort to understand ways of life in human societies needs to be concerned with the constitutive character of "institutional facts" that cannot be confined to words on paper. We need to turn to questions about how and why human beings have recourse to rule-ordered relationships in the constitution of order in human societies. The artifactual character of institutional arrangements turns on how ideas expressed through the language of rules are used to constitute patterns of human relationships. Playing football and watching football with an awareness of what is happening on the field of play depend on common knowledge and shared communities of understanding about the rules of the game and the enforcement of those rules in accordance with standards of fairness.

If citizens are essential players and the basic rule makers in the game called "democracy," which applies to diverse exigencies of life, we have the problem of determining how to hold officials accountable for the discharge of their responsibilities. In turn, we also have the problem of deciding how to hold citizens accountable to one another for the discharge of their responsibilities. Madison's concern about the Tyranny of the Majority occurs when winning coalitions gain control over the institutions of government. Tocqueville's concern about Majority Despotism arises when those who exercise the prerogatives of Government attempt to cope with all of the problems of life, sparing people the cares of thinking and the troubles of living. The whole moral and intellectual conditions of a people are placed at risk.

People who look to a single overarching unit of government as "a sole, simple, providential, and creative power" have lost the capability for pursuing and mediating conflicting interests through processes of conflict resolution. Such processes involve using ideas to pool, rearrange, and compromise interests in constituting shared communities of understanding about how to cope with the exigencies of life through reflection and choice in self-governing communities of relationships. These problems lay at a deeper level entailing the place of language and culture—the mass of ideas that constitute their character of mind—as these relate to the constitution of order in human societies. The intergenerational character of life means that people, who are children in successive generations, need to learn the rudiments of democratic ways of life by relating to others in the context of family and community. We cannot do away with childhood. We each live through that experience on our way to becoming adults and preparing ourselves for becoming citizens in democratic societies. Without appropriate arrangements for rearing and educating children, citizens across successive generations may lose the moral understanding and knowledge appropriate to a science of citizenship—the science of politics—necessary to their function as citizens.

The game of Parliamentary Government associated with British Government may be very different from the game of American federalism as conceptualized by the authors of *The Federalist,* in the same way that the games that both Americans and other nations call "football" are fundamentally different games. Principles of bureaucratic administration in British parliamentary government did not come to dominate public administration in England until the twentieth century. To presume that Parliamentary Government and Bureaucratic Administration are the true forms of government in democratic republics is like presuming that German *fußball* or English soccer is the true form of football or that the French Republic is the true form of democracy. If the players, officials, and spectators were uncertain about what games were being played, great confusion, I presume, would be the result. This level of confusion has come to prevail in American society about the constitution of the American system of governance during the twentieth century. Different sets of ideas are being used by players, officials, and spectators to give meaning to the American way of life. Mutual trust is giving way to confusion and distrust.

A "federal form of government" combining the advantages of a great republic with the advantages of small republics, which might even extend to what Thomas Jefferson called "ward republics," is a radically different conception of a system of government from one induced, overseen, managed, and directed from the Executive Office of the President. The latter creates "strange paradoxes," as Tocqueville had observed.

> The democratic nations that have introduced freedom into their political constitution at the very time when they were augmenting the despotism of their administrative constitution have been led into strange paradoxes. To manage those minor affairs in which good sense is all that is wanted, the people are held to be unequal to the task; but when the government of the country is at stake, the people are invested with immense powers; they are alternately made the playthings of their ruler, and his masters, more than kings and less than men. ([1835–40] 1945, 2:321)

What began as a War on Poverty has induced increasing poverty among the presumed "beneficiaries," creating what has been referred to as an "underclass" of broken families and homelessness, both of which have become characteristic of central cities in American society. Members of the ruling class who sponsored the War on Poverty became the principal beneficiaries. Books of a generation later bore such titles as *Losing Ground* (Murray 1984), *The Dream and the Nightmare* (Magnet 1993), *Rethinking*

Social Policy (Jencks 1992), and *The Good Life and Its Discontents* (R. Samuelson 1995).

Basic transformations have occurred in the American system of governance, from a system with such noteworthy features as a federal system having the advantages of both large republics and small republics to one of Presidential Government run from the Executive Office of the President exercising tutelage over an innumerable multitude. All citizens are presumed to be equal and alike, endeavoring to procure the petty and paltry pleasures with which they glut their lives, while turning to the Government as the sole agent and arbiter of their happiness, to paraphrase Tocqueville. These transformations suggest why I turn from the study of "government" to questions about the place of ideas, language, and culture in the constitution of order in democratic societies. An understanding of Tocqueville's diagnosis of Democratic Despotism, in contrast to the Tyranny of the Majority, requires attention to the place of language and culture in constituting their "character of mind" and shaping "the whole moral and intellectual condition" of people.

These transformations have occurred over approximately ten generations. Great changes have occurred in the material and technological conditions of life, including a very large metropolis on the southern California coastal plain and others in different regions of the world. What remains troubling is the transformation from a free, self-governing society with townships and judicial processes in which citizens participated both in tending to their common concerns and rendering judgment about the application and enforcement of laws to a society that turns to something called "the Government" to address the problems of life.

The Scope of This Inquiry

Tocqueville's basic challenge about the viability of democratic societies is still with us. His extended characterization of Democratic Despotism ([1835–40] 1945, 2:318–19, quoted earlier) suggests that the United States has proceeded on a course that is likely to contribute to the failure of American democracy. The concept of "liberal" Parliamentary democracy is vulnerable to autocratic dominance. I believe that the paradigmatic shift proposed by Woodrow Wilson will not make the world safe for democracy. It will lead instead to State-governed Societies that are likely to be destructive of the institutional arrangements essential to the constitution of self-governing societies. What I earlier addressed as an intellectual crisis (V. Ostrom [1971] 1987) pervades American society and has, consequently, become a cultural crisis that places both American society and contemporary civilization at risk.

Unfortunately, as a dweller in Plato's Cave, I cannot see the direct light of Truth. I can only hope to pursue this inquiry through an intellectual struggle with others who concern themselves with the sciences of human affairs in ways that contribute to "the mass of those ideas which constitute their character of mind" among peoples in democratic societies and comprise "the moral and intellectual conditions" of democratic peoples. The meaning of democracy turns on the relationship of ideas to deeds in the various activities and games of life. The idea that ideas articulated through the use of language permeate all of life is the key to understanding what it means to live a life in democratic societies. I can only hope, by drawing on the work of others, to explore a few basic aspects pertaining to the character of mind that contributes to the viability of democratic societies.

In the chapters that follow, I proceed in three steps. The first is concerned with the quest for a science of human affairs appropriate to democratic societies. My concern parallels Tocqueville's concern for a "new science of politics . . . for a new world." To press the inquiry further in chapter 2, I draw on James Bryce, John Dewey, and Harold Lasswell in what I regard as a quest for a science of politics appropriate to the study of democratic societies. In chapter 3, I draw on George Orwell's mode of analysis, suggested in an appendix to his novel *1984,* to examine the language of *The Communist Manifesto* and a parallel effort to examine the language of the Welfare State that I identify as the New Newspeak in contrast to "Science as a habit of mind, or a method of thought, irrespective of its particular branches" (Orwell [1949] 1983, 254). In chapter 4, I turn to what I hope is both a sympathetic and critical assessment of a tradition of scholarship with which I have worked. These efforts present serious shortcomings while offering important contributions for working with the diverse cultural and social sciences as they might contribute to a common science of human affairs. A strange anomaly persists: discourse about human affairs remains incoherent. Until scholars in the cultural and social sciences and those who participate in the governance of democratic societies establish the rudiments for a common language to discuss human affairs, we cannot reach from the ordinary exigencies of everyday life to problems of global concern. Our discourse is like that of blind men who rely on their sense of touch to portray an elephant.

In part 3—"Back to Basics"—I am concerned with basic conceptual, ontological, and epistemological problems in understanding the human condition and aspects of human affairs. All opportunities are accompanied by dangers. Human beings face difficulties in dealing with a world that is open to potentials for choice but always accompanied by basic limits. There is much about the mystery of being that cannot be known by mortal human beings. All systems of logic depend on presuppositions that cannot themselves be proved. We do not and cannot see the direct light of Truth. We depend on presuppositions grounded in the teachings of those who have expressed ideas of great wisdom in understanding human potentials. We also depend on skills of artisanship in achieving whatever human beings are able to achieve.

In part 4, "The Cultural Foundations of Creative Civilizations," I am concerned with exploring both common features and critical differences in comparing African and European experience and in comparing Western and Confucian traditions. I look on literate vernacular languages as key factors in explaining differences in African and European cultural development. In comparing East and West, I turn to both commonalities and basic differences in the teachings of the prophets and sages and to what these imply for science as a method of thought broadly applicable to the use of ideas in the exercise of problem-solving capabilities.

Finally, in the concluding section of this book, I explore the possibility of progress by attempting to resolve some of the puzzles explored in the course of this inquiry and by conjecturing about the development of a science of citizenship that might enable human beings to use the arts and sciences of association to diagnose their sources of trouble and to learn from their mistakes. My effort is to deepen the foundations implicit in Tocqueville's analysis so that we might recognize the theoretical merit of Tocqueville's achievements and begin to explore potentials for crafting democratic societies built on principles of self-governance. Our challenge is to create "freer institutions" rather than to "stretch [ourselves] at the feet of a single master." Democracies are viable only under limited conditions; and finding ways of meeting those conditions are the necessary means for achieving democratic ways of life.

PART 2

The Quest for a Science of Human Affairs Appropriate to Democratic Societies

If people are presumed, in some meaningful sense, to have self-governing capabilities, such that each mature individual is presumed to be one's own governor, capable of participating in communities of associated relationships and of being knowledgeable about public affairs, then questions arise about the scope of what is meant by the term *democracy.* Does the term apply only to forms of government, to ways of life, or to both? If ways of life are implicated, then what ways of thinking and ways of acting become features of rational discourse in democratic ways of life? How do we think about life in democratic societies without cutting ourselves off from essential features that are constitutive of democratic ways of life?

The idea that democracy in America was a great experiment—the focus of attention in Tocqueville's *Democracy in America*—poses a problem about how ideas were used to design the experiment. Those ideas relate to the meaning of democracy in America. I turn to the work of James Bryce, John Dewey, and Harold Lasswell to understand their efforts to conceptualize the meaning of democracy and use language appropriate to such an inquiry. In a chapter on Newspeak and Doublethink, I turn to languages of political rhetoric to address the problems of humanity at large and in the abstract, rather than in the ecological and cultural exigencies of human communities. I then turn to the application of economic reasoning to nonmarket decision making to reveal still more wide-ranging problematics about the use of language in political inquiry and the relationship of political inquiries to the constitution of order in human societies. These problematics reveal serious ambiguities and incoherence in the use of language both in scientific and political discourse.

The place of ideas in the architecture of choice has been seriously neglected. The choices that are made with regard to production, exchange, and use of goods and services as they are available in competitive market economies and open diversely organized public economies are different than the choices that are to be made with regard to the rules of a fair game used in constituting patterns of order in human societies. These, in turn, are different than the choices that apply to the warrantability of knowledge, which needs to be taken into account if we are to anticipate the consequences that follow from the ideas or conceptions being put into practice. Choices in human societies are not simple, straightforward, linear computations but multiple strands of interdependent computations that need to be considered as complements to one another.

CHAPTER 2

Conceptions of Democracy and the Language of Political Inquiry

On the register of the retina of our eyes, we *see* people relating to one another in the ordinary exigencies of life. We are more rarely witnesses to what they say to one another, and we never see the perspectives they hold as they relate to each other. When we look in the mirror, we cannot see the workings of our own mind. The best we can do to understand others is to use language to communicate with one another in interpersonal relationships. We confront a deep puzzle that much of what we see is how the Mind's Eye, so to speak, is prepared to read the images formed on the retina of the eyes and to receive messages conveyed by the other sensory features on which we rely. The Mind's Eye, as I use that metaphor, refers to the organization of human cognition as constituted by languages, experiences, thoughts, feelings, habits, and associations, some of which may be quite invisible to the retina and inaccessible to other sensory organs. Unfortunately, we may be *unconscious* of much that is constitutive of *human consciousness.* We face the difficulty of raising to consciousness much of what is neglected by the best-informed observers.

In this chapter, I explore the conceptual tools used by well-informed observers who have been concerned with the study of modern democracies. The focus of attention will be on their efforts to mobilize analytical tools that help us to understand how people learn to be self-governing. These are among the conditions necessary for establishing the viability of democratic societies. In a narrow sense, the political sciences might include law, journalism, public administration, public affairs, and political science, narrowly construed; but in a broader sense, the political sciences include the whole corpus of human knowledge bearing on choice. In pursuing this inquiry about the language of the political sciences and its relationship to human affairs, I shall presume, as Tocqueville did, that people in a democratic society need to achieve a level of knowledge and civilization that allows them to "discern the causes of their own wretchedness" ([1835–40] 1945, 1:231). In other words, they need to perceive their own troubles and be capable of formulating remedies by altering conditions to yield results that are more conducive to their common good.

In orienting ourselves to the problems of language in the constitution of knowledge with reference to systems of rule-ordered relationships in human societies, I turn to the language used in the work of three scholars concerned with modern democracies. The first is James Bryce, who served as British ambassador to the United States and in an array of other assignments in a distinguished career, and who authored *The American Commonwealth* ([1888] 1995) and *Modern Democracies* ([1921] 1931). Bryce worked with conceptions of liberal democracy, emphasizing representative government that closely parallels Woodrow Wilson's formulations. Bryce was notably uncomfortable with Tocqueville's formulations.

The second is John Dewey, the premier American philosopher of the twentieth century, who had a deep concern about the prospects of a democratic way of life. Dewey attempted to shift from a focus on "state" to "public" to get at the practical problems that underlay human relationships, but he failed to leap from the singular [state/public] to the plural [political systems/publics] in addressing *The Public and Its Problems* (Dewey 1927).

The third is Harold Lasswell, whom I regard as the premier American political scientist of the twentieth century, and who was strongly preoccupied with the development of a language for political inquiry and its relationship to democracy as a sharing of power. Lasswell's work reveals how concepts of "power" create serious anomalies for coming to terms with the meaning of democracy. Serious difficulties are also reflected in distinctions Lasswell makes between political myths, doctrines, and ideologies, on the one hand, and the political sciences, on the other. If the political sciences exclude beliefs associated with myths, doctrines, and ideologies, how are we to establish relationships between ideas and deeds? This key issue is addressed in this chapter and in several of the subsequent chapters.

In addressing the work of these scholars, we again confront a paradigmatic challenge. A language primarily devoted to the "form of Government," the "State," or "*power* relationships" may focus human perceptions in ways that neglect what needs to be taken into account. Does the concept of democracy refer to people and the way that structures of relationships get established so that people function in societies that govern themselves for themselves, to paraphrase Tocqueville? Or does the concept of democracy apply only to the form of government? If the language of the political sciences includes only a portion of what is constitutive of democratic societies, political scientists cannot understand how such societies *work*. They do not understand how the essential working parts relate to one another. What does it mean for people to govern? If our understanding is inadequate, our language is likely to be inappropriate.

Inquiries about Modern Democracies

James Bryce

James Bryce, a Briton of Scottish-Irish, Presbyterian heritage, was as strongly motivated as Alexis de Tocqueville to understand democracy in America and democratic potentials in the world at large. The sweep of Bryce's *American Commonwealth* is as great as Tocqueville's *Democracy in America* ([1835–40] 1945). Many of the details are more fully elaborated. Machine politics and boss rule in the post–Civil War era was examined with separate chapters on the "Philadelphia Gas Ring" and "Kearneyism in California." In his introductory chapter to *The American Commonwealth,* Bryce explicitly contrasted his mode of analysis with Tocqueville's, which he described as being grounded "on general and somewhat speculative views of democracy."

> . . . my object has been less to discuss its merits than to paint the institutions and people of America as they are, tracing what is peculiar in them not merely to the sovereignty of the masses, but also to the history and traditions of the race, to its fundamental ideas, to its material environment. I have striven to avoid the temptations of the deductive method, and to present simply the facts of the case, arranging and connecting them as best I can, but letting them speak for themselves rather than pressing upon the reader my own conclusions. ([1888] 1995, 1:3–4)

Bryce overstated the contrast; like Tocqueville, he offered his own conclusions. Like Bryce, Tocqueville was concerned with the history and tradition of the Anglo-Americans, with basic ideas, and with the material environment of the North American continent. Bryce was well grounded in "general" and "speculative" views about democracy. I am confident that his education was as comprehensive as Tocqueville's.

Yet there are contrasts. First among these are Bryce's reference to "the sovereignty of the masses," which has quite different connotations than Tocqueville's reference to the "sovereignty of the people," and the latter's view that each individual is first his or her own governor. Second, Bryce was more preoccupied with "facts." Deduction is an *inferential relationship* with regard to *propositions.* The relationship of ideas to actions and actions to outcomes [some future apparent good] as being either "factual" or "artifactual" is of critical importance with regard to how human experience is to be *construed*—whether as brute facts or as institutional facts. I believe that this is the key issue that Bryce and Tocqueville would have been required to clarify in determining the similarities and differences in their two inquiries.

Bryce asserted in the introduction to *Modern Democracies* that "It is Facts that are needed: Facts, Facts, Facts" ([1921] 1931, 1:12). That statement might rightly be viewed as evidence of "brute empiricism," as Lasswell and Kaplan (1950, x) asserted. Again, Bryce overstated his position; the role of ideas in "origins" is emphasized in his case studies of the six democracies that he examined. Yet the concept of the separation of powers is characterized as a "dogma" in the American case (Bryce [1888] 1995, 1:26). How ideas are to be construed in the conduct of a practical experiment is not explicitly addressed in detail by either Tocqueville or Bryce. Their work as scholars, however, is based on different presuppositions on this issue.

In addressing the object of his inquiry in the *American Commonwealth,* Bryce referred to "a national commonwealth" and indicated that there are "three main things that one wishes to know . . ., viz., its framework and constitutional machinery, the methods by which it is worked, the forces which move it and direct its course. It is *natural* to begin with the first of these. Accordingly, I begin with *the government*" (ibid., 1:4–5, my emphasis). He recognized these as having a "two-fold" reference to "national or federal authorities" and "states." The initial focus, then, is on "the government"; and within that context Bryce began with the "national government, whose structure presents less difficulty to European minds, because it resembles the national government in each of their own countries" (ibid., 1:5). The idea of federalism was accommodated to the European idea of the State. The unfolding of Bryce's analysis is by no means confined to "the government" but treats extensively, especially in the second volume, the party system, public opinion, and the "social institutions" characteristic of American society and the place that these have in American democracy as a way of life.

In *Modern Democracies,* we find the same focal emphasis and the same wide scope in the way that Bryce cast his net to get at the "Facts." He asserted, for example, that "Democracy really means nothing more nor less than the rule of the whole people expressing their *sovereign will* by their votes" (my emphasis). He then presumed that some features in all democracies are "everywhere similar, due to the fact that supreme power rests with the voting multitude" ([1921] 1931, 1:viii). Bryce then went on to assert:

It is of the Form of Government as a Form of Government—that is to say, of the features which democracies have in common—that this book treats, describing the phenomena as they appear in their daily working to an observer who is living in the midst of them and watching them, as one standing in a great factory sees the play and hears the clang of the machinery all around him. The actual facts are what I wish to describe, and it seems as if nothing could be simpler, for they are all around us. But the facts are obscured to most people by the half-assimilated ideas and sonorous or seductive phrases that fill the air; and few realize exactly what are the realities beneath the phrases. To those persons who, as politicians, or journalists, or otherwise, have been "inside politics," the realities of their own country are familiar, and this familiarity enables such experts to get a fair impression of the facts in other countries. But as regards large parts of every public that may be said which the cynical old statesman in Disraeli's novel *Contarini Fleming* said to his ardent son who wished to get away from words to ideas, "Few ideas are correct ones, and what are correct no one can ascertain; but with Words we govern men." (Ibid.)

It is hard to imagine how Bryce could present us with a deeper dilemma but one that is apt to characterize much of political "reality." Presumably, the insiders—those engaged in Statecraft—know the Facts, which are as close to the truth as it is possible to achieve. But it is "Words" that "govern men." Presumably, reality is a form of theater where Words, expressed in sonorous or seductive phrases, are disassociated from ideas. Human beings may or may not, Bryce might argue, be motivated by ideas in the actions they take.

If one stands in a great factory, observes activities, and hears the clang of machinery, there is another "reality." The design and creation of the factory, the machinery, and the activities of people are shaped by reference to ideas. The factory was built to produce something. Its structure represents the arrangement of present means to achieve some future apparent good, to paraphrase Hobbes's definition of power. The clang of machinery relates the theoretical realms of physics and the applied realms of mechanical and electrical engineering. To look at a factory without the ideas that went into its design, construction, and operation would be to cut oneself off from an essential understanding of what is transpiring on the factory floor. The physical character of the factory, the nature and layout of the machinery, and what is being transformed [produced] is what John R. Commons ([1924] 1968) referred to in his mode of analysis as the "plant"—an industrial facility. The operation of the factory as a plant turns on knowledgeable artisans knowing what they are doing. The people working in accordance with the "working rules" of the "going concern," in Commons's language, are constituted by a system of authority relationships. In the going concern is a governance structure that coordinates the efforts of people constitutive of the working relationships that keep the factory going and doing whatever it is that the factory does. No single workman may have complete consciousness of the way that ideas relate to what gets done; but how the factory works and takes its place in the context of a larger society or civilization turns on access to ideas associated with diverse bodies of knowledge. The constitution of the factory represents a complex configuration of relationships that functions simultaneously as an epistemic order, an economic order, and a governance [rule-ordering] structure in a system of social identities.

There are, however, problems in construing a "form of Government" with reference to a "whole people" where "supreme power rests with the voting multitude." Is it those acting on behalf of the "whole people" in a national government who speak on behalf of the people? Agents can easily become masters if it is only a national representative body that speaks on behalf of the whole people. In his chapter "Oligarchies in Democracies," Bryce concluded: "Thus Free Government cannot but be, and has in reality always been, an Oligarchy within a Democracy" ([1921] 1931, 2:550). When is democracy an illusion; when do illusions about democracy serve as cognitive screens to conceal an Oligarchy of the Few? Are human societies ordered by an "iron law of oligarchy" (Michels [1911] 1966)? When do "dogmas" about a separation of powers and federal systems of governance become necessary factors to be taken into account? In a footnote, Bryce suggested that the phrase *Will of the People,* a key phrase in his own system of ideas,

> seems to involve two fallacies, *or rather perhaps two implications* which induce fallacies, and they spring from the *habit* of conceiving of the People as One. The first is that the Will of the Majority is apt to be thought of as if it were the Will of All. The second is that as it comes from many it is thought of as issuing alike and equally from many, whereas in fact it originates in few and is accepted by many. ([1921] 1931, 2:548 n. 3, my emphasis)

Critical inquiry requires the clarification of conceptions about how something works. If inferences involve fallacies, critical problems need to be addressed in intellectual artisanship.

A "fact," following Hobbes, can be conceived as an event witnessed. There is always a problem of how an event witnessed is to be construed:

Does the sun revolve, or does the earth spin? Am I first my own governor in a democratic society, or am I only one of a great multitude who conceives of the People as One? Is the Will of All a fantasy of the imagination—a source of self-deception? "Where is the Will of the People?" Bryce asked (ibid.). Do fallible creatures dealing with an uncertain world act on the basis of a Will, meaning commitment, or is human artisanship more tentative, more experimental, more contingent than an exercise of Will?

How we address general ideas and speculative issues with reference to systems of governance was of critical importance in unraveling Bryce's impressions when he wrote:

> The absorption of men's minds with ideas and schemes of social reconstruction has diverted attention from those problems of free government which occupied men's minds when the flood-tide of democracy was rising seventy or eighty years ago; and it has sometimes seemed to me in writing this book that it was being addressed rather to the last than to the present generation. That generation busied itself with institutions; this generation is bent rather upon the purposes which institutions may be made to serve. (Ibid., 1:x)

The work of the one "generation" needs to be seen in relation to the other. What happened after "seventy or eighty years" is rather crucial in estimating the warrantability of the theory used, for example, in fashioning the design of the Soviet system (Kaminski 1992). Can people ignore the conceptions that went into the design of institutions in fashioning a system of government to secure accountability on the part of representative officials in the purposes they were intended to realize? The potentials for tomorrow depend critically on the tools and intellectual resources that were fashioned yesterday. How human beings deal with the constitution of knowledge affects the course of civilizations across generations, centuries, and millennia. Is democracy an object of manipulation; or does it offer significant potential in the emergence of human civilizations?

There is much to be learned from Bryce so long as his concern with Facts is supplemented by a reader's concern with general ideas and speculative issues. Working with human beings is quite different than the "sovereignty of the masses," as Bryce's candor revealed when he discussed the "Will of the People." People's intentions are important in what people attempt to do and get done. The relationship of ideas to deeds and to critical reflection about what has transpired seems essential to the emergence of political science, while commentaries about sonorous and seductive phrases in the drama of political theater appear to obscure the emergence of such a science.

John Dewey

John Dewey, an American of New England Congregational [Puritan] heritage, was preoccupied with the place of ideas in human experience and with an abiding faith in "democracy." That faith gained expression in a variety of works concerned with learning, education, inquiry, intelligence, logic, epistemology, and philosophy, but always with a preoccupation for the conditions of life in a democratic society. A small volume on *The Public and Its Problems* (1927) represents Dewey's effort to treat democracy as a system of governance. Dewey could be highly critical of what might be called arbitrary and dogmatic systems of thought. It is important, then, to give both sympathetical and critical attention to his effort to come to terms with political theory in the context of his preoccupations with democracy.

Dewey's inquiry begins with assertions that pose a challenge for his reader. "The concept of the state," Dewey asserted, "like most concepts which are introduced by 'The,' is both too rigid and too tied up with controversies to be of ready use" (ibid., 8). He proposed to approach his inquiry by a flanking movement rather than a frontal attack.

> The moment we utter the words "The State" a score of intellectual ghosts rise to obscure our vision. Without our intention and without our notice, the notion of "The State" draws us imperceptibly into a consideration of the logical relationship of various ideas to one another, and away from facts of human activity. It is better, if possible, to start from the latter and see if we are not led thereby into an idea of something which will turn out to implicate the marks and signs which characterize political behavior. (Ibid., 8–9)

Indeed, the concept of "The State" is bound up in logical relationships. Dewey proposed to turn his back on that problem and, like Bryce, to look for the "facts of human activity." This would be consistent with a presupposition that a political order exists. What he was searching for were "facts"—events witnessed—that "implicate the marks and signs which characterize political behavior." How a system of governance is to be found by such an inquiry and what its relationship to democracy might be is a problem of substantial proportions.

Dewey's inquiry is an interesting adventure. He begins with a search for the public. The public is conceptualized as those affected by the indirect consequences of human actions that are of sufficient importance to be controlled in ways "to secure some consequences and avoid others" (ibid., 12). The distinction between private and public turns, then, on the significance of consequences for those not directly involved in transactions. To exercise control requires recourse to agents who will do so.

The search for the public turned into the discovery of the state. The public is those affected by the indirect consequences of human actions. These indirect consequences are what economists might refer to as externalities or neighborhood effects. The agents responsible for the control of indirect consequences are officials—government. The state, then, in Dewey's inquiry, is conceptualized as both the government and the public as they interact with one another. The public acquires a consciousness of itself through the deliberations and actions taken by government.

In addressing the distinguishing characteristics of a "democratic state" to the *political* features of democracy, Dewey identified these characteristics with a "democratic mode of government" associated with "a specified practice in selecting officials and regulating their conduct as officials" (ibid., 82). Popular elections, short terms of office, and, thus, frequent elections are mechanisms for regulating the conduct of officials. Yet Dewey recognized that these mechanisms—general suffrage and officials chosen by plurality vote—appear to be associated with an erosion of "social and humane ideals" in which "the utilization of government as the genuine instrumentality of an inclusive and fraternally associated public" is lost (ibid., 109). The consciousness associated with conjoint effort is lost; and the public is eclipsed. Those who control the agenda of political discourse and enjoy the fruits of victory presumably do so in closed circles while using sonorous and seductive phrases that are not enlightening to others.

Unfortunately, using relationships pertaining to public, officials, and conjoint activities as terms for People, Government, and State in an effort to discover "the state" provides us with no resolution about whether "sovereignty"—the authority to make law—resides with the "government" or with the "public" as they are conjoined in a State. No reference is made to the problem of constitutional choice or to whether multitudes of such states can coexist with one another in associated systems of governance. Whether or not a monopoly of rulership prerogatives and control of the instruments of coercion will transform agents into masters ruling over subjects is not discussed. Instead, the eclipse of the public is associated with the emergence of the "Great Society," a problem addressed by Graham Wallas (1914) in a book by that title. The Great Society was a concept applied to interdependencies that reach far beyond the known horizons of each individual's personal experience. Dewey saw the eclipse of the public in the Great Society as calling for a "search for the Great Community." That search for Dewey required recourse to a problem of method—

methodology—in the mobilization of human intelligence to undertake conjoint activities.

Dewey did make interesting observations about the importance of language in scientific discourse.

> Science, in other words, is a highly specialized language, more difficult to learn than any natural language. It is an artificial language, not in the sense of being factitious, but in that of being *a work of intricate art,* devoted to a particular purpose and not capable of being acquired nor understood in the way in which the mother tongue is learned. (1927, 163, my emphasis)

Dewey further considered the problem of communication to be such that "In its deepest and richest sense a community must always remain a matter of face-to-face intercourse" (ibid., 211). How to engage the search for the "Great Community," achieve an articulate awareness of publicness, and do so by discovery of "the state" remained unresolved. Dewey, I argue, trapped himself by presuming that the "facts of human activity" would lead to a discovery of the state. Despite his warning about intellectual ghosts associated with the concept of "The State," Dewey's search may have been plagued by these same ghosts in his search for The Public.

Dewey did not acknowledge the possibility of a specialized language appropriate to a political science and a language of discourse that might be appropriate to the constitution of democratic societies. Apart from Dewey's use of the expression "The State," I am left with such ambiguities in studying Dewey's account that I cannot decide whether he implicitly uses a unitary conception of State to inform his analysis. I personally owe a great intellectual debt to Dewey. His emphasis on the hypothetical character of human knowledge was the source of an insistent demand on myself to come to terms with the relationship of ideas to design concepts and to actions.

Dewey is associated with an American school of philosophy identified with "pragmatism." The critical relationship in "pragmatism" is the relationship of science as a "highly specialized" and "artificial" language to practices that give critical attention to whether that language yields warrantable results in experimental circumstances. There are, then, critical issues bearing on the pragmatics of language. What relationship do ideas expressed in a highly specialized and critically assessed language have to consequences—the results achieved? How ideas affect what gets done needs to be determined. Unfortunately, Dewey, in turning to political inquiry, did not address himself to problems of language in the constitution of political orders as carefully as did Thomas Hobbes, Alexander Hamilton, James Madison, and Alexis de Tocqueville. He saw no tension between "democracy" and "large-scale collective planning" (Dewey 1946, 27). Dewey failed to diagnose the eclipse of the public as being associated with strong incentives to use deceptive language to create erroneous conceptions in democratic societies.

Among contemporary American politicians, the term *pragmatism* disassociates ideas from results achieved. A "pragmatist" in contemporary political discourse is one who cannot be bothered with ideas but is preoccupied with whatever works. What works is measured in individual success—in positions held and honors bestowed. These are the marks of achievement—indicators of performance. With reference to the pragmatics of language, I shall by contrast be concerned with the relationship of ideas—hypothetical conjectures embedded in conceptual-computational logics—to the results that are achieved by what gets done. Conceptions imply elements and relationships expressed as a computational logic. This was implicit in Dewey's work as a scholar. When he turned to a search to discover "the state" in a democratic society, however, he neglected the place of the *pragmatics of language* as being the essential link between ideas and what gets done. The results achieved must always be mediated by language—in thinking, in communicating with others, and in deciding what to do and doing what gets done. The pragmatics of language is an essential feature of pragmatism.

Dewey would have rejected Hobbes's effort in *Leviathan* ([1651] 1960) to render a hypothetical account of Man in a State of Nature. When people seek to realize Peace as an alternative to War through covenants, it is personal, face-to-face communication that nurtures the common understanding and patterns of social accountability that are constitutive of community. Hume's treatment of sympathy and fellow feeling as the source of justice (an artificial [artifactual] virtue), Adam Smith's theory of moral sentiments, Montesquieu's conception of republican virtue as necessary to the spirit of the laws in a republic, *The Federalist*'s theory of constitutional choice reiterated in a compounded system of federal republics, and Tocqueville's analysis of a great experiment in the constitution of a self-governing society would have afforded Dewey with better foundations for addressing the constitution of order in democratic societies than a quest for discovery of the state. His book might more appropriately have been entitled *The Publics* [in the plural] *and Their Problems.* Dewey's warning about the abstractness and rigidity of "concepts that are introduced by 'The,'" applies to The Public as well as to The State. If he had been guided by his own warning, he could have carried his analyses much further.

Harold Lasswell

Harold Lasswell, an American of Midwest Presbyterian heritage, undertook with Abraham Kaplan, an American of New York Jewish heritage, the task of formulating a language and a mode of analysis that would provide a general framework for the conduct of political inquiry and the basis for the development of a general theory that might apply to the "shaping and sharing of power" as patterns of order in human societies. I identify the analytical language formulated in *Power and Society* (Lasswell and Kaplan 1950) with Lasswell because it was at the core of his life's work and did not serve Kaplan's scholarship in a comparable way. I know of no other effort of such a fundamental magnitude since Hobbes's *Leviathan.* Lasswell was critically concerned with the revolutionary struggles of mankind that dominated the course of events in the twentieth century and, thus, with the place of democracy and contending patterns of order among different peoples.

It is difficult to imagine a scholar who was more knowledgeable of the literature in the social sciences and humanities or more sensitive to the "puny" character of the understanding of "any observer" "beside the gargantuan proportion of the facts" (Marvick 1977, 82) entailed in the patterns of order in human societies. Lasswell emphasized subjective [psychological] and external manifestations of life, the contextual and developmental aspects of human societies, the interactive character of social processes, and the nature and function of symbols in social processes. He emphasized that "the power process is not a distinct and separable part of the social process, but only the political aspect of an interactive whole" (Lasswell and Kaplan 1950, xvii).

Lasswell rejected the fictitious cleavage that separates the study of the "individual" from the study of "society," asserting, "There is no cleavage; there is but a gradual graduation of reference points" (Marvick 1977, 75). He presumed that these reference points applied to individuals as they interacted with one another with regard to multiple values identified as *power, respect, rectitude, affection, well-being, wealth, skill,* and *enlightenment.* The shaping and sharing of these diverse values occur in social contexts characterized by commensurate structures and processes.

Power as the Core Concept in Political Science

Lasswell considered *power* relationships to be the core of political science. Lasswell's analysis of the *power* relationship is grounded in two terms— *decision* and *power.*

DF. A *decision* is a policy involving severe sanctions (deprivations). (Lasswell and Kaplan 1950, 74)

DF. *Power* is participation in the making of decisions: G has power over H with respect to the values K if G participates in the making of decisions affecting the K-policies of H. (Ibid., 75)

Policy was earlier defined as a projected program of goal values and practices (ibid., 71) and *sanction* as a response to an act that is expected to modify future acts in the direction of conformity to some norm (ibid., 48). The point of emphasis is on *severe deprivation:* "power is a special case of the exercise of influence: it is the process of affecting policies of others with the help of (actual or threatened) severe deprivations for nonconformity with the policies intended" (ibid., 76). In this context, then, "the political process is the shaping, distribution, and exercise of power." This is where, in my judgment, great mischief begins creating opportunities for some to gain dominance over and to exploit others. Lasswell, however, added a parenthetical observation to his assertion that "the political process is the shaping, distribution, and exercise of power (in a wider sense, of all the deference values, or of influence in general)" (ibid., 75). The emphasis, however, is on political science as "the study of the shaping and sharing of power" (ibid., xiv) and of politics as the shaping and sharing of *power.* Our puzzle is whether the concept of democracy is associated with the constitution of the State as a political order narrowly construed or with the constitution of social orders broadly construed.

Lasswell's concept of power is consistent with the mainstreams of theoretical inquiry. Max Weber, for example, conceived of power as "the possibility of imposing one's will upon the behavior of other persons" (Rheinstein 1967, 323). Power is a form of domination established "by virtue of authority, i.e., power to command and duty to obey" (ibid., 324). "In other words," states Weber, "in our terminology *domination* shall be *identical with authoritarian power of command*" (ibid., 328, Weber's emphasis). Weber further elaborates his meaning by reference to the following situation.

The manifested will *(command)* of the *ruler* or rulers is meant to influence the conduct of one or more others *(the ruled)* and actually does influence it in such a way that their conduct to a socially relevant degree occurs as if the ruled had made the content of the command the maxim of their conduct for its own sake. Looked upon from the other end, this situation will be called *obedience.* (Ibid., Weber's emphasis)

Terms like *sovereignty, state,* and *government* received Lasswell's critical attention. *Sovereignty* is defined as "the highest degree of authority" (Lasswell and Kaplan 1950, 177), a *state* as "a sovereign territorial group" (ibid., 181), *governors* as "state authorities," and *government,* then, as "the practices of specified persons—the state authorities" (ibid., 184). In a more general context, Lasswell identified a State as "a manifold of events" where there is a "recognition that one belongs to a community with a system of paramount claims and relationships" (Marvick 1977, 75, 79).

In his critical reflections, Lasswell was careful to distance himself from concepts of unity, indivisibility, unlimitedness, or completeness that would be associated with a single [sole] center of Sovereign Authority. Instead, he took the position that "while there is always some form and degree of authority, this may occur in a multiple structure no component of which is superior to the others, and such that even the structure as a whole cannot be said to be superior to each of its components" (Lasswell and Kaplan 1950, 178). If I understand correctly, his referent, in summation, is to "the authority which renders a final decision, so that there is no appeal to a higher authority. And so on" (ibid., 181).

This is a key problem of concern to many great thinkers of the age: when does contestation cease; when is obedience exacted? Is the problem resolved by the determination of some mortal human being or is there a further appeal: To God; to "a general law, which bears the name of justice" (Tocqueville [1835–40] 1945, 1:259); to one's conception of truth; and to modifications of constitutional formulations? Contestation is important, but "decisions" cannot be delayed forever. These circumstances were the source of Socrates' and Jesus of Nazareth's travail. Jan Hus, for example, could not bear to render false witness against himself, be faithless to his God, and acquiesce to ecclesiastical and secular authority. He chose to be honest with himself and faithful to his God to the best of his own humble understanding and submitted to being burned at the stake (Spinka 1965). This was also the message conveyed in Martin Luther King's "Letter from Birmingham Jail" (1967). Some people cannot acknowledge falsehoods as truths and be true to themselves. They cannot engage in "symbolic politics" by manipulating "symbols"—sonorous and seductive phrases—to win elections, form coalitions, enact seductive phrases into law, and enjoy the spoils of victory. Constitutional processes in constitutional democracies always remain open to reformulations in light of a fundamental appeal to justice or to truth, even though injustices inevitably occur among fallible human beings. There can be no flawless system of order in human societies.

We come back, then, to the puzzle about the paradigmatic challenge of democracy—What is the place of individual responsibility, mutual understanding, social accountability, and trust with reference to conflict, contestation, and conflict resolution? These problems cannot be resolved by winning and losing elections or by an appeal to particular occupants of public offices. These matters require reference to a culture of inquiry in a search for justice and for truth. When State boundaries become permeable to crosscutting communities of relationships concerned with a quest for knowledge, the conduct of artisanship, and structures of relationships that transcend State boundaries, an appeal to the sovereignty of territorial groupings is seriously attenuated. Naked power, as Lasswell fully appreciated, breaks the bonds of individual responsibility, common understanding, social accountability, and mutual trust.

The Conception of Democracy

In addressing the topic of democracy, the concept of power as pertaining to relationships involving severe sanctions posed serious difficulties for Lasswell. In treating "anarchy" as conditions where the scope of effective power is minimal, Lasswell was driven to the following observation.

> As a rule approximates anarchy, it ceases to have the character of a rule at all. The scope of power shrinks to a minimum—in the limiting case, *no* coercion is exercised. Social control remains, of course, in the various forms of influence; but the control is noncoercive. Whether the weight of noncoercive influence is sufficient to maintain social organization cannot be settled a priori or in a general way. An anarchical society is by definition not a body politic, but it might conceivably retain its societal character. Because anarchy does not come within the range of political science, it cannot be said to be impossible; what does not exist for one observational standpoint might nevertheless be discoverable from other standpoints. We introduce the concept as specifying a limit; whether or not cases do or could exist at the limit falls outside the present inquiry. (Lasswell and Kaplan 1950, 223, Lasswell's emphasis)

In his subsequent treatment of democracy, Lasswell went on to observe:

> Democracy is thus defined here by three characteristics of the power process: (1) Power is exercised with a maximum of self-responsibility. Democracy is incompatible with any form of authoritarianism, regardless of the benefits accruing from such concentration of responsibility. (2) The power process is not absolute and self-contained:

decisions are conditional and subject to challenge. Democracy is incompatible with arbitrary and uncontrolled exercise of power, regardless of the majorities by which it is exercised. (3) The benefits of the power process are distributed throughout the body politic. Democracy is incompatible with the existence of privileged castes, regardless of expectations concerning the assumed "common interest." (Ibid., 234)

Where the scope of effective power is increased, Lasswell used the term *regimentation;* where it is decreased, he used the term *voluntarization.* With this in mind, Lasswell further treated the attributes of a democracy in the following way.

Other characteristics are related to these, both empirically and by definition. Thus a democracy is liberal rather than totalitarian (voluntarization is maximized, regimentation minimized), by the definition of libertarian in terms of self-responsibility. It is equalitarian (the elite constitutes an open class rather than a closed caste) by the definition of commonwealth in terms of impartiality. It is republican rather than autocratic (an inclusive rather than restricted oligarchy), as an empirical condition of impartiality. And the rule is balanced (dispersed) rather than dictatorial (concentrated) as an empirical condition of juridical defense. Thus an equivalent definition might have been formulated in terms of other combinations of characters, and indeed different characteristics or combinations of them have been taken by various writers as *the* definition of "democracy," all of them being in fact involved in one way or another. (Ibid., 234–35, Lasswell's emphasis)

Lasswell emphasized that "a democratic regime [i.e., the structure of political forms] is . . . only a necessary but not a sufficient condition for democracy" (ibid., 238). His summary treatment of the concept of democracy includes the following points:

(1) The formulations throughout are descriptive rather than normatively ambiguous. The question of how democracy is constituted and may be maintained is dealt with in terms which, it is hoped, lend themselves to the proliferation of empirical inquiries rather than the elaboration of metaphysical ideals and justifications.
(2) The concept of democracy is analyzed so as to exhibit a content of great complexity, rather than in terms of some single characteristic like "self-government" or "freedom."

(3) This is of particular significance as leading to a consideration of the complexity of conditions on which democracy rests. Democracy is not simply a matter of this or that feature of the social structure; *the social order, the regime and the control structure are all involved.*

(4) Thus democracy is dealt with as a possible, though difficult, pattern of *social organization.* (Ibid., 239, my emphasis)

Democracy, if I read Lasswell correctly, cannot be understood by reference only to the concept of "power" as he defined that concept. Political science viewed as the study of only *power* relationships, one might conclude, affords an unsatisfactory conceptual language for the study of democratic societies. Democracies come within the range of Lasswell's political science only to a limited degree. Lasswell's attributes of democracy imply a system of order minimally related to his concept of power relationships. Political scientists following such concepts of power cannot adequately address themselves to the constitution of democratic societies.

There are potential frontiers to be explored with regard to noncoercive patterns of social control that extend beyond the "range of political science" ["anarchy"] but within the "range" that applies to "democracy." Concepts of self-responsibility, voluntarization, impartiality, dispersal of authority, contestability [juridical challenge and defense], and balance are the attributes that Lasswell used to characterize democracy. Each of these attributes is consistent with what Tocqueville referred to as a self-governing society, in contrast to a State-governed Society.

If I read Lasswell correctly, he was also asserting that how democracies are constituted and maintained depends on "the proliferation of empirical inquiries." Relying on theories alone and acts of Will does not suffice. Rather, there are the problems of working with ideas, of learning from experience, and of extending the frontiers of knowledge as people in democratic societies learn to use ideas to establish common knowledge and to work with one another through language in shaping mutual understandings, patterns of social accountability, and trust. Difficult questions we confront are (1) How are societies, which have the attributes of self-responsibility, voluntarization, impartiality, dispersal of authority, contestability, and balance, to be constituted? (2) How are the processes for making decisions—policies involving severe sanctions (deprivations)—to be resolved with these attributes of democratic societies in viable systems of governance?

Lasswell's emphasis on language as being fundamental to political or social inquiry is a recognition that language is fundamental to the constitution of knowledge. Hobbes's *Leviathan* has a comparable preoccupation with language as the essential tool with which man, the artificer, comes to terms with the conception, design, and constitution of commonwealths. In contrast, Bryce is amusingly candid about the fundamental shortcomings of his own use of language. Dewey's reference to "science" as a "highly specialized," "artificial," but not "factitious," language was not used to inform himself about the design of the American system of governance or to explain why officials as agents of The Public contribute to the eclipse of The Public.

Lasswell presents us with an anomaly that the key concept in his conceptualization of a political science—*power*—may have only limited application to the study of democratic systems of governance characterized by self-responsibility, voluntarization, wide dispersion and sharing of authority [egalitarian], impartiality, challengeability, and equilibrating tendencies. The way that Lasswell defined *power* as the focus of inquiry in political science is not consistent with the characteristics that he associated with "democracy." If the essential characteristics of democratic societies are not "a matter of this or that feature of the social structure" and require reference to the "social order" as a whole, we are, I believe, required to raise the possibility that "paramount claims and relationships" may be constituted by patterns of order that transcend the boundaries of "sovereign territorial groups" characteristic of Nation-States. Serious conflicts may arise over paramount claims and relationships that cannot be resolved by States.

The Place of Enlightenment and Wealth in the Social Order

Lasswell's characterization of the social process as pertaining to the shaping and sharing of values also had reference to "enlightenment" and to "wealth." Enlightenment is associated with knowledge and the place of knowledge in an epistemic order—the development, communication, and use of knowledge. Wealth pertains to an economic order concerned with production, exchange, and use or consumption of goods and services. To these considerations we need to add Dewey's reference to the "highly specialized" and "artificial" languages of the sciences. To the extent that scientists fashion a common knowledge that deals with universals, the features characteristic of that common knowledge are incorporated in vernacular and literary languages that take those bodies of knowledge into account in the more general constitution of knowledge and the conduct of human artisanship. The languages of mathematics, physics, the geological and geographical sciences, and increasingly the biological sciences, as these have gained expression in industry, commerce, and agriculture, are the bases for fashioning epistemic orders that transcend the territorial boundaries of "sovereign" States.

Furthermore, the imperial thrusts of the various European empires together with Hugo Grotius's conception of freedom of the seas and Adam Smith's conceptions of free trade in competitive market economies meant that a global economic order was being put into place. A *res publica* of commerce and a *res publica* of science had begun to emerge in the larger world. Further, conceptions emerging from Dutch, British, American, and French revolutionary struggles were becoming a part of the larger consciousness of human potentials for dealing with rule-ruler-ruled relationships.

We now confront a serious puzzle in the human condition. Peace, advances in human knowledge, the extension of "free trade," and "the general law which bears the name of justice" approximate the conditions of being pure public goods. Everyone would be better off if these possibilities were generally available to all of mankind. Such public goods would be universal public goods not confined to isolable publics.

All human capital—all human productive capabilities—is tied up with the pragmatics of language and the way that languages function as a basis for common understanding, social accountability, and mutual trust in human communities. Languages are no longer confined to kinships, tribal groupings, or nation-states. Instead, languages, including scientific languages, have become complex structures giving access to diverse bodies of knowledge and expression in equally diverse forms of artisanship. Patterns of human association are no longer confined to States as systems of paramount claims and relationships. Communication is mediated in language systems in which beliefs of a universal character have become a part of the heritage of much of mankind. Yet the artisanship that makes use of these diverse bodies of knowledge depends critically on intelligible communication of a face-to-face character in applying knowledge to time and place specificities (Hayek 1945). These conditions challenge Lasswell's conceptualization of *power* [coercive] relationships as providing the basic analytical concept for a political science. Power is important; but it does not provide us with the core concept for coming to terms with the constitution of order in democratic societies. We are, I believe, required to associate rule-ruler-ruled relationships with the potentials for people in language communities to achieve lawfulness in a more general context that reaches to global proportions.

If the place of language and the constitution of knowledge are fundamental to the constitution of rule-ordered relationships, attention needs to be given to the place of ideas in the constitution of political orders. The paradigmatic challenge of democracy raises issues about the ontological and epistemological foundations of the political and social sciences. An important issue, then, is how ideas are addressed in the political and social sciences. I turn now to the way that Lasswell addressed this issue.

The Problem of Ideology

I draw on Hobbes's work to presume that all human actions associated with the voluntary nervous system are grounded in thought. Speech and knowledge acquired through language are the foundations for human artisanship. Hobbes's concept of power, as the use of present means to obtain some future apparent good, is broader than Lasswell's concept of it, as the exercise of influence on others by recourse to severe sanctions to secure conformity to explicit standards of conduct [policies]. The emphasis in Lasswell's concept is on *power over* associated with command and control of instruments of coercion. Those who are the "decision makers" engage in making policies—projected programs of collective action—and in exercising *power over* others to implement policies.

The task of elaborating a framework for political inquiry—the objective undertaken by Lasswell in *Power and Society*—is one in which "the elaboration of hypotheses presupposes, logically, a conceptual framework in terms of which clear hypotheses may be formulated" (Lasswell and Kaplan 1950, x). A distinction is made between *political doctrine* and *political science.* The focus in *Power and Society,* then, is on "an attempt to formulate the basic concepts and hypotheses of political science" (ibid., xi).

It is important to recognize that the basic concepts and hypotheses pertaining to the political process and to a political science may exclude political doctrine and may also treat democracy as more concerned with patterns of social organization broadly implicating the social order rather than the political order per se. This issue is, in part, alluded to in the following observation by Lasswell.

> Thus in a sense all of the social sciences have an identical subject matter, but they adopt toward this subject matter varying observational standpoints (frames of reference) leading to different sets of problems. Hence, though political science as here conceived is characteristically concerned with polities, it is not [need not be] limited to that concern ("science of government," "science of the state," and so on), but deals with the social process in its entirety, though always in its bearings on power. (Ibid., 215)

It is possible that the shaping and sharing of values affect the structure of incentives embodied in mutual understandings and patterns of social accountability in ways that might minimize reliance on the need to seek conformity through recourse to severe sanctions [deprivations]. Preoccupations with *power over* relationships may need to shift to patterns of association more concerned with mutual understanding, consensus, reciprocity, and social accountability—that is, *power with* relationships (Follett [1924] 1951). The enforcement of mutually accepted standards of conduct turns on monitoring and sanctioning arrangements at work among people in their associated relationships. Persons who are in nonofficial roles have a place to play in the articulation of a "public's" consciousness of itself.

Lasswell emphasized the importance of "a principle of symbolization" in the human condition (Lasswell and Kaplan 1950, xviii). The realm of speech and language is concerned with the "nature and function of symbols." This is in contrast to the world of events reflected either in human activities or objects [sets of events viewed as entities and relationships] being acted on. The world of political symbols is indefinitely large, complex, and multifaceted and is the subject of one of ten chapters in *Power and Society*. Political symbols are defined as "symbols that function to a significant extent in power practices" (ibid., 103). A most troubling assertion is made in the introductory discussion: "All political symbols, then, have causes and consequences in power relationships" (ibid., 104). Is symbolization—the act of naming—causally ordered or artifactually created? Are languages "open" and "productive" in the sense of tools that can be used in "creative" ways? I cannot presume a causal ordering of the human imagination that places symbols in a causal ordering of *power* relationships. Rather, I presume that the exercise of the imagination is a process for inducing potential variety in the human articulation of language and communicable to others by engaging their imaginations. I communicate not simply by the use of words but in an effort to stimulate others to use their imagination in a way that is commensurate with how I am using my own imagination. We may need to introduce new conceptions and modify the articulation of language. The nature of this process of ordering involves great latitudes of innovation and inventiveness. I cannot conceive of such processes as being "caused" in some determinate way. We are addressing problems of creativity. Needless to say, profound difficulties are involved.

Similarly, I am troubled by the assertions that "political symbols circulating among the power holders correspond more closely to the power facts than do symbols presented to the domain" and that "the distribution of enlightenment corresponds to the power pattern" (ibid., 110). "Insiders" are presumed to be better informed than ordinary people. Facts as events witnessed are variable with time and place exigencies; enlightenment depends on arrangements for acquiring and transmitting knowledge and information. If indiscretions of speech place people at high risks of severe deprivations (Custine [1839] 1989) and "facts" are extracted by torture, the level of enlightenment among power holders may be extremely low and severely distorted. The filtering and distortion of information transmitted in bureaucratic structures may adversely affect the enlightenment of those in positions of command (Tullock 1965). Rulers may be more vulnerable to misinformation and misconceptions than are peasants. I do not expect the distribution of enlightenment to correspond to patterns of dominance.

The principle of symbolization in particular political orders, Lasswell held, is expressed as a *political myth*—"the pattern of the basic political symbols current in a society" (Lasswell and Kaplan 1950, 116). These are the "'fundamental assumptions' about political affairs." *Political doctrine,* then, is "the part of the political myth that formulates basic expectations and demands"; the *miranda* "consists of basic symbols of sentiment and identification" (ibid., 117). Political doctrine, Lasswell asserted, is typically set forth in constitutions, charters, and formal declarations. I presume that "expectations and demands" are similar to what I specify as "terms and conditions" by reference to constitutional formulations. Lasswell correctly asserted, then, that "Political theory is normatively ambiguous to a high degree," that "No clear separation is made between hypotheses of political science and the demands and expectations of political philosophy" (ibid., 118). *Ideology* is identified as "the political myth functioning to preserve the social structure" and *utopia* as a political myth functioning to "supplant" an ideology (ibid., 123). This distinction was made by Karl Mannheim in *Ideology and Utopia* (1936). I construe casual references to political ideology, including references to both political doctrine and miranda and to ideology and utopia, to be equivalent to political myth.

At this point, I find myself in deep intellectual difficulties. It is as though ideas—ideologies—have only a most tenuous relationship to political "reality." There are several grounds for holding to that position. One is a presumption that those who exercise effective rulership prerogatives face an altogether different reality—*raison d'état*—than those who are subjects. The reality is one set of contingencies; the symbolization of power by way of rituals, ceremonies, celebrations, festivities, pomp, and display is another set of contingencies—to enchant subjects, distract their minds, and hold their allegiance. These are the "realities" of Statecraft and the theatrics of *power.*

When literacy and public opinion begin to enter political considerations, the realities of rulership need to be complemented by skills in manipulating political symbols to control public opinion. Lasswell would use the term *propaganda* to identify this complement (Lasswell and Kaplan 1950, 111). The ruling elite is associated with a political reality that is accompanied by an ideological component: the maintenance of the traditional social structure as against contending utopias. Still another variant of the reality and the illusion of *power* is presumably manifest in "democratic" politics where slogans are articulated to create "bandwagon" effects in winning elections. Democracy might be a pretentious fraud; and the reigns of *power* reside in the hands of small ruling elite. Viewed from a general perspective of human artisanship, action is always mediated by an effort to obtain some future apparent good. Wishes do not suffice. The exercise of artisanship requires some present means. An arraying of conjectures pertaining to "present means" to obtain some future apparent good entails "expectations and demands," in Lasswell's terminology. The realization of some apparent "good" always implies a demand—an expression of preference. Expectations pertain to conjectures about how present means might be transformed to obtain some future apparent good. This is the essential relationship entailed in hypotheses as if-then statements.

We face a critical issue: the fate of democracies may turn more immediately on quests for votes than on strivings toward enlightenment and justice. The place of ideas in the discourse about public affairs may be subject to a selective bias in which glittering generalities, slogans, and sonorous phrases are used to appeal to voters. Such an array of ideas may then be used to build governing coalitions claiming popular mandates to enact public policies. Strong incentives exist for deception and self-deception. Frequent repetition of slogans and positive reinforcement by popular acclaim enhances prospects of self-deception. Distinguishing political ideologies from the concerns of the political and social sciences immunizes the realm of politics from critical scientific inquiry. Ideas set forth in constitutions, charters, and formal declarations and used to justify policy decisions are presumed to have no truth value and to be political doctrine rather than political science. Under these circumstances, political discourse in liberal democracies, addressed abstractly to Nations as a Whole, inevitably produces false illusions and misconceived policies. The vulnerability of democracies arises from circumstances in which a quest for votes has no necessary relationship to truth and justice and in which political scientists preoccupy themselves with the art of manipulation.

Complex sets of contingent relationships are presumably involved in rule-ordered relationships in human societies. We might anticipate these as being put together in different ways—in accordance with varying doctrines and formulas. Articulations of political doctrine associated either with some prevailing "ideology" or some "utopian" formulation when reflected in the actions of successive Governments has the prospect of yielding a jumble of inconsistent legal requirements. Strong selective biases exist for political discourse to become incoherent and for political processes to make profuse and potentially conflicting commitments. When such commitments are activated and transformed into artifactual states of affairs, the aggregate is vulnerable to spinning out of control. The aggregate pattern of "commonwealths" is something other than common wealth.

Tocqueville's reference to a "great experiment" to "construct society upon a new basis" by relying on "theories hitherto unknown or deemed impracticable" was presumably of substantial importance for those concerned with a political science. This was especially the case when Tocqueville suggested that the effort was "to exhibit a spectacle for which the world had not been prepared by the history of the past" ([1835–40] 1945, 1:25).

These assertions, made in the closing paragraph of chapter 1 in *Democracy in America,* escaped Lasswell's attention. He warned the reader against "the gathering of 'facts' without a corresponding elaboration of hypotheses" and referred explicitly to Tocqueville's "descriptive" efforts, which sometimes appeared to him to come "dangerously close" to "brute empiricism" (Lasswell and Kaplan 1950, x). I am sensitive to this problem because I too neglected to give proper attention to Tocqueville's formulations in the sense of making them a part of my critical, conscious awareness. It took me a long time to learn to read Tocqueville with a consciousness of the critical importance of that paragraph to the meaning of the whole two-volume work. I was unconscious of what had been constitutive of Tocqueville's conscious effort to write about a great experiment that had occurred on the North American continent, where I have lived my life. In self-governing societies, the conduct of great experiments is always done by those who design and who carry out the experiments. An experiment works only if it endures as a conscious effort. Do the experimenters know the significance of the experiment they are conducting, or are they pursuing other more expedient opportunities?

Addressing political ideas in a context of utopias and ideologies, and doctrines in a context of political myths, runs great risks. Partisans of a traditional version of a Golden Age and partisans of a Revolutionary version of Utopian Salvation can tear societies apart if ideologies and utopias are contested at every election. We are apt to view political thought in our Mind's Eye as "make-believe"—as fictitious allusions—without appreciating that all thought is in some sense a "fiction" [creation] of the mind in the same way that Hobbes referred to all expectations about the future as being "fictions" of the mind. The pragmatics of language is critical to the use of words as "fictions"—intellectual constructions—that are essential to communication, the organization of knowledge, and the conduct of artisanship.

To emphasize alternatives as "ideologies" and "utopias" is to presume that political choice pertains to whole systems of order. It is either the prevailing myth justifying the status quo or a competing myth encouraging the creation of a whole new social order. This was the myth of the French Revolution and the source of the tragedies associated with the Reign of Terror, the Napoleonic dictatorship, and the political instabilities of the French system of governance. When the tenure of a Government is limited to a few months or a few years without a fundamental transformation in the way people think and order their relationships with one another on a day-by-day basis, it is unrealistic to presume that whole new social orders can be constituted by a change of Government. The authors of "ideologies" and of "utopias," as Lasswell conceptualizes those terms, are likely to presume that "States" rule over "Societies" and that domestic political struggles involve warring factions bent on using the *power* of the State to destroy one another. This is not an appropriate cultural or political context for democratic societies.

The analysis of any problematic situation in human societies requires a conscious awareness of what aspects in the status quo ante are the sources of troubles. How can those conditions be addressed as isolable elements that, if modified, might yield appropriate changes in the consequent state of affairs? This is the basis for achieving an adaptive response by a change in policy at an appropriate level of analysis. Rejecting the prevailing system of social order for a whole new system conceptualized to replace the prevailing order would, in the course of time, either tear societies apart or lead people to discount the world of politics as absurd games played by cynical manipulators, fools, or madmen. When real troubles in the lives of people arise under such conditions, revolutions and coups d'état become the methods for achieving change. Such methods of change imply that one set of autocrats is replacing an existing set of autocrats, assuring the persistence of autocracies.

Serious difficulties would presumably arise from Tocqueville's concern about the erosion of language in a democratic society and about the risks that people in a democratic society might bear if they were to ignore the place of "ideas" in the constitution of societies. An exclusive preoccupation with the pursuit of "interests" would, for Tocqueville, be "as if human opinions were reduced to a sort of intellectual dust, scattered on every side, unable to collect, unable to cohere" ([1835–40] 1945, 2:7). This expectation is parallel to Dewey's concern about the *eclipse* of the *public*. Under such circumstances, the realm of public discourse dominated by the hustling of the mass media can create the illusion that people can be spared "all the care of thinking and all the trouble of living" (ibid., 2:318) and that scholars studying public opinion are concerned only with expressions of attitudes as articulations of preferences rather than with discourse about ideas.

The place of political myths, doctrines, ideologies, and utopias carry with them a concept of Statecraft that exists apart from the beliefs that are used to rationalize and justify activities being undertaken in particular societies. It is as though States were mutually exclusive sovereign territorial units constitutive of Societies and as though the place of a political theory in a political science were distinct from the ideas used to rationalize and justify the patterns of order constitutive of societies. If "state" boundaries in "democratic societies" are relatively open, many of the aspects of social orders associated with a *res publica* of science, a *res publica* of commerce, and a *res publica* of laws need not conform to national boundaries. Societies may take on different configurations of order than States. Rulers and their speechwriters and propagandists may then be viewed as creators of political myths who do not necessarily believe their own assertions. Statecraft can easily become an exercise in fabricating Noble Lies—patterns of deception and self-deception. Citizens and politicians can be egoistic pursuers of strategic opportunities of an expedient sort rather than persons concerned about coping with common problems.

Conclusions

We face the irony that, rather than presuming that rule-ordered relationships are constitutive of the institutional facts of life in a way that rules of a game are constitutive of the play of a game organized in accordance with a coherent system of rules, both Bryce and Dewey, as well as Woodrow Wilson, sought to look at the "facts" of human behavior to discover "reality." Bryce's disassociation of "Words" that "govern men" from ideas indicates that a deep erosion of critical awareness can occur. If a new generation is bent on accommodating institutions to the diverse and expedient purposes that they can be made to serve, freedom can be lost in the process. Seeking to "escape from theory" and search for "facts" "without allowing" oneself "to be confused by a knowledge of what that government was intended to be," as Woodrow Wilson proposed to do ([1885] 1956, 30), is destructive of the potentials for a political science and for societies of men to use reflection and choice in constituting systems of governance.

Lasswell and his generation, who were my teachers, presumed political science to be a science of State, or a science of Government. Lasswell attempted to break out of that mold. Lasswell's genius was his deep appreciation that the characteristics of a democratic society did not conform to a theory of command and control by relying on some single center of Supreme Authority. Those who aspire to being political scientists or to serving in professions critically concerned with law and human affairs bear a special responsibility for dealing with the warrantability of assertions apart from winning cases, dominating decisions, and peddling books or intellectual productions. Democracies cannot be viable systems of order if there is not a strong concern for "truth" viewed as warrantable assertions.

Yet the magnitude of the difficulties is reflected in the efforts of three premier scholars of the twentieth century to address themselves to the constitution of democratic societies. Lasswell, for example, showed a deep appreciation for the meaning of democracy as pertaining to self-responsibility, voluntarization, impartiality, dispersal of authority, challengeability, and balance. All of these attributes apply to Tocqueville's concept of self-governance, in which each individual is first one's own governor and then capable of working out appropriate patterns of rule-ordered associations with others through mutual agreements based on common knowledge and shared understanding as the foundations for conjoint activities in communities of relationships. Such conditions were marginal, however, to Lasswell's framework for conceptualizing a political science based on *power* relationships. Instead, democratic societies are as much realized through the shaping and sharing of such values as respect, rectitude, affection, well-being, enlightenment, skill, and wealth as through power relationships broadly construed. Human beings seek to influence and be influenced in matters of mutual concern. I listen to others to learn from what they have to say about matters of mutual concern. From this perspective, I consider Tocqueville to be correct in his presupposition that democratic societies are self-governing societies, not State-governed Societies.

Yet I must confront the anomaly that Lasswell, an abler scholar than I, did not, in my judgment, understand the sweep and depth of Tocqueville's analysis. If Lasswell were alive today, could I have convinced him of the merit of the assessment I have made? In light of many hours of extended discussions with Lasswell and some of his more devoted students, I would hope so.

This conjecture leaves me with another anomaly in addressing the relationship of ideas to deeds. Ideas as such are not enough to accomplish deeds. Nor are democracies a matter of Will. I use the term *Will* here to express commitment and determination rather than an openness to choice, for which some great theologians have used the term *Free Will*. The Will of the People is without meaning unless it is grounded in continued learning based on the experience of working with ideas as they are manifest in results achieved. Ideas need to be accompanied by the experience of working with ideas in the course of bringing deeds to realization. There is a sense in which democracies, as ways of life, cannot be taught by recourse to ideas alone. Instead, democracies as ways of life are brought to realization by learning to live and work with others in ways that are commensurate with self-responsibility, impartiality, respect for the autonomous authority of others, contestability as a road to conflict resolution through mutual enlightenment, the shaping of common knowledge, mutual understanding, and trust in patterns of associated relationships that reach out to larger communities of relationships. These foundations give meaning to democratic ways of life.

Myths and the misplaced use of abstractions to apply to Societies as a Whole need to be recognized for what they are—less than empirically warrantable assertions. I turn next to the way that arguments have been used to justify political actions in undertaking major political experiments to achieve communism and to realize social welfare through the instrumentalities of the State.

CHAPTER 3

Newspeak and Doublethink:
The Delusion of Ideologies

In his novel *1984,* written in 1948, George Orwell focused on the corruption of language associated with the development of what he called "Newspeak." In that book, Big Brother was an obvious reference, I have presumed, to Joseph Stalin, and Newspeak and Doublethink were analogous to the basic difficulties that were inherent in the language used by the ruling party in the Soviet Union to undertake its revolutionary mission to make Society free of human exploitation. That era in human experience, at least so far as Russia and Eastern Europe were concerned, came to a close as the Soviet Union itself came to an end. But are the problems of Newspeak and Doublethink confined to the Soviet experiment and to Marxist-Leninists formulations?

We may have witnessed the emergence of a New Newspeak in the United States and in other Western Societies. As the twentieth century comes to a close, the worst imaginable tragedy is that people who have had to endure Marxist-Leninist Newspeak might confront still further tragedies that will inevitably unfold if the New Newspeak transforms the quest for Democracy into still more tragic failures. Unless the problem of the New Newspeak can be effectively resolved, we can anticipate that the peoples of both North America and Western Europe may find themselves trapped in deep troubles.

In pursuing this inquiry into the problem of Newspeak and Doublethink, I shall first identify some superficial examples of its manifestation in the contemporary world. I shall then attempt to identify the source of this problem with languages as institutions. After this, I shall offer a brief examination of the language problem inherent in *The Communist Manifesto* (Marx and Engels [1848] 1967), and I shall explore the language of the New Newspeak characteristic of contemporary political discourse in the United States. I conclude this chapter by indicating the paradigmatic challenge that both forms of Newspeak pose for life in democratic societies.

Some Examples of Newspeak at Work in the Contemporary World

During the twentieth century, the peoples of the world have witnessed two world wars of immense destructive force. Ironically, the destruction of those two world wars was exceeded with regard to human life and suffering by the oppression, warfare, and genocide practiced by those who exercised rulership prerogatives over their own people. That irony is compounded by the fact that oppression, internal warfare, and genocide were practiced by those who proclaimed the Liberation of Mankind and identified themselves as Liberators. These tragedies were witnessed by much of mankind, who willingly celebrated the end of Imperialism but rarely took notice of the suffering and genocide imposed by rulers on their own subjects. Those were the purely internal affairs of sovereign States. The twentieth century became an age of holocausts—not confined to the holocaust of European Jews by Nazi Germany.

After the end of World War II, much of the world welcomed the end of the British, French, Dutch, and Portuguese Empires. A "cold war" ensued. The Gorbachev era was marked by a candid acknowledgment of troubles in the Soviet Union. When an attempted coup in August 1991 failed to preserve the Soviet autocracy, the Soviet Union collapsed. The American President and Secretary of State were left in helpless disarray. Without Gorbachev to relate to, they were lost. Why should this have been the case?

The paradoxes of language in this situation were multiple. The name Union of Soviet Socialist Republics was itself a manifestation of Newspeak, as Antoni Kaminski has suggested in *An Institutional Theory of Communist Regimes* (1992). The word *union* commonly implies a voluntary association. *Soviet* means council. *Republic* implies a system of government conducted in the context of an open public realm operating in accordance with so-called republican principles of open discussion and debate about public affairs and about public measures to be taken by open processes of collective choice. The term *socialist* had strong Marxist connotations but is a word to which I cannot assign meaning except for a presumption that happiness can be assured by the State. The demise of self-proclaimed empires was generally applauded; but autocratic empires that proclaimed themselves as republics and as unions of socialist, soviet republics were embraced by the heads of governments as lawful states.

Similarly, the efforts to create a Free World to replace the exercise of imperial authority in the British, French, Dutch, and Portuguese Empires were accompanied by the rise of new States that preyed on their own subjects. For example, the Government, military, and organized militias in

Rwanda, dominated by partisan Hutu factions in 1994, engaged in massacres of Tutsi people in a manner not unlike the massacre of Huguenots that occurred on St. Bartholomew's day with the knowledgeable support of clerical and royal authorities in sixteenth-century France. Such matters are presumed to be the purely internal affairs of sovereign States. Systems of State-to-State aid have enhanced the capabilities of State authorities to oppress and exploit their own peoples (Copeland 1969; V. Ostrom [1988] 1993; Davidson 1992). This process has gone on in some parts of the world in ways that far exceed the oppression exercised by the British, Dutch, or French Empires. I point to these exigencies not to justify imperial authority but to puzzle about the way that language can seemingly confuse thinking. Something is wrong in the way that human beings experience themselves, think, and act in relation to one another.

A Preliminary Assessment of Languages as Institutions

I presume that languages are the most fundamental institutions in human societies and, as such, serve as the essential matrices in all systems of social and political order. They are used to shape and articulate thought, to conceptualize what might be done, and to shape the actions taken in whatever is accomplished. Systems of thought and ways of life, if based on warrantable conceptions, would reflect one another by being different sides of the same coin, so to speak: thought and actions; thought and artisanship. Introducing new conceptions of revolutionary proportions would presumably require radical alterations in the construction of language systems.

A Copernican conception of a sun-centered solar system, in contrast to an earth-centered universe, had radical implications for the physical sciences (Koestler 1959). In the course of time, radical transformations have occurred in the languages of astronomy, geology, geography, physics, and many other fields of knowledge. Friedrich Engels, in his speech at the graveside of Karl Marx, asserted, "Just as Darwin discovered the law of development of organic nature, so Marx discovered the law of development of human history" (Tucker [1972] 1978, 681). If Marx and Lenin offered the equivalent of a Darwinian shift in perspective about the development of human history, we should expect major shifts to occur in the languages pertaining to ways of life in human societies. The key questions, then, are whether the new language associated with the Marxist-Leninist conception of relationships in human societies (1) provided a way to formulate and express ideas that were constitutive of a new way of life and (2) enabled people in their diverse situations to yield results consonant with the newly conceptualized way of life. If not, the use of ideas in action yields great disparities between conceptions articulated in public discourse, the actions people take, and results achieved. Thoughts lose their coherence. Actions lose their meaning. And people lose their sense of orientation to the world in which they live. They come to recognize that explanations being offered by political authorities are nothing but fabrics of falsehoods.

The Instrumental Features of Language

In addressing the instrumental character of language, several aspects of language systems affect both *thinking* and *productive* potentials in the games of life that are constitutive of human societies. If activities are based on warrantable knowledge, both thinking and productive potentials should presumably mirror one another. One such instrumental feature of languages bears on basic orientations to be taken in confronting unknown and ambiguous situations. This is a pervasive problem because human artisanship is always oriented toward some future possibility. Distinctions exist between, for example, basic orientations that encourage people to fight when confronted by unknown or ambiguous situations and basic orientations that encourage a problem-solving approach. Such precepts as "love thy neighbor as thyself" have quite different implications than "liberate the oppressed; destroy the oppressors." I would expect to find basic metaphors, parables, and proverbs in all language systems that afford people with basic orientations for confronting unknowns. Such features of languages have important implications for scientific inquiry and the exercise of problem-solving capabilities, because human beings are always plagued by unknowns reflecting the limits of human knowledge.

A second feature of language systems bearing on the constitution of order in human societies pertains to human efforts to *make distinctions* that lay the foundations for rendering normative judgments of a moral character. The terms used to express concepts are based on distinctions. Distinctions are reflected in the classificatory schema that are constitutive of languages. How distinctions relate to one another is a critical feature of all languages. All languages have reference to moral distinctions, and members of human societies cannot function without making some such distinctions. There can be no social science without a recognition of the importance of moral distinctions to ways of life in human societies. There need be no single universal standard, but the problem of how normative distinctions are made is a necessary feature of ways of life in human societies.

A third feature of language systems pertains to the establishment of *deontic requirements* that give rules their binding effect. All societies are required to come to terms with making rules binding in the ordering of human relationships, even though such arrangements may be variable across human societies. Grammars of rules, languages of law, and structures of authority relationships exist in all societies and are reflected in the languages people use in communicating with and acting in relation to one another.

A fourth feature of all language systems is the expression of *hypothetical contingencies* as if-then relationships. This is the source of what might be referred to as "positive" knowledge: if certain conditions exist and some elements are activated in appropriate ways, then specifiable consequences can be expected to occur. When hypotheses are acted on under specified conditions and are reproducible by anyone following appropriate procedures under specifiable conditions, they accrue public warrantability and are presumed to have universal application and to be "true" in some limited meaning of that term. An important complement to the language of hypothetical contingencies is the use of the imagination to offer questioning conjectures—what-if speculations. Such conjectures are the source of new conceptualizations that may lead to radical paradigmatic shifts. The Copernican formulation was a paradigmatic shift associated with a what-if conjecture: what if the earth spins instead of the sun revolving around the earth? Speculative flights of the imagination may also be the source of fantasies of absurd proportions requiring critical scrutiny to demonstrate their lack of empirical warrantability and public reproducibility.

A fifth feature of language systems is the articulation and organization of knowledge, by reference to *conceptual-computational logics,* into aggregated bodies of knowledge that become constituent parts of the general corpus of knowledge. For example, electricity has to do with the flow of electrons, water supply with the flow of a common chemical compound H_2O. These resources function with regard to different modes of analysis, but both have characteristics of common-pool, flow resource systems. Life on earth depends, in part, on the liquidity of water and the flow of electrons. Conceptual-computational logics are cumulative and come to be expressed in language systems. All five of the above features affect the pragmatics of language. If appropriately acted on, they are embodied in the way that knowledge gets expressed in human artisanship and in creations of an artifactual character of existence in human societies.

The Importance of Mutual Understanding

The use of knowledge in human societies is not confined to the "positive" features of hypothetical [if-then] contingencies but depends on the levels of *mutual understanding* that pervade human relationships and that derive from basic orientation, criteria for making linguistic and normative distinctions, and the binding [deontic] character of rule-ordered relationships. Mutual understanding shared with one another establishes the *foundations for communication.* Human knowledge is not confined to the external world but turns on the character and degree of common knowledge, mutual understanding, social accountability, and trust. The pragmatics of language is concerned, then, with the relationship of ideas expressed in language to thought and with the relationship of thought to actions and to what is achieved through coordinated actions based on communication among those participating in associated efforts.

These features in the pragmatics of language are *the foundations for all forms of capital,* if capital is conceptualized as the means available to enhance human productive capabilities. Narrowly construed, *human capital* (Schultz 1961) can be defined in relation to the acquisition and use of knowledge and skills. *Social capital* (Coleman 1990, 302) can be conceptualized as the aspects of social structures—norms and institutional arrangements—that facilitate productive capabilities. *Physical capital* (Lachmann 1978) can be conceptualized as physical tools and facilities used in production, exchange, and consumption of goods and services. The place of language and its relationship to the transmission and use of knowledge in human artisanship mediates these diverse forms of capital in achieving human productive capabilities.

Newspeak and Doublethink

In an appendix to *1984,* George Orwell gives a brief presentation of the "Principles of Newspeak." The purpose served by Newspeak, he asserts, is "to provide a medium of expression for the world-view and mental habits proper to the devotees of Ingsoc [English Socialism; "England" is the setting for *1984]"* and simultaneously "to make all other modes of thought impossible" ([1949] 1983, 246). Language, Orwell asserts, has reference to three sets of vocabulary. One set pertains to everyday languages—"for such things as eating, drinking, working, putting on one's clothes, going up and down stairs, riding in vehicles, gardening, cooking, and the like" (ibid., 247). A second vocabulary consists "of words which had been deliberately constructed for political purposes" (ibid., 249). This is a language of discourse in partisan politics. The third vocabulary consists "entirely of scientific and technical terms" (ibid., 254). Presumably these three sets of vocabulary might be brought together in a common language of discourse in which a belief in the unity of knowledge might prevail.

What is distinctive about Newspeak is the separation of a language of political discourse from the language of everyday life and the languages of the sciences and technologies. In Orwell's conception of Newspeak, a language used in political discourse assumes the dominant position. The language of everyday life is confined to those areas devoid of political implications. Scientific and technological discourse is even more narrowly confined to particular areas of application and is devoid of a vocabulary for "expressing the function of Science as a habit of mind, or a method of thought, irrespective of its particular branches" (ibid.), including the realms of politics and everyday life. Habits of mind and methods of thought are presumably to be dominated by a language of political discourse—the core of Newspeak—rather than by methods of science as a mode of solving problems. The language of partisan political discourse represented by Newspeak is presumed to be the true language for the construction of a new social reality: communism.

Doublethink occurs when a language of political discourse diverges radically from the language of everyday life and from the languages of science and technology. Ideas are denied merit by deliberately misinterpreting or reinterpreting evidence. Everyone is forced to think in two ways: the way expressed in political discourse and the way people think as they experience everyday life and engage in productive technologies. Except for the occasional "election," citizens experience themselves as spectators in political processes rather than as participants in something called "democracy." No commonly accepted "habit of mind" or "method of thought" applies to the exercise of problem-solving capabilities in all aspects of life. Ideas are not treated as having hypothetical significance but as *ideologies* ambiguously characteristic of political discourse.

While these features of language may have taken an exaggerated form in the Soviet Union, there are strong manifestations of comparable tendencies elsewhere in the contemporary world. The problems of Newspeak and Doublethink focus, then, on the corruption of language that occurs in the context of partisan political discourse. A transformation occurs in which the character of political discourse comes to dominate other uses of language. The drama manifest in the political arena is what constitutes "news." It is purveyed by mass media through television, radio, and the press, as though the public character of life were a drama being acted out on the stage of a theater, in which citizens are spectators who register their response through opinion polls and voting. The language used in the discourse of political officials and their contenders, as reported and discussed by journalists, becomes the New Newspeak—sonorous phrases mumbled with great incoherence. The features of life pertaining to general orientation, making distinctions, establishing normative criteria, and rule-ordered relationships become transformed into languages of political discourse, with the people having less than a conscious awareness of what transpires. Actions grounded in partisan political discourse amplify propensities to err and generate a sense of helplessness on the part of a disoriented people. I turn next to the language of *The Communist Manifesto* and to the language of the New Newspeak currently being used in the United States of America, to explore the fundamental incoherence of political discourse during the twentieth century.

The Language of *The Communist Manifesto*

In analyzing the relationship of thought and action, I rely on three presumptions: (1) that the pragmatics of language in human experience depends as much on mutual understanding as on assertions about the external world, (2) that mutual understanding is instrumental to the actions taken in whatever is done in human societies, and (3) that ideas expressed in thought are used to transform present means to realize some future apparent good. I use these presumptions to examine what Karl Marx and Friedrich Engels say in *The Communist Manifesto.* The language of *The Communist Manifesto* is global and sweeping in its referents. Through all historical time and in all countries, a class struggle is presumed to exist between "oppressors" and the "oppressed." The struggle can end only in "a revolutionary reconstitution of society" or "in the common ruin of the contending classes" (Marx and Engels [1848] 1967, 79). Historical time, according to a footnote added by Engels, is to be associated with the use of written languages.

Marx and Engels maintain that the modern manifestation of that struggle occurred with reference to "two great hostile camps . . . : Bourgeoisie and Proletariat" (ibid., 80). The Bourgeoisie exploit the labor of others. The Proletariat work and are exploited by the Bourgeoisie. According to the *Manifesto,* "The executive of the modern State is but a committee for managing the common affairs of the whole bourgeoisie" (ibid., 82); "Thus the whole historical movement is concentrated in the hands of the bourgeoisie" (ibid., 89). The whole system is "based on class antagonisms, on the exploitation of the many by the few" (ibid., 96). The *Manifesto* asserts that "the physician, the lawyer, the priest, the poet, the man of science" have all been converted into "paid wage-labourers." The family has been reduced to "a mere money relation" (ibid., 82). "The average price of wage labour," according to the *Manifesto,* "is the minimum wage" necessary for "subsistence" (ibid., 97). The *Manifesto* states that laborers "sell themselves piecemeal" as a "commodity." It asserts that "Wage decreases" in proportion as "the repulsiveness of the work increases" and that "the burden of toil also increases" as "the use of machinery and division of labour increases" (ibid., 87). Workers are the exploited, helpless ones.

These patterns are presumed to fit within a revolutionary scheme subject to constant change in modes of production, with "constantly expanding markets" reaching to global proportions and giving "a cosmopolitan character to production and consumption in every country" (ibid., 83). According to the *Manifesto,* "The cheap prices of [this revolutionary scheme's] commodities are the heavy artillery with which it batters down all Chinese walls. . . . It compels all nations, on pain of extinction, to adopt the bourgeois mode of production: it compels them to introduce what it calls civilization into their midst, i.e., to become bourgeois themselves. In one word, it creates a world after its own image" (ibid., 84).

A redemptive potential arises, however, from a competitive dynamic that increasingly concentrates power in a decreasing portion of the population constituting the Oppressors, while it concentrates a lack of power in an increasing portion of the population constituting the Oppressed class. This is the source, then, of the revolutionary potential that can be expected to yield the collapse of the existing Bourgeois social order and the emergence of a new social order.

For the reconstitution of Society at large to occur, the *Manifesto* advances the thesis that as the class struggle "nears the decisive hour . . . a small section of the ruling class cuts itself adrift, and joins the revolutionary class, the class that holds the future in its hands" (ibid., 91). The Proletariat is the revolutionary class; but it needs leadership to realize its revolutionary potential. That leadership has the advantage of "clearly understanding the line of march, the conditions, and the ultimate general results of the proletarian movement" that distinguishes them from "the great mass of the proletariat." Their immediate aim is the "formation of the proletariat into a class, overthrow of the bourgeois supremacy, [and] conquest of political power by the proletariat" (ibid., 95). This is the mission of the self-proclaimed Communists in the *Manifesto.*

The statement of the mission of self-proclaimed Communists is accompanied by a strange disclaimer: "The theoretical conclusions of the Communists are in no way based on ideas or principles that have been invented, or discovered, by this or that would-be universal reformer" (ibid., 95–96). If I understand correctly, Marx and Engels are associating themselves with historical determinism and disassociating themselves from individual moral responsibility for the ideas they profess and the actions that they propose. The course of history runs in a determinate evolutionary path established by what were presumed to be the eternal laws of history rather than an emergent pattern of evolutionary development reflecting human thoughts, choices, and actions. Their theoretical conclusions, let me again emphasize, are *not,* according to Marx and Engels, based on ideas or principles invented or discovered by would-be universal reformers: Eternal laws of history operate apart from the role of ideas in human affairs. History is shaped by a larger Rationality that has nothing to do with the way that mortal creatures think about the constitution of order in human societies. Consistent with such an interpretation, the *Manifesto* also asserts, "But Communism abolishes eternal truths, it abolishes all religion, and all morality, instead of constituting them on a new basis; it therefore acts in contradiction to all past historical experience" (ibid., 103).

The Communist Manifesto asserts that "the theory of the Communists may be summed up in the single sentence: Abolition of private property." Marx and Engels reject the position that a worker has a property right to his or her own labor and, thus, is neither a serf nor a slave. Capital is identified as "that kind of property which exploits wage labour" (ibid., 96)—a unique way of conceiving the term *capital*. An appropriation of the products of labor that "is made for the maintenance and reproduction of human life" and "leaves no surplus wherewith to command the labour of others" is recognized as a proper exercise of "personal appropriation." If I understand correctly, something that might be called "theft" in a "Capitalist" society, would be a form of "personal appropriation." The aggregate product of labor, then, is viewed as "accumulated labor." It follows that "in Communist society, accumulated labour is but a means to widen, to enrich, to promote the existence of the labourer" (ibid., 97). The term *accumulated labor* refers to "accumulated productive capabilities." The problem, then, if I understand correctly, is how to organize the accumulated productive capabilities in a society so that the Class of Laborers—the Proletariat—can enjoy the products of those accumulated productive capabilities.

The position of Communists, according to the *Manifesto,* is to exercise leadership on behalf of "the proletarians as a whole." This might be hypothetically extended to "the *common* interests of the *entire* proletariat, independently *of all nationality*" (my emphasis). At whatever stage of development, Communists "always and everywhere represent the interests of the movement as a whole" (ibid., 95). The *Manifesto* asserts that when "the more or less veiled civil war, raging within existing society" (ibid., 93) is terminated by the conquest of political power, "the first step in the revolution by the working class, is to raise the proletariat to the position of ruling class, to win the battle of *democracy*" (my emphasis), with leadership presumably to be exercised by Communists. According to the *Manifesto,* "The proletariat will [then] use its *political supremacy* to wrest, by degrees, all capital from the bourgeoisie, to centralize all instruments of production in the hands of the State, i.e., of the proletariat organized as the ruling class [led by Communists]; and to increase the total of productive forces as rapidly as possible" (ibid., 104, my emphasis).

The Communist Manifesto then indicates the following measures that would be "pretty generally applicable, . . . in the most advanced countries":

1. Abolition of property in land and application of all rents of land to public purposes.
2. A heavy progressive or graduated income tax.
3. Abolition of all right of inheritance.
4. Confiscation of the property of all emigrants and rebels.
5. Centralization of credit in the hands of the State, by means of a national bank with State capital and an exclusive monopoly.
6. Centralization of the means of communication and transport in the hands of the State.
7. Extension of factories and instruments of production owned by the State; the bringing into cultivation of wastelands, and the improvement of the soil generally in accordance with a common plan.
8. Equal liability of all to labour. Establishment of industrial armies, especially for agriculture.
9. Combination of agriculture with manufacturing industries; gradual abolition of the distinction between town and country, by a more equable distribution of the population over the country.
10. Free education for all children in public schools. Abolition of children's factory labour in its present form. Combination of education with industrial production, &c., &c. (Ibid., 104–5)

When such measures are acted on, the *Manifesto* anticipates that (1) all production will have been concentrated "in the whole nation," or presumably in the whole world; (2) all class distinctions will disappear; and (3) "*public power*" will lose its *political character*" (my emphasis). According to the *Manifesto*, "*Political power,* properly so called, is merely the organized power of one class for *oppressing* another" (my emphasis). Communists acting on behalf of the Proletariat as a whole, by definition, do not exercise Political Power—they act on behalf of the Proletariat and do not oppress the Proletariat. Communists are acting on behalf of the Proletariat as a whole, who have assumed the prerogative of the State to use the Accumulated Labor [productive capabilities] on behalf of those who labor. It is under those conditions, then, that *The Communist Manifesto* concludes, "we shall have *an association,* in which the free development of each is the condition for the free development of all" (ibid., 105, my emphasis). The relevant domain is not specified but is presumed to be the Nation-State.

If we view such a formulation as a statement about the constitution of order in human societies, important orienting and normative positions are asserted. The referent is global. The time horizons include all of history. Societies are class struggles between Oppressors and the Oppressed in which occasional transformations occur in the reconstitution of Societies at large. Life is more or less a veiled "civil war" that can yield the "common ruin" of all. Society through all History, then, is class warfare. Material forces determine the course of history, and words are but the reflection of that reality. No "eternal truths," "religion," or "morality" has standing in the presence of reality—a Truth—that is in "no way based on ideas or principles that have been invented, or discovered, by this or that would-be universal reformer." Marx and Engels both used ideas and denied the merit of ideas—an anomaly of radical proportions. They removed themselves from the human condition and entered the circle of the gods.

The burden of ordinary mortals is somehow to understand the laws of History and to struggle against and liberate themselves from Oppression by a dominant class. The liberation of mankind turns on a revolutionary struggle to seize the instrumentalities of State power. When people clearly understand "the line of march" [the course of history] and "the conditions and the ultimate general results of the proletarian movement" [the nature of order], we have circumstances where those who see the direct light of Truth can exercise leadership on behalf of Accumulated Labor as the aggregate productive capabilities of Mankind. Such "an association" is perceived to be the basis "in which the free development of each is the condition for the free development of all." This is one version of a presupposition that the State is an association for the common good of all despite the anomaly that the State throughout recorded history has been an instrument of exploitation and oppression. Lenin's formulation of the revolutionary mission of the Communist party in *What Is To Be Done?* ([1902] 1932) turns on much the same presuppositions: the unity of a few professional revolutionaries who exercise leadership by acting in accordance with strict secrecy and strict discipline in the discharge of their responsibilities.

If, however, self-proclaimed Communists do not see the direct light of Truth, we would expect an effort to realize the mission proclaimed in *The Communist Manifesto* to fail. That was the judgment rendered by Milovan Djilas, a former member of the ruling circle of the Communist party in Yugoslavia. He observed that the reverse happened from the expectations held by the leaders of the Communist party who had achieved dominance over the instruments of State power in the U.S.S.R. A distant observer relying on a variety of accounts of the era when Stalin exercised leadership of the Communist party might view the actions taken to be consistent with the precepts and conceptions of *The Communist Manifesto* and with

Lenin's conception of the revolutionary mission of the Communist party. One need not presume that Stalin was an intentionally evil man. A dedicated commitment to the conceptualizations advanced in the *Manifesto* would be sufficient. The language of the *Manifesto* provides a basic formulation for understanding the design of the Soviet experiment. Instead of achieving "an association, in which the free development of each is the condition for the free development of all," the Communist party itself became the new ruling class. Autocracy prevailed; and the struggle for democracy endured its most severe assault from those who sought to strengthen democracy and achieve the withering away of the State.

The problem of rule-ordered relationships in human societies was pervasively ignored in the Communist quest for the Liberation of Mankind by revolutionary struggle. The neglect of critical attention to the binding character of rules, to rule-ruler-ruled relationships, and to the possibilities of achieving self-governing capabilities through general orientations, conceptual distinctions, and methods of normative inquiry consistent with the quest for peace in complementary communities of relationships were ignored. The burdens of the erstwhile "Oppressed" became the more oppressive as their self-proclaimed Liberators imposed burdens of "equal liability of all to labor," "the establishment of industrial armies, especially for agriculture," and so on.

Orwell's problem of Newspeak was only one of the multifaceted problems engendered by the Soviet experiment. We can only hope that hindsight gives a clearer vision than foresight. The overwhelming dominance of political discourse articulated by the leadership of the Communist party in Soviet society yielded one of the most extreme tragedies experienced during the twentieth century. Those exercising a power of command insisted on a language of public discourse that diverged from the realities of life as people experience those realities. Mutual understanding, social accountability, and trust were not realized. The matrix of the language used was a fabric of falsehoods (Solzhenitsyn 1979). The regime eventually tottered and collapsed. A great experiment became a monumental disaster. The burden of ordinary mortals is to study the relationship of ideas to deeds, to consider the sources of failure, and to learn from experience.

The Language of the New Newspeak in the United States of America

The New Newspeak is a radically different language of political discourse emerging during the twentieth century. This language of discourse is associated with basic changes in the political order of American society. As a consequence of these changes, I have reached the conclusion that American society is in deep trouble. Michel Crozier, in *The Trouble with America: Why the System is Breaking Down* (1984), has reached similar conclusions. A report by the Associated Press, which purported to be a survey of the current situation, alluded to "America's current outrage and anxiety" (*Herald-Times* [Bloomington, Ind.], April 21, 1992). Using the New Newspeak, the media justified the burning of south-central Los Angeles, which occurred a week later (beginning on April 29, 1992), as an *acceptable* expression of "outrage" in response to an *unacceptable* expression of "outrage" construed as "police brutality." When "rage" and "outrage" characterize public discourse and gain expression in police brutality, pillage, and arson, civilization is placed at risk. Common courtesies associated with civility and civilization are no longer presumed to prevail among members of Society. What are the roots of this affliction?

The Language of Abstraction in Political Discourse

The overwhelming amount of political discourse in the mass media, among students and faculty on university campuses, and in casual discussions contains references to "America," "Society," "the Nation," and "the Government." These abstractions presumably apply to the country as a whole and to the aggregate population within the political boundaries of what is identified among the nations of the world as the United States of America. "The Government" usually has a more specific referent: the central institutions of Government in Washington, D.C. This is another version of the presupposition that the State is the unique association for the common good of all.

The Activist Scientist

In the interests of science, we must accept the necessity of playing by Washington's rules and speaking the Washington language.
                    (Editorial by Jaleh Daie, *Science* 272, May 24, 1996:1081)

Any set of attributes assigned to Society or the Nation as a Whole is an abstraction. Poverty, then, is an attribute of the Society as a Whole and is applicable to that set of the total population whose monetary income falls below a specified criterion designated by Governmental authorities. A general image of impoverishment is presumed to apply to that population as an aggregate Class of the Society as a Whole. Treatment of categories applicable to Children, Women, the Handicapped, the Poor, the Disadvantaged, the Unemployed, the Wealthy, Race, the Homeless, or whatever the referent may be is to an abstract Class associated with Society as a Whole. References to the Environment, the World, and the Earth have a global referent analogous to the *Manifesto's* global orientation applying to all mankind; but the predominant focus in contemporary American language is to America, the Nation, the Society, Mankind, or the Environment as abstract references to the Whole. Leading political partisans presume the Government to be the Principal Actor exercising tutelage over and responsibility for the Nation—managing Society as a Whole.

Reference to such abstract entities is accompanied by strong feelings of compassion similar to those expressed by Marx and Engels in *The Communist Manifesto.* Terms like *Abuse, Children, Women, Handicapped,* and *Homeless* provoke strong sentiments of compassion that are unameliorated by the experiences of relating to particular individuals who may be characterized by such attributes and may be required to cope with different, unique, and difficult exigencies of life. Franklin Roosevelt, for example, suffered from the crippling effects of poliomyelitis, but that did not make him a Handicapped Person among his contemporaries. Discourse shifts to human rights and entitlements of a universal character without correlative responsibilities in the context of discrete communities of associated relationships.

When referents shift to such levels of abstraction, the Democratic form of Newspeak provides opportunities for some small fraction of the population to exercise leadership and to speak on behalf of those who, as a class, stir strong sentiments of attachment and identification. Known as Activists, they are attracted to participate in the Political Process and serve in the Government. Activists, like Communists, know what is good for the Disadvantaged and the Oppressed. The Government becomes the all-purpose problem solver. Problems are to be resolved by general uniform Policies that are to be applied to the Society as a Whole. General formulations of Law are to be supplemented by the expenditure of money, which is subject to more elaborately specified general administrative rules and regulations, all of which are presumed to be a part of the Law. Law becomes a system of command and control for managing Society as a Whole through a Bureaucracy, using administrative methods to exercise tutelage over Society. A concept like *Race* is presumed to apply to all individuals in discrete categories; and the Struggle against Racism necessarily requires recourse to racism in a reverse order. It is as though races were categories of pure types.

The well-intentioned efforts of compassionate Activists relying on the New Newspeak can be transformed into madness when General Programs are applied to Society as a Whole. Size and diversity in the material conditions and in the cultural exigencies of life are confounding conditions. The United States of America and the Russian Federation are vastly larger in the size and diversity of territorial domains and populations than Iceland or Denmark. These conditions of size and diversities are compounded when General Programs expressed in abstract categories, applicable to Society or the Nation as a Whole, are related to what might be referred to as the "moral hazards" and "Catch-22 situations" in which individuals make their choices.

Moral Hazards and Catch-22 Situations

The term *moral hazard* has reference to some implicit standard of rightness but is subject to hazards that occur when standards of rightness are placed at risk. Creating a system of fire insurance to ameliorate the individual losses suffered from fire may, for example, create opportunities for people to collect insurance by deceptively and illegally setting fire to buildings. Systems of insurance for personal injuries can be expected to create new afflictions and stimulate a whole new industry called "injury law." An opportunity to gain an advantage may also arise with regard to morally ambiguous actions that can be justified because others act in the same way. The consequence of unmitigated moral hazards are higher costs for everyone. Alternatively, efforts to mitigate moral hazards may involve the imposition of costly bureaucratic procedures. A *Catch-22* situation, identified with a novel by that name (Heller 1955), refers to situations where individuals confront unfavorable circumstances in whatever choice they might make—that is, to forced choice among undesirable alternatives. It is entirely possible for moral hazards and Catch-22 situations to become so complexly configured in relation to one another that individuals in societies find themselves trapped in helplessness and frustrations that burst into outrage and violence.

As a casual observer of the American scene, I am struck by the way that so many of the major cities in the United States include extended areas that have been reduced to rubble. Yet the destructions of warfare have not visited the North American continent during the twentieth century. I am forced to conclude that major portions of American cities have been reduced to rubble by their own residents. How do such circumstances occur?

I presume that there is no single cause for such states of affairs. The way that institutional arrangements are put together is likely to have profound effects. New housing may be subject to poor craftsmanship that leads to the abandonment of whole blocks of housing. Publicly guaranteed loans relieve builders and financial agencies of responsibility for monitoring the quality of the construction when buildings are being put together, a time when potential defects can be observed. A site with which I am familiar was appropriately constructed; but residents used the sewer system to get rid of hot liquid fat from cooking pans. The building was abandoned by the managing agency that functioned as its nominal owner with Government-guaranteed loans. Anything that could be detached and removed was "salvaged" by passersby, windows were smashed, and a shattered building became rubble in the landscape. It is possible for people to throw garbage out the window and feed insects and rats, for children to urinate when the necessity moves them, for young adolescents to test their strength on any movable object, and for both adolescents and adults to take pride in sexual conquests. If you mix these propensities together with sticky fingers and with pride in the display of conspicuous wealth, human beings acquire destructive potentials equivalent to carpet bombing.

One of the great tragedies afflicting individuals in all human societies is the death or permanent departure of a father in a family. Human compassion may seek for a universal solution to be attained by using the powers of the State to supply a source of income for families with dependent children to meet their essential needs. A criterion inherent in the conception of such a program would be the absence of a man in the household. The source of income would then presumably be subject to termination if there were a man in the household. A cost—a moral hazard—occurs in reestablishing family ties, because a source of income would be lost. The presence of female-headed families without adult males in households implies that a cohort population of unattached males is likely to occur. Cohorts of unattached males during the most sexually active period of their life are serious sources of trouble in any society. Families without fathers become viable in some minimal sense of survival; but populations reared in fatherless families may not contribute to "civic" cultures and "civil" societies consistent with the requirements of "civilizations." Such societies, in which moral hazards are combined with Catch-22 situations, are vulnerable to breakdown.

The burden confronting single mothers with dependent children involves relationships that cannot be successfully monetized in any society. Money as a medium of exchange meets the criteria of being a purely private good. The payment of money to supply a source of income can be used only to procure those goods and services available through market-exchange arrangements. Assistance in coping with nonmonetized features of family, kin, and community life turn on the availability of attentive eyes and helping hands capable of doing what money cannot buy. Rearing children to become citizens cannot be achieved simply by buying and selling in market-exchange relationships. The most fundamental source of human and social capital in any society is family households as they function in speech communities in which patterns of associated relationships are constituted in neighborhoods.

Furthermore, the amount of monetized income made available for aid to single mothers with dependent children is likely to be subject to maximum specified limits of a minimal sort. Persons in such circumstances have incentives to acquire supplemental income, but at the risk of reduced welfare payments or of violating the "Law." One way "welfare mothers," in many circumstances, can make ends meet is to supplement their income by violating the Law. Recourse to such potentials for deriving supplemental income can become a way of life in a community; it is hard to imagine more perverse circumstances in human societies (Jencks 1992). Good intentions and moral hazards have contributed to the breakdown of both family and community life. Public programs create incentives to break the Law. It is entirely possible that the best-intentioned efforts of a Welfare State have ameliorated some tragedies and greatly compounded other tragedies to the net detriment of everyone involved. Freedom from want and freedom from trouble cannot be "guaranteed" by "The State."

Dutch Welfare State Springing New Leaks

There are signs of a growing malaise in the Netherlands. Even Prime Minister Ruud Lubbers has been saying the country is "sick."

The signs include evidence of increasing disgust with the swelling ranks of slackers receiving state assistance. With a sagging economy, this puts an ever greater burden on the employed, who now pay the highest tax rate in Europe—53.1 percent.

There are officially 914,018 invalids in the Netherlands, one-fourth of them 35 or younger. That gives Holland, which has a population of 15 million, the world's highest proportion of the infirm. The Rotterdam social affairs office believes that fraud is involved in half of all welfare cases, according to the daily Suddeutsche Zeitung of Munich.

There is talk of reform, but skeptics point to the forest of rules and regulations that would have to be felled—more than 300 merely in the areas of jobless and illness benefits. Earlier attempts to pare the state's bounties have brought energetic protests.

The glory days—the hardworking Dutch once reputedly built 1,000 ships a year, and they assembled a naval fleet twice the size of the British and French fleets combined—seem ever more distant.

(Brian Knowlton, *International Herald Tribune*, March 4, 1993)

I cannot pursue comparable conjectures about all of the diverse measures that have become a part of the program of Welfare States. I cannot presume that all such programs will manifest the same structure of perverse incentives that I have portrayed. These can be expected to vary with time and place exigencies requiring more careful specification as elements affecting the structures and logics of situations. The critical lesson to be learned about the Welfare State is to *beware* of gross *abstractions*. Similar problems are not common problems. Common policy programs may be inappropriate ways for resolving similar problems, such as all problems having to do with "housing." Highly abstract concepts like States, Markets, and Societies may foreclose much more extended opportunities to explore and analyze problems and consider alternatives at diverse levels of analysis. Counterintentional and counterintuitive contingencies prevail in all human societies. Critical scrutiny and comparative analysis is required if standards of empirical warrantability and public reproducibility are to prevail. The concept of a Welfare State runs the risk of creating a short-term illusion that offers a promise of well-being accompanied by risks of increasing impoverishment and eventual breakdown that may be as serious as the breakdown of the Soviet experiment. Relying on a Welfare State to solve the problems of Market Economies is likely to neglect many of the essential features in an economy of life that are mediated by nonmonetized patterns of reciprocity in family and kin relationships and in diverse associations and communities of relationships. The pursuit of material gains reflected in monetized accounts runs the risk of eroding essential conditions of life that cannot be mediated through market transactions. Privatization offers no general solution to the failure of the Welfare State.

We face, then, a serious anomaly. Many of the essential features in the constitution of order in human societies are not visible to the human eye. We see overt activities within our range of vision. We do not see the thoughts that give access to alternatives and the calculations that inform choice. Price, as an indicator of exchange value, can be measured; but money may be an exceedingly poor yardstick as a general measure of values. We cannot see the fellow "feelings" that permeate human relationships or the communities of understanding that accrue over time through the use of language in talking and working with one another. We can gain access to those invisible features characteristic of human societies only by talking to knowledgeable participants and coming to share the mental images and feelings to which they have reference in discrete situations.

For those whose lives are caught up in these processes of destruction, any one particular individual is likely to experience an endless series of counterproductive situations. The distant compassionate observer, who is a spectator watching "news" *produced* on television screens, sees the Plight of the Poor or Homeless and finds it rationally necessary to identify some cause like Poverty or Race and then to consider some remedy like Money. If the distribution of money is viewed as the ultimate source of the problem, then we view the Wealthy as the Cause of human misery, which brings us back to visions of the Oppressed and their Oppressors.

Activists who advance the cause of the Poor and the Homeless by offering some remedy like the transfer of money have strong incentives to deny critical evidence that suggests that spending more money has little or no material effect on Poverty or Homelessness. Spending more money does not necessarily improve the quality of life in households or neighborhoods. The quality of many services depends largely on the coproductive efforts of the individuals involved, as in the case of educational and health services and in many aspects of welfare services.

The problem of moral hazards and Catch-22 situations permeates the political system as a whole, including the system of "justice." A presumption that any problem can be resolved by passing a law can easily become ensnared in a bramble of legal provisions. The first step is to prohibit a general class of activities. The second step is to delineate a narrowly defined scope of activities that are *permitted.* Permits *require* recourse to administrative procedures. When legislation is formulated in comprehensive or omnibus enactments of several hundred pages that are supplemented by administrative rules and regulations encompassing thousands of pages, no one can be aware of everything that the law prohibits, permits, or requires.

The use of administrative methods mixes together service activities with enforcement and adjudicatory functions. Efforts to procure help in securing a public service is apt to be accompanied by dangers of being trapped for violation of some rule. The potential dangers in seeking help from public servants may be of such a magnitude that the potential benefits are forgone.

The viability of any enterprise, voluntary association, public agency, or "subordinate" unit of government depends on numerous and heterogeneous factors being put together in complementary ways. Diverse attributes of each factor can be subject to universal rules that adversely affect the viability of going concerns as workable endeavors. Statutory enactments and administrative rules can establish a legal bramble that places the rule of law at risk. Entitlements to human rights can be formulated in ways that create servitudes as their necessary legal complements.

I do not want to imply that my conjectures are the "true" explanations. Human tragedies can accrue from many different "causes." My point is that we need to inquire—to search; to investigate—in order to understand. For remedial actions to be taken, it is necessary that those who live in a culture of poverty immersed in a system of command and control come to understand the nature of their situation and what might be done to better it. Activists beating drums and shouting slogans in Demonstrations are likely to be a distracting form of public theater preparing people to war on one another. These same Activists are likely to participate in efforts to win elections, create dominant coalitions, and enjoy the fruits of victory. We need critical inquiry, not the drums of warfare.

Unfortunately, the drama of public Demonstrations and mass media communications affects how people think. Abstract explanations may come to be accepted as "true." Candidates for public offices in democratic societies are exceedingly sensitive to the winds of public opinion as it is expressed in the partisanship of party politics. The way to solve problems is to pass laws. The language of the "law," enmeshed in complex and elaborate rules and regulations uniformly applicable to Society as a Whole, places people at risk of becoming offenders of a "law"; it entraps people in conspiracies of silence and deception, using the "back door," and going "underground." Law becomes an instrument of entrapment, eroding trust, social accountability, and mutual understanding.

Stealth Legislation

Pension Rules Tacked Quietly on Trade Bill Portend Vast Changes

Some Big Companies Won Key Concessions but Still Face Enormous Outlays

Retirees May Be Hard Hit

When a lame-duck Congress voted to liberalize world trade late last year, little noticed were 129 pages of pension provisions tacked awkwardly onto the end of the bill.

But ever since then, calls have been pouring into offices of benefit consultants and members of Congress as people realized that these pages contained the most significant pension-funding changes in 20 years. The changes had coasted quietly into law on the back of an effort to pay the costs of introducing unrelated new global trade rules under auspices of the General Agreement on Tariffs and Trade.

Worried Employees

In addition, thousands of employees are phoning corporate and brokerage offices that deal with pension benefits to ask whether, as they have heard, an obscure new law . . . can directly affect their wallets.

(Albert R. Karr and Ellen E. Schultz, *Wall Street Journal,* March 15, 1995)

The Philosophy of the New Newspeak

What I would regard as a philosophy of the New Newspeak is articulated in *The Search for Meaning* (1989), which proclaims in its subtitle the "new spirit in science and philosophy." I refer to this volume edited by Paavo Pylkkänen, particularly to its essay by Srinivas Aravamudan, "Deconstruction, Somasignificance and the Implicate Order: Or, Can David Bohm and Jacques Derrida Have a Dialogue?," to have a specific referent to illustrate the general problem. We are informed by Aravamudan that Jacques Derrida "is engaged in a radical critique of Western philosophy, which takes the form of 'deconstruction'; of what Derrida calls 'the metaphysics of the presence'" (Pylkkänen 1989, 239–40). Western philosophy, according to this explanation of Derrida's metaphysics, is associated with a mode of inquiry that "systematically hides its dependence on language and metaphor in order to communicate a hidden agenda of 'metaphysical' and ideological positions." To illustrate that agenda, Aravamudan asks the reader to

consider the 15 sets of oppositions listed below:

Man	Woman
Speech	Writing
Presence	Absence
Reason	Imagination
Work	Play
Origin	Derivation
Author	Reader
Host	Parasite
Central	Peripheral
Meaning	Language
Soul	Body
Inside	Outside
Essence	Structure
Truth	Rhetoric
Philosophy	Literature.

(Ibid., 240)

The task of deconstruction, then, is to reveal "that Western philosophy has systematically attempted to characterize the ideas in the second column as inferior to, or derivative from, and secondary to the first column" (ibid.). A dichotomy of opposites presumably conceals a hierarchy of dominance. "Deconstruction," then, according to Aravamudan, "dismantles the authoritarianism of binary oppositions for the heterogeneous multiplicity, polyvalence and 'free-play' of the linguistic sign" (ibid., 241).

The "metaphysics of the presence" apparently has its analogue in the metaphysics of Scientific Materialism: a struggle between Oppressors and the Oppressed. Concepts such as Man and Woman are viewed as opposites reflecting a concealed hierarchy of dominance. Women's Liberation is viewed as a struggle to free Women from the dominance of Men. Any set of binary distinctions can be arrayed as opposites, requiring a struggle to perform a deconstruction that "dismantles the authoritarianism of binary oppositions." Binary distinctions are easily transformed into binary oppositions of an abstract character that are associated with more general abstractions about Society as a Whole. Languages, as classificatory schema, are dismantled as "deconstructionists" exclaim, resulting in great incoherence, a "free play" of linguistic signs.

If people were to use such a language of political discourse to inform their thinking and the actions to be taken with reference to one another as members of classes assigned to Binary Opposites, such people would find themselves in a Catch-22 situation analogous to Hobbes's State of Nature. Binary Opposites would struggle with one another to achieve what Marx and Engels referred to as "a revolutionary reconstruction of society" or "the common ruin" of the contending sets. If the revolutionary reconstruction of society turns on the conquest of the instrumentalities of State power to dismantle the "authoritarianism of binary oppositions," then a more or less veiled form of civil war could be expected to yield a new autocracy—a new form of Democratic Despotism. Interest Groups become Warring Factions. Elections become grotesque forms of political theater mobilized by Activists serving as cheerleaders and drumbeaters. Outrage and anxiety prevail in everyone's helplessness to do anything about the patterns of madness prevailing in Society. Is the New Newspeak another form of monumental disaster in the making?

The Paradigmatic Challenge of Democracy

A radically different conception of American society is represented by Tocqueville's thesis that the American "experiment" represented the constitution of a self-governing society where society governed itself for itself. He anticipated that the emergence of democracy would require a "new science of politics" for a "new world." This assertion, I presume, is to be construed with reference to two later assertions.

> In democratic countries the science of association is the mother of science; the progress of all the rest depends upon the progress it has made. ([1835–40] 1945, 2:110)

> The art of association then becomes . . . the mother of action, studied and applied by all. (Ibid., 117)

An art and science of association links the world of science and technology, the constitution of patterns of rule-ordered relationships, and the conduct of artisanship, in all its diverse forms, to ways of life in self-governing societies. When human artisanship brings the vocabulary of the sciences and technologies together with the vocabulary of the arts and sciences of association, the language of political discourse takes its proper place in the vocabulary of everyday life and of the way people live their lives in self-organizing and self-governing societies. Each is first his or her own governor and is then responsible for fashioning mutually productive relationships with others.

Once we recognize that democratic societies turn on self-organizing and self-governing capabilities, we can also appreciate that Peter Kropotkin's *Mutual Aid* ([1902] 1972) and Pierre-Joseph Proudhon's *The Principle of Federation* ([1863] 1979) have an important place in thinking about the constitution of democratic societies. William Edgerton's *Memoirs of Peasant Tolstoyans in Soviet Russia* (1993) demonstrates how the teachings of Leo Tolstoy formed the foundations for establishing patterns of collective farming with radically different characteristics than the Soviet form of collectivization. Tocqueville's *Democracy in America* ([1835–40] 1945) is an important complement to the contributions of both Kropotkin and Proudhon, to Pieter Geyl's history of the emergence of the Dutch Republic ([1932] 1988, [1936] 1989), to Adolph Gasser's *Geschichte der Volksfreiheit und der Demokratie* [History of freedom and democracy] (1939), and to many other works dealing with self-governing associations [syndicates, *Genossenschaften, Eidgenossenschaften*] and communities [communes, *Gemeinde*] (Grossi [1977] 1981). Microconstitutional systems of self-governing associations can be conceptualized in a macroconstitutional order in which the diversely associated instrumentalities of governance are organized as complementary patterns of associated relationships (E. Ostrom 1989, 1990). The "mir" of the village is related to the "mir" of the planet Earth—the local to the global (Turgenev [1861] 1939, 185). The State need not be destroyed by violent means. Processes of constitutional choice can be put in place through open public deliberations in the diverse exigencies of life. Under those circumstances, States as monopolies of authority relationships and instruments of force can be expected to wither away, if they are no longer monopolies, in the same way that absolute monarchs and emperors have withered away in the course of modern history.

Such possibilities turn on a pragmatics of language where the elements in classificatory schema are not viewed as binary opposites but as complements to one another. The distinction arrayed as Man and Woman, for example, applies to two distinct elements in a classificatory schema pertaining to gender. Those distinct elements in a binary set may be distinguished as opposites, but those opposites fit in complementarities that pertain to sexuality and to other features in the constitution of life in human societies. Orwell's "proles" [proletarians] would find it difficult to understand the "radical" critique of "deconstruction." Instead, they would view Man and Woman as complements in the most enduring bonds of human relationships. Where classificatory distinctions are made, the terminological expressions of those distinctions always reflect some rationale for making a distinction. Any distinction used to sort one term from another is expressive of some "reason" for making a distinction and for understanding a principle of complementarity for relating distinguishable elements to one another. A principle of complementarity, not oppositions, applies to the logic of sets that are meaningful in the constitution of social orders.

Ludwig Lachmann's concept of "capital" is the equivalent of Marx and Engels's "accumulated labor." Lachmann argues that a principle of heterogeneity is always operable in assembling the diverse factors and tools to accomplish something. I presume that such a principle applies to production, to exchange relationships, and to the consumption and use of whatever is consumed, used, or enjoyed. Lachmann sees these heterogeneous elements as always being related by a principle of complementarity to achieve the transformations to yield artifactual creations—products, artifactual states of affairs. I rely on these principles in such diverse activities as making bread and thinking about the way patterns of order are constituted in human societies and about how I constitute my relationships to others, presuming that I am my own governor and am capable of constituting associated relationships with others.

Lachmann's terminology can be applied to the logic of languages. Any classificatory schema—distinctions expressed in words—will reflect heterogeneities. Gender reflects heterogeneous elements—male and female—that apply to diverse forms of life and diverse aspects of life in human societies. However, these heterogeneities also reflect complementarities; the latter must always be taken into account with reference to the former. All elements in subsets are *associated with* sets in classificatory schema. Private is the complement of public; thought, a complement of action; ideas, a complement of what gets done. These are among the features that need to be seriously reconsidered in exploring the way that the constitution of languages affects how people think, how thought affects actions, and how actions affect what occurs in constituting order and what is achieved in human societies.

Democracy, then, is a condition where people learn how to cope with conflict and engage in inquiries about problematic situations to achieve conflict resolution through conscious problem-solving efforts to acquire common knowledge, mutual understanding, social accountability, and trust in their diverse relationships with others. People strive for complementarities in their diverse relationships. Uniformity in the presence of great diversities will inevitably entrap mankind in Catch-22 situations. Human beings who aspire to freedom will find themselves in a situation, as Rousseau asserted, where everyone is bound in "chains" ([1762] 1978, 46). So we come back to an eternal struggle. The struggle is associated with a quest for complementarities among intelligible creatures in which our capacity to *communicate with* one another and exercise *power with* others in patterns of association is grounded in common knowledge, mutual understanding, social accountability, and trust (Follett [1924] 1951). Recourse to instruments of coercion cannot be eliminated. If no coercion were available in a lawful system of order, the most perverse predators would be free to prey on others. The challenge is to find ways to limit coercive potentials to standards of legitimacy associated with both liberty and justice.

To act "in contradiction to all past historical experience" is to render human beings helpless. We cannot know the Truth. We can, however, attempt to develop a critical awareness of the relationships of the languages we use to thought, the relationships of thought to the actions we take, and the relationships of communicating, associating, and working with others to what is achieved. The institution of languages is the fundament of order in all human societies. The problem of Newspeak implies the corruption of language, the failure of communication, the loss of problem-solving capabilities, and the erosion of political and social orders. Michel Crozier, writing in the year 1984, was, in my judgment, correct in anticipating that America, too, is moving toward what the Russians would call Times of Trouble. Antoni Kaminski, in a working paper entitled "The New Polish Regime and the Specter of Economic Corruption" (1996), demonstrates how the corruption of language pervades economic and political corruption. The term *privatization* has become "a fertile ground for foul practicing" (ibid.). The term *self-government* as it is used in the Polish Industrial Self-Government Act enables party officials and the bureaucratic nomenclature to create a facade for bureaucratic immunity.

Karl Popper, writing during the war years of the early 1940s in *The Open Society and Its Enemies,* warned that the transition from a closed society to an open society involves a transformation in which an open society becomes increasingly an "abstract society." He went on to observe that

There are many people in modern society who have no, or extremely few, intimate personal contacts, who live in anonymity and isolation, and consequently in unhappiness. For although society has become abstract, the biological makeup of man has not changed much; men have social needs which they cannot satisfy in an abstract society. ([1945] 1963, 1:174–75)

The abstraction of scientific generalizations mixed with the art of political manipulation among people who live in anonymity and isolation is a recipe for disaster. New versions of Newspeak inevitably emerge as ideas get confounded by partisan politics with ideologies, and no one knows what to think.

Can the methods of thought and habits of mind characteristic of science as a method of coping with problems irrespective of its particular branches be used to apply to diverse facets of life? As a way of reflecting about these potentials, I turn to a critical assessment of a tradition of scholarship with which I have been associated. We face problems of coming to terms with diverse criteria of choice in a common framework that gives us some minimal degree of intellectual leverage in coherent ways of thinking.

CHAPTER 4

Epistemic Choice and Public Choice

At the intersections of anthropology, economics, law, political science, public administration, and sociology, a sufficient body of literature had accumulated from interdisciplinary research efforts by the mid-1960s to support a new approach to the study of public decision making. Those inquiries were stimulated by a growing awareness that problems of institutional weaknesses and failures in market arrangements could not be corrected simply by recourse to governmental decision processes that were themselves subject to serious limits. How did we develop a better understanding of the structure of decision making and performance in the "public sector"? What were the limits applicable to collective choice and its relationship to collective action? Now, in the presence of three or four decades of cumulative efforts in the Public-Choice tradition, how does one assess the prospects for the next generation?

My conclusion is that the most important potentials have been associated with diverse thrusts on the peripheries of work in the Public-Choice tradition rather than with efforts at the core of the tradition to apply "economic reasoning" to "nonmarket decision making," as the Public-Choice approach has been conceptualized by the mainstream of Public-Choice scholars. The "core" of the Public-Choice tradition involves economic reasoning that places primary emphasis on a *nontuistic, self-interested, rational actor* approach to *methodological individualism. Nontuism* implies *not* taking account of the interests of others; *self-interest* implies taking account of one's own preferences. *Rational actors* in economic theory seek to maximize their own net advantage. *Methodological individualism* involves taking the perspective of hypothetical individuals in choice situations. By "thrusts on the peripheries," I refer, for example, to Gordon Tullock's (1965) focus on the way that bureaucracies filter and distort the transmission of information to create systemic propensities for deception and for error, to James Buchanan's (1979a) emphasis on the artifactual character of human individuality, to Douglass North's (1990) insistence that ideas and institutional arrangements are important, and to James Coleman's (1990) concern that norms are important sources of productive potentials.

Work on the peripheries is where important advances at the frontier are most likely to occur. The leading contributors to the Public-Choice tradition have never confined themselves to a "core" built on extreme rationality assumptions. A. K. Sen's article on "Rational Fools" (1977), Karl Popper's essay on "Rationality and the Status of the Rationality Principle" (1967), and Brian Barry and Russell Hardin's collection of essays on *Rational Man and Irrational Society?* (1982) are indicative of some of the social dilemmas and puzzles that pervade human societies. Perhaps the important challenge for Public-Choice scholars is to address how basic anomalies, social dilemmas, and puzzles can be resolved in human affairs, rather than to apply economic reasoning, narrowly construed, to nonmarket decision making.

A question of some importance is whether these efforts at the periphery of the Public-Choice approach are only miscellaneous idiosyncratic accretions. In that case, the literature will exceed human cognitive limits and become fleeting fads among Towers of Babel. Or are there ways that these cumulative inquiries can be ordered as contributions to diverse elements, foci, and levels of analysis that are complementary to one another and that meet standards of scientific warrantability? This, too, is a matter of "public" choice at an epistemic level about what is worthy of inclusion in the corpus of knowledge. The attribute of publicness as applied to the corpus of knowledge is not confined to collective choice implicating institutions of government. Rather, the public-good character of knowledge evokes important potentials for economic and political development—in all aspects of market and nonmarket decision making. The public-good character of knowledge is not decided by Governments but by those who are artisans engaged in the creation and uses of knowledge. Public choice need not be decided by elections and coalitions claiming popular mandates. Furthermore, the principles of choice applicable to the warrantability of knowledge are different than the principles of choice applicable to a choice of goods in market and public economies. These are different than the principles of choice applicable to the constitution of rule-ordered relationships in accordance with standards of fairness. Principles of consensus among participants can apply to each, but the criteria of choice vary among different types of choice.

If an intellectual apparatus can be developed to give complementarity to the diverse thrusts in inquiries pursued over the last three or four decades, we might also expect to achieve a greater coherence among much longer traditions of inquiry in the social or cultural sciences. Edwin Haefele, for example, called attention to an assertion made by Aristotle—"For that which is common to the greatest number has the least care bestowed upon it" (Aristotle 1942, bk. 2, chap. 3, sec. 3)—to reject Plato's argument about the ideal polity expounded by Socrates in *The Republic,* a title that is itself a misnomer drawn from the Latin language. Aristotle's assertion indicates a long-standing awareness of collective-action dilemmas. If a public facility or service were to be collectively provided, any narrowly rational actor would take advantage of what became freely available, while declining to bear responsibility for a proportionate share of the burdens and costs. Under these circumstances, levying a tax through some instrumentality of government would serve as a proxy for a market price. People could not be expected to pay taxes voluntarily.

A new approach not only opens potentials for future work but allows for a better appreciation of how to select from and build on prior achievements. Problems of epistemic choice—the choice of conceptualizations, assertions, and information to be used and acted on in problem-solving modes—must necessarily loom large. If the Public-Choice approach will continue to contribute to the advancement of knowledge, that future depends on meeting the requirements of epistemic choice. In this chapter, I first give attention to the problem of epistemic choice and then relate that problem to the arraying of elements in a framework implicit in the Public-Choice tradition.

The Problem of Epistemic Choice

Fundaments of Epistemic Choice

Thomas Hobbes, David Hume, Adam Smith, and others give us foundations for dealing with language, learning, knowledge, communication, artisanship, and moral judgment in the exercise of choice. In considering the problem of epistemic choice, the contingencies of language and their relationships to knowledge, choice, and action are at the focus of attention. The conceptions formulated, the words used, and the assertions made are all significant because symbolic expressions stand for referents. Symbols used in interpersonal communication refer to events in the world: elements [things named] and relations [motions, action tendencies, transforms] functioning in subject-predicate-object relationships, in hypothetical if-then relationships, and in factor-function-product relationships. Distinctions relate to classificatory schema that identify sets and subsets in patterns of associated relationships.

Three criteria can be used for establishing the warrantability of assertions: (1) logical coherence among complementary assertions in bodies of knowledge presuming a unity of knowledge; (2) empirical warrantability—hypothetical assertions withstand critical scrutiny in light of experience—and (3) public reproducibility—empirical results, achieved by

some, can also be replicated by others if assertions are appropriately formulated and acted on. The important associations between linguistic formulations and referent events are accompanied by parallel associations
occurring in the patterns of thought characteristic of inferential [if-then]
reasoning. This is complemented by thinking associated with the use of the
imagination to array speculative what-if conjectures. Human thought may
evoke fictions of the mind that differ substantially from those sets of assertions that withstand the tests of logical coherence, empirical warrantability, and public reproducibility.

In an epistemic context, I find Thomas Hobbes's analysis "Of Man"
([1651] 1960, 7–108) to be far more helpful for establishing the conceptual
foundations for human understanding than Jeremy Bentham's formulation, which emphasizes something Bentham called "utility" ([1823] 1948).
Hobbes argued that speech [language] is the factor that distinguishes
Homo sapiens from other creatures, like lions, bears, and wolves. Science is
a "knowledge of consequences" associated with hypothetical assertions.
Thought permits the arraying of alternative possibilities. Choice involves a
weighing of those alternatives in relation to internal indicators of individuals reflecting their appetites and aversions [preferences]. Hobbes asserted
that "The POWER [action potentials] *of a man,* to take it universally, is his
present means, to obtain some future apparent good" ([1651] 1960, 56,
Hobbes's emphasis). I conceptualize Hobbes's definition of power to
equate purposive action with artisanship—the use of present means to
obtain some future apparent good. His basic postulate is then formulated,
"So that in the first place, I [Hobbes] put for a general inclination of all
mankind, a perpetual and restless desire of power after power, that ceaseth
only in death" (ibid., 64). I interpret that assertion to indicate that the general inclination of all mankind is a continual striving to use present means
to obtain some future apparent good, in successive efforts that cease only
with death. Saints, for example, presumably strive through prayer and
meditation to bring themselves closer to God, rather than maximizing
their net assets in a system of financial accounts. Scholarship need not be
concerned with maximizing wealth, even though scholars, like everyone
else, need to meet the economic requirements of life. Languages, then, not
only act as devices that enable human beings to convey signals to one
another but are the means for constituting knowledge, organizing
thought, arraying alternatives, ordering choice, and taking actions in
arranging present means in appropriate ways to realize future apparent
goods. Choice is mediated by human cognition and action potentials articulated through language. But language can, unfortunately, also be used to
fool oneself and others.

Hobbes's Man in a State of Nature is, I believe, a hypothetical thought experiment of presuming human beings to be *devoid of speech* and, thus, comparable to animals like lions, bears, and wolves. In referring to the frailties of the mind in chapter 13 of *Leviathan,* Hobbes proposed "setting aside the arts grounded upon words" (ibid., 80). Individuals would seek their own good; but, in the absence of speech, in the presence of scarcity and the existence of others, they would end up fighting with one another. Fighting is a recurrent and persistent phenomenon among *Homo sapiens.*

The precariousness of conflict situations is indicated by Kenneth Boulding's essay "Toward a Pure Theory of Threat Systems" (1963). Boulding presumes speech; but an exchange of threats involves a form of speech in which someone demands, *"You* do something *good* for *me* or *I* will do something *bad* to *you."* The person confronted with a threat is presented with a choice between two bads because doing something good for the other will require a cost to oneself. To defend oneself in such a circumstance, an even stronger counterthreat is easily made. Threats, as such, are mere words. The vulnerable point in an exchange of threats occurs when the credibility of a threat is made a matter of honor. One or the other is required to follow through and make his or her threat credible or to apologize for being offensive. Conflict involving an exchange of threats has a very strong tendency to escalate into violent confrontations yielding more destructive effects than were intended by those who initiated an exchange of threats. Destruction can easily escalate into uncontrolled violence.

Toward a Lawful Order and a Culture of Inquiry

In adopting a problem-solving mode as an alternative to fighting, Hobbes explored a set of principles that would be constitutive of Peace as an alternative to War. Achieving peace requires taking account of the interests of others; nontuism does not work in that context. Rather, Hobbes argued that a method of normative inquiry grounded in the rule *"Do not that to another, which thou wouldest not have done to thyself"* ([1651] 1960, 103, Hobbes's emphasis) is necessary to the achievement and maintenance of peace. As a method of inquiry, Hobbes suggested that such a rule can be made "intelligible even to the meanest capacity" by using the following approach.

> [If,] when weighing the actions of other men with his own, they seem too heavy, . . . put them into the other part of the balance, and his own into their place, that his own passions, and self-love, may add nothing to the weight; and then there is none of these laws of nature [articles of peace] that will not appear unto him very reasonable. (Ibid.)

A method of normative inquiry grounded in the Golden Rule is available for reconsidering one's own preferences in relation to the preferences of others when interdependent interests require *impartiality* in arriving at a judgment pertaining to joint interests. John Harsanyi (1977) and Reinhard Selten (1986) have adopted a similar approach as a broader foundation for evaluating rules of action and not simply action alone. I summarize the set of principles Hobbes derived from this method of normative inquiry in table 4.1. These can be viewed as necessary conditions for the constitution and reform of human communities in accordance with basic normative precepts taught in the Jewish, Christian, and Islamic traditions. Similar precepts prevail in other civilizations. They are steps to be pursued in the resolution of conflict as a way of peacefully resolving problems in human relationships. Conflicts associated with interdependent individual interests suggest commonalities that require attention to how individual interests relate to communities of interdependent interests. A method of normative inquiry in a problem-solving mode is available among members of speech communities to explore options for resolving conflict in relation to all different forms of choice.

This method of normative inquiry is a way of making interpersonal comparisons and arriving at rules of reason. Hobbes viewed these rules of reason as accessible to anyone who draws on his or her fundamental resources as a human being, mediated through the use of language, to build shared communities of understanding. Mutual trust is established by performing covenants made. For Hobbes, a fool would deny such rules of reason without appreciating the destructive potentials involved. The terms *nature* and *natural* are associated with different meanings when referring to man in "a state of nature" and to "the laws of nature." This tension reflects puzzles about the place of language in "human nature" and the place of culture in human societies. Rules of right reason are presumed to be expressive of human nature even though they accrue as human cultural achievements and are not evoked by genetic reproduction alone.

David Hume (1948) and Adam Smith ([1759] n.d.) relied on a sentiment of sympathy, modified by the generality of language in human communication, to arrive at a standard of justice for mediating human relationships. In "An Enquiry concerning the Principles of Morals," Hume wrote:

> The distinction, therefore, between the species of sentiment [i.e., sympathy or fellow feeling in contrast to those connected with any other emotion or passion] being so great and evident, language must soon be moulded upon it and must invent a peculiar set of terms in order to express those universal sentiments of censure and approbation which

TABLE 4.1. Hobbes's Laws of Nature [The Way to Peace]

1. That one seek peace and follow it, but be prepared to defend oneself.

2. That one be willing, in the quest for peace, when others are willing, to lay down one's right to all things and be content with so much liberty against others as one would allow others against oneself.

3. That individuals perform their covenants made.

4. That one act in relation to others so they will have no cause for regret.

5. That everyone strive to accommodate oneself to the rest.

6. That upon caution of future time, a person ought to pardon the offenses past of them that, repenting, desire it.

7. That in retribution of evil for evil, persons look not at the greatness of the evil past but at the greatness of the good to follow.

8. That no one by deed, word, countenance, or gesture declare hatred or contempt of others.

9. That everyone acknowledge another as one's equal by nature.

10. That at the entrance into the conditions of peace, no one reserve to oneself any right which one is not content should be reserved to every one of the rest.

11. That if one be trusted to judge between one person and another, one deals equally between them.

12. That such things as cannot be divided, be enjoyed in common, if it can be, and if the quantity of the thing permit, without stint, otherwise proportional to the number of them that have right.

13. That such things as cannot be divided or enjoyed in common require that the entire right to the whole thing, or else, making the use alternative, be determined by lot.

14. That distribution by lot be determined by an agreement among the competitors or by first seizure.

15. That all who mediate peace be allowed safe conduct.

16. That they that are at controversy submit their right to the judgment of an arbitrator.

17. That no one is a fit arbitrator of one's own cause in relation to the interest of another.

18. That no one in any cause ought to be received for arbitrator to whom greater profit or honor or pleasure apparently arises out of the victory of one party rather than another.

19. That in controversies of fact those who judge should give no more credit to one witness than to another but should call additional witnesses until the question is decided by the weight of evidence.

Summary Rule: *Do not that to another, which thou wouldest not have done to thyself.*

Source: Hobbes [1651] 1960, chaps. 14 and 15.

arise from humanity or from views of general usefulness and its contrary. Virtue and Vice become known; morals are recognized; certain general rules are framed of human conduct and behavior; such measures are expected of men in such situations. This action is conformable to an abstract rule; the other contrary. And by such universal principles are the particular sentiments of self-love frequently controlled and limited. (1948, 254)

The moral quality arises from fellow feelings expressed as general rules: "Virtue and Vice become known; morals are recognized; certain general rules are framed of human conduct . . . ; such measures are expected of men in such situations. This action is conformable to an abstract rule; the other contrary." Hume was emphasizing the *coevolutionary* and *configured* development of sentiments, languages, the foundation of morals, the articulation of meaning, and the basic foundations of law as these might apply to epistemic choice and other forms of choice.

Following his well-known passage about distinguishing "is" and "ought" statements, Hume indicated that it is necessary to "look within" to find the standards for rendering moral judgment. Those standards are ascertainable by the use of methods of normative inquiry to make interpersonal comparisons mediated through speech. Without a background of common knowledge, a shared community of understanding about making appropriate normative distinctions, a system of social accountability for monitoring and enforcing rules, and a substantial degree of public trust that rule-ordered relationships will be adhered to, there is no basis for assigning autonomy to individuals to exercise responsibility for the actions they take in the governance of their own affairs and in relating to others. The conditions stipulated in Hobbes's laws of nature are the foundations for both a lawful order and a culture of inquiry. The use of extreme rationality assumptions in economic theory runs the risk of stripping away and ignoring essential epistemic and moral considerations that are constitutive of human affairs.

The Basic Epistemological Problem

Walter Eucken ([1940] 1951), the German economist associated with the development of *Ordnungstheorie* [theory of order], writing in the late 1930s, called attention to what I regard as the basic epistemological problem in the cultural and social sciences. Eucken asserted that economic theorists rely on a single, simple, general model that is presumed to have universal application in the conduct of economic analysis. By so doing, he argued that economists increasingly distanced themselves from economic "reality." Abstractions lose meaning, theory is confined to doctrine and lacks contact with "reality." Hans Albert (1984), a German philosopher concerned with problems of epistemology in the Popperian tradition as applied to economics and the social sciences, refers to this as a problem of model-thinking. A fully specified model bounded by limiting assumptions is presumed to have universal applications. Model thinking may serve the purposes of rigorous mathematical reasoning but neglects empirical "realities" and problematics in human affairs. Eucken contrasted the empirical inquiries of economic historians of his time as heaping facts on facts without relevance to economic theory. The result was a "great antinomy": abstract doctrine on the one hand, and the accumulation of facts, on the other, without critical attention to how theory and facts—ideas and deeds—relate to one another in establishing the warrantability of what was being asserted. Eucken's "great antinomy" yields a basic incoherence in discourse about human affairs. Contemporary work by Douglass North (1990) and Harold Berman (1983) and a virtual flood of similar inquiries represent major advances in this regard. The ambiguous and pervasive uses of the term *model* among economists and among many social scientists, however, leave me grasping for words to gain understanding.

At this point, it is important to recall Hobbes's assertions about the use of language that might make one "excellently wise" by acting on scientifically warranted conceptions in contrast to "excellently foolish" when acting on absurd doctrine—"senseless speech" ([1651] 1960, 22). In Hobbes's judgment, being excellently foolish was worse than simple ignorance. People of simple ignorance do not indulge in genocide and holocausts. Rather, those who engage in such conduct are presumably infected with some form of intellectual "virus," so to speak. Prudence, which Hobbes associated with experience, is a way of distinguishing sensible from senseless uses of language. Absurd doctrines can meet standards of logical rigor and mathematical proof but yield disastrous consequences when used to inform actions. Human action needs to draw on general principles that can be applied to particular time and place exigencies that vary with ecological and cultural circumstances.

Eucken presumed that different systems of economic order exist in different times and places. His concern was how to identify and develop basic elements and relationships so that a commensurate framework could be used to specify structured variants—morphologies—to allow for comparative assessments of performance. He presumed that all systems of economic order require planning—the uses of knowledge and information. His concern was with the differences in planning processes that occurred, for example, in contemporary "market" and "command" economies, rather than with a presumption that there are some "planned" and other "unplanned" economies. He further presumed that all economic orders function in a context of political orders.

Eucken's presumption that planning takes place in all economic activities is commensurate with Hobbes's presumption that all action is grounded in thought. This poses an issue with regard to Friedrich von Hayek's use of the concept of "spontaneity" (1973, 36–54), and Adam Smith's concept of the "hidden hand" ([1776] n.d.), in the creation and maintenance of social orders. Are such terms to be applied to relationships viewed as "brute facts" or "institutional facts" that reflect self-organizing and self-governing capabilities among knowledgeable and intelligible human beings? Can "hidden hands" be expected to work spontaneously in the constitution of order in human societies viewed as systems of natural order—"brute facts"? If Hayek's spontaneity and Smith's hidden hand depend on the intelligent use of the arts and sciences of association among the members of societies, we in the Public-Choice tradition bear a substantial burden in elucidating and making use of the sciences and arts of association. Coming to terms with problems of institutional weaknesses and failures depends on the development of analytical capabilities commensurate with the sciences and arts of human association.

Neoclassical economic theory relies on a "model" presuming a perfectly competitive market economy in which fully informed actors participate as buyers and sellers when a price equilibrium is achieved at a point where demand at that price equals the supply offered at that price. With an indefinitely large number of market participants, the actions of particular buyers and sellers will not alter the price equilibrium. So price provides crucial information about economic opportunities. Market decisions about price are nontuistic in the sense that a perfectly competitive market would determine price on an impartial basis without regard for others. A rational actor in such circumstances would act in a way that maximizes individual self-interest.

Social dilemmas arise, however, when individuals select strategies to maximize their own gains that diverge from the aggregate gain that might have been realized. Each individual acting on the basis of a best response without regard for others need not achieve the highest joint benefit (common good). Individual success in acquiring wealth is not the appropriate measure of a contribution to "society," "civilization," or "human welfare." Many human relationships are not monetized exchange relationships. Individual rationality in maximizing "utility," as Bentham used that term, could yield Sen's "Rational Fools" and Barry and Hardin's "Irrational Society."

As a purely abstract intellectual enterprise, neoclassical economic theory in the Anglo-American tradition has considerable merit; but it is bound up with seriously limiting assumptions. Among these are fully informed actors whose actions are governed by law and order. Ordinary theft, violence, and the exappropriation and seizure of property are assumed away. The *necessary* conditions for the constitution and operation of a market economy depend on establishing conditions approximating these assumptions by reference to the proper operation and performance of a political system, an epistemic [knowledge and information] system, and a moral order. These patterns of order operate concurrently. Habituated patterns of conduct are not sufficient. Self-conscious awareness of the way that economic, political, epistemic, and moral contingencies may work in complementary ways is necessary to the sustainability and reformability of patterns of order in human societies.

The emphasis on maximizing "utility" or "wealth" means that primary attention is being given to preference orderings; other aspects of the political economy of life are excluded from the focal attention of inquiry and swept into the background. The principle of maximizing Utility, also referred to by Bentham as the "happiness principle," presumably applies universally to people everywhere for choosing among bliss points without regard to language, culture, or the constitution of order in particular societies and ways of life. The place of knowledge and of information, the place of a moral order as constitutive of fiduciary relationships, the place of law and the requirements of justice, and the requirements of intelligibility in human artisanship are treated as outside the focus of inquiry. Such circumstances are susceptible to self-deception. If attention is given only to preferences, there is a danger that the "whole moral and intellectual condition of a people" will be reduced to "intellectual dust," as Tocqueville asserted ([1835–40] 1945, 1:299, 2:7).

Continuing to adhere to an orthodox way of applying "economic reasoning" to nonmarket decision making does not allow for learning to occur. An openness to uncertainty, social dilemmas, anomalies, and puzzles as presenting problematics, allows for learning, innovation, and basic advances in knowledge to occur. This is why all scholarship in the social and cultural sciences needs to be sensitive to the artifactual character of language and the intellectual constructions that are used to frame inquiry. The existence of conflict should serve as a reminder that our intellectual constructions may be at fault. Recognizing different ways of conceptualizing problematics may be the key to the achievement of conflict resolution. Different ways of conceptualizing the intellectual enterprise within and among the social and cultural sciences is of basic importance in working out the essential relationships of ideas to deeds in human societies.

The Problem of Lawful Order

If we recognize that Jeremy Bentham, the early exponent of the concept of Utility as a single, linear scale of values, was a philosopher with a strong interest in jurisprudence, we can begin to appreciate some of the difficulties that can arise in applying economic reasoning grounded only in Utility theory to nonmarket decision making. Bentham's concept of Utility served as a single summary measure for preference orderings implying a single selection principle applicable to all human choices. Both Hume and Adam Smith used the term *utility* to mean "usefulness" rather than a summary measure for all values. Maximizing Utility for Bentham also meant the achievement of the greatest good for the greatest number.

Bentham's way of addressing the problem of rule-ordered relationships was to presume that men of goodwill could know what would provide the greatest good for the greatest number and, thus, what was good for others. Such men could be relied on to establish a rational code of law that would avoid the irrationalities of relying on the Common Law, an accretion of precedents derived from the accidents of historical decisions accumulated from the past. The problem of representative government could be resolved by the selection of an assembly of men of goodwill rather than of aspiring politicians seeking to win elections and form governing coalitions to enjoy the fruits of victory. The criminal law for Bentham was the core of the law because it established the bounds of lawful conduct and was, presumably, made effective by enforceable sanctions. A fear of punishment rather than a sense of justice motivates men to obey rules. Bentham's solution to the problem of men governing men placed reliance on principles of command and control, in contrast to Madison's solution of using power to check power in a search for conflict resolution in accordance with principles of freedom and justice. If potentials for deception and self-deception prevail in human societies, a way to cope with such ambiguities is to rely on principles of contestation among opposite and rival interests. Checks and balances are necessary to make such systems work. But then the question is how to achieve commonalities.

We face a puzzle posed by Hobbes of whether the unity of commonwealths turns on the unity of the Sovereign *representative* or the unity of the *represented.* Hobbes presumed that the unity of the commonwealth could only be achieved by the unity of the Sovereign representative. The American federalists, by contrast, presumed that the application of covenantal methods to conflict and conflict resolution was the appropriate way to create the conditions of common knowledge, shared understanding, social accountability, and mutual trust that were viewed as essential to self-governing communities of relationships and to the achievement of the conditions of peace and other public goods.

If command and control by a single power are not the key design principles, how do we devise the rules for a fair game? These rules require the experience of communicating and relating to others in the context of a prior background of common knowledge, shared understanding, social accountability, and mutual trust. Human beings are always drawing on prior experiences, but they need not be the slaves of precedents. Systems of rule-ordered relationships depend on change, adaptability, and reformulation. What methods of normative inquiry should be applied to the construction and alteration of rule-ordered relationships?

Hobbes presumed that standards of fairness depend on informed consent: "It is in the laws of a commonwealth, as in the laws of gaming: whatsoever the gamesters all agree on, is injustice to none of them" ([1651] 1960, 227). This assumption implies standards achieved through informed consent—general agreement, not majority rule. Hobbes warned that "Unnecessary laws are not good laws; but traps for money" (ibid., 227–28). Adherence to the Golden Rule as a method of normative inquiry is an appropriate way to devise the rules of a fair game that are consistent with rules of equity and informed consent. If the Common Law of England had been constructed by relying on the principles of equity inherent in God's law, the Common Law might then be revised by relying on principles of equity appropriate to a search for equitable solutions. Covenantal methods are constitutive of covenantal societies. This would be an alternative to Hobbes's sovereign or to Bentham's reliance on men of goodwill to formulate a rational code of law presuming criminal law to be the core of positive law.

The cost calculus introduced by Buchanan and Tullock (1962), emphasizing expected decision costs as time and effort expended on the making of decisions and expected external costs as the deprivations likely to be suffered from adverse decisions—or the mutual advantage gained from favorable decisions—goes some distance in taking account of factors that would enter into a method of normative inquiry appropriate to the formulation of rules for a fair game. Their cost calculus is an effort to array expected costs consistent with Utility calculations. Estimating "costs" applicable to both monetized and nonmonetized relationships does not provide the basis for formulating a fair set of rules as such. Jurisprudence still has its place. A cost calculus is a useful mode of computation in estimating what is worth doing, as a complement to other standards of performance.

Human choice involves contingent relationships grounded in knowledge *plus* the capacity to weigh and choose among alternatives in relation to criteria of choice. The important contribution by Buchanan and Tullock was to recognize that the logic of choice applied to the choice of rules is different than the logic of choice applied to the selection of persons to serve in positions of political authority or the expenditure of money to buy vendable services and products. How to select "men of goodwill" is always problematic. How to achieve equitable resolutions by using power to check power turns critically on the achievement of a culture of inquiry to pursue a problem-solving mode of inquiry applicable to conflict and conflict resolution.

Eucken's critique and the analyses offered by Hobbes, Montesquieu, Hume, Adam Smith, and others addressing similar questions in the seventeenth and eighteenth centuries have led me to conclude that the requirements of epistemic choice cannot be met by universal models alone. Differently conceptualized systems of order in human societies do exist. Such systems are constituted in different ways. Establishing commensurability for treating variable characteristics requires reference not to an infinite plenitude of "facts" but to common elements in a framework that can take on variable characteristics.

Features of an Analytical Framework

In my judgment, the innovative thrust in early Public-Choice efforts was to bring together concerns about "methodological individualism," "the nature of goods," and "decision-making arrangements" [institutions] as distinct elements to be taken into account in addressing market and non-market decision making (V. Ostrom [1973] 1989). These were elements of a general framework that could be used to specify the logic of prototypical situations in human societies. An epistemic element—the place of common knowledge and communities of shared understanding in decision situations—was neglected. The accompanying schematic in figure 4.1 is a representation of such a framework.

Unlike a universal model that is presumed to apply to human experience everywhere, a framework uses basic elements that can be brought together to conceptualize different patterns of order in human societies. By drawing on human agents to be the active elements that make the system work, it is possible to consider competing hypotheses about differently conceived systems of order, provided that people in human societies are willing to engage in the experiments. Criteria applicable to epistemic choice might then be applied to conjectures about different systems of political order. It would be appropriate to conjecture whether societies of men might constitute "good governments" by reflection and choice, pro-

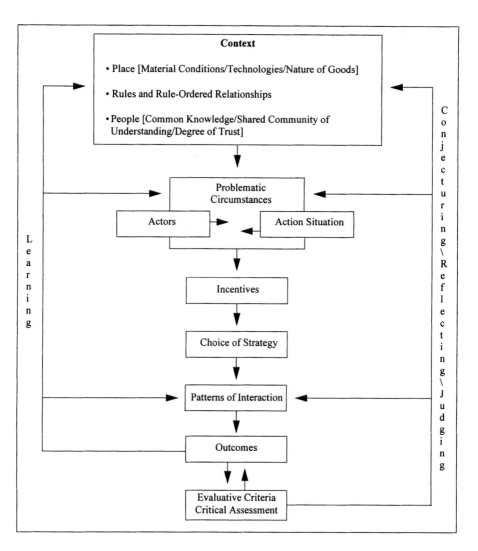

Fig. 4.1. A framework of elements and stages in institutional analysis and development. *Actors* perceive *incentives* (opportunities and constraints) in *problematic circumstances* in light of the structure of *action situations* set in a more general *context.* These incentives affect their *choices of strategies* in *interactions* affecting *outcomes.* These processes are *evaluated* through *conjecturing, reflecting,* and *judging.* Individuals in such situations *learn* to modify the structure of the situation or their strategies in an emerging or destabilizing system of order. (For similar frameworks, see Kiser and E. Ostrom 1982; E. Ostrom 1990; and Oakerson 1992.)

vided that they are willing to specify their standards of judgment. Under these circumstances, the "political doctrine" used to formulate "basic demands and expectations" typically set forth in constitutions, charters, and formal declarations, as expounded in Lasswell's formulation, might be treated as relevant hypothetical conjectures within "political science" and the related cultural and social sciences.

Tocqueville used a similar framework for his study in *Democracy in America.* Before addressing himself to the institutional arrangements characteristic of the American system of governance, he explicitly considered the physical circumstances of the North American continent, where the Anglo-Americans had settled and lived in relation to the aboriginal population. The origins—historical background—of the Anglo-Americans and their general social condition were also considered as the context for specifying the institutional arrangements characteristic of their system of governance. His analysis of the particular factors that contributed to the maintenance of the American federal republic turned explicitly on the elements in his framework:

I.   The peculiar and accidental situation in which Providence has placed the Americans.
II.   The laws [rules and rule-ordered relationships].
III. The manners and customs of the people. ([1835] 1945, 1:288)

The analytical problem, then, is how contextual elements fit together to create action situations that are relevant to the choices being made by actors who are acting with reference to that situation. The more fully the situation can be specified, the less burden needs to be placed on the particular rationality postulates being asserted for hypothetical actors. A postulate of complete or perfect information can be avoided if situational conditions pertaining to common knowledge and shared communities of understanding can be specified. Thus, Tocqueville presumed that manners and customs of the people apply to moral and intellectual conditions that are characteristic of those who are participants in action situations. The weaker form of such a postulate would be a combination of Hobbes's conception of power as the use of present means to obtain some future apparent good when combined with the assertion of "a perpetual and restless" striving that persists so long as life endures. Active agents are motivated to act in ways that will leave them better off, rather than worse off, as they conceptualize the importance of fundamental values, including peace, knowledge, freedom, justice, and well-being, but not necessarily limited to those values.

A framework is necessary in specifying the features that need identification in any analytical effort. Indicating how some activating factor can be used to drive transformations to be achieved is a way of specifying hypothetical if-then contingencies to account for cause and effect relationships. This is a way of formulating theoretical explanations. Moving toward a more precise specification of the necessary and sufficient conditions for achieving a transformation is the specification of a model. Working with frameworks, theories, and models is necessary for achieving general explanations in the cultural and social sciences and in such fields of study as history, journalism, jurisprudence, and public administration. Model thinking alone is not sufficient. The intellectual enterprise requires moving back and forth across frameworks, theories, and models so as to appropriately fit limiting conditions, opportunities, and hypothetical contingencies into the multidimensional facets characteristic of the artifactual nature of human habitation.

The rudiments for such a framework can be built by drawing on the early work of Public-Choice scholars. Methodological individualism is a way of postulating active agents. These agents act in light of knowledge and information and in relation to material conditions and technologies, to affect the nature of the goods that function in the economy of life. Relationships are mediated by decision-making arrangements set within the moral and intellectual conditions that affect how individuals relate to each other.

Methodological Individualism

I use the term *methodological individualism* to presume, as Lasswell did, that the fundamental feature of human societies is "acts performed by individuals who are not merely biological entities but persons who have an individual 'ego' and a social 'self'" embedded in a cultural heritage (Lasswell and Kaplan 1950, 3). Individuals, as egos and social selves, function in the social and cultural context of normative processes with an autonomous sense of personal existence, without being confined to the extreme rationality assumptions of microeconomic theory. Self-interest considered in light of the interests of others is a way of reaching shared communities of understanding. Calculations pertaining to warrantable knowledge, standards of fairness, other normative considerations, and material well-being are deserving of complementary attention. Collectivities may act in concert and function as actors, but group actions are always to be understood as patterned forms of individual actions.

I presume that the perspective of methodological individualism is necessary in the cultural and social sciences, even for inquiries in societies that do not recognize the autonomous standing of individuals in the constitution of those societies. We, as individuals, use our own resources as human beings to attempt to understand others, presuming as Hobbes did that there is a basic similitude of thoughts and passions characteristic of all mankind. Confucian societies, for example, have not traditionally recognized the standing of individuals apart from family units (Yang 1987). Any such conception has consequences that are important, as individuals act either with reference to family ties and the webs of obligation and opportunities among kin or as outcasts required to come to terms with radically different conditions of life. Outcasts, for example, can associate together in secret societies, organized as brotherhoods, and function at the margin of society, engaged in some combination of organized crime and as enforcers for those who cannot rely on the formal system of authority relationships. It is entirely possible for such outlaw societies to achieve an honorable place in societies with repressive regimes, as did Robin Hood and his men. Political realities include reference to Mafias of diverse nationalities, implying universal tendencies.

Whether "lawful" or "unlawful" regimes best serve the interests of "people" is an open empirical question. Where indiscretions of speech are treated as high crimes, as in the characterization of imperial Russia by Marquis de Custine ([1839] 1989), standards of legality lose their relationship to standards of moral judgment. Former inhabitants of prison camps in the Soviet Union testify that professional criminals were treated as the elite among the prisoners and cooperated with camp authorities to maintain "order" within the camps in return for opportunities to prey on political prisoners. Mafias were being nurtured in the confines of prison camps. State authorities who view "private property" as an evil might also view ordinary theft with ambiguity about who is the offender—the "thief" or the "victim." Under such circumstances, individual entrepreneurship would be difficult to distinguish from organized crime; and "lawful" activity may be difficult to distinguish from theft. Those issues can only be resolved by determining who is preying on whom with reference to basic standards of moral judgment. *Who* has standing with regard to *what* is a critical question in establishing patterns of order in human societies. Economic orders turn on moral contingencies. A proper economic order would, presumably, be a moral economy (Scott 1976; Popkin 1979).

The place of moral contingencies in the constitution of a moral order needs to be understood in relation to the patterns of character structure that affect individual choice in the context of more extended patterns of human association. This is why Tocqueville identified religions as political institutions in American society even though religious institutions took no direct part in the function of governmental institutions as such. The question remains whether human beings can use their resources as human beings to understand how other human beings can be expected to draw on a cultural heritage, with its ontological, moral, and epistemological contingencies, to anticipate what choices actors would be prepared to make in hypothetically specified situations. We are still dealing with hypothetical actors confronted with the problem of making choices in hypothetical situations.

Knowledge and Information

Factors pertaining to common knowledge and asymmetries of knowledge and information are among the reasons why "applied theoretical" economists concerned with the empirical investigation of industry structures do not undertake studies of markets in general but focus on particular markets involving closely substitutable goods in which commensurable bodies of knowledge and technologies occur in a nexus of market relationships. We are back to Eucken's problem of whether a single, simple, abstract, universal model of a perfectly competitive market allows comparisons to be made; again we must identify how exogenous parameters and endogenous variables function in establishing the empirical warrantability of theoretical conjectures.

Competitive markets are important "public" institutions. They play a significant evolutionary role in generating common knowledge about the place of price as a measure of value, for equilibrating supply and demand [production and use], and for establishing conditions of individual rationality. The experience of buying and selling in competitive market economies evokes levels of information and common knowledge placed on a scale of value expressed in prices that is not only advantageous to buyers and sellers but informative to any entrepreneur who may seek to take advantage of opportunities that are available. Anglo-American economic theory emphasizes the equilibrating features of competitive market economies. Austrian economists emphasize the information-generating features and their role in entrepreneurship (Kirzner 1973). When the latter is combined with innovation and advances in knowledge and technologies, equilibrating tendencies are continuously being challenged by disequilibrating tendencies that are affected by advances in knowledge, skills, and technologies, including the institutional arrangements that serve as modes of production, exchange, and consumption or use (Dosi 1984).

The problem of common knowledge and asymmetries applicable to the generation and use of knowledge and information occur in the context of speech communities, in the crafts and professions, in the context of individual and collective choice, and generally in relation to whatever human beings do. The assertion of private property rights and their enforcement depend on communities of shared understanding. Common knowledge is of fundamental importance for coordinated activities in human societies. All knowledge conditions cannot be directly resolved by market exchange. Complementary criteria are required to supplement benefit-cost analysis. Presuppositions of methodological individualism need to be related to communities of shared understanding as fundamental elements in a framework for the analyses of decision situations (Kiser and E. Ostrom 1982; E. Ostrom 1990; Oakerson 1992).

Material Conditions, Technologies, and the Nature of Goods

Material conditions as they are transformed by technologies and institutional arrangements have a decisive effect on the conditions of life as these affect the nature of goods. Two sets of variables that pertain to exclusion and to subtractability or jointness of use can initially be used to construct a typology of goods as illustrated in table 4.2. Other factors related to domain and scope add further dimensionality.

The *exclusion* principle has long been recognized as a criterion essential to the feasibility of market organization. Two sets of criteria—difficulty of exclusion; jointness of use—have been variously used in efforts to conceptualize public or collective goods as distinguished from private goods (Head 1962; Olson 1965). I emphasize jointness or subtractability of use rather than rivalry or nonrivalrousness of Utility considerations. Treated as variables, these two sets could be conceived as independent of one another; and dichotomizing the sets with on [yes] or off

TABLE 4.2. Types of Goods

	Jointness of Use	
Exclusion	Alternative Use	Joint Use
Low cost	*Private Goods:* bread, shoes, automobiles, haircuts, books, etc.	*Toll [Club] Goods:* theaters, nightclubs, telephone service, toll roads, cable TV, libraries, etc.
High cost	*Common-Pool Resources:* water pumped from a groundwater basin, fish taken from an ocean, crude oil extracted from an oil pool, etc.	*Public Goods:* peace and security of a community, national defense, mosquito abatement, air pollution control, fire protection, weather forecasts, etc.

Source: V. Ostrom and E. Ostrom 1977, 12.

[no] settings could be used to create a two-by-two matrix, including private goods, toll [club] goods, common-pool resources, and public goods.

This simple logical construction reflects abstractions put into dichotomized logical sets. The logical construction is used to clarify sets of distinctions. In practical circumstances, factors pertaining to potentials for exclusion and to use or consumption are likely to represent continua of more or less and in some combination. For example, excludable goods and services are amenable to market organization, but competitive markets allow open access to buyers and sellers who make joint use of market arrangements. Open competitive markets themselves have the characteristics of public goods, while trading in markets applies to private goods. Discrete markets or shopping centers with assigned locations have the characteristics of common-pool resources. Money as a medium of exchange has the characteristic of a private good; money as a unit of account in a monetary system is a public good. The set of logical categories needs to be used with caution in addressing the exigencies of human experiences. These categories provide ways of addressing essential elements in an analytical schema available to scholars in the cultural and social sciences.

In addition to factors pertaining to exclusion and those pertaining to subtractability or jointness of use, other factors of basic importance pertain to *domain* and *scope,* implying multidimensional matrices. *Domain* bears on factors of territoriality [space], ranging from small third-party neighborhood effects to those of global proportions, as in the case of fallout from nuclear explosion or cumulative changes in the chemical composition of the atmosphere and stratosphere. *Scope* pertains to the independence of one or another type of good or service so that units of a good or service are distinguishable from other goods and services. If the state of affairs subject to joint use and consumption implicates a domain of small magnitude, the relevant public—those affected—might be organized with regard to something appropriately called "neighborhoods." There is no necessary identity between the domain of Nation-States and the domain characteristics either of natural phenomena [e.g., watersheds] or of the way that human habitation is accompanied by neighborhood effects.

Scope contingencies apply to functional specialization, leading to distinction among goods and services. Both water and electricity have the characteristics of common-pool, flow resources that must be kept isolable from one another. Electrical engineering requires careful attention to "insulation." Flows of storm water, sewer water, and domestic water require separable consideration. Diverse opportunities exist in how enterprises associated with such services might be put together in ways that are accountable to the people being served, to develop a consciousness of the interdependencies among productive, distributive, and consumptive aspects of a public economy in contrast to a private market economy. Where considerable autonomy exists in the exercise of self-organizing and self-governing capabilities, various combinations might be achieved in which the character of specialization is resolved by complementary sets of decisions worked out within particular collectivities and in the interrelationships among particular collectivities. Such arrangements are open to mutual accommodation depending on the problematics arising in discrete situations; we need not presume that uniform rules apply to Society as a Whole.

Critical problems arise for the organization of joint consumption aspects among communities of users in public economies. Diverse opportunities available for organizing production functions allow for the creation of quasi-market conditions in a public economy, depending on the alternatives that are available. Scholars with strong applied and theoretical interests in the Public-Choice tradition have faced many of the same problems as applied theoretical economists in industrial organization. Problems confronting fishers are quite different than those confronting irrigators, even though fisheries and irrigation systems both have characteristics associated with common-pool resources (E. Ostrom 1990; Schlager and E. Ostrom 1992). Furthermore, the interface between the resource base and its use implies that common-property relationships are closely bound up with the "private" property rights of individual users. Variations in the scope and domain of toll goods, common-pool resources, and public goods have substantial implications for how communities of relationships are affected and for what standing those communities have within systems of governance for exercising collective choice and taking collective action. We could expect to find multitudes of collectivities operating in systems of governance that simultaneously function as public economies (V. Ostrom, Tiebout, and Warren 1961; Bish 1971; Advisory Commission on Intergovernmental Relations 1987).

The relationships of private property to public thoroughfares, such as sidewalks, streets, and highways, are closely correlated. How the interests of diverse publics are to be taken into account is of substantial importance. Collective organization on a small scale is essential to the interest of smallholders because collective organization enables them to better articulate their joint interests rather than acting as isolated individuals in relation to State authorities. The relationship of the property rights of individuals to complementary forms of social ownership, including various forms of cooperative associations and private, municipal, and public corporations, is of substantial proportions in all human societies (Grossi [1977] 1981; Netting 1993; E. Ostrom 1990).

Decision-Making Arrangements

The great diversity of potential public goods and common-pool resources, where exclusion of individuals may be difficult to achieve and where variable patterns in jointness of use may prevail, implies many communities of interests of varying scope and domain. Efforts to escape these complexities by reference to the concept of "the State" are inevitably confounded by the diversity of decision-making arrangements applicable to choice in human societies. The specter of simplified allusions to "the Market" and "the Government" [State] haunts a large proportion of the work in Public-Choice theory. Such uses of language evoke allusions to "Capitalism" and "Socialism" under circumstances in which I cannot understand whether the term *capitalism* refers to what Adam Smith meant by *free trade* or *mercantilism* or both. An allusion to something called "the Government" does not clarify what the term refers to. If the reference implies that the instrumentalities of collective action are organized as a single firm—the Government—occupying a monopoly position with regard to (1) authority relationships and (2) the legal instruments of coercion, we are conceptualizing Public Choice as occurring under conditions specified in Hobbes's theory of sovereignty. Eucken's conjectures about different ways of conceptualizing systems of order would suggest that alternatives of economic, epistemic, and political significance may exist. Concepts of "States" and "Markets" are not effective ways of articulating the intellectual revolution that is stirring in our midst. As intellectual constructs, they are too gross to be useful; they run the risk of being misleading and are the source of serious forms of deception and misconceptions.

To make rules binding, criteria grounded in moral distinctions must be enforceable, and enforcement may depend on imposing deprivations [punishment] for failure to conform to rules. There are thresholds of choice where coercion is a necessity for the maintenance of order in human societies. As a consequence, I expect no human society to exist without coercive capabilities. Should the exercise of coercive capability be based solely on a power of command without contestability or on some other way of constituting authority relationships?

One way of coping with a theory of sovereignty is to sort out diverse levels of choice. Buchanan and Tullock's *Calculus of Consent* (1962) began that important task by distinguishing between constitutional choice and collective choice. They argued that a base rule of *conceptual unanimity* is important in establishing consensus about the terms and conditions applicable to the exercise of collective choice. There are situations where a rule of unanimity might be relaxed by unanimous agreement to prefer other, less encompassing decision rules in light of the time and effort required to achieve unanimity and the strategic opportunities available to holdouts. The operational significance of coerced choice can be subject to levels of mutual understanding and public scrutiny that achieve informed consent or voluntary agreement in establishing standards of legitimacy. Distinctions can be made among constitutional, collective, and operational choices as the necessary and continuing complements to one another if standards of legitimacy are to prevail. Standards of legitimacy, conceptual unanimity, and informed consent mirror one another, but they need not function through single collectivities applicable to whole societies. If constitutional choice is exercised by military coups or revolutionary struggles and if collective decisions are made by ruling elites engaged in predatory exploitation of others, we would expect very limited opportunities to be available for choice in organizing ways of life. A unitary power of command implies servitude for subjects, not choice for persons and citizens.

Efforts to achieve binding effects by putting words on paper take us back to conceptual-epistemic problems. Words by themselves do not convey meaning but depend on communities of shared understanding among members of speech communities. The language of the *Constitution of the United States* has been used to draft constitutions in other parts of the world but without much effect. This has led many scholars to conclude that constitutions are meaningless fictions or, at most, positive morality, not positive law. The problem cannot, however, be resolved at that level. Statutory enactments and administrative rules and regulations are also words on paper. What are the grounds for legitimacy? Officials can command; but individuals do not necessarily obey. Patterns of deception and self-deception may pervade human relationships. We are back to problems of publicness in language, communication, meaning, common knowledge, consensus about basic norms or criteria of choice, and social accountability. In the absence of consensus, conflict is possible. In the presence of conflict, a problematic situation may exist requiring the adoption of a problem-solving mode of inquiry to reestablish shared communities of understanding. Such circumstances suggest that epistemic difficulties exist and that problems of epistemic inquiry about the relationship of concepts and information to problematic situations have priority in deciding what is to be done. A single, universal, comprehensive, and workable code of law applicable to all mankind is an empirical impossibility. So is a single, simple, universal "model" of "economic" reasoning applied to "nonmarket" decision making.

Back to Epistemic and Cultural Factors

Words in the realm of science and technology do not convey meaning apart from knowledgeable, skilled, and intelligible individuals who know how to act with reference to the meaning assigned to words. No experiment can be appropriately conducted by uninformed experimenters or "strategic opportunists" who wish to rig the results to their own advantage. The conduct of any viable enterprise depends on knowledge, skill, and intelligibility among those who constitute the enterprise. Any viable enterprise, public as well as private, turns on the use of knowledge in whatever gets done, set in a context of economic potentials mediated by patterns of rule-ordered relationships as essential complements to one another.

The importance of epistemic and cultural factors in the constitution of different patterns of order can be illustrated by contrasting the republican character of covenanting [federal] societies with despotic systems of order. The concept of *res publica*—the public thing—implies an open public realm in which public affairs are openly considered and decisions are reached through open public deliberation. Cooperative activities depend on undertaking contingent agreements subject to plausible commitments. The promises made need to become binding commitments consistent with contingent agreements. If some participants are played for suckers, trust is broken and a moral offense has been committed. Openness of deliberation in processes for mediating conflict and achieving conflict resolution need to be designed to elucidate information, articulate arguments bearing on contending interests, and reach resolutions in light of mutual and public consideration of complementarities. Individual interests need to be understood as having commonalities bearing on shared communities of interest.

How individual interests relate to common interests needs to be clarified through processes of conflict and conflict resolution that serve the correlative purposes of generating common knowledge and shared communities of understanding that create a consciousness of complementary social identities. The structure of incentives needs to be such that the quest for cooperative endeavors is reinforced in ways that are compatible with fundamental values, such as peace, enlightenment, liberty, justice, or well-being; such values should have the potential for becoming universal public goods. Incentives compatible with "republican virtues" need to be the basis for the design of decision structures that give expression to decision processes consistent with the enlightenment of the open public realm.

In autocratic systems of order, which are constituted with reference to a single center of Supreme Authority and which rely on law as command uniformly applicable to people under diverse ecological conditions, the pursuit of cooperative endeavors runs the risk of violating the letter of some legal formulation having the proclaimed force of law. Instead of plausible commitments to be resolved by commonly accepted standards of enlightenment and justice, advantage is likely to accrue by pursuing a strategy of plausible ignorance. Resolutions are sought through secret accommodation. These circumstances occur where regulatory prohibitions are subject to granting conditional licenses and permits by administrative methods. The confidential character of administrative methods encourages favoritism. Regulatory measures become potential sources of corruption and traps for money. Administrative methods that focus on legalities become destructive of a rule of law. Under such circumstances, each individual's task becomes a lifelong endeavor of achieving special connections to cope with the problems of life. The standard response is to plead ignorance rather than trying to be helpful to others and acquiring a public reputation for being helpful to others.

What Tocqueville refers to as "the whole moral and intellectual tradition of a people" accrues in the course of living a life. Problems are worked out through time, in structures mediated by processes at work in everyday life. In this way, people form habits of the heart and mind with less than conscious awareness of the changes that transpire in the course of time. Yet the viability of democratic societies depends on continuing the function of the *res publica* conditions, while maintaining the continuities of a rule of law that is itself subject to change through time, and while meeting the requirements of freedom and justice. Incentives to seek special advantage through the art of manipulation always exist. Random solutions will not suffice. Instead, knowledgeable, skilled, and intelligible creatures confront the challenge of learning how to correct errors and how to respond to problematic situations in constructive ways.

Viable democracies are neither created nor destroyed overnight. Emphasis on form of government and the binding character of legal formulations are not sufficient conditions to meet the requirements of democratic societies. The moral and intellectual conditions of those who constitute democratic societies are of essential importance. This is why building common knowledge, shared communities of understanding, patterns of accountability, and mutual trust is as essential as producing stocks and flows of material goods and services. The epistemic and cultural contingencies of life are at least as important as the economic and political conditions narrowly construed.

My sense is that the more innovative contributions to the Public-Choice tradition of research have come from contributors who were concerned with a better understanding of basic anomalies, social dilemmas, or paradoxes, rather than with applying a single abstract model of economic reasoning to nonmarket decision making. The latter concern becomes an exercise in the application of an orthodox mode of analysis in price theory; the former opens important new frontiers of inquiry.

Conclusions

Language and its place in the articulation of knowledge is the most fundamental source of productive potentials in human societies. No human mortal can be presumed to know the Truth. The conditions for establishing the warrantability of what we presume to know are the foundations for developing a culture of inquiry appropriate to addressing ambiguities and unknowns in efforts to identify and resolve that which is problematic. The future of Public Choice will be determined by its contributions to the epistemic level of choice in the cultural and social sciences and to the constitution of the epistemic order with which we live and work. Increments to knowledge in research programs require conceptual ordering for what is to be taught. All processes of choice are mediated by languages that enable human beings to acquire capabilities not achieved by lions, bears, and wolves.

Rationality is affected by access to knowledge and communities of shared understanding; every individual is fallible; and everyone endures the costs of choices made under ignorance, misconceptions, deceptions, and strategic manipulations. Both the systems for making epistemic choices and those for making market choices contribute to the elucidation of knowledge and information essential to systems for making public choices. I cannot imagine a modern society without some form of exchange arrangements characteristic of market organization. A key question is how variable structures among market arrangements affect conduct and performance. If the range of inquiry is extended to the epistemic realm, our concern is with how variable conceptions [ideas] affect the design of structures, the organization of processes, patterns of conduct, and performance. The concept of a perfectly competitive market can serve as an important conceptual yardstick and an initial point of departure. Whether such a conceptualization serves as an adequate basis for discriminating observation about different types of market structures is questionable.

That problem is made more difficult by the potentials for strategic collusion between economic entrepreneurs and political entrepreneurs in setting the rules of the political and economic games to facilitate the dominance of the few in relation to the many. Potentials for collusion and intrigue are greatly enhanced when political orders are constituted as monopolies in the exercise of rulership prerogatives and in control over the instruments of coercion in societies. The application of economic reasoning to public choices cannot be advanced very far using the postulates of perfectly informed actors participating in competitive markets operating in unitary States directed by a single center of Supreme Authority. Equilibrating tendencies under those circumstances are likely to sacrifice market rationality to bureaucratic rationality and both market rationality and bureaucratic rationality to corruption. We need to go back to basics to reconsider the human condition and what it means to be a human being relating to other human beings in the world in which they live.

PART 3

Back to Basics

If you and I are to be self-governing, how are we to understand and take part in human affairs? It is important that we attempt to clarify the human condition and how that condition establishes essential foundations for what it would mean to become self-governing. We need to clarify the human condition as it applies to human potentials in the world at large rather than to the parochial circumstances of the United States of America as such.

Chapter 5 on the human condition is concerned with adaptive potentials that arise from the general characteristics associated with patterns of adaptation, the place of choice, and the constitution of systems of order that have both evolutionary and coevolutionary characteristics. Language becomes the key factor giving rise to cultural adaptation to complement processes of genetic adaptation and learning as these are associated with biological evolution. Complementary uses of language yield coevolutionary aspects that apply to diverse facets of life in human societies.

Chapter 6 gives further attention to the place of language in the political economy of life. Many aspects of language usage are so transparent that human beings lack a critical self-consciousness about the place of language in human societies. This inquiry is further extended in chapter 7 to consider the ontological foundations of human understanding. Important considerations grounded in religion and philosophy serve as basic orientations toward life and toward how to address problematic situations of unknown proportions. These strands of thought are tied together in chapter 8 with regard to artisanship-artifact relationships, which are viewed as the key to human potentials.

CHAPTER 5

The Human Condition: Life, Learning, Language, Knowledge, Culture, and the Problem of Order

The phenomenon of choice—of being able to consider alternative possibilities and to select a course of action—is a universal feature of the human condition. Choice is a basic aspect of all adaptive arrangements. Before we can understand the place of the constitution of order in human adaptation, we need to consider the more general structure of adaptive arrangements. Human beings have access to extraordinary endowments for adaptive potentials that derives from genetic and cultural factors.

This inquiry into the human condition—a condition that both you and I share—will focus on adaptive potentials and the problems associated with adaptation. This inquiry is accessible to both of us when we use our own resources as human beings to understand others. Engaging in such an effort is a humanistic version of the methodological individualism discussed in chapter 4. I shall turn first to the various forms of adaptive behavior and their contribution to human development. These potentials are plagued by numerous threats or dangers. These threats pose fundamental dilemmas that are sometimes marked by tragedy and sometimes resolved by tenuous arrangements that fail when improperly understood and not given attentive care. An appreciation of the tenuous nature of order in human society is the most important lesson to be learned about the human condition.

The human animal is, as Robert Ardrey has observed, the wolf among the primates (Marais 1969). It adapted to a meat-eating diet and learned to use tools to kill and to defend itself, at a very early stage in hominid development. I use the term *Wolf among the Primates* as a metaphor to refer to an omnivore with a long life and working brain capable of storing large amounts of memory, thinking in linguistic articulations, and using a creative imagination. With such capabilities, this omnivore can easily learn to pillage, plunder, and prey on others and to achieve great creative potentials.

Wolves achieve relatively sophisticated levels of teamwork in their pursuit of prey and in their transmission of learning across generations, even though their communication is characterized by the articulation of signals, in contrast to the predominantly symbolic character of human language. The level of adaptation accrued through genetic adaptation, and that which turns more specifically on learning acquired by the young through the experiences associated with maturation, is relatively greater among primates than among other mammals. The "invention" of languages—invented in small accretions with occasional bursts in new modes of articulation—and their continuing development is the critical factor in the emergence of human civilization, though features pertaining to territoriality, cognition, habituation, dominance, sexuality, preferences, and criteria of choice have phylogenetic foundations. Frans de Waal in *Good Natured: The Origins of Right and Wrong in Humans and Other Animals* (1996) explores the biological foundations of morality, sympathy, rank and order, quid pro quo relationships, and community.

Hobbes identified "SPEECH, consisting of *names* or *appellations,* and their connexion; whereby men register their thoughts; recall them when they are past; and also declare them one to another for mutual utility and conversation" as "the most noble and profitable invention of all other." He went on to assert that without language, "there had been amongst men, neither commonwealth, nor society, nor contract, nor peace, no more than amongst lions, bears, and wolves" ([1651] 1960, 18).

I do not suggest that the Wolf among the Primates can only pillage, plunder, and prey on others. Dogs, as man's best friend, presumably share a genetic endowment derived from wolves or their common ancestors. We do, however, need to recognize a strong genetic bias that easily predisposes human beings toward fight sets and the escalation of conflict into destructive violence. The course of constructive, creative efforts is much more demanding and difficult to realize than destruction. Care is more demanding than neglect.

The dual features of genetic evolution and cultural evolution imply a duality in human nature—as an animal and as an artifactual being. This duality need not be viewed as contradictory. The animality of mankind does not need to be denied for cultures and civilizations to achieve their aspirations. Profound tensions do, however, inevitably exist. For human beings to enjoy the opportunities of a civilized existence requires them to be aware of their animal impulses and to learn how to govern themselves so as to achieve the opportunities that become available through peaceful coexistence. The distinction between successful achievements and failures is not easy to make, especially if the relevant time horizon transcends generations. The duality of phylogenetic conditions and human cultural potentials is the source of profound tensions that each of us is required to experience and attempt to reconcile in our own efforts to govern ourselves.

The human capabilities for learning, as we shall see, pose a potential threat of chaos. The solution to that threat implies a Faustian bargain in which human beings are required to have potential recourse to instruments of evil to advance their joint or common good [common wealth]. The threat of chaos and the creation of order from chaos, in turn, pose a threat of tyranny. The amplification of human capabilities for learning necessarily means that all human efforts to plan are plagued with uncertainties. These threats are compounded by a threat of increasing relative ignorance that accompanies modern efforts to stimulate innovations with the growth of new knowledge. All of these conditions need to be taken into account in an assessment of the human condition and in critical reflections about what is constitutive of human potentials.

Adaptation

Adaptation implies a covariant relationship, not a determinate one-way relationship. As defined in a standard dictionary, the term *adapt* means: (1) to make suitable to requirements or conditions, (2) to adjust or modify fittingly, or (3) to adjust oneself to different conditions and environments. Adaptive organisms, mechanisms, or entities have a capability to induce variety in their conduct in relation to variations in their environment and to do so in ways that are *suitable, fitting,* or *appropriate.* Adaptations are thus covariant relationships in the sense that variations in the environment, which affect essential values, will evoke variations in response. The higher the degree of adaptability attained by a living organism, the larger the potential repertoire of variety that is available to it in responding to variations in its environment. Simpler forms of adaptation are always covariant relationships; the more complex forms of human adaptation are multivariant relationships of great complexities.

A statement of these principles of adaptation is an application of what W. R. Ashby (1956) has called "the law of requisite variety." It takes access to potential variety to respond to variety in a way that maintains some essential value or values within limits. To sustain life in a highly variable and potentially threatening [dangerous] environment requires access to commensurate capabilities. To achieve fit is to hold essential values within limits. Access to variability in adaptive strategies implies capabilities to adapt to greater varieties of variable situations.

The essential structure of adaptation, then, suggests first the existence of some mechanisms or arrangements that are capable of *generating poten-tial variety.* This potential variety is next subject to *selection,* if an *appro-priate fit* is to develop between adaptive entities and the events that com-prise their environments. Appropriateness of fit is determined first by whether essential values are kept within limits [e.g., limits of survival among others]. If adaptations are to persist through time, selection must occur with elements of regularity or constraint. Successful adaptations must, further, be subject to *retention* through time if they are to persist. An evolving system of order always involves (1) variation, (2) selection, and (3) retention. An understanding of adaptive systems of order requires a capacity to account for patterns of variation, selection, and retention.

Where selection occurs within constraint and regularity, and where that constraint and regularity can be named, we can identify a principle of selection. Choice is a particular form of selection on the part of organisms that can array alternative possibilities [i.e., have access to potential vari-ety]. To choose is to select from an array of possibilities.

The processes of generating potential variety, selection, and retention yield *effects* over time that are not necessarily confined to conscious means-ends planning. The process of selection, as much as the goal to be achieved, is of critical importance. If I wish to go to a place of work, for example, I get there by the choices I make along the way. How I act depends on what others do. The "what-to-do" contingencies depend on the "how-to-proceed" contingencies. I never adhere strictly to advanced planning. I proceed by taking account of diverse contingencies with regard to the performance of an automobile, the conduct of others, the conditions of the thoroughfare, the weather, and so on. A barrier indicating that a road is under construction requires modification of plans in driving to work.

The adaptive potential among human beings derives from different forms or modes of adaptation. Among these are (1) genetic adaptation associated with biological evolution, (2) learning as a form of adaptation that occurs among all animals or organisms that have nervous systems and motor facilities, and (3) cultural adaptation that occurs when organisms nurture the young and use signals to condition the response of others. Among human beings, the adaptive potential is greatly amplified through language, the shared learning transmitted by language, and the artifacts created by reference to language. Culture among *Homo sapiens* can broadly be conceptualized as that which is learned and derived from learn-ing through the uses of language. The use of language to acquire learning implies that learning is shared among those communicating and relating with one another. Such forms of learning are social and cultural in nature. I will briefly consider each form of adaptation in turn.

Genetic Adaptation

Genetic evolution occurs among all living organisms. Life for any one organism is of limited duration; and the transmission of life depends on reproduction. Reproduction involves an opportunity for the generation of variety whenever a new life-form differs, however slightly, from an existing life-form. Whenever life is transmitted with imperfect reproduction, especially variants associated with mutation, we would expect variations to occur in new life-forms. The new will not be an identical reproduction of the old. Thus, imperfect reproduction offers the prospect that the chain of life will become anywhere from one to many transformations, where new life-forms cannot be predicted with certainty from the characteristics associated with old life-forms.

Sexual reproduction, in particular, amplifies access to the potential variety that is available to each new living organism and is accompanied with a significant degree of autonomous individuality. A union of cells derived from different lineages, but joined by a union of reproductive elements, increases the potential for genetic variety in the transmission of life. The process of selection occurs with the survival of the populations that continue to transmit life by reproduction. Conditions in the environment, including the existence of competitive life-forms, affect potentials for survival.

Life-forms that do not survive to reproduce are not represented in future populations. New variations in life-forms that have a greater capability to adapt to their environment survive to reproduce. The environment thus selects those characteristics that survive. Since Darwin, this principle of selection has been called *natural selection.* Retention of the selected form of life depends on reproducible modifications in the gene structure of those that survive. Forms of life that have potentials for learning also have prospects of searching out adaptive niches in their environments, reducing the degree of environmental determinism. I shall discuss learning as a form of adaptive behavior momentarily.

Genetic adaptation apparently occurs only in relation to reproduction. Species that produce large numbers of offspring with short generations are capable of substantial genetic adaptation over shorter periods of time than those with few young living over long generations. However, little genetic adaptation will occur within the lifetime of an individual organism except as long-lived organisms have access to short-lived forms of life, such as digestive systems and immune systems, as a part of their biotic constitutions. Genetic adaptation thus occurs in an *intergenerational* context, and each individual member of a species or living entity inherits a genetic endowment that remains relatively constant throughout its lifetime. Biotic entities may also emerge through symbiosis and achieve complementary patterns of adaptation.

Learning as Adaptive Behavior

Over very long periods of genetic adaptation, a wide variety of life-forms have emerged. Among the life-forms that have experienced genetic adaptation are species that have access to nervous systems that enable them to "learn" or to adapt during the life span of each individual member of a species. Those life-forms that have the capability of learning gain access to another form of adaptive behavior. Learning can thus be viewed as an amplification of adaptive potential. Human beings, through an extended process of genetic adaptation, have been endowed with a form of life that gives them access to extraordinary capabilities for learning.

Any organism that is capable of learning has access to genetic endowments that provides it with (1) sensory mechanisms to derive information from the environment; (2) cognitive facilities for comprehending, retaining, and working with information about recurrent events, regularities, or constraints in the environment; (3) internal sensations or feelings that serve as potential indicators about disturbances and states of well-being, experienced as desires or aversions; and (4) reacting parts or motor facilities that enable animated life-forms to act with variety in relation to dangers and/or opportunities in their environments.

By using these genetic endowments, any animal with a nervous system can (1) derive information about events in its environment, (2) organize such information in some form of image or cognitive mapping, (3) assess or weigh this information in relation to its own internal indicators or feelings, and (4) act in a way that will facilitate its relative well-being and survival. Learning organisms are able to adapt to a variety of environmental circumstances within the course of their individual life spans.

Sensory mechanisms are important in giving organisms information about potential opportunities and dangers or disturbances in their environment. So long as constraints exist in the environment, in the sense that potential variables behave like constants over given time horizons or vary in a recurrent rather than random way, an organism with cognitive facilities is able to form stable images about elements in its environment. If it can conceive of potential moves or acts in relation to those relatively stable elements in its environment, it can then weigh those possibilities by reference to its own internal indicators or feelings and act in a way that will leave it better off rather than worse off. The complement of these capabilities suggests that adaptive potentials depend on autonomy as an essential feature of learning.

W. R. Ashby has emphasized that *"every law of nature is a constraint"* (1956, 130). Laws of nature are linguistic statements about regularities in recurrent events; recurrent events presumably occur with regularity in nature. Ashby also demonstrates that learning can occur only in the presence of constraint (ibid., 134).

Given constraints in an environment and a capacity to perceive of potential acts or moves in relation to those constraints, we can now conceive of learning as depending on the generation and selection of different images, conceptions, moves, actions, and possibilities. When a barrier exists, we learn to get around, go over or through, or remove it. The source of variety resides in the cognitive and motor facilities of animated beings. The association of successful actions with conditions and consequences is retained in memory and informs future actions in like circumstances. Search behaviors associated with so-called trial-and-error methods can be used to generate associations as stable images. If a trial is unsuccessful when measured by internal indicators, an organism can change its behavior until it is successful. If it can then retain information about its successful moves and conceptualize ways to use information to deal with similar events in the future, it will have learned. Learning thus occurs by generating several trials, by selecting, by conceptualizing images, and by retaining information about successful trials. When like circumstances characteristically occur, an environment is transformed into a knowable situation with regard to the actions to be taken in that situation.

Internal indicators—feelings, emotions, sentiments—are essential features in a choice process. They provide a learning organism with a series of readings about its well-being and serve as a basis for understanding essential values or preference orderings. These internal indicators function as modes for weighing alternative possibilities and thus govern selection. Selection occurs with reference to an array of possibilities, when an organism acts on the possibility that will leave the organism better off rather than worse off. Memory about essential associations between antecedent conditions and consequences is the means of reproducing the particular associations that yielded selective advantage.

Learning, then, can be defined as that form of adaptation that depends on the discovery of constraint or regularity in the environment, the formation of an identifiable image or pattern of association, and the capacity of an organism to act with variety in response to that situation, to select from the array of possibilities those that will leave it better off rather than worse off, and to retain in its memory essential associations [images] that enable it to repeat an appropriate response when similar events [situations] reoccur.

Critical elements in the learning process occur internally to a learning organism. Much of the essential information for understanding learning as a form of adaptive behavior is difficult to procure. Norms imply standards or criteria of choice—principles of selection. Choice implies evaluation and selection. These need to be raised to consciousness—made explicit—if we are to understand patterns of order in human societies. What are sometimes referred to as "values" are criteria of choice, principles of selection, *and* the emergent states of affairs that are derived from using principles of selection as criteria of choice in creating patterns of order.

Social orders are the patterns that derive from processes of selection and choice. What criteria of choice are used and how these work in the constitution of order in human societies is an essential part of social "reality." Values should not be dismissed as unintelligible nonsense because they lack embodiment as tangible, material artifacts apart from the symbolization of language. Instead, values get embodied in artifacts with reference to such criteria as balance, fit, beauty, economy, freedom, justice, truth, and so on. Each criterion of choice can be subject to judgment on a scale of better or worse. Values depend on methods of inquiry for making interpersonal comparisons in hypothetically specifiable situations and occur as features of patterns of order in ways of life. The assertion "Do unto others as you would have others do unto you" implies making interpersonal comparisons.

Learning as a form of adaptive behavior significantly amplifies potentials for adaptation beyond those available through processes of genetic adaptation. Learning gives those organisms with nervous systems and motor facilities the capability for modifying their patterns of behavior during the life span of a single organism in relation to events that occur within its environment. Genetic adaptation, as I have noted, occurs only in an intergenerational context. Those organisms that are genetically endowed with nervous systems and motor facilities have greatly amplified their potential for adaptive behavior by being able to make *intragenerational* adaptations. This endowment, in turn, unquestionably facilitates the survival of species that develop more complex nervous systems and thus gain access to a larger repertoire of adaptive potentials.

The radical limit confronting most species is the circumstance that life, for individual organisms, is of limited duration. Learning and the use of what has been learned is embodied in mortal creatures (Fodor 1987). The learning acquired by each member of a species is largely lost when life expires. All mammals are creatures endowed with food supplies for prolonged immaturity of the young and the maintenance of some patterns of social organization. Eugène Marais demonstrates in *The Soul of the Ape* (1969) that baboons achieved elaborate structures of social organization characterized by cultural diversity among bands or troops living under the diverse ecological conditions of dense forests, mixed savannas, and open grasslands. Learning by the example of others reinforced by messages conveyed by sounds and bodily expressions, even in the absence of developed languages, allowed conditions of cultural variants to emerge. Marais conjectured that the features of the brain capable of making causal associations and the working of something we call the imagination allowed for relatively high levels of innovation and adaptation among baboons. Language, however, radically amplified further adaptive potentials and cultural variations among human beings. The intergenerational tie in the transmission of human cultures is of critical importance to the continuity of civilizations.

Cultural Adaptation and Cultural Evolution

The characteristic of adaptation that distinguishes *Homo sapiens* from other forms of life has been the development of language as a facility [instrument, tool] for radically amplifying human capabilities to acquire and transmit learning. Languages are highly specialized symbol systems in which sounds and markings can be used to stand for or to represent events and relationships. Symbols organized as words and articulated in assertions can be used to express ideas and associations of ideas in complex patterns of thought. By inventing words to stand for events and relationships and by using sequences of words to express thoughts, human beings can communicate their thought processes to one another when words as symbols are used as media for thought and communication. Such thought processes can be extended into a realm of ideas [conceptualizations] that goes far beyond the bounds of immediately observable events.

Because of the triangulation between (1) events and relationships, (2) words or symbols, and (3) ideas, images, or thoughts, words, in serving as media of communication, can be used to transmit learning from one individual to another in contemporary or succeeding generations. So long as ideas and trains of thought can be translated into words, learning acquired by one individual can be transmitted to others for their use. New knowledge or discoveries can be acquired by those who have access to a common language, without everyone having to make each discovery anew from individual trial-and-error experience. The development of languages has enabled human beings to accumulate increasingly large aggregations of knowledge that gives them access to extraordinary accumulations of learning. Experience, skill, and memory are, however, lost with death, creating a significant problem of discontinuities among human beings and a distortion of learning that emphasizes abstractions associated with symbolization.

The type of learning that has accrued as a part of human cultural adaptation reaches far beyond the bounds of individual conduct to be constitutive of what Searle referred to as institutional facts—the social reality that is itself an artifactual construction by relying on norms and rule-ordered relationships. In turn, the combination of learning that affects individual adaptation and the form of learning associated with socially constructed institutional arrangements enable people in human societies to increasingly transform the material conditions of their environment into a habitat shaped by human knowledge, skill, and intelligibility. This threefold adaptive potential—individual adaptation, social adaptation, and ecological transformation of the environment—implies that human adaptation involves interactive configurations of relationships reaching far beyond simple causal, or stimulus-response, explanations. An understanding of human artisanship in its diverse manifestations is necessary to an understanding of the human condition.

The capacity to transmit learning from one generation to another depends on the types of language that are available to human beings. Where humans have reference only to a spoken language, we expect substantial difficulties to arise in the amount of knowledge that can be stored and transmitted to successive generations. Where a language cannot be recorded as a material object in some written, printed, or electronic form, the connection between the conveyor of knowledge and the receiver of acquired knowledge must be made by chains of direct interpersonal communication.

Great varieties of information may be organized as knowledge by specifying regularities or principles at work and transmitting them from generation to generation by spoken language. The relationship of regularities as "organizing principles" to "concepts," or equivalently "ideas," to action, and to "information" implies two different uses of the term "information." One is factual, the other artifactual. Ideas and actions can be used to transform factual elements into artifactual creations. Conceptualizations [ideas] and information can also be easily lost and distorted. Ideas and information transmitted through long chains of oral communication will be altered and distorted to a greater degree than will messages transmitted as material objects and conveyed from one person to another person in written, printed, or electronic form. Societies that depend only on spoken language may, however, rely on cumulative narratives as registers of knowledge. The narrators of those registers become the sources of accumulation and transmission of knowledge and occupy places of distinction in preliterate societies. Literate castes also occupy places of distinction in predominantly nonliterate societies.

The constraints inherent in spoken languages imply substantial limits to the aggregate pool of knowledge that can be transmitted across generations. As a consequence, we would expect any society relying exclusively on a spoken language to be associated with relatively more "primitive" civilizations by modern standards but to be more sensitive to discrete conditions in its environment. Difficulties in communication are such that we would also not expect societies without a written language to be an adequate basis for the large-scale patterns of global organization associated with modern conditions.

The development of writing and the later development of printing and electronic communication have greatly altered human capabilities to record, store, and transmit increasingly large bodies of knowledge. With the availability of writing, printing, and electronic communication, knowledge and information can be transmitted over greater distances in both space and time, with less loss of symbolic content, when conveyed to knowledgeable and intelligible recipients. Knowledge also becomes more easily accessible to people who acquire basic literary skills. Communication, however, is placed at risk if the symbols [words] used on the part of the conveyor and the receiver do not refer to commonly understood referents. Shared images [*Gestalten,* as in Gestalt psychology] give meaning to symbols as human imaginations [minds] are at work in using language to communicate with one another. Shared images are the basis for common knowledge and shared communities of understanding that are the cultural foundations for human communities. What can be transmitted through symbolic representations always needs to be complemented by the practical experience of engaging motor facilities as necessary complements to the symbolic features of thought. Skill and intelligibility must necessarily complement those features of thought that are acquired by symbolic representations, if ideas are to be transformed into artifacts.

While languages have been of central importance in human cultural evolution, they are still imperfect instruments for transmitting and organizing knowledge. Each word stands for a class of events or relationships. Thus, all languages introduce elements of simplification in human communication that cannot take adequate account of the variety that exists in referent contextualities. Furthermore, the triangulation between (1) events and relationships, (2) words or symbols, and (3) ideas, images, or thoughts lacks sufficient reliability to avoid creating ambiguities about meaning. This is especially true where words are used as the basis for reflecting about subjective experiences and constituting systems of order in human societies that are themselves grounded in language. The concept of justice, for example, has reference to events that only have meaning as they apply to human relationships, which are themselves organized by reference to key words that refer, at least in large part, to subjective states, intentions, and conceptualizations. Much of political "reality" is not accessible to the retina of the eyes but depends to a very large extent on accumulated conceptions embedded in language and used to organize thought. Paradigmatics, the mind-sets we use to organize our thinking, are of critical proportions in the cultural and social sciences.

Changes in the nature of language systems are critical variables that affect the potential for development in human civilization. More "advanced" civilizations become possible as human beings develop new language systems that give them greater capabilities to organize, store, transmit, and use knowledge and information with higher degrees of fidelity.

Recent developments in machine languages will profoundly affect the organization of tools for communicating with one another and, thus, for coordinating production and communication flows in complex patterns of relationships. The development of scientific languages amplifies the application of reasoned inferences in elaborate structures of association that enhance the capacity of human beings to organize large bodies of knowledge. The development of new language systems and the acquisition of skills in the use of those language systems can be expected to affect the future course of human civilization. The weak link is the image-to-image relationship in construing meaning as these mental states relate to activities and what gets done.

We confront serious puzzles with reference to language that may contribute to an erosion of meaning in the use of language. The meaning associated with the triangulation of images [mental states], events and relations [the objects and states of the world referred to], and words or symbols [names assigned to events and relations] involves a shared community of understanding among language users. Tacit levels of understanding go beyond the mere use of words and of definitions stated in a more profuse use of words, as in dictionaries. In a sense, an "organic" tie pervades intelligible communication by reference to the tacit common understandings that are fashioned by communities of language users. The organon is the mind, not the gonads. The essential link is language. Language associates thoughts, ideas, and knowledgeable articulations of skill in actions to what gets done—ideas to deeds. A basic tension is highlighted by Michael Polanyi's (1962) reference to "tacit knowledge" in contrast to Karl Popper's (1972) reference to "objective knowledge." Both are at work within the cultural and social milieu of speech communities.

As the milieu of human communication is transformed by mass media, the tacit knowledge associated with intelligible communication is likely to erode. The interjection of "ya' know" in sentences during interpersonal communication is an indicator of the tenuous character of meaningful communication. A language common to increasingly large populations of people and territorial domains may tend toward increasing simplification in its levels of abstraction, with increasing loss of meaning with reference to contextualities. Unless compensatory, crosscutting uses of specialized languages occur, serious abuse of communication, the stereotyping of illusory abstractions, and misunderstandings can emerge. These potentials are most likely to occur in political discourse involving mass media. Politicians are more concerned with using glittering generalities to create favorable public "images" and to win votes than with facilitating critical inquiry. Such circumstances create opportunities for strategic manipulation. The deceptions inherent in gross oversimplifications may evoke self-deceptions. Those who fool others are likely to fool themselves, and they may threaten the viability of human societies.

The invention of new techniques for observation has also pressed the frontier of observables beyond immediate sensory perception. New tools expand the potential for human action in transforming the natural environment into a realm shaped, in part, by human knowledge. The elaboration of language into structures of theoretical inference and the development of research methodologies for experimentally testing inferences against observables imply that human beings learn strategies for testing associations that go well beyond trial-and-error methods. With these strategies, human beings might be said to be capable of *learning how to learn.*

By an explicit understanding of strategies relevant to the development of new knowledge, human beings can learn how to improve their capabilities for generating new knowledge. When combined with the development of printing and new forms of language, the rise of the modern sciences following Kepler, Galileo, and Newton has contributed to a virtual explosion of knowledge and the transformation of the conditions of life in modern times. This explosion of knowledge and the transformation of human civilization has largely occurred in the last five hundred years, with the so-called Copernican and Darwinian revolutions and the application of the technologies of printing to literate languages. A half millennium is a surprisingly short time in the existence of *Homo sapiens.*

When human capabilities to acquire, organize, and transmit knowledge are taken into account with the extension of human motor skills through the use of tools and machinery, human beings have developed radical potentials for transforming their environments from a configuration of natural events into cultural or artifactual states of affairs. Human beings have learned, for example, how to transform elements of the geosphere and biosphere into an agriculture where much of the landmass of the earth is subject to human cultivation [culture]. Human knowledge has worked such a transformation of the earth that the noosphere—the sphere shaped by human knowledge and artisanship—as distinguished from the geosphere and the biosphere, has assumed global proportions (Teilhard de Chardin [1955] 1965; Turchin 1977).

Language as a medium for the communication of ideas and thoughts is itself an artifact of the interpersonal level of human experience. Symbols can only have meaning to the extent that human beings possess a shared understanding about the meaning to be attributed to symbols. There can be no purely private language. To invent linguistic codes to assure secret communications among a small set of individuals requires great skill and effort on the part of those involved, who use a form of knowledge called "cryptology." Language is always a common facility shared by a community of persons who maintain patterns of communication with one another. New concepts and terms may be introduced by individuals, but they become a part of a language only when the meaning and use of new terms are shared as a basis for communication with others.

Languages, and systems of meaning derived from language, come to have a *quasi-autonomous* existence of their own. Individual persons are born into the world, acquire languages, and use those languages through a lifetime, often without having had much effect on the nature of the language itself. Some individuals with exceptional skill in the use of language and in conveying meaning to others may, like Shakespeare, have a profound influence on the emergence of a literate vernacular language, such as English. However, a language can exist only so long as it continues to be acquired, used, and monitored as an instrument of communication and of actions constitutive of ways of life. Fidelity in the use of a language depends on the potential for a critical response to improper uses of language. In this sense, languages can at most be thought of as semiautonomous cognitive systems—cultural artifacts. Languages have meaning only in the context of human association; and human knowledge has the conventional characteristics of being embodied in language systems. David Hume, in my judgment, was correct in referring to the conventional character of human knowledge. This does not mean that any "convention" is, by being conventional, warrantable knowledge. Rather, it means that *human knowledge and rationality* are *grounded in and bounded by* conditions that apply to *languages and their uses.*

Artifacts such as languages, number systems, and patterns of human association can, in turn, be subject to inquiry with regard to the underlying structures inherent in those artifacts. Grammar, linguistics, and metalinguistics; arithmetic, algebra, and the theory of numbers; anthropology, sociology, economics, jurisprudence, and political science—all these sciences are engaged in the study of artifactual systems that have their semiautonomous, cognitive, and conventional properties grounded in languages and that turn on the place of languages and their uses in what gets accomplished in human societies. The transmission of learning from one generation to another depends on processes of education, broadly construed to include enculturation, socialization, and the acquisition of skills. Each new generation must make a substantial investment in learning what has already been learned by others. The generation of new knowledge adds to the repertoire of prior learning.

Thus, that language enables human beings to communicate learning from one individual to another in contemporary or succeeding generations has, as indicated earlier, greatly amplified the adaptive potential that human beings have derived from their genetic heritage. Learning is accumulated across generations, to evoke new forms of cultural evolution that have quite different characteristics from genetic evolution. So long as human capabilities for learning and ordering their learning can be accumulated across generations, the development of human civilization is a progressive endeavor. The rate of progress depends on the growth and accumulation of new knowledge in ordered relationships that enable human beings to act in ways that are presumed to leave them better off rather than worse off. If languages erode and those who presume to be "modern" reject the learning accrued from prior generations, it is also possible for civilizations to decline—for civilizations to be "trampled underfoot," a possibility Alexis de Tocqueville expressed ([1835–40] 1945, 2:47).

The attributes of human cultural evolution depend on personal learning in the sense that each individual must acquire the knowledge that gives access to potentialities for action. Thus, we cannot speak of a culture or civilization apart from the people who comprise the population that is constitutive of that culture or civilization. Individual persons are the learners, the thinkers, and the doers. If individuals fail to acquire and transmit the accumulated learning that forms a part of their cultural heritage, that learning can be lost. Civilizations can decline and disappear if succeeding generations of people do not maintain the continuities of language and learning and of the meaning to be assigned to words and their referents. What we call Grecian civilization is not associated with the population of modern Greece. The despotisms of the Roman, Byzantine, and Turkish Empires took their toll. The Chinese people have closer ties to what we call Confucian civilization despite recent efforts to achieve a Cultural Revolution and create a Marxist-Leninist civilization.

Problems of Order and Change

In my discussion of adaptation, I have indicated how various modes of adaptation have greatly expanded the repertoire of possibilities available to human beings in relating themselves to events in their world and to one another. I have avoided many of the implications that pose difficulties associated with these potentials for adaptive behavior, apart from the problem of the transparency of language and its threat to linguistic competence. I use the term *transparency* not to mean "visibility," as it often occurs in current public discourse, but to refer to conditions that are largely invisible to the retina of the eye. A window is transparent; I can see through it to what is beyond it. The transparency of large windows in urban settings is often fatal to birds that do not see the glass, and people are known to bump into plate-glass doors.

I use the term *threat* to refer to the way that patterns of human interaction may yield consequences of destructive proportions to those who interact with one another. Such threats need not involve an intentional exchange of threats like that considered in Kenneth Boulding's "Toward a Pure Theory of Threat Systems" (1963). Actions may also yield threats as a consequence of unanticipated patterns of interaction among human actors. My use of the terms *threat* and *risk* is associated with vulnerability to destructive potentials, whether or not intentionality is involved. This usage is different than that introduced by Frank Knight in *Risk, Uncertainty, and Profit* ([1921] 1971), where risk is associated with estimates of probabilities.

An understanding of human institutions—which are largely transparent—as patterns of order in human societies requires us to come to terms with several potential threats. The first such difficulty is the threat of chaos that derives from amplifying potential variety. The creation of a social order poses, in turn, a threat of tyranny. The generation of new knowledge always presents threats of uncertainty provoked by dynamic adaptations and innovations that places limits on efforts to plan for the future and renders some aspects of prior knowledge obsolete. A further threat arises from the inability of individuals to master and use more than relatively limited bodies of knowledge within the duration of their lifetime. The pursuit of opportunities is always accompanied by dangers that pose potential threats to human beings. I shall pursue each of these circumstances in turn.

The Threat of Potential Chaos

I have already characterized adaptive behavior as being associated with three processes or mechanisms. One process arrays or *generates* possibilities, which gives access to *potential variety*. Another *selects* from that array of possibilities. A third *retains* the selected possibilities. In dealing with learning in contrast to genetic adaptation, the mechanisms for arraying possibilities involve recourse to cognitive processes—images, conceptions, ideas. Any organism with a rich imagination has substantial capabilities for arraying different possibilities.

If we temporarily set aside considerations of selection and retention, we can begin to perceive what access to large accumulated bodies of knowledge implies. When human beings have learned about constraints inherent in events in their environment and can then act with variety in relation to those events, they gain access to a very large repertoire of potential variety in their behavior. If all of the potential variety in human behavior were to be acted on in a random way, rather than in highly selective ways, human beings would face a state of affairs approximating chaos. Casual observation of human affairs indicates substantial anxiety about the threat of chaos and the problem of maintaining order in human relationships. Access to a very large repertoire of potential variety thus carries with it a threat of chaos.

I have indicated in the earlier discussion of learning as a form of adaptive behavior that learning can occur only in the presence of constraint. Constraint gives rise to regularities that can be observed and acted on. Human beings thus face a paradoxical situation: they need order or constraint in their environment as a necessary condition for learning; but learning gives rise to new possibilities for increasing the potential variety of human behavior. Increasing potential variety in human behavior threatens the maintenance of a predictable order in which learning can occur. As the human adaptive potentials increase, we would anticipate that *mechanisms for ordering or constraining choices* must *simultaneously* occur if human development is to advance beyond very primitive levels. Features of human societies depend on *coevolutionary* patterns of development.

In the previous discussion of learning, I have also indicated that any organism that has the capability for learning will act subject to a constraint, in that it will select or choose that possibility that is expected to improve its well-being as measured by reference to its own internal indicators. Thus, we would expect all organisms to show constraint in the actions that are selected rather than to randomly pursue all possibilities that are perceived to be available. All animals can be expected to manifest regularities in their patterns of behavior, even though we are unable to predict each act that any particular animal will pursue at any single point in time. We would predict general behavioral tendencies on the basis of *assumptions* about internal states, levels of learning, and the principle of selection that will be used in choosing among alternative possibilities. Denying food to an experimental animal is a way to establish motivation in the animal's conduct during learning experiments.

The development of order out of chaos requires that each human being establish a basis for anticipating how others will behave, so that each person can act with an expectation that other persons will act with constraint. Common knowledge and shared communities of understanding are the foundations for shared expectations about how others will behave. Individuals may, of course, act in ways that enhance their own well-being at a potential cost to the well-being of others. The individuals who suffer adversely will, as intelligent creatures, pursue strategies to reduce potential deprivations. Such patterns of interaction may result in destructive conflict—fighting—which leaves each individual worse off (Boulding 1963).

Since human beings are unable to directly read each other's minds, the task of developing a method for ordering behavior in relation to one another again requires recourse to language. Language now becomes the basis for stipulating rules, so that disparate individuals can act with expectations that others will behave in accordance with those rules. Decision rules are means for constraining potential variety. They partition the array of all possible actions into subsets, with some possibilities *constrained* as inadmissible or unlawful forms of behavior. Decision rules thus enable two or more persons to interact with one another under conditions where some possibilities are excluded and other possibilities are included within the range of choices available to each individual. The excluded possibilities establish the constraints on choice. The included possibilities establish the opportunities or capabilities authorized in human conduct. Decision rules use language to introduce constraint into human relationships and establish the basis for social organization.

If people act with reference to a common set of decision rules, individuals can pursue their interests in relation to one another in an orderly and predictable manner. Any automobile driver, for example, is able to act in relation to thousands of other automobile drivers by knowing the common rules of the road. Such knowledge enables each driver to arrive at one's destination with a very high degree of predictability, without knowing the destinations of any other driver. If, in the absence of a common set of decision rules, all automobile drivers were to act randomly in relation to one another, the potential variety of all possible actions would preclude anyone from reaching one's destination in an orderly and predictable manner. Each driver would instead be confronted by a threat of chaos that would leave one helpless, disoriented, anxious, and unable to act in many situations.

Reliance on decision rules as means for creating order from potential chaos indicates why we can refer to human beings as political animals. Decision rules become a basis for ordering choice and for creating order in human relationships. We can anticipate that rule-ordered arrangements go hand in hand with the growth of human knowledge and the development of human civilizations. The growth of human knowledge must be accompanied by the creation of social order based on shared concepts, expressed in words, and formulated in rules. Institutions are social artifacts created through human cognition and choice and built on languages pertinent to rule-ordered relationships among communities of people drawing on common knowledge and mutual understandings.

The use of language to create ordered social relationships by reference to rules represents a peculiar form of order that has interesting implications for human beings. Decision rules create only a partial form of ordering, where distinctions are made between the conduct that is *permitted* and that which is *prohibited* or *required*. Inherent in the distinction between that which is prohibited, permitted, or required are criteria for making such distinctions. How such criteria are formulated, understood, and applied to rule-ordered relationships in human societies poses a problem of normative inquiry: How do human beings make distinctions pertaining to what is right and wrong as a basis for distinguishing what is prohibited, permitted, or required? Such distinctions are articulated with reference to modal verbs, such as *must not, may,* and *must* (Wright 1951, 1963; Commons [1924] 1968; Hohfeld 1964; E. Ostrom, Gardner, and Walker 1994; Crawford and E. Ostrom 1995). In most circumstances, a wide range of options are still available. Human societies can then be considered as relatively open systems of order. Constraints are introduced into human relationships, but those constraints do not exhaust potentials for choice.

At the level of social organization, human beings attain a partial form of selection that implies that learning is being embodied in the rules that order social conduct. Out of the range of potential variety, individuals are being constrained from exploiting all possibilities and are being limited in their choice to a smaller range of possibilities. Rules thus provide the basis for a first order of selection that takes account of the interdependent interests of others and yield states of affairs reflecting the cultural values that are derivative from adhering to criteria of selection used in the exercise of choice. By relying on rules and the patterns of organization implied by systems of rules, human beings are able to move to more elaborate patterns of individual and social adaptation. They can take account of the interest of others and draw on each other's capabilities in pursuing opportunities of mutual advantage. By maintaining the continuity of systems of rule-ordered relationships over generations, human beings might accumulate bodies of learning that are entailed in systems of rules and rule-ordered relationships.

The Threat of Tyranny

By themselves, decision rules are only words. As such, they are not self-generating, self-applying, or self-enforcing. Social order, as a consequence, depends on human agents who can formulate, apply, monitor, enforce, and alter decision rules. This condition is the basis for distinguishing governmental institutions from other institutions in any society. Governmental institutions are those decision-making arrangements that are specialized to formulating rules, monitoring adherence to rules, determining conflicts, enforcing rules, and altering decision rules that affect interpersonal relationships among communities of people. Systems of rule-orderings are thus always accompanied by systems of governance. *Authorized relationships,* pertaining to authority to act, are always accompanied by *authoritative relationships,* pertaining to authority to monitor adherence to rules, determine the appropriate application of rules, enforce rules, and formulate and reformulate rules (Commons [1924] 1968, chap. 4).

The development of rule-ordered relationships depends on collective decision-making arrangements if individuals are to partake of the advantages that are to be gained from social organization. Collective action implies that some persons, who have authority to formulate rules, resolve conflicts, enforce decisions, and alter legal relationships affecting others, will necessarily be assigned an authority that is subject to radical inequalities when compared to the authority of those who are subject to that governing authority. If a system of rule-ordering is to prevail, some decision makers must be able to make decisions that can determine and enforce legal relationships among others. Words could not be given effective meaning in the maintenance of ordered relationships among individuals if each individual were free to determine for oneself which rules apply. Collective action always implies organized inequalities in interdependent, rule-ordered relationships. Rules thus imply both rulers and ruled. How that set of relationships is to be organized is the core problem in the constitution of order in human societies. The most fundamental source of inequalities in human societies derives from the use of rules to order human relationships.

The capacity to enforce rules and maintain order in human relationships depends, in turn, on the use of sanctions to enforce conformity to rules and to punish those who violate rules. My use of the term *sanction* carries a negative connotation associated with "punishment" and with deprivations—in much the same way that Lasswell's concept of power did. Positive sanctions have their place in extending recognition and honor to those who perform in meritorious ways, but breeches of the law are not normally honored. The enforcement of lawful standards of conduct thus depends on assigning authority to those who govern, so that they may use instruments of coercion to impose punishment [deprivations] on others. Organization in human societies, then, depends on a Faustian bargain—a bargain with evil—where imposing deprivations on others via instruments of evil, that is, sanctions, including those of organized force, necessarily leaves some worse off rather than better off.

These conditions—the radical inequalities between rulers and ruled and the lawful use of organized force as prerogatives of rulership—present the most fundamental tensions and dangers for the organization of human societies. On the one hand, an inequality of decision-making capabilities and a capacity to impose potential sanctions are *necessary conditions* for creating and maintaining ordered relationships among human beings. On the other hand, these necessary conditions are clearly *not sufficient conditions* for maintaining *orderly and productive* relationships. The sanctions necessary for maintaining ordered social relationships may be used to compound wrongs as well as right wrongs.

The conditions of political constraint can be used as instruments of oppression and tyranny as well as to support productive and mutually beneficial relationships. This circumstance necessarily implies that political relationships are sensitive relationships and, like fire, need to be treated with care when we are devising solutions to the structuring of decision-making arrangements in human societies.

If used with skill, sensitivity, and constraint, the conditions of political choice can be used to encapsulate conflict and to enable persons to contemplate the consequences of their actions before making decisions and forcing others to bear the practical effects of those consequences. In short, the political process can be used to encourage deliberation, to reduce the prospect of error, and to enhance the calculation of more general, long-term interests. In this way, advances in justice and in human welfare can be attained in light of reasoned contention among self-interested and fallible human beings.

Conversely, relying on illusory concepts and strategic bargaining to formulate rules and on coercive capabilities for ordering human relationships can exacerbate conflict, suppress recourse to human reason, and provoke strategies of preemptive reprisals. Threats and counterthreats, challenges and reprisals, can easily escalate into violence, tyranny, and warfare (Boulding 1963). The facilities for political choice can be used to generate a vicious circle of events leading to the compounding of wrongs. Those who govern have access to instrumentalities that offer them prospects of dominating the allocation of values in a society. By control over the making of rules that have the force of law, rulers can alter the rig of the games of life so that some people are systematically advantaged and others are systematically disadvantaged. By control over the instruments of coercion, they can oppress and tyrannize others. A few people can function as rulers and dominate all others who are subject to their rule. If the concept of State is based on a monopoly over rulership prerogatives and the use of force in a society, States will be among the most predatory institutions in human societies (V. Ostrom, Feeny, and Picht [1988] 1993; Yang 1987; Kaminski 1992; Sawyer 1992; Loveman 1993).

The characteristics of a Faustian bargain in which instruments of evil are used to do good create circumstances where strong incentives exist for the pursuit of perverse opportunistic strategies. Milovan Djilas, in the conclusion to *Conversations With Stalin* (1962), asserts that, except for Lenin, Stalin must be regarded as the most grandiose figure in the history of Communism. Djilas explains that Stalin championed the "ideas of Communism" and "brought them to realization in a society and state," but that from "the viewpoint of humanity and history, history does not know a despot as brutal and cynical as Stalin was. He was methodological, all-embracing, and total as a criminal. He was one of those rare terrible dogmatists capable of destroying nine tenths of the human race to 'make happy' the one tenth" (ibid., 190). He built Russia into a major industrial and military power. "All in all," Djilas continues, "Stalin was a monster who, while adhering to abstract, absolute, and fundamentally utopian ideas, in practice recognized, and could recognize, only success—violence, physical and spiritual extermination" (ibid., 191). Control over the instrumentalities of State power made Stalin immune to criminal proceedings. Many who had actively and willingly participated in the system were led to their own destruction.

Even in democratic societies, as I showed in my discussion of the New Newspeak, temptations exist to rely on deceptions in political discourse, and such deceptions transform ideas into ideologies and lead to pervasive human tragedies. Presuming to do good can be an illusion when the path to political success is indicated by winning elections, forming ruling coalitions, enjoying the fruits of victory, and reorganizing systems of government to eliminate checks and balances and to gain easier access to instruments of evil to do good.

The most difficult aspects of the Faustian bargain that are embedded in all systems of political order are the temptations afforded by instruments of coercion to create strategic opportunities, which themselves pose moral hazards, where the short-term advantage of some people accrues at the cost of others or even to their own long-term disadvantage. Shirking and opportunistic behavior can occur among Marxist workers as well as on the part of "capitalists" who profit by using the assets of others. Politicians too can make promises and authorize programs that constitute moral hazards for opportunistic citizens. No society anywhere is immune to the strategic opportunism and moral hazards engendered by the Faustian bargain requiring access to instruments of evil to realize the common good.

A critical issue, then, is whether the principles of rule-ordered relationships can be extended to place limits on those who exercise governmental prerogatives, by recourse to a constitutional level of choice. The terms and conditions for the exercise of governmental authority are then subject to lawful specification, in which processes of constitutional choice are exercised through decision processes beyond the reach of governmental officials as such. So long as appropriate limits can be maintained with regard to the exercise of governmental prerogatives, citizens, through their exercise of constitutional choice and their willingness to challenge those who infringe on those limits, can be said to make the "political laws," as Tocqueville asserted ([1835–40] 1945, 1:55–58). When such processes are themselves controlled by governmental officials, those who are agents easily become masters. Opportunistic citizens who turn to the Government to solve all of their problems cannot maintain appropriate constitutional limits. Such conditions are viable only when citizens develop a sufficient moral consciousness to appreciate that opportunism can be destructive of self-responsibility and mutual respect. Such conditions, however, need to be reinforced by institutional arrangements that can be effectively monitored, are subject to contestability, and afford access to effective modes of conflict resolution.

There remain problems associated with what Tocqueville referred to as "habits of the heart" (ibid., 1:299). The metaphor of referring to public officials as "public servants" implies an effort on their part to extend a helping hand to cope with and achieve resolution to public problems. Unfortunately, the routinization of the "habits of heart" associated with a "helping hand" too easily engenders impersonal routine responses that are far less than helpful. The routine way of saying "no" is to seek justification in rules that deny access to remedial efforts; and the routine way of avoiding responsibility is to plead ignorance.

The Threat of Uncertainty

As human capabilities for learning, organization, and communication have increased, the aggregate pool of human knowledge has expanded in substantial ways. As a consequence of this development, an accelerator principle seems to operate in the development of human civilizations. Substantial investments in research and development continue to generate new knowledge, seemingly at an increasing rate.

The growth of new knowledge also has the effect of disrupting existing or established relationships and expectations about future developments. New knowledge gives rise to new possibilities. New possibilities, if acted on, manifest themselves as new events, relationships, or occurrences that could not have been anticipated by those who failed to take account of those new possibilities in anticipating the future course of events.

These conditions generate a basic paradox for social planners and social forecasters. Under conditions of rapidly expanding knowledge and technological developments, long-term comprehensive planning and long-term forecasting are subject to radical limitations. Any creature that continues to learn, to acquire new knowledge, and to act on expanding bodies of knowledge necessarily confronts uncertain futures. Human capabilities for learning and generating new knowledge necessarily imply that human beings cannot accurately anticipate the future course of human development.

Long-term, comprehensive plans that are designed to serve as blueprints to predetermine the future course of events will fail to be realized. Long-term, comprehensive planning is thus an impossibility. Creatures who are capable of generating new knowledge and of creating new possibilities are necessarily foreclosed from long-term comprehensive planning if they are to take advantage of the new knowledge and new possibilities. Planning can be an essential strategy for arraying knowledge and organizing information in an assessment of alternative possibilities, so long as time horizons are limited and crude magnitudes of uncertainty can be specified in relation to the generation of new knowledge and the obsolescence of old knowledge. The magnitude of ignorance cannot be specified, and human beings always confront potentials for surprise associated with either good or bad "fortunes." As Milovan Djilas observed in *The Unperfect Society,* "History does not exactly abound with instances of thinkers' predictions having come true, least of all those relating to social patterns and people's attitudes and way of life" (1969, 150).

If long-term forecasting and long-term planning are subject to severe limits, a relative advantage may be gained by relying on the constraints inherent in rules to order relationships among individuals where the particular techniques and modes of production are left open to choice. The constraints introduced by rule-orderings are, however, soft, in the sense that they operate only as a matter of human choice. Yet if we can know how such constraints order choice and affect patterns of behavior, we can anticipate general patterns of social development without knowing precise technologies, their relationship to the array of all products produced by human effort, and their precise value in relation to one another. Such knowledge about general patterns of association should also enable us to understand how rules constrain choice and affect behavior in ways that are likely to generate social pathologies under changing conditions of interdependencies. Such knowledge might then be used to change rules, create new patterns of behavior, and affect how human beings relate to one another, under circumstances that avoid those pathologies and generate more constructive patterns of human relationships. Changing rules and patterns of rule-ordered relationships means that human institutions and the constitution of order in human societies are subject to alteration and can be "reformed" under appropriate circumstances, though not under any and all circumstances. Reformability is itself subject to limits.

This analysis also leads to the conclusion that human beings are unable to order conduct that is "rationally" directed only at attaining "the good life" or the "common good." The most that fallible creatures with imperfect knowledge can do is use evaluative criteria as the basis for choice with regard to the multitude of choices that everyone makes every day. Operational objectives or goals can then be selected by reference to appropriate yardsticks, if we think of evaluative criteria as yardsticks—measuring devices—for making interpersonal comparisons. Human development unfolds as humans decide which successive actions and steps to take by weighing each choice according to principles or criteria of selection without knowing the "ultimate goal" or "end state" of human development. Capabilities achieved today affect the potentials that are available for tomorrow. Human beings must journey through time, measured in lifetimes, without knowing the ultimate fate of the species *Homo sapiens,* the ultimate fate of the planet Earth, or the ultimate fate of the universe.

Institutional conditions will be mutually productive when self-interested individuals choose strategies to enhance their well-being with reference to particular decision-making arrangements and structures of opportunities that leave no one worse off. This condition is sometimes referred to as the Pareto criterion. Pareto optimality would imply that all such moves had been exhausted—an impossibility for fallible creatures subject to significant degrees of ignorance, uncertainty, and innovative potentials. Social pathologies are generated when the opposite occurs, that is, when the consequences of self-interested individuals choosing strategies to enhance their own well-being with reference to particular decision-making arrangements and structures of opportunities leave oneself and/or others worse off—a necessary danger associated with the use of sanctions to impose deprivations on others. The State cannot be accurately conceived as an association for the common good of all.

The conditions of institutional weaknesses and institutional failures that generate social pathologies exist in many different forms. Modifications in decision-making arrangements can transform patterns of human interaction from unproductive pathological relationships to mutually productive relationships. Such possibilities have substantial ramifications for human development but are always accompanied by serious dangers and risks. The general veil of ignorance that obscures human vision about the future course of events and the veil of ambiguities in the use of languages are aggravated by the limited mastery that each individual can attain in relation to the aggregate pool of knowledge. I turn next to the threat of increasing relative ignorance as a factor affecting potentials for human development.

The Threat of Increasing Relative Ignorance

Adam Smith, in *The Wealth of Nations* ([1776] n.d.), identified specialization of labor as a factor that contributes to increasing productivity in human societies. Smith illustrated the operation of this principle by reference to pin-making. Without any division of labor, it might well take an individual the better part of a day to make a single pin. When pin-making can be organized with reference to appropriate materials, tools, and a few simple operations, a crew of ten men, according to Smith's illustration, can make something like 48,000 pins per day. Specialization of labor and the appropriate development of materials and tools increases the productivity of each individual from 1 pin per day to something like 4,800 pins per day, each individual's share of the joint productive effort (ibid., 4–5).

But Smith went on to argue, at a later juncture in *The Wealth of Nations,* that there is another side to this same coin. Each pin-maker, whose activities are confined to a relatively few simple operations, will find the opportunities to extend one's learning to be seriously confined. Each comes to know more about less. Smith articulated the implications.

> He naturally loses, therefore, the habit of such exertion [the exertion of his mind], and generally becomes as stupid and ignorant as it is possible for a human creature to become. The torpor of his mind renders him, not only incapable of relishing or bearing a part in any rational conversation, but of conceiving any generous, noble, or tender sentiment, and consequently of forming any just judgment concerning many even of the ordinary duties of private life. Of the great and extensive interests of his country he is altogether incapable of judging; and unless very particular pains have been taken to render him otherwise, he is equally incapable of defending his country in war. . . . His dexterity at his own particular trade seems, in this manner, to be acquired at the expense of his intellectual, social, and martial virtues. But in every improved and civilized society this is the state

into which the laboring poor, that is, the great body of the people, must necessarily fall, unless government takes some pains to prevent it. (Ibid., 734–35)

Smith implied that the productive gain derived from specialization, getting work done, is accompanied by a loss of general knowledge and social skills.

Peter Kropotkin, the author of *Mutual Aid* ([1902] 1972), might have looked at Smith's example of the pin-makers from the perspective of having studied cooperative enterprises among Siberian peasants and Swiss watchmakers. Kropotkin would have concluded that, instead of becoming slaves to machines, workers might constitute enterprises under terms and conditions where they could participate in the governance, management, and operation of that enterprise as it functions in more extended networks of relationships. The contingencies of pin-making can be ordered in different ways, with different incentives, opportunities, and consequences for pin-makers. Nevertheless, in a system that emphasizes aggregate growth of knowledge, we can expect a tendency for each individual in the system to confront a problem of specialization—of knowing more about a more confined field of knowledge.

The Spanish philosopher José Ortega y Gasset, in *The Revolt of the Masses* ([1932] 1957), advanced a thesis that specialization of knowledge has a similar effect on those who pursue professional and scholarly interests. Specialization of knowledge has produced a "new barbarian," according to Ortega y Gasset, whom he identifies as a "learned ignoramus." As the aggregate pool of knowledge increases, there is a correlative increase in the relative ignorance of every individual in relation to that aggregate body of knowledge. Individuals are necessarily limited in their capacity to master large bodies of knowledge and to understand their contextualities. Following Ortega y Gasset, we might identify this problem as the paradox of the learned ignoramus. Human beings thus confront the circumstance that no one can "see" or "know" the "whole picture." All who exercise choice—who make decisions—are fallible. In systems of rule-ordered relationships, the rendering of choice associated with the assignment of authority—the capacity to decide—is vulnerable to the learned ignoramus. No one, including government officials, can know all of the consequences that flow from one's decisions and actions—and be aware of the larger contextuality in which essential distinctions and combinations apply to human artisanship. All decision making is subject to error.

The problem of the learned ignoramus is radically amplified by the serious hazards associated with the intergenerational cycle of life. The prolonged period of childhood and adolescence is a period of socialization, enculturation, and learning essential to the intergenerational transmission of a culture. The period of youth is marked by both sexual maturation and the bonding of what Ortega y Gasset would refer to as coeval age groupings. The more such generational bonds are reinforced and isolated from intergenerational continuities, the greater the propensity for each generation to presume that it is the master of its own fate, free to disregard both the prejudices and the wisdom of its forebearers. The intergenerational transmission of knowledge and skill is placed at risk.

Learned ignoramuses, like myself as one immersed in the traditions of Western civilization, are likely to become so other-directed and preoccupied with patterns of ordered relationships that they focus on the constitution of human societies as it pertains to contemporaries only. The synchronic character of life in human societies, however, needs to be viewed as complemented by the diachronic character of life cycles occurring through time, including the intergenerational cycle of life itself. Asian civilizations, in contrast to Western civilizations, place a much stronger emphasis on the developmental feature of life through time. When each generation turns to its own peers for standards of judgment and rejects the standards of judgment associated with elders, essential continuities in the cultural evolution of human civilization are placed at risk.

We in the West are apt to presume the autonomy of individuals and to presume universal human rights without considering the place of language in the constitution of common knowledge and shared communities of understanding. Some of us presume that a single, comprehensive, and uniform code of law might apply to all mankind. Critical reflection about the diversity of conditions under which human beings live their lives and the place of languages in the emergence of cultural diversity would lead me to conclude that a single, comprehensive, uniform, and enforceable code of law for all humanity and for many nation-states is an impossibility. Yet the constitution of human societies has, in the last half millennium, become increasingly global. We face the problematics of relating family households and other communities of interests, which in some languages would be conceived as "households" [*eco* in *ecology* and *economy* derives from the Greek word *oikos,* meaning "household"], that extend to features of a global "household." These problematics cannot be resolved by a single global center of Supreme Authority or by any single criterion of choice.

The relation of the vocabularies of particular sciences and technologies can be ameliorated by recourse to science as a method of inquiry or way of thinking, as George Orwell ([1949] 1983, 254) suggested in his discussion of language. By relying on such a method of inquiry or way of thinking, human beings can extend their horizons of inquiry and gain access to specialized vocabularies and bodies of knowledge without acquiring the skills and intelligibility necessary to become a fully articulate artisan in every field of knowledge. The commonality afforded by methods of inquiry and ways of thinking are, then, the essential features for building common knowledge, shared communities of understanding, patterns of social accountability, and mutual trust in human relationships. These derivatives do not just happen as spontaneous features of life in a state of nature; they require intelligibility and skill on the part of human beings who know how to think and use their rational facilities to solve problems and constitute mutually productive relationships with one another.

We come back then to a paradigmatic problem of whether systems of governance turn critically on command and control or whether governance is conceived as working with communities of people in creating and maintaining public facilities and states of affairs. The conduct of public affairs requires the pooling, rearranging, and compromising of existing interests—in the constitution of common knowledge, shared communities of understanding, patterns of social accountability, and mutual trust—that are subject to challenge and to being reestablished and reaffirmed through processes of conflict resolution. Obedience in a system of command and control is ostensibly simpler to understand. The use of methods of inquiry and ways of thinking associated with science, in its larger sense, presumes that the political and social sciences and the humanities are grounded in a science of culture, meaning the sciences appropriate to the cultivation of diverse creative potentials.

When everyone is assumed to be fallible, error proneness can be reduced by the development of error-correcting procedures in the organization of decision-making processes. The organization of decision-making processes that facilitate error-correcting strategies requires reference to specialized decision rules that involve opportunities to challenge and contest different perceptions, the arraying of arguments, and the assessing of evidence. Where error-correcting procedures can be built into the structure of decision-making arrangements, we can view such procedures as organizing processes that facilitate learning and create a culture of inquiry. Systems of organization, including systems of government, can be viewed as arrangements that facilitate or repress opportunities for learning to occur and for a culture of inquiry to develop. Issues bearing on the methodologies of choice and the ways that such methodologies are taken into account in the structure of decision-making arrangements affect our estimate of error proneness or error-correcting capabilities that occur in human decisions. Potentials for learning through processes of conflict and methods for conflict resolution are of essential importance.

The Problem of Coevolutionary Development

In conclusion, we as human beings confront a difficult problem of coevolutionary development. All of the tensions arising from the dual character of biological and cultural evolution have the potential to plague every individual and every human relationship. Problems of desire and rationality are not easy to resolve. Problems of coevolutionary development are especially difficult because the system for constituting order in human societies is marked by significant degrees of openness, which means that each individual is, to some degree, capable of shaping one's own futures (Fromm 1947; Buchanan 1979b). This pertains to the acquisition of skills and what one strives to make of one's life, including the type of character structure that one's conscience will allow expression while one is learning to relate to others and to cope with the problems of life. We usually associate this character of evolutionary development with something that we call "maturation." Persons become the focal referents in relation to the semiautonomous cognitive-cultural-social-artifactual structures in which we live our lives. A "conscience," a character structure, and a personality emerge in coping with the multifaceted aspects of life as a coevolutionary process. Freedom means to acquire autonomy in governing one's life while taking account of one's relationships with others and of the fundamental limits that are constitutive of life and the world in which we live.

The semiautonomous cognitive-cultural-social-artifactual structures with which we live also have an existence of their own. Systems of knowledge have their own existence with reference to subject matters, courses of studies, and what presumably comes to be articulated in what we call "schools" and "universities." They become constitutive of patterns of common knowledge, shared communities of understanding, social accountability, and trust that are operable in human societies. These systems also bear on crafts and professions and on what is created by artisans functioning in diverse skills, crafts, and professions. The organization of systems of knowledge, and those who make it a craft to work with systems of knowledge, can be identified with the constitution of *epistemic orders.*

And so we can think of semiautonomous cognitive-cultural-social-artifactual structures that become operable in nurturing life in the sense of producing, exchanging, consuming, using, and enjoying what becomes and is made available. Such patterns of organization might be identified with the constitution of *economic orders.* Rules and rule-ordered relationships in the diverse contexts in which human beings maintain regularized relationships with one another can also be viewed as semiautonomous cognitive-cultural-social-artifactual structures. Such patterns of organization can be identified as *juridical or political orders* that apply to *authorized relationships,* which pertain to authority to act; *authoritative relationships,* which pertain to authority to monitor, determine, enforce, and alter authorized relationships; and *constitutive relationships,* which set the terms and conditions of governance with regard to both authorized and authoritative relationships.

Since all of these semiautonomous orderings are language mediated, we would expect these diverse orderings to be related to language communities that are often identified with nationalities and civilizations. *Nationalities* and *civilizations* are systems of identity with which people recognize and associate themselves and their relationships with others. These systems of order are not coterminous with political jurisdiction but are likely to interpenetrate one another in complex configurations of relationships. How these systems of order emerge in the future development of human civilizations will depend on how human beings like you and me choose to live our lives and give attention to ideas, actions, feelings, and achievements in relating to one another. The relationships of ideas to deeds are enmeshed in these patterns of coevolutionary development that make complementary uses of language systems.

The constitution of order in human societies involves complex configurations of multivariant relationships that pose a most serious challenge to the limits of human cognitive capabilities. In some basic sense, all of us are learned ignoramuses. Limits to cognitive capabilities in the cycles of life need to be much better understood to allow for a realistic assessment of the magnitude of change that is culturally feasible in human societies. Presuppositions that the Old Order can be replaced by a complete New Order are absurd. How change is to take place in the lives of people will be determined by the opportunity that people have to participate in the consideration and realization of those changes as they impinge on their lives as ordinary mortals. Otherwise, revolutionary impulses will always be checked by counterrevolutionary reactions. The only way such reactions can be avoided is to exterminate the opposition. This inevitability is the principal source of genocide and holocausts in the twentieth century.

Being the kinds of creatures we are, we keep striving. The quest is elusive. The adventure can be enlightening. The problem of human development requires that we live our lives in nested configurations that bring together conditions of life embedded in genetic and cultural heritages whose origins and destinations we cannot know, but whose evolution we may come to appreciate. We might develop some small measure of sympathetic appreciation about what unknowns might imply about essential mysteries in life. We can pursue inquiries about those conditions that enhance meaning for peoples living in human communities and how those might be taken into account so that human beings retain a sense of humanity in relating both to one another and to the world in which we live.

When we ignore such conditions, human beings are capable of the most profound evils. A tolerable life cannot be lived by relying simply on a principle of "one individual, one vote, majority rule." Nor can a tolerable life be lived under a single, comprehensive, and uniform code of law subject to a single overarching system of command and control. We need to reconsider the conditions under which knowledgeable, skillful, intelligent, and clever creatures can learn to live with one another in ways that are consistent with their own shared sense of what can be achieved in working with and relating to one another. Learning to live a productive life among the Wolves of the Primates requires more than being a wolf. One must come to appreciate, like the *Steppenwolf* (Hesse [1927] 1963), that human adaptive potentials require the unfolding of many layers of evolution, development, meaning, and enlightenment. These are the conditions of life—the human conditions—that we must attempt to understand as we address ourselves to the puzzle of what it means to live in democratic societies.

CHAPTER 6

An Institutional Analysis of the Place of Languages in the Political Economy of Life

Languages and the diverse uses of languages give the distinctive quality to the ways of life lived by *Homo sapiens*. To address the problematics of language, I propose to undertake an institutional analysis of the place of languages in the political economy of life in human societies, using the framework developed in chapters 4 and 5. To gain contextuality, I assume that all human activities occur in action situations that have material and environmental exigencies that affect their use as resources in the political economy of life. The nature of goods and the technologies associated with their production and use are essential factors requiring specification. Further, all action situations occur within a context that has reference to rules and rule-ordered arrangements, which need specification. All action situations also occur in a context in which it is necessary to specify the common knowledge, the shared community of understanding, and the identities that exist among those acting with reference to others in any given action situation.

Presuming hypothetical individuals functioning in action situations, we expect that there exist (1) technological possibilities with reference to the production and use of specifiable goods and services, (2) specifiable rule-ordered relationships, and (3) shared communities of understanding and identities, which are interrelated with one another to create structures of incentives and constraints that lead to choices of strategies. Given the situation and the choices made by others, such choices of strategy create patterns of interaction that, in turn, yield consequences. The problematic for the analyst is whether the specification of the action situation and the structure of incentives confronting actors in action situations is sufficient to allow the analyst to estimate the likely choices of strategies, patterns of interaction, and the consequences that will follow. The aggregate structure has the positive analytical character of a hypothetical [if-then] arrangement. The positive analysis also has normative content and implications depending on the standards of choice applied to interpersonal relationships and the relationship of positive analysis to intentionality. Whenever counterintentionality and counterintuitivity prevail, normative ambiguities arise, and normative formulations require that positive contingencies of a counterintuitive and counterintentional character be taken into account with regard to social dilemmas. This mode of analysis, discussed in chapter 4 and represented in figure 4.1, is more fully developed in Elinor Ostrom's *Governing the Commons* (1990).

In this analysis, I presume *hypothetical individuals* in the context of *any* speech community. Only the most limited assertions can be made about environing and material conditions, the rule-ordered relationships applicable to specifiable situations, and the specific character of the shared community of understanding [culture] prevailing in any specific speech community. Even with these radical limitations, an analysis might hopefully reach some nontrivial conclusions.

In applying such a mode of analysis, I shall first review the general analysis of human adaptive behavior made in chapter 5. I shall attempt to specify the nature of the good and technological contingencies that I associate with the "thing" that you and I experience as "language." I shall then turn to patterns of use associated with the functions or uses of languages. These can only be approached in a preliminary way. To go further would require another book. I shall then face the problem of conjecturing about the aggregate structure of events and the ordering principles that we would expect to occur in the choices of strategies in hypothetical situations and the assessment of consequences that follow from the nature of the good, technologies, and potentials for the uses and misuses of language.

Presumptions about Hypothetical Individuals

I am prepared to follow Thomas Hobbes in his introduction to *Leviathan* ([1651] 1960) in presuming that all human beings everywhere share a basic similitude of thoughts and passions that derive from a genetic endowment associated with *Homo sapiens* as a species. As I discussed in chapter 5, I also assume that all human beings share with all other animals a capacity to adapt to the circumstances in which they find themselves. There are thus some universal commonalities that apply to "human nature." Those commonalities need to be distinguished from the great variations acquired through linguistic and cultural achievements.

Two levels of adaptation—the genetic and the cultural—lead to problems. First, information derived from the environment is reproducible as memory in the biological tissues of the nervous system. This potential is subject to the severe limit that information acquired as memory in individuals is erased biologically with certain malfunctions of the central nervous system and death. This is why language is of such fundamental importance in serving as the instrument for conceptualizing elements and relationships in the milieu of human experience and for the accumulation of knowledge and information on an intergenerational basis, associated with cumulative patterns of cultural evolution accruing to the members of language communities. Languages provide access to the stocks of knowledge and flows of information available to human beings. Individual learning associated with the cumulative experiences of living a life are, however, largely lost with senility and death.

A second problem arises from efforts of scholars to postulate conditions applicable to Man in a State of Nature. I view such efforts as important sources of theoretical conjectures about action tendencies in situations where creatures having the biological characteristics of human beings, but no common language, might interact with one another. There is, however, an anomaly. It is difficult to imagine how a species with such deep and prolonged childhood dependencies could survive without the social capabilities associated with language. I presume, then, that the evolution of language among *Homo sapiens* has been associated with biological evolutionary patterns that have occurred over a very long period of time—millions of years. Given the openness of the central nervous system to imprinting and retention of memory about events in the environment, I presume that the physical features of the nervous system are especially susceptible to coevolutionary development. Thresholds that occur in the technologies of language formations radically transform human potentials associated with the emergence of cultures and civilizations. Communication by signaling is very widespread among species in the animal kingdom, and the rudiments of intergenerational transmission of learning exist among all mammals, as species biologically equipped with food supplies for the long-term dependency of the young (Bonner 1980). Species among the primates, such as baboons, for example, develop cultures, which vary substantially among troops living in diverse environmental conditions (Marais 1969).

A key question, then, is: When, in the biological evolution of hominids, was phonetic signaling transformed by a process of naming and the assignment of names—sounds, words—to designate elements and relationships in a way that became associated with both syntax as a technique of linguistic expression and semantics as a way to convey meaning? Once the concept of naming occurred, that concept was easily extended to wide-ranging symbolizations characteristic of speech in human communities (Keller [1902] 1965; Langer 1972). There seems to be no specifiable limit to its extensions to new frontiers of inquiry.

I presume, then, consistent with Noam Chomsky's (1968) formulations, that the biological characteristics of the nervous system allow for the imprinting of what is acquired through learning to establish patterns of association with reference to linguistically transmitted and syntactically ordered patterns of speech that form the basis for communication and cognitive transmission of meaning. Communication depends on shared communities of understanding. This means that the use of language always occurs in the presence of the reciprocal exercise of human intelligibility. A listener or reader always brings some background of knowledge, skill, and intelligibility in assigning meaning to be conveyed by words. Words as symbols used to express meaning may serve as signs to reveal further levels of meaning.

Within a given speech community, individuals may conceive of themselves and their relationships with others in diverse ways. Tocqueville refers to two quite different cultures existing on the Ohio River: one in Ohio, on the northern side of the river; the other in Kentucky, on the river's south shore. Stefan Zweig presents Marie Antoinette, in his biography of her, as conceptualizing herself and her relationships to others as the "Queen of Rococo," with minimal awareness of what it meant to be Queen of France, until the signs of revolutionary tragedy had pervaded her domain as the Queen of Rococo and had become a threat to her very existence as Queen of France and as a living human being (1933, 89–103). A culture of rococo was a part of the French culture in a context of European cultures, but with quite different meaning and significance from the aggregate cultures of France and of Europe. The daughter had, as a consequence, quite a different place in history than her mother, Maria Theresa of Austria.

I assume, then, that all "normal" human beings are capable of learning and have access to the necessary rudiments of intelligibility to function as language users and to assign meaning to language as a consequence of having acquired and learned to use a language within some language community. What this may imply turns on proceeding further in our analysis of language as a "good" and of some of the technological potentials associated with the uses and misuses of languages.

Language as a "Good"

A standard mode of analysis associated with modern scholarship in political economy typically has recourse to at least two different factors that critically affect potentials for exchange relationships and market organization as discussed in chapter 4. One pertains to whether anyone can exclude others from gaining access to the good without meeting the terms and conditions of the owner, vendor, or supplier. This condition can be specified as a criterion of exclusion: others can be excluded from appropriating a good or enjoying its benefits unless they meet the terms and conditions for using or acquiring the good or service. Such relationships are embedded in conceptions of law pertaining to "private" property rights. Depending on how costly it is to achieve exclusion, it is possible to dichotomize this factor and treat it as a variable. Another factor is whether the use or consumption of a good or service occurs under circumstances where its use or consumption by someone is subtractive or whether the good or service is nonsubtractive and subject to joint use in some community of users. Goods that are subtractable in use—where my use forecloses your use— and subject to exclusion as applied to individual possession are most amenable to competitive market-exchange relationships. These factors are arrayed in chapter 4, in table 4.2.

The first step in this analysis, then, is to view language as a "thing" and to ascertain its "nature" as a "good." In a world where the thing referred to would be the English language, I would first recognize that my use of the English language does not subtract from its use or enjoyment by others. Further, there is no advantage to me, as one who is in possession of English-language capabilities, to exclude others from using the language. Advantages accrue to me as more and more people use the English language. Indeed, my having acquired English as a vernacular language is one of the more valuable assets that it was my good fortune to have acquired. The more universal its use becomes, the greater the benefit to me. The cost of efforts to achieve exclusion is revealed by the difficulty in creating secret languages associated with such concepts as cryptography and cryptology.

While I am aware of my good "fortune" to have acquired English as a vernacular language and to enjoy the benefits that accrue from a widely used language, I also have an awareness that humanity is the richer for the way that diverse languages have contributed to different civilizations, reflecting the multiple experiences of peoples having lived through both overwhelming tragedies and heroic achievements in many different circumstances. If my conditions of life were threatened by the dominance of some people, I would have substantial incentive to communicate with others through discrete signs and symbols that could be identified with discrete communities of relationships. Such conditions are a part of the larger "fate" of mankind; and my good fortune was built in part by both military and economic imperialism and by the resistance offered to British imperialism.

In viewing language as a "thing" that has the latent characteristics of a *universal public good,* a serious qualification arises. Viewing language purely as a "thing" would require us to include in our analysis of languages "archaic" or "dead" languages no longer in common use for purposes of general communication. It is essential to the characteristics of a "living" language that it be a language-in-use. Any effort to deal with language as a thing apart from its use severs language from its essential contextualities. Languages-in-use relationships are of fundamental importance to the constitution of order in human societies and to how we create bodies of knowledge to be shared with others.

The widely held presumption about value being associated with scarcity seems not to hold in the case of language as a latent universal public good. Rather than scarcity, we confront problems of linguistic profusions. The limit in such circumstances is the cognitive capability of human beings to cope with linguistic profusions. The limits of nature apply to human cognition and motor facilities.

Another limitation arises from the degradation or erosion of meaning associated with a language because of the misuses or abuses that individuals make in their enjoyment and use of a language. This gives rise to a problem in which the use of language may be subject to ambiguities and confusion in the way that language is being articulated. It is possible for some to mumble intentionally with great incoherence. It is possible for others to talk or express themselves in writing with only a superficial awareness of what they say and write. Such circumstances might be referred to as a Tower-of-Babel problem, which places a culture and its associated ways of thinking and acting at risk.

These preliminary reflections lead me to the conclusion that public goods are likely to involve some nonmonetized relationships not directly relevant to a theory of public expenditure. Such a conclusion poses difficult questions about the place of investment and about who makes what investments in public economies. Individual persons, as essential coproducers, are likely to play important roles. Thus, Governments as such cannot govern alone. What people choose to culture—meaning to create, to cultivate, and to nurture—is constitutive of language communities and ways of life. Only some limited features of life are marginally affected by State authorities. These problems are especially important in realizing the potentials for democratic societies. The efforts of economists, including Paul Samuelson (1954), to address the theory of public goods as a theory of public expenditure inevitably introduces a selective bias that excludes universal public goods and the way that such goods function in the political economy of life.

The public-good character of languages, the potential profuseness of linguistic articulations, and the Tower-of-Babel problem point to the critical importance of biological limits characteristic of *Homo sapiens* and of how these limits interact with linguistic articulations to yield characteristic patterns in the constitution of speech communities. One source of the problematics involved in the constitution of speech communities is limits on the cognitive capabilities and motor facilities available to human beings. These, in turn, are related to the technologies of linguistic expression. Among the technologies of linguistic expression, I shall rely on crude distinctions applicable to (1) body language [signaling and the interpretation of signs], (2) spoken language, (3) written language, and (4) electronic language and its potential for simultaneously conveying pictographic, phonetic, and written representations. In shifting attention to the constitution of speech communities, I shall be concerned with how biological limits and language potentials interact with one another in ways that are constitutive of speech communities, in a context in which reliance is placed mainly on body language and spoken language.

The Constitution of Speech Communities

Limits among Elements and Relationships

The first biological limit and the most fundamental constraint in the constitution of speech communities is the limit that human beings cannot simultaneously speak, listen to, and understand what is being said. They can, however, observe body language and tonal features while speaking *or* listening. I presume that the connection of sensory mechanisms associated with listening and the motor facilities associated with the articulation of speech are such with reference to the central nervous system that both cannot simultaneously function in a way that is consistent with attention and comprehension. Individuals cannot both speak and listen simultaneously. A preoccupation with what one wants to say is likely to attenuate what one hears. Requirements of human intelligibility cannot be met for either a speaker or a listener in the presence of a simultaneity of listening *and* speaking in an interpersonal context. Communication is subject to serious biological limits.

This fundamental constraint has the most profound and obvious implication: human beings functioning in speech communities are required to give attention to one another. This, I presume, is the foundation for dealing with moral contingencies—taking account of others and establishing the basis for considering the self in relation to others and how interpersonal relationships are to be mediated in processes of *communication.* How those conditions are to be made operable in human relationships turns on allocational arrangements and on how such arrangements function in human affairs. Moral contingencies pertain to rules of propriety. I presume, then, that the speaking-listening relationship entails reference to prescriptive rule-ordered relationships that are coevolutionary aspects in the development of speech among *Homo sapiens* everywhere. Attention to others in *communication* implies that the realm of norms—*nomos*—is closely bound up with the logic—*logos*—of assertions.

Listening has a profound place in political processes. The Greek emphasis on rhetoric may have had an unfortunate bias in distorting the character of human communication in political processes. The good listener may be more important than the good speaker in acquiring problem-solving capabilities. Neither aspect can be seriously neglected. A selective distortion in patterns of communication emphasizing speech to the neglect of listening will, however, have its inevitable pathologies.

At the biological level, we can take a further step to consider symmetries and asymmetries in speaking-listening [communicative] relationships. In the context of a two-person speech relationship, there is an opportunity for each person to take turns in carrying on a conversation. Taking turns is an allocational rule consistent with reciprocity among individuals who have a mutual regard for one another in conversational relationships. The presumption is that each has something to offer to the other in the give-and-take of a conversation, yielding the prospect that each is better off by virtue of what is shared in common [communication]. Each seeks to influence and is prepared to be influenced by another. Other allocational rules learned by children include "share and share alike" and "first come, first served."

Speaker-listener relationships are also subject to substantial asymmetries. If, instead of assuming a two-person speech relationship, we assume an indefinitely large number of persons in a speech relationship, we are bound by the circumstance that the members of an N-person speech situation can listen to only one speaker at a time. Substantial symmetry in taking turns and maintaining the continuity and coherence of discussion can occur in small groups. When such a group exceeds approximately five to ten individuals, stress begins to occur both in taking turns and in the incoherence of the discussions. As the number of persons in a deliberative group increases in size, the order of the proceedings depends on an alteration in the structure of authority relationships.

Proceedings are facilitated if someone exercises the prerogatives of "host," "chair," "speaker," or "master of ceremonies." The generalization has been advanced by James Madison in *The Federalist* (No. 58) that the larger the group, the more dominant the leadership will be in exercising control over the agenda and over the conduct of proceedings (Hamilton, Jay, and Madison [1788] n.d., 382). Strong oligarchical tendencies prevail in the organization of large democratic assemblies. When applied to elections, the organization of political parties and parliamentary bodies, such tendencies have been referred to by Robert Michels as an iron law of oligarchy ([1911] 1966), where the few exercise power over the many.

How large deliberative assemblies are to be constituted poses serious difficulties. Is the choice of a chair to be mediated by standards of impartiality and fairness or by the desire to expedite and control proceedings? Is each participant to be given equal opportunity to speak, and in what sequence may those allowed to speak do so? Is speech to be confined, for example, to those occupying the "front" benches, with "backbenchers" serving as a cheering section, as in the British House of Commons? Madison asserted that in large deliberative assemblies, the larger the group, the more incoherent the deliberations. This generalization was accompanied by the assertion that "had every Athenian citizen been a Socrates, every Athenian assembly would still have been a mob" (Hamilton, Jay, and Madison [1788] n.d., 361). Very large public assemblies reaching into the tens or hundreds of thousands can be easily transformed into bedlam. The presence of a small band of secret conspirators could, under appropriate circumstances, easily turn any large crowd into bedlam or into a mob capable of storming lightly defended fortresses or presidential palaces. The attributes characteristic of individuals are dominated by the structure of the situation.

A second biological constraint affecting the constitution of order in human societies is what I shall refer to as a limited span of attention. A similar concept identified as "span of control" applies to systems of command and control in bureaucratic structures. Human cognition, as I experience myself, requires focused attention. I am able to give attention to and focus my conscious thought on only one problematic and chain of thought at a time. Chains of thought take the form of sequencing what-if and if-then conjectures. Linguistic capabilities are only gradually acquired and are accumulated as memory reinforced by practice and habituation. Memory and habituation allow for what might be called the "stacking" of accumulated linguistic capabilities (Sproule-Jones 1993). Skills in phonetic ciphering and deciphering, in the morphology of word usage, and in the syntax appropriate to the expression of meaning are only gradually acquired and are reinforced in habituated responses that preoccupy several of the first years of life and that occupy, to some significant degree, all of the remaining years of life.

As this mastery of phonetics, morphophonetics, syntax, and semantics is acquired and becomes thoroughly habituated, conscious attention need not be given to those features of a language. Instead, these skills are used with substantial automaticity, while the primary focus of attention is directed to what is being said verbally by the speaker and by the attentiveness of the listener. The same phenomena occur in all of the arts, all forms of artisanship, and all forms of human activities. Much of what has been learned is not subject to conscious efforts to recall. It becomes an integral part of habituated responses that permeate habits of thoughts, feelings, and the exercise of motor facilities. The very limited capabilities that each of us can devote to conscious thought draws, then, on a much larger accumulation of learning that functions subconsciously through residual memory and habituation.

An increase in the automaticity of habituation is likely to be inversely related to a consciousness about the place of language in human cognition, communication, and shared communities of understanding, unless individuals give special attention to the artisanship involved in linguistic articulation. The skilled artisan has an appreciation for the way that habituated skills express cumulative accomplishments. The place of language, however, is apt to become transparent—both invisible and subconscious—in casual communications. Attention is given to the meaning of what is being said rather than to linguistic media. When a skilled artisan acquires the capabilities for functioning as a "coach," or a "master" artisan working with apprentices, the relationship of practice to habituation and to skill is given knowledgeable and conscious attention. When language becomes transparent to a user, that language user presumes to see "reality" devoid of a conscious awareness of the paradigmatics [mind-sets] given expression in language. Without a critical awareness of the artisanship inherent in language usages, an individual may achieve the minimal cumulative capabilities necessary for participation in a speech community and at the same time become a slave to that way of thinking and its habituated routines. One's consciousness is imprisoned by the way that habituation conserves on the limits of focal attention and allows for habituated responses at a subconscious level of awareness: one presumes directly to see "reality"— the sun "rises" and is intuitively presumed to revolve around the earth.

A third limit on human cognitive capabilities applies to conceptualizing dimensionality in more than two-dimensional surfaces or three-dimensional space. These problems get built into the basic structure of languages. The aggregate corpus of "knowledge," viewed as subjects to be understood, implies dimensionalities far beyond the bounds of three-dimensional space. The world of rule-ordered relationships, as only one aspect of language usage, is tied together in complex configurations of authority relationships that might be conceptualized in a three-dimensional world as applying to constitutional rules, collective choice rules, and operational rules, each of which are associated with discrete structures and processes of choice.

Distinguished scientists can proceed on a presupposition that putting language on paper, mandating requirements, will suffice to solve global problems in the absence of an intelligible awareness of what is required to make words expressing rules binding among peoples of diverse languages living in different ecological niches. It is as though words bind human conduct without reference to shared communities of understanding and agency relationships pertaining to monitoring conduct and enforcing rules among the diverse dimensions embedded in systems of authority relationships. A sorcery of words can be presumed to be sufficient to achieve fantasies about what ought to be. Lawyers, legislators, and administrators can too easily focus on compromises to achieve agreement on words to be used in a legal instrument, with little or no attention to what is implied for action in discrete situations.

A fourth limit on human cognitive capabilities is that all human beings are subject to radical limits on the aggregate accumulation of learning and skills that are subject to effective utilization in the functioning of each individual's cognitive capabilities and motor skills. No single individual is the master of the diverse forms of language usage characteristic of language communities. Further, continued practice is necessary to maintain and improve skills. No human being has access to complete or perfect information, and this limit is well illustrated in our limited command of languages.

Basic limits applicable to communication [speaking and listening], span of attention, memory, habituation, and multidimensionality thus pose challenges for the elaboration of languages. The loss of consciousness associated with habituation is challenged by the necessity of transmitting linguistic and cultural achievements to successive generations. The greater accumulation of knowledge and skills accompanying specialization and division of labor requires commensurately greater self-conscious efforts in transmitting cultural traditions across successive generations, into the future and among diverse speech communities. These are the burdens borne by those who are concerned with the organization and transmission of knowledge in human societies. In democratic societies, each person is required to bear these burdens.

Patterns of Communication in Speech Communities

Human languages are crafted in concurrent patterns of communication in associated relationships that are constitutive of ways of life among contemporaries. Contemporaries craft and make use of the artifacts that are also constitutive of a livelihood in an intergenerational cycle of life. Attention is variously given to fashioning the architectonics of bodies of knowledge and systems of rule-ordered relationships to cope with mutual expectations about the symmetries and asymmetries that pervade life in human societies. This implies a complexity that exceeds the limits of individual cognitive capabilities. The reality that is constituted as ways of life in human societies has reference both to norms for ordering human relationships and to the logics of association that apply to what needs to be done. Both are needed to enable human beings to function in relation to one another, to the environing and material conditions in which they live, and to a future that is different than the past.

Individuals are not the exclusive measure of life in human societies. Human beings are required to live and work with the environing and material conditions of "nature" and with one another in unique ecological niches. Human life cannot be nurtured by talking and listening alone. The condition for maintaining a livelihood depends on the ways that language can be used in acting knowledgeably in discrete time and place exigencies to achieve a viable living. The environing and material exigencies of life must be drawn on to sustain a livelihood under conditions of an intergenerational cycle of life that requires access to knowledge, skill, and productive potentials that bring together diverse symmetries and asymmetries in language-mediated relationships.

Teamwork entails complementarities in skills and coordinated actions achieved through the use of signaling and the spoken word. A hunt, for example, requires coordination both to achieve success and to allocate the catch among those participating in the hunt. Communication in the context of living a life and gaining a livelihood, then, gives meaning to the names used in the articulation of semantics expressed in a grammar of subject-predicate-object relationships and in a logic of purposive action. Learning to use a language and the regularized use of language in coming to terms with the meaning of life are the bases for the shared communities of understanding and common knowledge that give meaning to the words and syntax used in a language. Diverse relationships are mediated by and bound together through language usages that permeate all aspects of life among intelligible beings functioning in speech communities.

Human cognition is, however, profoundly affected by the way that languages give expression to ways of conceptualizing what human beings experience in the course of living their lives. Wilhelm von Humboldt observed, "By the same process whereby he spins language out of his own being, he ensnares himself in it; and each language draws a magic circle round the people to which it belongs, a circle from which there is no escape save by stepping out of it into another" (quoted in Cassirer [1946] 1953, 9).

The possibility exists, then, that individuals become the slaves of their linguistic and cultural tools unless they develop a critical awareness of the potentials and limitations inherent in languages as the cognitive-social-working "machinery" that is an essential part of life in human societies. The biological [genetic] constraints pertaining to speaking and listening, then, affect fundamental patterns of association in human communities and represent commonalities that are constitutive of order among different human societies.

I presume, then, that Tocqueville was correct when he asserted that "villages," "towns," or "tithing" exist in "all nations" ([1835–40] 1945, 1:60). Wherever a number of people collect themselves in such communities of relationships, they seem to constitute themselves in ways that are "perfectly natural." Such communities are not the only patterns of association but include reference to families in households and compounds whose members become associated in cooperative exchange relationships and potential conflicts with other householders (Netting 1993). Diverse patterns of association of varying symmetrical and asymmetrical forms become constitutive of speech communities that have the characteristics of neighborhoods, tithings, villages, townships, parishes, communes, and so on, which give expression to communities of relationships associated with essential complementarities for gaining livelihoods and giving meaning to an intergenerational cycle of life. Institutions in such contextualities lay the foundations for the self-organizing and self-governing arrangements in which neighbors in human societies learn to cope with both the inconveniences and the opportunities that neighborhood brings. Tocqueville considered the existence of such communities to be "coeval with that of man" among all mankind ([1835—40] 1945, 1:60).

Diverse "settlements" of kin and neighbors get embedded in larger structures of authority relationships. The latifundia of Peru, Chile, and Brazil were constitutive of aristocracies reflecting diverse systems of imperial authority (Freyre 1946, 1963, 1970; Loveman 1976). The great imperial estates of the Russian tsardom following Ivan IV were vastly different than the latifundia of the Portuguese Empire in Brazil and the plantations of the American South (cf. Beaumont [1835] 1958b; Freyre 1946; Pipes 1974). The "townships" in the Old Northwest in the United States were units of land measurement intended to embody settlement patterns and institutions of a different order of magnitude than the latifundia of Brazil, the imperial estates of Russia, the plantations of the American South, and the collective farms of the Soviet Union. Yet similarities among these institutions exist as *Homo sapiens* in speech communities are required to cope with the conditions of life. These similarities and differences should not be glossed over. They need to be deeply understood and appreciated as being constitutive of systems of order in human societies.

The way that the speech communities of villages, towns, tithings, estates, and plantations get put together in the larger configuration of speech communities turns on the way that the larger patterns of order get put together. Boundary conditions apply to limits, and the problems of dealing with these limits are represented by eternal struggles among peoples everywhere. These struggles have fueled imperial aspirations through all of recorded history. The way of resisting imperial aspirations turns on creating distinct cultural and linguistic patterns that distinguish "us" from "them" in ways that can be distinguished by those seeking to sort themselves out from others.

The more open relationships are, the greater the ease of communication and the assorted pattern of relationships that apply to the uses and misuses of languages. These uses and misuses of languages are potentially productive of common knowledge, shared communities of understanding, patterns of social accountability, and mutual trust, or of the contrary attributes that reflect the absence of such potentials. Common knowledge represents shared expectations about one's relationships to one's world. Shared communities of understanding represent shared expectations about measures of value that serve as standards of judgment about how to relate to one's world. Agreement about joint activities turns on shared standards of evaluation that serve as a basis for both agreement and patterns of accountability presuming complementary efforts to keep and maintain complementary sets of relationships among those who associate with each other. Mutual trust is derivative of keeping promises and striving to maintain complementary patterns in more general communities of relationships. An openness of boundary conditions permits the emergence of open public realms characteristic of the *res publica* condition that allows for emerging potentials. The circumstance applicable to universal public goods means that human beings have incentives to seek out new relationships in which, if latent potentials could be brought to realization, everyone would be better off if all others had access to those potentials. The misuse and abuse of language places them at risk.

Diverse and Complementary Uses of Language

In what might be called "the political economy of life," any productive effort requires the use of diverse means [resources and tools] to achieve some future apparent good, as implied by Hobbes's definition of the term *power:* "present means, to obtain some future apparent good" ([1651] 1960, 56). This relationship is characteristic of all artisanship and all purposive activities. There are always problems in dealing with interdependencies in alternative and joint uses of necessary means, and any effort to achieve some future apparent good is likely to yield an array of effects—products, by-products, and residuals. The range of contingencies applicable to human artisanship can be constrained with reference to both domain [spatial dimensions] and scope [the factor-function-product or present-means → future-apparent-good relationships]. These contingencies are important in addressing potentials for isolability, permitting autonomies, and taking account of interdependencies in some fields of effects, or states of affairs, while recognizing other interdependencies that may transcend any given boundary conditions.

We confront a most difficult conceptual and ontological problem. We make distinctions, classify, and relate elements to one another in diverse levels of analysis because of the radical limits that apply to human cognitive and action potentials. We presume potentials for isolability because we could not function to realize creative potentials without presuming some significant degree of autonomy and some significant degree of openness in the patterns of ordered relationships that are constitutive of the universe in which we live. Thus, we search for alternatives, for opportunities to exercise choice, but with an awareness that alternatives are subject to being joined to still other conditions that are not included in an analysis. The standing of individuals from a perspective of methodological individualism needs to recognize that human individuality is joined to biological, linguistic, cultural, and social contextualities that function in the jointnesses of complex configurations of relationships. Our effort to come to an understanding of the place of language in the political economy of life in human societies requires that we view the diverse uses of languages as being alternative uses but that we recognize at the same time that diverse uses occur with complementarities that have features of jointness.

The problematic can be illustrated with reference to the study of what might be called a "water industry" (Bain, Caves, and Margolis 1966). A variety of joint and alternative uses of water fit into the political economy of life anywhere. These typically have to do with navigation, floods and flood control, drainage, discharge and dissipation of wastes, power generation, domestic consumption, municipal and industrial uses, irrigation, fish and wildlife preservation, and so on (V. Ostrom 1968). Such uses can be specified, assessed in relation to supply and demand in discrete situational exigencies, and evaluated based on how structure and conduct relate to performance.

In *The Production and Distribution of Knowledge in the United States* (1962), Fritz Machlup attempted such an analysis of what might be alluded to as the "knowledge industry." The use or consumption aspects in Machlup's study were neglected. The production-exchange-consumption functions of an economic ordering as used in economic analysis often neglect the use or consumption aspects, with serious implications for the analysis of "household" [eco/*oikos*] economies. A "language industry" that applies to a delimited scope of attention pertaining to easily accessible substitutes is not possible for me to imagine. Rather, languages transcend all the realms of communication and discourse in human societies and all aspects of life. We need, despite all of the difficulties involved, to focus on diverse language usages in an effort to explore the place of language in the political economy of life in human societies.

At this juncture, it is also necessary to recognize the poverty of language. Learning depends on making meaningful distinctions. Yet distinctions in classificatory schema may not yield mutually exclusive and exhaustive sets and subsets. The earlier reference to a variety of joint and alternative uses of water resources recognizes that jointness may coexist with the availability of alternatives. Alternative uses imply alternatives forgone, which at some contingencies of supply in dealing with water supply systems means the sacrifice of other potentials that are conjoined to the use being made. This is a potential source of difficulty in all classificatory schema, because the elements in a subset are bound together by some form of complementarity that gives coherence to the meaning associated with the set and subset distinctions: elements function in sets accompanying some ordering principle. There is no single ordering principle. My reference set of water usages—navigation, flood control, drainage, discharge and dissipation of wastes, power generation, domestic consumption, municipal and industrial uses, irrigation, fish and wildlife preservation, and so on—is not a mutually exclusive and exhaustive set but an ambiguous set of joint and alternative uses that might, in turn, be associated with in-the-channel uses and on-the-land uses. These classifications are human conventions that serve human purposes. Human beings do not possess a level of intelligibility to perceive all levels of discreetness functioning in all configurations of relationships.

An effort to make distinctions in patterns of joint and alternative uses of human languages might include the following: (1) communicating, including signaling; (2) thinking; (3) arraying alternatives; (4) ordering choices [specifying standards of selection]; (5) planning; (6) acting to realize potentials; (7) assessing consequences; (8) critical reflection and explanation; (9) constituting the corpus of knowledge; and (10) fashioning patterns of identities and meanings. Each of these uses or functions of language works in ways that is complementary among joint and alternative uses. Given the limits to human communicative and cognitive potentials, each use is potentially a distinct "object" of focal attention, but the coherence of linguistic articulations and of cultural manifestations means that each of these uses has its fit in complexly configured relationships. Scholars like Hannah Arendt, Ernst Cassirer, Susanne Langer, George

Steiner, and Tzvetan Todorov are likely to use quite different categories than I have used to characterize the uses of language.

A concern with language and culture in constituting order in human societies suggests a preoccupation with the pragmatics of language that bears on the relationship of "ideas" to "deeds," as Milovan Djilas has expressed the basic pattern of relationships in human societies. In *The Unperfect Society,* Djilas has asserted that, "The idea and the deed are indivisible because an idea is always an idea of a deed, an idea of creation . . ." (1969, 230). The difficulty is how to come to terms with the relationship of ideas and deeds. If they were "indivisible" in some radical sense, there would exist a unity: One—a fully joined entity. My reference to ten uses or functions of language implies a ten-dimensional configuration of relationships. Any such possibility exceeds my cognitive limits. I cannot comprehend the world of ideas and of deeds as though they were One. I must acknowledge my own fallibility and presume the fallibility of all individuals who are *Homo sapiens.* Our challenge, then, is how to take languages that run the risk of profuse babbling and use them in ways that enhance the responsible use of human knowledge, skills, and intelligibility within meaningful expressions of artisanship in processes of being and becoming.

We might, instead of presuming an intuitive comprehension, give successive attention to each dimension and develop an awareness of how these different dimensions relate to one another. An example of the simplest type of intuition in relating ideas to deeds is my experience in working with a cabinetmaker. An "idea" [conception] for a coffee table with a free-form design occurred to me while I was looking through an assortment of boards. Two boards, some tools, screws, glue, sandpaper, and finishing oil were used to create a unique table far different than a mere sum of the parts. Anyone with an intelligible understanding of furniture making would know what had occurred to transform a few items into a table of a distinctive sort and would know how to make proper use of that table. But it did not just happen. It was wrought from the material resource of "nature." It could be explained, but only by reference to human intelligibility and human artisanship. Every use of language entails an artisanship relevant to its function in some artifactual creation that then may require commensurate patterns of use as it functions in ways of life. That table continues to have an important place in the household that is my home. So, too, do the books and authors with whom I live and work.

The potentials for making use of languages in relating ideas to deeds are significantly modified by the technologies implicit in the structure of languages. The spoken language greatly amplifies human capabilities as applied to the diverse uses of languages, in contrast to a reliance on signaling alone. In turn, the technologies of writing and printing greatly amplify human potentials. So, too, has the development of electronic languages in the uses of tools and in the potential for simultaneously transmitting pictorial images, speech, and the printed word. These technologies are thus potentially interactive in cumulative ways. However, they are subject to the limiting conditions that involve their *use* and *misuse* by fallible human beings. Communication and its relationship to learning, memory, habituation, a very limited span of attention, and conceptions of dimensionality operate within the limits of each individual's aggregate capabilities to achieve effective mastery of ideas and skills. Whatever any single individual can accomplish is severely limited. Those limits can be modified only by intelligible communication in which mutual understanding is grounded in common knowledge and shared communities of understanding, which are the bases for assigning meaning to words and achieving coordination in diverse forms of associated activities to yield deeds in specific time and place exigencies.

The radical transformation achieved by technologies of writing and printing might be illustrated by a few allusions to how technology has affected the constitution of the corpus of knowledge. I presume that some form of symbolic representation by physical depiction has long been a part of human experience. The Chinese characters remain a part of a long tradition of pictographic written symbolic expressions. The use of an alphabet based on phonetics is confined to no more than the last five or six millennia of human experience. The application of printing to an alphabetical language is of much more recent origin, something like five or six centuries. Biologically we might calculate five generations to the century, fifty to a millennium. The transformation in the technologies of languages wrought in the last five millennia has been of radical proportions, greatly transforming the cultural, social, and material conditions of human life, even though the basic conditions applicable to "human nature" in a biological sense have changed relatively little.

I presume that the traditions associated with Moses, Confucius, Plato, Aristotle, and the Buddha have been made possible only by access to written languages. Eric Voegelin identifies Confucius, Lao Tzu, the Buddha, Isaiah, Pythagoras, and Heraclitus as "members of the same generation" (1957, 20). These traditions continue to shape the emergence of human civilizations, and each of these traditions in themselves has brought together substantial achievements in reflecting about and in giving order to the corpus of human knowledge, which, in turn, has made its contribution to important literary traditions. The magnitude of these achievements associated only with the Hebraic, Greek, and Roman traditions, as great as they are, was seriously diminished by the destruction of great libraries in Alexandria, Athens, Antioch, Baghdad, Constantinople, and Rome. Handcrafted manuscripts were plundered and burned by men of pride. When Hobbes wrote "Of Man" in *Leviathan,* he provided only the barest outline when addressing the several subjects comprising the corpus of knowledge. Diderot and the French *philosophes* created an encyclopedia as a general way of formatting the corpus of knowledge. As important and useful as such efforts have been, they inevitably demonstrate their limits. The very corpus of knowledge continues to unfold in ways that could not have been anticipated by fallible creatures.

In the world of human experience associated with the uses of written languages, the profusions of what has been produced are enormous—beyond my limited capabilities to imagine. These profusions even within the confines of a single language—English—are extraordinary: all accumulated writings, records, archives, libraries, and so on. Michel Foucault, in *The Archaeology of Knowledge* ([1972] 1982), uses the metaphor of an archaeological investigation as the mode for investigating these linguistic accumulations. Yet the essential relationship of "ideas" to "deeds" depends on discrete individuals in discrete language communities achieving complementarities in their uses of language. The meaning of language connects signaling, communicating, thinking, arraying alternatives, ordering choice, planning, acting, achieving deeds, assessing results, reflecting critically on what occurred in shared communities of understanding, and constituting a corpus of knowledge among people whose actions are mediated with reference to complementarities in rule-ordered relationships as ways of ordering choice.

Not every idea or every use of words is of equal significance in what can be accomplished. There are, however, "necessities" in the relationship of specific ideas to particular deeds. In the realm of artisanship, ideas pertaining to the use of some necessary means to achieve some future apparent good imply intelligible use of ideas, mediated by skillful actions exercised on the necessary means to achieve what gets done. At the same time, the necessary components in creating any artifact turns on the place of particular ideas in a more general corpus of knowledge and in structures of authority relationships by which individuals are associated with others in configurations of rule-ordered relationships involving varying degrees of symmetry and asymmetry in complexly structured social realities. An operational realm in acting on material conditions is necessarily complemented by an epistemic realm having to do with thought, knowledge, and aspirations and by a social and political realm of acting with reference to others in rule-ordered relationships. These are simultaneously at work in the constitution of order in all human societies and are brought together with regard to systems of identity and identification that bear on the "spiritual" and aesthetic qualities of life.

Given the immense profusion of linguistic utterances expressed in written forms, the enhancement of human productive potential is threatened by inundations of babbling. The "pollution" of the physical environment is dwarfed by comparison to potentials for the pollution of the human mind without the acquisition of greatly enhanced capabilities in learning how to make more critical and disciplined uses of language and without the development of criteria for the ordering of choices and for the critical assessment of human experience. Every use of language entails selection, and processes of selection are applicable to craftsmanship, which, in turn, implies that principles of selection are manifest in what is achieved. The uses, misuses, and abuses of language play a critical role in relating ideas to deeds in whatever it is that human beings do and accomplish. The concept of "free speech" cannot resolve the problem of language. Heaping profusions on profusions only implies superabundant profusenesses in linguistic articulations. Problems of Newspeak and Doublethink are likely to prevail in patterns of deception and self-deception evoked by political rhetoric. An "economy of superabundance" in linguistic articulations can be a greater evil than an "economy of scarcity": silence in due proportions is necessary to thought. The essential problem is how to select from and order the superabundant brambles of linguistic articulations. What is required, then, are disciplined, responsible, and intelligible uses of languages, and those requirements depend on a deep and coherent comprehension of the place of language in the political economy of life in human societies. I have merely posed the problem and laid the foundations for further inquiries that can be extended much further. My own efforts are only a few small steps along the way.

All of life in human societies is bound up with the matrices of language and the uses made of languages. In a concluding paragraph to his discussion of rational choice in economics and psychology, Vernon Smith, an experimental economist, recognizes the pervasive character of the contextuality of language usage and of the rules used to govern everyday affairs.

> Language learning in children occurs in a social context. Without contact with people, children do not learn to speak. If they have such contact, they learn to speak in the total absence of formal instruction. But the same case can be said of decision making: I could substitute "make market decisions" for "speak" in the last two sentences and they would apply to what we have learned in the laboratory about

adults. On the basis of cognition alone, without the language of the market and ongoing social interaction with other agents, rational decision is frustratingly illusive. (1991, 894)

Until we develop a greater self-consciousness of the importance of languages and the modes of artisanship in the proper uses of languages, we are likely to find ourselves becoming isolable and helpless individuals adrift in oceans of words. In such circumstances, we are apt to lose ourselves in fantasies, fall back on the phylogenetic resources of Wolves among the Primates, and begin to prey on one another.

The Constitutive and Transformational Character of Language

The critical reader in the Public-Choice tradition of inquiry will recognize that in the course of this inquiry about the place of language in the political economy of life, I have variously referred to language as "rule-ordered relationships," to language as a "good," and to language in "the constitution of speech communities." I have thus associated language with the characteristics of each of the basic elements used in the mode of analysis that I characterize as "institutional analysis." That critical observation is indeed correct. Instead of being separable, these basic elements are conjoined in multifaceted ways that pervade human relationships. Man spins language out of his own being, to paraphrase Humboldt, and ensnares himself in it. That condition can only be transcended by stepping out of one's vernacular language into other languages, to acquire the capabilities for reflecting about the human condition in the context of diverse language communities aware of the extreme limits of human cognition and actions in making proper use of languages in human affairs.

At the individual level, language is a set of rule-ordered relationships that can be regarded as an institution. At the level of collectivities, language is a public good within the boundary conditions of any particular collectivity. The learning, use, and alteration of language articulations is constitutional in character, applicable to the constitutive character of human personality, to patterns of human association, and to the aggregate structure of the conventions of language usage. While important aspects of languages can be carefully delineated in elements and relationships and can be treated with logical rigor, the way in which the aggregate structure of languages function in human societies suggests that the aggregate configurations of meaning and their function are not subject to simple quantification and explication. The way languages are associated with institutions, goods, cultures, and personality attributes means that we find languages permeating all aspects of human existence as we have come to know the human condition.

The human condition itself is transformed by the way that language functions in a transformational way to affect the artifactual nature of life that is shaped by the use of human knowledge. The nature of the *senses* themselves are transformed as instruments of measurement, and instruments for working with materials are developed and skillfully used in whatever human beings accomplish. The disparate *senses* of a biological endowment are both integrated and extended with a *sense of participation* in whatever human beings learn to do and to perfect through skillful applications drawing on normative standards of judgment. These extensions of the meaning of *sense* accruing from the social character of human existence mean that the *sense of participation* becomes associated with what can be thought of as *common sense*. Standards of judgment come to be reflected in a *common sense of virtue* that includes reference to diverse virtues. These accrue as a function of human achievements that are worthy of emulation. Such standards of judgment are not statistical artifacts about human population but measures of aspiration and achievement. When put together in skillful ways, the Great Societies that reach to global proportions are capable of remarkable achievements. Graham Wallas's Great Society was not, however, a society confined to Nation-States.

The problematics of Graham Wallas's Great Society are greatly compounded when we add the conjecture offered by Henry Sumner Maine in *Ancient Law*. Maine saw the patterns of development from the ancient law of preliterate societies to modern "progressive societies" as a general evolutionary "movement *from Status to Contract*" ([1861] 1864: 165). This movement was accompanied by presumptions of individual competence and autonomy marked by essential equality implying that each individual as a mature and independent being is capable of making binding commitments in relation to others in interdependent relationships. This poses a challenge for individuals who occupy the positions of persons and citizens to become sufficiently knowledgeable in the acquisition, use, and development of the arts and sciences of association to function in *free* societies consistent with requirements of liberty and justice.

The transformations of languages achieved through writing, printing, and electronic communication are inevitably accompanied by both opportunities and dangers. These developments in language, communication, and the practice of human artisanship have been associated with the emergence of modern civilization. Electronic communication has brought both voice and pictorial representations into the presence of nursing infants at the beginning of natal life, if not into their experience of prenatal life. The whole world of human experience, intensified to achieve dramatic effect, is accessible to every infant and growing child through the electronics of the television tube. Such technologies put at risk the notion that learning is to be nurtured with regard to precepts to be transmitted through the reflective experience of parents, grandparents, prior generations, and the common sense accruing among friends and neighbors in human communities. The drama of violence, the passions of sexuality, and the presence of tragedy, rage, and outrage are amplified by cinematic magic to attract and occupy attention. The habits of the heart and mind that are constitutive of the moral and intellectual tradition of a people are placed at risk: violence, passion, tragedy, rage, and outrage become commonplace.

Study: Americanizing Can Ruin Dream

Baltimore—The more American customs the children of immigrants adopt, the less likely they are to do well in school and chase the dream that brought their families here, researchers said Friday.

The researchers found that nearly all immigrant children prefer to speak English instead of the language of their parents. They also found these children generally outperformed U.S.-born children in school, and spend more time on homework and less watching television.

But "the longer they have lived in the United States and among those who were born here, there is a tendency toward lower grades and lower aspirations," said Ruben G. Rumbaut, a sociologist at Michigan State University.

(Associated Press, *Herald-Times,* February 10, 1996)

How human beings will respond to such circumstances I cannot say. If events take their own course, motivated by short-term audience appeal, we can expect the spectacle of Spectator Democracies to unfold as a farce for everyone to see on their farseeing tubes. I doubt, however, that such a scenario will be the end of the story. The opportunity for critical reflection in light of experience and the prior accumulations of critical reflections about the human experience means that human beings need not be the passive victims of deception; we have the potentials for learning and innovation. Languages are not simple determinants of human existence but essential working tools that are themselves alterable by human creativity. How that creativity will manifest itself in the future I cannot know. I still live in Plato's Cave, with others with whom I can communicate and who have access to libraries, farseeing tubes, and all of the other potentials that can be used and abused. What will happen in the unfolding drama of Plato's Cave I cannot know; but languages provide us with access to whatever stocks of fantasy and knowledge and to whatever flows of information and misinformation are available to us as human beings.

CHAPTER 7

The Ontological Foundations of Human Understanding

I have attempted to address the place of language in the political economy of life in a way that gives some analytical leverage that goes a few steps beyond the analysis of the human condition. Adaptive potentials are accompanied by threats that pose problems for the constitution of order. Before those threats can be resolved, human beings confront the *necessity* of coming to terms with the artisanship applicable to the constitution of systems of order of their own creation. A basic paradigmatic challenge arises from at least two contrary ways of constituting order. One way relies on a single ultimate center of Supreme Authority constituted as Sovereign, which exercises a power of command and control over people as members of a Society. A contrary theory relies on power to check power amid opposite and rival interests. The latter approach depends on shared communities of understanding among individuals and requires the mediation of conflict and the achievement of conflict resolution consistent with the creation of shared communities of understanding under changing conditions of life occurring in the context of continued learning and cultural evolution.

I earlier explored the problem of Newspeak and Doublethink and noted the close parallel between Orwell's version of Newspeak and the New Newspeak I refer to as increasingly characteristic of American and European political discourse. No Great Experiment is immune to the threat of becoming a monumental disaster. This threat is a manifestation both of the Faustian bargain necessary to the achievement of order in human societies and of the circumstance that dangers exist whenever and wherever adaptive potentials are available.

Such possibilities pose serious anomalies for what might be called "a political science"; and those anomalies apply to all of the social and cultural sciences and humanities and to anyone preoccupied with the meaning of democracy. The modern world has widespread aspirations for something called "democracy." Those aspirations pose questions about the feasibility of systems of governance in which people as citizens exercise basic rulership prerogatives rather than being subjects under the command and control of some single center of Supreme Authority.

My analysis of the place of language in the political economy of life has recognized that language, like peace, justice, or free trade, is a type of good that increases in value as it is shared among more people. The greater the number of people who enjoy justice, peace, free trade, and common languages, the better off people will be. The condition of scarcity does not apply. Problems arise in the patterns of use; and these problems have their roots in the biological condition affecting communication, thinking, and action potentials of *Homo sapiens* as a genetically endowed form of life. Potentials for learning, communicating, thinking, choosing, and accomplishing whatever people might aspire to accomplish depend on the maintenance of standards bearing on proper performance. *Nomos/logos* relationships are closely associated in the constitution of speech communities and of affecting coevolutionary facets of life in human societies. Methods of logical thinking are themselves rule-governed; languages are rule-governed.

In undertaking this inquiry about the ontological foundations of human understanding, I take as my point of departure Eric Voegelin's effort to address himself to "the new science of politics" (1952), which I shall juxtapose to Alexis de Tocqueville's assertion that "A new science of politics is needed for a new world" ([1835–40] 1945, 1:7). I have referred to Tocqueville's allusions to a science and art of association in which "the science of association is the mother of science" in democratic countries. According to Tocqueville, "the progress of all the rest depends upon the progress it has made" ([1835–40] 1945, 2:110), and the art of association is "the mother of action, studied and applied by all" (ibid., 2:117).

Voegelin made no reference to Tocqueville in his five-volume work *Order and History*, in *From Enlightenment to Revolution* (1975), or in *The New Science of Politics* (1952). Yet I am persuaded that both Voegelin and Tocqueville addressed fundamental issues about the ontological foundations of human understanding necessary to the viability of democratic societies. As one who aspires to being both a political scientist and a citizen of a democratic society, I am required to render my own judgment about the place of ontology in the constitution of democratic systems of order. Voegelin's preoccupation was with the place of God in the community of being. Hobbes's Sovereign was accountable only to God. Tocqueville was also preoccupied with the place of religion in democratic societies. In addressing the place of religious precepts in systems of knowledge, I shall indicate the complementarities in Voegelin's, Hobbes's, and Tocqueville's analyses and carry the analysis forward to indicate my own conclusions about the transcendental character of order that establishes the basis for coherence in systems of knowledge. Religious precepts, I conclude, have a fundamental place in systems of knowledge.

I shall then turn to the place of "science" in the interpretation of history. This problem became a preoccupation for Ibn Khaldûn, a fourteenth-century Islamic historian of Spanish ancestry. In my judgment, his fundamental conceptualization has been reinforced by Tocqueville's analysis, which presumes that the culture of a democratic society must be grounded in a culture of inquiry. This implies that histories are accounts of evolutionary paths associated with the uses of language and knowledge and with the conduct of artisanship in problem-solving ways of life. A science of culture and cultural evolution must necessarily be open to innovation and change. Unfortunately, different types of error may abound. Habituation may be sufficiently strong to preserve erroneous concepts against challenge. Other fundamental concepts may be challenged for the wrong reasons.

The Place of Religion in Systems of Knowledge

Voegelin's Statement of the Problem

In *Israel and Revelation,* the first volume of *Order and History,* Voegelin opened his introduction with the following assertion.

> God and man, world and society form a primordial community of being. The community with its quaternarian structure is, and is not, a datum of human experience. It is a datum of experience in so far as it is known to man by virtue of his participation in the mystery of its being. It is not a datum of experience in so far as it is not given in the manner of an object of the external world but is knowable only from the perspective of participation in it [the mystery of being]. (1956, 1)

The quaternary [fourfold] features of human existence require reference to (1) God, (2) man, (3) world, and (4) society and to the way these are related to each other. Much of existence in the sense of *being* and *becoming* is *not* given in "the manner of an object of the external world." Existence cannot be seen as having a fully "objective" reality.

There is, then, some "reality" that can only be known by "participation in the mystery of being." The mystery of being implies recourse to the nonmaterial spiritual feature of existence. There is, then, a fundamental aspect of ignorance at "the decisive core of existence" (ibid., 2). And that decisive core of existence pertains, as Hobbes has expressed the problem, to the thought that "there is some cause, whereof there is no former cause, but is eternal; which is it men call God" ([1651] 1960, 68). A critical feature at the core of existence is a decisive ignorance that cannot be surmounted. This leaves human beings with a quality of blindness at the core of their existence.

> At the center of his existence man is unknown to himself and must remain so, for the part of being that calls itself man could be known fully only if the community of being and its drama in time were known as a whole. Man's partnership [participation] in being is the essence of his existence, and this essence depends on the whole, of which existence is a part. Knowledge of the whole, however, is precluded by the identity of the knower with the partner, and ignorance of the whole precludes essential knowledge of the part. (Voegelin 1956, 2)

The core in the mystery of being cannot be seen or touched. That aspect of what Voegelin referred to as the community of being cannot be experienced in a finite and knowable way by participating in the mystery of being. The ideas—the conceptions—of a Transcendent Order of Being can potentially be experienced at a level of apperception and symbolization by human participation in the mystery of being. We only know by the way we experience ourselves as participants in the mystery of being. Charles Darwin reported his experience of seeing the panorama from the crest of the Cordillera as like "hearing in full orchestra a chorus of the Messiah" ([1839] 1958, 278).

Such possibilities, however, give rise to extraordinary opportunities for fantasy and free association. Aspects of being are required to be consonant with the whole and thus are potentially capable of withstanding critical reflections. We are left with the circumstance, expressed to me by Filippo Sabetti, that Carlo Cattaneo identified the search for the eternal as an *ontological necessity* and as a *necessary epistemological contingency*. There are metaphysical presuppositions that cannot be proved and that provide the ontological foundations for epistemological standards of judgment.

A Restatement of the Problem

My problem is that I cannot know the answer to the mystery of being. Even if I acknowledge the possibility of divine intervention in the revelations of prophets, like Moses and Muhammad, I still face inevitable limits in the symbolization of language. I assign meaning to the words on the printed page, and the meaning I assign is grounded, as a first approximation, in the conventions of the speech communities in which I participate. What I comprehend turns, then, on my efforts to use my intelligibility to construe what is being said about the mystery of being, which must, in some fundamental sense, be and remain a mystery. Yet I presume that there is a mystery that must of necessity be accepted as a "reality"—an ontological necessity—and that such an ontological necessity is an epistemological contingency. This position is consistent with Gödel's formulation that there can be no complete system of logic—that there are necessary ontological/metaphysical presuppositions that cannot themselves be proved.

The problem is compounded both by the opportunities for fantasies and free associations about such a mystery and by the dogmatism with which beliefs are held about the characteristics associated with that mystery or with which the existence of such a mystery of being is denied. The dogmatism with which the mystery of being is denied has been identified as the source of the crisis of Western civilization. That dogmatism, in turn, was provoked by the dogmatism where words on paper were assigned meaning in the context of paradigmatic challenges associated with the Copernican and Darwinian formulations. One of the problematics confronting a scholar concerned with something called "political theory," as that pertains to a political science and the relevance of that theory for something called "democracy," turns on ontological necessities that function as necessary epistemological contingencies.

For Voegelin, the community of being had reference to God, man, world, and society. I might translate *world* and *society* as "place" and "people." The way that people in their world relate to one another in societies is a way of achieving adaptive potentials. I cannot claim to have had any direct personal divine inspiration. Yet coping with multitudinous problem-solving efforts and observing the world in which I live evokes an openness to a mystery of being that I cannot deny. Critical reflection leads me to believe that an awareness of such mysteries is a necessity in the constitution of order in democratic societies. If religion is a necessity in the conceptualization of paradigmatically diverse formulations, religion might be viewed as a necessary element in a system of knowledge pertaining to the constitution of order. We do, however, face the problem of those systems of order that were constituted under circumstances of explicitly *rejecting* religion as a necessary feature in their constitution. We have the potential, then, of those who reject religion becoming the *prophets* of new *secular religions*. What we call "ideologies" may be the source of the most profound pathologies in human personal and social disorders. I shall next refer briefly to the way that both Thomas Hobbes and Alexis de Tocqueville treat religion as a necessity for the constitution of order in their dif-

ferent paradigmatic formulations. I shall then advance some tentative conclusions.

Hobbes's Analysis

Hobbes took the position that thought requires making distinctions. He
held that "whatsoever we imagine is *finite*" ([1651] 1960, 17, Hobbes's
emphasis). He then asserted, "When we say any thing is infinite, we signify
only, that we are not able to conceive the ends, and bounds of the things
named." He continued, "And therefore the name of God is used, not to
make us conceive him, for he is incomprehensible; and his greatness, and
power are inconceivable; but that we may honor him" (ibid.). Hobbes's
use of the third-person masculine pronoun in reference to God is, I presume, both literary license and literary convention consistent with
Voegelin's mystery of being. Honor is due from those who are participants
in the community of being, but there remains a mystery of being that cannot be known apart from a participatory awareness about mysteries of
being.

Hobbes, at a later juncture, explicitly tied the search for knowledge to
an allusion to God.

> Curiosity, or love of the knowledge of causes, draws a man from the
> consideration of the effect, to seek the cause; and again, the cause of
> that cause; till of necessity he must come to this thought at last, that
> there is some cause, whereof there is no former cause, but is eternal;
> which is it men call God. (Ibid., 68)

In a separate chapter, "Of Religion," Hobbes took the position that "there
are no signs, nor fruit of *religion,* but in man only . . . ; that the seed of *religion,* is also only in man; and consisteth in some peculiar quality . . . not to
be found in any other living creatures" (ibid., 69, Hobbes's emphasis).
Only human beings preoccupy themselves with the mystery of being. The
consequences yielded [fruits] are to be observed only in human beings with
reference to human actions and deeds accomplished. His analysis points to
diverse motives on the part of those who are the authors [creators] of religions, including those rulers "whose ends [are] only to keep the people in
obedience" (ibid., 75). What Hobbes referred to as a "true religion" is that
associated with the kingdom of God by covenant with his chosen [choos-
ing] people.

Hobbes's formulation of his "natural laws" were based on the Golden
Rule, which Hobbes stated as "*Do not that to another, which thou wouldest
not have done to thyself*" (ibid., 103, Hobbes's emphasis). Jesus of

Nazareth is reported in the Gospel according to Matthew as saying in the Sermon on the Mount, "Therefore all things whatsoever ye would that men should do to you, do ye even so to them: for this is the law and the prophets" (Matt. 7:12). Hillel, the great Jewish teacher who was contemporary to Jesus of Nazareth, regarded this principle as the fundamental rule when he asserted, "What is unpleasant to thyself, that do not to thy neighbor is the whole Law, all else is but its exposition" (*Encyclopaedia Britannica*, 1967, XI: 496). Confucius, when asked if any one word could be adopted as a lifelong rule of conduct, in a similar way articulated a principle of "sympathy"—"Do not do to others what you would not like yourself" ([1910] 1937, bk. 15, chap. 23). For Hobbes the Golden Rule suggested a method of normative inquiry that would enable ordinary mortals to take account of their own interests and the interests of others so as to discount their own "passions and self-love" and arrive at agreeable standards of fairness and justice. I have, in chapter 4, table 4.1, characterized Hobbes's exposition of his "natural laws" as articles of peace that would serve as the foundations constitutive of human communities.

In his chapter "Of the Kingdom of God by Nature," Hobbes explicitly identifies his "laws of nature" with the "Divine laws" associated with "God's sovereignty." An *explicit* reference is made to "the fourteenth and fifteenth chapters of this treatise [*Leviathan*]" ([1651] 1960, 235). To worship God is to honor God, and "obedience to his laws, that is, in this case to the laws of nature, is the greatest worship of all" (ibid., 239). Hobbes also identifies worship with the Latin term *cultus,* which refers "properly, and constantly, [to] that labor which a man bestows on any thing, with a purpose to make benefit by it" (ibid., 235). He distinguishes between agriculture as being subject to the cultivator, in which the profits yielded accrue to the cultivator, and circumstances where labor is bestowed on those who are *not subject* but are to be won by "good offices," that is, through what might be called "goodwill." This is the sense of culture that applies to a Sovereign *serving* his people. *Cultus Dei,* the worship of God, also involves the "culture" of and by a people with reference to cultivating the peace, concord, and prosperity of a commonwealth. To culture is to cultivate.

In Hobbes's theory of sovereignty, the unity of law depends on a unity of power, meaning that the source of law resides in a single Supreme Authority, which for juridical purposes is the source of law, above the law, and cannot be held accountable to a rule of law by "subjects." The single source of law exercises, then, a monopoly of authority relationships and the lawful instruments of coercion in a society. That source of authority is consequently unalterable, complete, indivisible, and absolute in the sense that a Sovereign can do no legal wrong and is not accountable to other human beings. No legal remedy is available; therefore, no legal wrong can exist. The logic of Hobbes's theory of sovereignty, then, turns to a Sovereign's accountability to God; "subjects" are also bound to observe God's law. The Sovereign, in his accountability to God, is responsible to supervise the worship of his subjects on a presupposition that *"a kingdom divided in itself cannot stand"* (ibid., 119, Hobbes's emphasis).

The chapter dealing with the accountability of a Sovereign to God is accompanied by a warning about the natural punishments that will follow from a Sovereign's neglect of his accountability to God.

> Having thus briefly spoken of the natural kingdom of God, and his natural laws [Hobbes's chaps. 14 and 15], I will add only to this chapter a short declaration of his natural punishments. There is no action of man in this life, that is not the beginning of so long a chain of consequences, as no human providence is high enough, to give a man a prospect to the end. And in this chain, there are linked together both pleasing and unpleasing events; in such manner, as he that will do any thing for his pleasure, must engage himself to suffer all the pains annexed to it; and these pains, are the natural punishments of those actions, which are the beginning of more harm than good. And hereby it comes to pass, that intemperance is naturally punished with diseases; rashness, with mischances; injustice, with the violence of enemies; pride, with ruin; cowardice, with oppression; negligent government of princes, with rebellion; and rebellion, with slaughter. For seeing punishments are consequent to the breach of laws; natural punishments must be naturally consequent to the breach of the laws of nature; and therefore follow them as their natural, not arbitrary effects. (Ibid., 240–41)

Hobbes's association of natural punishments with the "laws of nature" would imply that a "true religion" reaches to a level of moral understanding that is the foundation of both community and jurisprudence. Not any command will serve a Sovereign equally well—only those that are grounded in methods of normative inquiry inherent in the principle of "Do unto others as you would have others do unto you." Applying that principle enables one to arrive at standards of fairness and justice. These standards apply to those participating in identifiable communities of relationships bound together in an overarching faith that any and all problems are tractable to resolutions by rendering honor to the mystery of being that is the Source of all Creation. *Cultus Dei* is an integral part of the diverse forms of *culture*—meaning both "to cultivate" and "shared learning and that derived from shared learning"—undertaken by human beings "with a purpose to make benefit by it." Human creativity is appropriately nurtured by honoring the Source of Creation in what one does.

Hobbes, however, warns that belief systems that pass for religion are not of equal merit with *cultus Dei,* even though religion is a necessary foundation for his theory of sovereignty. The necessary and sufficient conditions for a peaceful and prosperous commonwealth depend on faithful adherence by both subjects and Sovereigns to God's law. To avoid the anxieties provoked by "false religions," Hobbes assigns to his Sovereign responsibility for doing honor to God on behalf of the people of the Commonwealth: *"a kingdom divided in itself cannot stand."*

In the concluding chapter of *Leviathan,* "Of Commonwealth," Hobbes saw the constitution of order in his Commonwealth as being derived from "the principles of natural reason," but his reference to *natural* reason turns on the kingdom of God by *nature,* including reference to God's law as the basic principles that apply to his *natural laws* and reference to "moral philosophy" as being the "science of virtue and vice" (ibid., 104) and a "science of natural justice" (ibid., 241). God's law is thus a necessary element in the constitution of "right reason." Wolves among the Wolf of the Primates must learn to cultivate God's laws of right reason if they are to realize creative potentials beyond preying on others. Hobbes concludes that "the science of natural justice, is the only science necessary for Sovereigns and their principal ministers; and that they need not be charged with the sciences mathematical." God's law requires knowledgeable and intelligible application to become workable in human affairs. The "theorems of moral doctrine" that lay the foundations for a science of "natural justice" are the basis by which "men may learn thereby, both how to govern, and how to obey" (ibid.). God's law is an ontological necessity and a necessary epistemological contingency for Hobbes's theory of sovereignty.

The necessary and sufficient conditions for the peace and prosperity of Hobbes's commonwealth turn critically on both "subjects" and a Sovereign who adhere knowledgeably and intelligibly to God's law as articulated in Hobbes's "natural laws." The "natural laws" are "rational"—consistent with "right reason," presuming that human beings "naturally" seek to do what is "right" and that peace is the achievement of rightful relationships. There are fundamental ways in which religious precepts pertain to the foundations of right reason and *cultus Dei*—the worship of God. This *cultus Dei* would imply an investment in oneself to achieve a more meaningful and constructive orientation to the *being* and *becoming* relationship associated with participation in the *mystery of being* and the achievement of rightful relationships with others, with Creation, and with the Source of Creation. The term *nature* is being used in a different way than in Ashby's statement that *"every law of nature is a constraint"* (1956, 130). Choice is implied; but choice always occurs within constraints. The place of man-made constraints constituted as rule-ordered relationships require ontological foundations consistent with the Source of Creation and its Creation.

Tocqueville's Analysis

In chapter 2 of *Democracy in America,* immediately following his reference in chapter 1 to the American experiment as a "great experiment," Tocqueville identified the covenantal theology of the Puritans as "the germ of all that is to follow and the key to almost the whole work" ([1835–40] 1945, 1:28). Its formulation in the *Mayflower Compact* acknowledged the standing of the colonists as "loyal subjects of our dread Sovereign Lord King James" and the nature of their undertaking, "for the glory of God, and advancement of the Christian Faith, and the honour of our King and country" (ibid., 1:35). That undertaking was "to plant the first colony" in what was to become "New England." In that compact, they claim that they

> covenant and combine ourselves together into a civil body politick, for our better ordering and preservation, and furtherance of the ends aforesaid: and by virtue hereof do enact, constitute, and frame such just and equal laws, ordinances, acts, constitutions, and offices, from time to time, as shall be thought most meet and convenient for the general good of the Colony: unto which we promise all due submission and obedience. (Ibid.)

I construe this act as being a constitutional precommitment to use covenantal methods grounded in biblical traditions and in the traditions of the first Christian congregations for the constitutions of all civil bodies politic as those occasions might arise.

This key idea is at the constitutional level of analysis. The idea was constitutive of a self-governing society by which communities of covenanters chose to address themselves to the problems of constitutional choice and the maintenance of a self-governing system of constitutional governance. This is clearly associated with Hobbes's reference to God's law and to the methods of normative inquiry inherent in the Golden Rule as a means of establishing an equitable—just and equal—system of law. Such a system had been in practice among New Englanders within the British Empire for a century and a half before the *Declaration of Independence* and the establishment of the United States of America, first, in association with

Continental Congresses, in the *Articles of Confederation* and, then, with the document known as the *Constitution of the United States.* The first amendment to the Constitution, added during the ratification process in what has become known as the Bill of Rights, was a provision that Congress shall make no law regarding the establishment of religion. Such language is formally a prohibition with regard to the exercise of legislative authority by the Congress of the national government of the United States and carries the correlative implication that such authority is reserved to the states or the people. The doctrine of the freedom of religion was widely adhered to among state constitutions as a basic constitutional principle in American society.

In these circumstances, Tocqueville devotes nearly one-half of a chapter concerned with the principal causes that tend to maintain democracy in the United States to what can be regarded as an essay on religion as a political institution. The opening paragraph of that discussion asserts:

> By the side of every religion is to be found a political opinion, which is connected with it by affinity. If the human mind be left to follow its own bent, it will regulate the temporal and spiritual institutions of society in a uniform manner, and man will endeavor, if I may so speak, to *harmonize* earth with heaven. (Ibid., 1:300, Tocqueville's emphasis)

I construe this passage to mean that human beings strive to deal with patterns of order in coherent ways. Presuppositions associated with a spiritual or transcendent order will be accompanied by principles used to constitute and justify political orders commensurate with characteristic ways of life.

The initial settlement of "British America" was undertaken by people who brought with them a form of Christianity that rejected the authority of the Pope for a "democratic and republican religion" (ibid.). These people committed themselves to "covenant and combine" themselves into civil bodies politic. Catholic immigrants to New England, especially from Ireland, brought with them a Catholic clergy that accepted the separation of the ecclesiastical from the secular realm. This was articulated in the papal dictate of Gregory VII in 1075, which provided a basis for the acceptance of Catholic religious doctrine together with a political doctrine associated with democratic and republican institutions. Common precepts in both the New and Old Testaments in the biblical tradition were the basis for transcending theological differences.

Citizens who covenant and combine themselves together to form civil bodies politic in diverse communities of relationships still draw on basic religious precepts about the transcendental nature of order in organizing the way they think and how they relate to one another. A commitment to freedom of choice with reference to the organization of religious congregations still means that citizens, as the source of sovereign authority, rely on basic metaphysical precepts to constitute their way of thinking and relating to one another in democratic societies. It is in this sense that religion, as distinguished from sectarianism, can be considered a "political" institution.

If there is to be a political science, then the place that basic precepts about the mystery of being have in forming the foundation for conceptualizing systems of order also need to be included in efforts to understand and explain the constitution of order in human societies. In this sense, we can appreciate Tocqueville's assertion that "In the United States the influence of religion is not confined to the manners, but it extends to the intelligence of the people" (ibid., 1:304). Religion not only influences "the habits of the heart" as people relate to one another but "the habits of the mind" as people articulate their intelligibility in their use of knowledge in the constitution of order. This, then, is fundamental in societies where citizens are the source of duly constituted political authority by methods of constitutional choice in systems of constitutional government.

There is a mystery, then, about the mystery of being. The dogmatics of elevating definitions to become the "ultimate reality" in the exercise of scholarship is insufficient for people trying to understand the meaning of democracy. Rather, there are ontological necessities that are necessary epistemological contingencies in relating ideas to deeds. A failure to appreciate the place of the mystery of being as an ontological necessity implies that simple exercises in spinning definitions can be a trap in which words lose their meaning. Yet we human beings bear the burden of conveying meaning by the words we use in communicating with one another. A deep awareness about the mystery in the mystery of being is an ontological necessity and a necessary epistemological contingency. The mystery is most fully appreciated in face-to-face communication and in how we act and what we do in living and working with others. It is not enough to repudiate others and to defend one's own view of the world; it is necessary to attempt to search out common grounds for understanding while being honest with oneself and one's understanding of what it means to participate in the larger order of Creation.

These considerations then led to Tocqueville's conclusion: "Religion in America takes no direct part in the government of society, but it must be regarded as the first of their political institutions; for if it does not impart a taste for freedom, it facilitates the use of it" (ibid., 1:305). What shapes the way people think about themselves, their relationship with others, and their world in realizing productive [adaptive] potentials is an essential ingredient in shaping the constitution of order in human societies. Basic presuppositions about the transcendent character of order associated with the mystery of being are thus essential elements in constituting human societies as communities of being.

Some Preliminary Reflections about the Necessity of Religion in the Constitution of Order

My own presumptions about human fallibility and the propensity to err do not take one very far in dealing with the problem of knowledge. Being a philosophical *agnostic* is no resolution to the problem of *gnosticism* as pertaining to faith in knowledge. We need to give critical attention to the problem of cognition—the relationship of human perception to understanding. We must also attend to what human beings do and accomplish— the relationship of ideas, expressed in words, to deeds.

Uses and Abuses of Language

The relationship of ideas to deeds is an issue that Hobbes addressed with regard to the uses and abuses of language. The following passage is deserving of careful attention.

> So that in the right definition of names lies the first use of speech; which is the acquisition of science: and in the wrong, or no definitions, lies the first abuse; from which proceed all false and senseless tenets; which make those men that take their instruction from the authority of books, and not from their own meditation, to be as much below the condition of ignorant men, as men endued with true science are above it. For between true science and erroneous doctrines, ignorance is in the middle. Natural sense and imagination are not subject to absurdity. Nature itself cannot err; and as men abound in the copiousness of language, so they become more wise, or more mad than ordinary. Nor is it possible without letters for any man to become either excellently wise, or, unless his memory be hurt by disease or ill constitution of organs, excellently foolish. For words are wise men's counters, they do but reckon by them; but they are the money of fools, that value them by the authority of an Aristotle, a Cicero, or a Thomas, or any other doctor whatsoever, if but a man. ([1651] 1960, 22)

In dealing with the "copiousness" of language, human beings run serious risks of becoming "excellently foolish," especially by the abuse of language among men of letters. This is the source of the problem of

Newspeak and the New Newspeak. The natural punishments that accrue as a consequence of rulers not giving critical attention to their own limitations is, then, the source of monumental disasters that affect both Sovereigns and subjects—all members of a commonwealth. Hobbes's necessary conditions for the peace and prosperity of a commonwealth were a Sovereign's accountability to God, a Sovereign's responsibility to exercise tutelage over the religious and civic instruction of subjects, a Sovereign's responsibility to govern in accordance with God's laws, and efforts on the part of subjects to relate to one another in accordance with God's laws. Hobbes is preoccupied with a "lawful" Sovereign. Sovereigns who rely on a doctrinaire adherence to religion or on the ideologies of secular religions are especially vulnerable to forcing their peoples to endure monumental disasters.

In Tocqueville's analysis, citizens in a self-governing society are sovereign in the exercise of the "right to make laws" through covenantal methods. Citizens in a democratic self-governing society bear the equivalent of Hobbes's formulation pertaining to a Sovereign's accountability to God—a source of potential failure in a democracy. "Despotism," Tocqueville asserted, "may govern without faith, but liberty cannot." According to Tocqueville, religion "is more needed in democratic republics" than in any other form of governance ([1835–40] 1945, 1:307). Tocqueville's phrase "self-interest rightly understood" ([1835–40] 1945, 2:125) turns on the idea that if individuals who are informing their thinking with reference to actions to be taken—what is to be done—rely on a covenantal ontology and the use of covenantal methods, they can achieve a right understanding that ameliorates self-interest with an appropriate accounting for the interests of other participants in their community of being. According to Harold Berman, the Western concepts of law were developed under circumstances where "the need for legal systems was not merely a practical political one. It was also a moral and intellectual one. Law came to be seen as the very essence of faith" (1983, 521). These are the grounds for the common knowledge and shared community of understanding among the peoples constituting democratic societies.

If sovereignty is to reside not in a Sovereign "representative" but in the sovereignty of those who are "represented," the essential source of unity is in the ontological presuppositions that are the foundations for right reason and for the virtues and sentiments appropriate to Peace as an alternative to War. These are the foundations on which a unity of knowledge can be fashioned through the science Orwell refers to as a method of thought and habit of mind not confined to particular sciences and technologies. The ontological presuppositions, methods of thought, and habits of mind are what governs in human affairs as people search out adaptive potentials for relating to one another and making constructive use of the opportunities available to them in the world in which they live.

Tocqueville's assessment of the long-term viability of American democracy in a multigenerational perspective turned, then, on considerations at work with reference to the problem of human cognition in a democratic society. Tocqueville asserted that people in democratic societies acquire a taste, if not a passion, for general ideas—abstractions that apply to everyone in the Society: "[I]n politics as well as in philosophy and in religion the intellect of democratic nations is peculiarly open to simple and general notions" ([1835–40] 1945, 2:289). Such simple and general notions might lead a people to become "excellently foolish," in Hobbes's terms. Such simple and general notions lead people to form a "favorite conception," claimed Tocqueville, of "a great nation composed of citizens all formed upon one pattern and all governed by a single power." "The very next notion . . . which presents itself to the minds of men in the ages of equality," said Tocqueville, "is the notion of uniformity of legislation. . . . [U]niformity of legislation appears to him to be the first condition of good government" (ibid.). Tocqueville asserted that "every citizen," then, "is lost in the crowd," and that "This *naturally* gives the men of democratic periods a lofty opinion of the privileges of society and a very humble notion of the rights of individuals" (ibid., 2:290, my emphasis). According to Tocqueville, the concept of citizens covenanting with one another in exercising the right to make laws is lost to a presumption that Government is "a sole, simple, providential, and creative power" (ibid., 2:291)—"the only arbiter of that happiness"—until nothing remains "but to spare them all the care of thinking and all the trouble of living" (ibid., 2:318). Tocqueville maintains that when such conditions occur, "the vices of rulers and the ineptitude of the people would speedily bring about its [the Society's] ruin" (ibid., 2:321). Democracies are vulnerable to the vices of rulers and the ineptitude of people; and great experiments become monumental disasters.

Rome was conquered by barbarians. "If the light by which we are guided is ever extinguished," Tocqueville asserted, "it will dwindle by degrees and expire of itself. By dint of close adherence to mere applications, principles would be lost sight of; and when the principles were wholly forgotten, the methods derived from them would be ill pursued" (ibid., 2:47). Struggles to dominate decisions do not necessarily yield enlightenment, justice, or well-being.

The concept of equality itself derives from religious precepts based on presuppositions that individuals are equal in their standing before God, and it is reinforced by Christian passions for the humble and the promise of redemption. The ultimate appeal is to the responsibility of the individual for one's own salvation and for establishing standards of judgment not motivated by envy but by a faith grounded in precepts to honor God above all else, love thy neighbor as thyself, and do unto others as you would have others do unto you. Tocqueville appealed to these precepts as the grounds for peace and for liberty and justice in seeking what is rightful. Tocqueville expressed his own judgment that "if faith be wanting . . . he [an individual] must be subject; and if he be free, he must believe." According to Tocqueville, self-seeking individuality under conditions of equality tends to isolate people from one another, "to concentrate every man's attention upon himself." Tocqueville maintained that "it lays open the soul to an inordinate love of material gratification." Contrariwise, argued Tocqueville, "there is no religion that does not place the object of man's desires above and beyond the treasures of earth and that does not naturally raise his soul to regions far above those of the senses. Nor is there any which does not impose on man some duties towards his kind and thus draw him at times from the contemplation of himself. This is found in the most false and dangerous religions" (ibid., 2:22).

Tocqueville's reference to "false and dangerous religions" and Hobbes's effort to come to terms with what he referred to as the "true" religion raise the most puzzling problems with regard to a theory of knowledge and its relationship to Voegelin's mystery of being. We may face the anomaly that a manifestation of the mystery of being occurs as an essential feature among those who deny or repudiate the idea of religion. If religious presuppositions are ontological necessities and necessary epistemological conditions in the constitution of systems of knowledge in communities of being, we would expect those presuppositions to manifest themselves among those who explicitly reject a belief in religious presuppositions. Following Voegelin's conceptions about the community of being, in which human beings are denied knowledge of the Whole, we would expect to find *prophets* of *new secular religions* who presume to have *knowledge of the Whole.*

New Secular Religions

As I examined the language of *The Communist Manifesto* in chapter 3, it became quite clear to me that Marx and Engels explicitly reject religious presuppositions in their assertion "But Communism abolishes eternal truths, it abolishes all religion, and all morality, instead of constituting them on a new basis; it therefore acts in contradiction to all past historical experience" ([1848] 1967, 103). Yet *The Communist Manifesto* promises the Salvation of Mankind by freeing the Oppressed of the world from their Oppressors in what is a form of class warfare that had existed through "all hitherto existing societies" (ibid., 79). According to the *Manifesto*, the revolutionary struggle led by Communists would be the penultimate war to end all civil wars and would achieve the Liberation of Mankind. This was a new form of secular religion that was being expounded while explicitly repudiating religion. This is why in chapter 3 I referred to Marx and Engels as having joined the "circle of the gods." They were expressing themselves as prophets [authors] of a new secular religion based on "Scientific Materialism" viewed from a transcending height that rejects "eternal truths," "all religions," and "all morality." Aspirations for material gratification reigned supreme in the *Manifesto*, with an exercise of moral fervor destructive of *balanced judgment,* which could be called "right reason."

In *The Old Regime and the French Revolution* ([1856] 1955), Tocqueville saw the French Revolution as a religious movement inspired by a passion for a universal rationality promising the Liberation of Mankind from the shackles of Religion and Tradition: "the French Revolution aspired to be world-wide . . . it created a common intellectual fatherland whose citizenship was open to men of every nationality and in which racial [cultural] distinctions were obliterated"; "its only parallel is to be found in certain *religious* revolutions" (ibid., 10, Tocqueville's emphasis). In commenting on the course of the Revolution, Tocqueville observed:

> the more it revealed its aspect as a grim, terrific force of nature, a new-fangled monster, red of tooth and claw; when, after destroying political institutions, it abolished civil institutions; when, after changing laws, it tampered with age-old customs and even the French language; when, not content with wrecking the whole structure of the government of France, it proceeded to undermine the social order and seemed even to aim at dethroning God himself; when, worse still, it began to operate beyond the frontiers of its place of origin, employing methods hitherto unknown, new tactics, murderous slogans— "opinions in arms," as Pitt described them. Not only were the barriers of kingdoms swept away and thrones laid low, but the masses were trampled underfoot—and yet, amazingly enough, these very masses rallied to the cause of the new order. (Ibid., 3)

The Revolution took on the characteristics of a religious crusade and became another tragic disaster. Deep passions of a religious character moved men who sought "to systematize the philosophy of God" (Voegelin 1975, 190, referring to and quoting Saint-Simon). Men moved by the "true reason of Enlightenment" destroyed great human achievements, like the cathedral at Cluny, as they ravaged Europe with the engines of warfare.

A problem to be addressed is the relationship of ideas to deeds with regard to "ideologies." The religious fervor associated with the French Revolution, Russian Revolution, Chinese Revolution, and numerous other "revolutionary" movements have become human tragedies. Why? Can the cultural and social sciences afford to dismiss the realms of ideologies as fictions of the mind that have little to do with political and social realities? If they do, are they neglecting "a grim, terrific force of nature, a newfangled monster, red of tooth and claw" to quote from Tocqueville, which is capable of "destroying political institutions," abolishing "civil institutions," and undermining "the social order."

In *The Devils of Loudun,* Aldous Huxley addresses the problem of "transcendence," which he presumes to be "man's deep-seated urge" to escape the isolation and helplessness of individuality ([1952] 1959, 313). Some efforts to achieve transcendence rely on intoxicants, such as chemicals, to stimulate feelings and illusions of the spirit; but such substances poison both the body and the soul. Other people induce trances and fantasies by repeating sounds—articulated as chants in sermons and slogans in speeches—and making repetitive movements. Words may have the most far-reaching implications in relating ideas to deeds. Huxley asserts:

> Language is the instrument of man's progress out of animality, and language is the cause of man's deviation from animal innocence and animal conformity to the nature of things into madness and diabolism. Words are at once indispensable and fatal. Treated as working hypotheses, propositions about the world are instruments, by means of which we are enabled progressively to understand the world. Treated as absolute truths, as dogmas to be swallowed, as idols to be worshipped, propositions about the world distort our vision of reality and lead us into all kinds of inappropriate behavior. (Ibid., 300–301)

Indicating the kinds of inappropriate behaviors, Huxley adds:

> Far more dangerous than crimes of passion are the crimes of idealism—the crimes which are instigated, fostered and moralized by hallowed words. Such crimes are planned when the pulse is normal and committed in cold blood and with unwavering perseverance over a long course of years. In the past, the words which dictated the crimes of idealism were predominantly religious; *now they are predominantly political. The dogmas are no longer metaphysical, but positivistic and ideological.* (Ibid., 301, my emphasis)

The irony is that Sovereigns, being the authors of laws, are above the law and cannot be held legally accountable for "crimes of idealism" when those crimes are being committed by State authorities. So far as nominal standards of legality are concerned, Sovereigns and State authorities are immune from prosecution for crimes of idealism. As a consequence, Sovereigns and the instruments of State power are able to war on their own peoples. Scholars who presume that ideologies are purely fictions of the mind see no essential connection between a theory of sovereignty and the forms of holocausts and genocide practiced by rulers pursuing fantasies of an idealistic character in relation to their own people.

Unfortunately, those scientists who treat propositions as working hypotheses in the confines of the experimental sciences also find it easy to presume that their understanding of the world can be imposed on others by relying on the mandatory authority of the State. What holds hypothetically and is presumed to be true can be imposed on others. We witness a form of Gnosticism—faith in Knowledge—when dogmas are swallowed and idols are worshiped without regard to the choices that people make in their discrete adaptations to the ecological niches in which they live. Ironically, those who renounce religion become unaware—unconscious—of the ontological or metaphysical stances that they take in presuming to use instruments of evil to do good. They presume themselves to be gods. We also face the further puzzle that the character of authority relationships within organized religion is vulnerable to corruption in much the same way that all authority relationships are subject to corruption.

The human mind is sensitive, closely bound up with emotions, and highly unstable. It needs anchoring. If individual cognition is to be the anchor, those who eat fruit from the Tree of Knowledge face the danger of conceiving themselves as gods. If the State becomes the ultimate anchor, practice of the art of manipulation leads to despotism. People in a democratic society depend on a Transcendent Order, whether called God or the Way of Heaven, to recognize the place of human nature and nature as being grounded in a common Source of Creation. Human *artisanship*, as constitutive of both institutional facts and artifacts, needs to find *its* place in Creation. Human rationality depends on establishing some coherent ground for right reason and stable feelings.

The Role of the Imagination in the Organization of Thought

I have referred repeatedly to the close association of the *nomos*/*logos* relationships. The formulation of a logic turns on the application of rules as norms that are characteristic of rule-ordered relationships. A logic of inference is accompanied by rules of "right" reason in a quest for rightfulness. There are standards to be applied with reference to any formulation. These standards are of human creation—human artifacts. These artifacts, as linguistic devices, do not apply themselves but rely on human agency in their proper—knowledgeable and intelligible—use. Appropriate methods apply to the use of linguistic tools, dependent on a shared community of understanding among the relevant community of language users. These relationships are critical to any theory of knowledge. They turn on the role of something that I have referred to as "imagination." I can only appeal to you to know what I mean by your having had the experience of using your own "imagination."

I find the work of Ibn Khaldûn useful in addressing fundamental questions about the problem of imagination. Ibn Khaldûn was a Tunisian scholar who lived from 1332 to 1406. His ancestors came from Andalusia, in southern Spain. He functioned as ambassador to the kingdoms of Granada and Castile, spent much of his life in Cairo, served as an emissary to Tamerlane, and addressed himself to the theory of history. He worked with Greek and Islamic traditions of scholarship. Here I refer to his *Muqaddimah,* which is translated as "An *Introduction* to History" (my emphasis) by Franz Rosenthal (1967). Muhsin Mahdi's *Ibn Khaldûn's Philosophy of History* (1964) is a thoughtful and stimulating exposition of Ibn Khaldûn's work. The organization of thought is central to Khaldûn's treatment of humanity, his consideration of Greek philosophy, and what I presume to be an Islamic conception of intellectual processes that pertain generally to human intellectual processes. I proceed on an assumption that as we try to clarify alternatives, we enhance prospects for extending the horizons of human understanding.

The association of symbols with referents in a context of speech communities can be viewed as a source of common knowledge and common understanding, which Ibn Khaldûn associates with "common sense." Lions, bears, and wolves presumably share a common sense of "being" with other lions, bears, and wolves in social units bound up with territoriality. Language communities, one might conjecture, involve levels and ranges of common sense that extend far beyond those of lions, bears, and wolves and that are thus characteristic of human beings in their diverse patterns of relationships. Given a common-sense level of cognition among language users, we face a critical question of cognitive processes associated with the imagination. These Hobbes, for example, treated as making distinctions with reference to perceptual images in separating elements of images and combining them in imaginary ways that become "fictions" of the mind. Imaginary creations, like fairies and mermaids, come into being with mythological accounts. The imagination is also the basis for the Platonic concept of Idea—a concept that gives meaning to form and to the Hebraic concepts of revelation and prophecy.

In his critical reflections on Greek philosophy, Ibn Khaldûn viewed the development of Aristotelian logic as the formulation of norms applicable to human thought that enabled distinctions to be made between proper and improper inferences in a system of logic. This use of the imagination arrives at standards of judgment about human reasoning that are associated with the use of language. Principles are to be applied in separating and combining. Greek preoccupations with characteristic functions and limits of number systems, for example, was the imagination at work in examining the characteristics of an imaginary [intellectual] creation. One might allude to the invention of a further level of abstraction associated with algebra, the name of which came to us from the Arabic language. The working of the imagination can yield diverse levels of abstraction that, in some sense, are stacked on one another in metalinguistic systems of discourse.

Two important problems arise with regard to the working of the imagination. First, is there a realm that goes beyond sense perception as applied to what we call the senses—seeing, hearing, smelling, touching, and so on? I am forced to respond in the affirmative. Second, is there a realm that might be associated with "extrasensory" perception? Again, I am forced to respond in the affirmative, but there must be limits, given the genetic conditions of life. What these are I do not know. Hypnosis is possible. I cannot know the limits of all possibilities; but I can be knowledgeable of impossibilities.

A third problem pertains to the important formulation advanced by Hobbes about moving from the effect to the cause, then to the cause of that cause, until we come at last to that which is eternal and men call God. The unfolding of such a causal ordering requires recourse to intellectual creations of the human imagination. Hobbes's reference is not to a direct causal ordering in nature but to patterns of association in an artifactual intellectual ordering, with the further reliance on the human imagination to go beyond to establish intellectual constructions reaching to the mystery of being. How these get related is suggested by what Ibn Khaldûn referred to as *intelligibilia* in relation to *existentia,* as these are mediated with reference to *sensibilia.*

The relationship of *intelligibilia, existentia,* and *sensibilia*—a triad—poses a critical problem in a theory of knowledge. Voegelin's formulation in the opening paragraph of *Israel and Revelation* implies two forms of *sensibilia.* One is associated with the senses as straightforward sensory perception—seeing with the eyes, for example—reinforced by symbolization and the use of language in human communities. The other is a "sense" derived from "participation" in a "community of being." The "sense" used by Scottish philosophers to refer to "moral sense" makes use of sympathy as a "sentiment" that comes from participation in a community of being. Consciousness of a "sense" of participation in a community of being, then, involves much more than being noble savages like lions, bears, and wolves—Wolves among Primates. Participation in working with *intelligibilia* constructed by the human imagination [intellect] involves a sense that might be associated with a larger awareness of functioning in the cultural heritage of human civilizations.

How far do such processes of working with the imagination reach? What are the processes for mediating such efforts? How are they to be judged in relation to their "truth" value? I cannot judge. Ibn Khaldûn and numerous others, including Blaise Pascal and Alexis de Tocqueville, referred to the "soul" as mediating the working of the mind between the world of *intelligibilia* and *sensibilia* in levels of apperception that can only be achieved by striving to make "sense" of the "Whole." This sense is associated with "inspiration" presuming "spirituality" and can only be "known" from the "sense" of participation in being. Such a "sense" is derived as "insight" that is "extrasensory"—beyond direct sensory perception. It is impossible to see the Whole by reference to eyesight; the Whole can only be "seen" by a "sense" of participation in being that is not confined in time and place and that is associated with the universal/eternal in the mystery of being. These reflections are consistent with my own experience in struggling with the meaning of democracy and what I presume to be characteristic of human efforts to conjecture about the constitution of order in human societies.

Whenever human beings reach beyond the limits of common knowledge of the mundane features of their world, they have recourse to elaborated intellectual constructions [semiautonomous cognitive structures] that are created by the working of the mind and that reach toward an understanding of the Whole. In extending their reach, they are moving to levels of *sensibilia* that ancients in the tradition of Voegelin's *Israel and Revelation* would refer to as "holiness." Are these efforts "excellently wise" or "excellently foolish"? To accept such intellectual constructions at face value while relying only on intuitive impressions is, in my judgment, being excellently foolish.

For this reason, I view inquiry about the mystery of being as an ontological necessity and a necessary epistemological contingency of special significance for democratic societies. I also regard current rulings of the Supreme Court of the United States requiring that the expressions of prayer be banned in public functions, such as high-school graduation ceremonies, to be a manifestation of extraordinary foolishness. To have government by discussion, as Walter Bagehot recognized (1908), requires listening to others, taking account of what others have to say, reaching one's own resolution about a proper course of action, and expressing oneself accordingly. I presume that the same principle applies to the public articulation of a prayer. Such a public expression is not a threat to my function as a responsible person and as a citizen in a democratic society. Any expression honoring a Transcendent Being anywhere is worthy of my respectful attention; but I bear my own responsibility for how I participate in the mystery of being. Freedom of religion does not imply the shunning of religion and disrespect for religious expressions in public places.

How the whole of being is put together I cannot know. I do know, however, that the copiousness of words can threaten my own participation in the nature of being. The distraction of talking pictures makes demands on my mind that foreclose serious thought. Provision for seclusion and quiet becomes necessary for my intelligible function in the realm of intellectual craftsmanship [*intelligibilia*]. I cannot deny the efficacy of prayer and meditation. They are consistent with my own experience of myself. My effort to be honest with myself has reference to my "conscience," through which my "soul" presumably "speaks" to me. Both Moses Maimonides and Thomas Aquinas taught that the study of God's Creation opens a way of coming to a better and deeper appreciation of the Source of that Creation.

Ibn Khaldûn, in his critical assessment of Greek philosophy, conceded that secondary *intelligibilia* can be built on primary *intelligibilia* more closely related to sensory perception by a reliance on the standards of reasoning associated with logic. The coherence of logical argument is important for working with the imagination and building the structures of *intelligibilia*. He went on to observe, "However, we must refrain from studying these things, since such (restraint) falls under (the duty of) the Muslim not to do what does not concern him" (1967, 401, Khaldûn's parentheses). Unfortunately, I do not know Islam well enough to know the context for the fuller meaning of this assertion. Such an assertion cannot be understood without an inquiry that goes much deeper than reference to words. I can be aware, however, of the serious abuses that can arise from misplaced abstractions in the use of language and from the strange admixture of moral passions and cold-blooded calculativeness that occur in what Huxley refers to as "crimes of idealism."

I am not able to render judgment about basic precepts taught by Muhammad, Maimonides, and Aquinas. I rely on the metaphor of Jacob wrestling with God. Jacob struggled with God not to destroy his God but to better understand him. His faith in God required a struggle to under-

stand and then to act in a way that was consistent with a deeper understanding of the Source of Creation, rather than in blind obedience to God.
It was for this characteristic of struggling with God that Jacob was given
the name Israel, meaning "the one who struggled with God." I can be sympathetic to an injunction not to involve oneself in what does not concern
one, which in my vernacular might apply to "busybodies"—those who
stick their noses into other people's business where they do not belong. We
are touching on a problematic of profound importance to the experience
of participating in communities of being in which both the problematic
and the experience must necessarily include unknowns reflecting mysteries
of being.

There is a context, however, when acting on precepts, which cannot
themselves be proved, *does have consequences.* Such precepts bear more on
an orientation toward participation in communities of being that creates a
selective bias with reference to what is given consideration, what is viewed
as problematic, and how processes of inquiry elucidate alternatives and
affect potentials for development. Selective biases associated with principles of selection can be expected to yield their fruit as consequences, which
are manifest in what is selected and what is forgone. The place of principles
of selection in the ordering of choice is important, then, both for the constitution of order in human societies and for those concerned with a political science viewed as a science of human association. The place of religion
in systems of knowledge cannot be ignored. Religion requires both sympathetic and critical attention for its place in the constitution of systems of
knowledge and in the constitution of ways of life. The fruits borne by
ontological presuppositions turn more on fundamental principles used in
constituting ways of life than on the names of particular religious doctrines. What prophets as great teachers have had to say is worthy of
respectful and sympathetic consideration.

Citizenship in democratic societies thus requires critical attention to
the problems of intelligibly working with those constructions we call
knowledge [*intelligibilia*] that can only be understood by the disciplined
use of the imagination and of doing so with an openness to innovations
that enhance human adaptive potentials. I presume that Spinoza, Pascal,
and Einstein, for example, reached far beyond the bounds of sensory perception in their efforts to comprehend the wholeness of what Ibn Khaldûn
referred to as *existentia* and that such effort required reference to both
intelligibilia and *sensibilia* that can only be gained from participation in the
community of being, in the sense that Voegelin referred to participation in
mysteries of being. I cannot know the Truth; but I can struggle to understand. It is my burden to attempt to better understand "the duty of the

Muslim," as well as the duties of Christians, Jews, and the adherents to other forms of religious and ontological teachings.

Basic paradigmatic shifts in intellectual perspectives can create intellectual necessities for reformulating the way that the intellectual constructions we call knowledge get put together. A shift in perspective from viewing the earth as the unmoving and immovable center of the universe to one of seeing the earth in motion required a basic alteration of the *intelligibilia* associated with the physical sciences and of the way that human beings view the mysteries of being. The possibility of a single source of Creation was, however, not challenged. Similarly, Darwin's theory of evolution, as a set of intellectual conjectures, was contradictory to the account of Creation presented in the Book of Genesis but does not contradict presuppositions bearing on a single Source of Creation. If the origin of species were pressed back through the chain of life to address questions about the origin of life, we would still not exhaust the mysteries of being (Polanyi 1962). The origin of species implies both origins and emergent properties that do not deny a Source of Creation.

The concept of revelation that Ibn Khaldûn defended in his "refutation" of Greek philosophy presents an interesting insight and poses a problem within its own formulation. The insight presumes that revelation is an essential foundation of "true" knowledge. Hobbes stated that "true" revelations are consistent with standards of right reason in the Kingdom of God by Nature. Presuming that Muhammad was a true prophet and capable of experiencing "pure intellection" associated with the Source of Being, a problem remains in the articulation of such an experience in human language. "When the Almighty himself condescends to address mankind in their own language," as James Madison asserted, "his meaning, luminous as it must be, is rendered dim and doubtful by the cloudy medium through which it is communicated" (Hamilton, Jay, and Madison [1788] n.d., 230). The "Word" of God, as a Divine Message, when communicated through the vehicle of human language, can only be imperfectly understood. The source of these imperfections is inherent in the one-many association between each word and its numerous referents in classificatory schema. Resolving such ambiguities always turns on the knowledgeability and intelligibility of the reader. Words do not speak for themselves. It would take a "true" prophet to accurately read the work of another "true" prophet, in the same way that it takes a poet to translate the work of a poet. A careful, sympathetic, and critical reading and study of a "true" prophet might enable an ordinary mortal like myself to penetrate puzzles, resolve anomalies, and reach to a deeper level of understanding, but such study could not allow comprehension of the "pure intellection" of God's Message.

Access to a deeper level of understanding is difficult for an Orthodox believer to achieve if his or her own reading of *words* in a text is presumed to convey the ultimate meaning. Orthodoxy runs the risk of being the ultimate conceit in presuming that one *knows* the Mystery of Being while achieving no more than worshiping idols. To understand dogma as words on paper requires reaching beyond dogma by recourse to sympathetic and critical reflections. I cannot know in any conclusive, empirically warrantable way when a human being reaching beyond "words" begins to become cognizant of the mysteries of being. Nor can I deny the mystery of being. What Muhammad, or any prophet, has to say is addressed to mankind in language, an imperfect tool created by and used by mortal human beings, and depends on appropriate levels of knowledge and intelligibility to understand.

The problem remains that participation in life involves mysteries of being that I cannot hope to penetrate. It is, however, essential that one be open to the mysteries of life in the search for meaning. Those whom some regard as "dead old men" have, in my experience, achieved an immortality with which I can live and work. I can experience an immortality of the soul through my participation in that community of being. There are basic precepts that constitute an essential foundation to the processes of inquiry as an adventure into the realm of the imagination that is accompanied by important potentials for rewards and for disappointment. Whether that orientation is to class warfare and the Liberation of Mankind from Oppression or to a search for peace, freedom, and justice in a context of rightfulness is of fundamental importance in coming to terms with the meaning of democracy and meeting the requirements of life. Such basic precepts are the foundations on which the place of knowledge in order and history are built, through the potentials for creativity achieved by those who were presumed to have been created in the image of the Source of Creation and whose creativity is an enduring contribution to Creation.

The achievement of "peace," as a universal public good, might serve as an inspiration for all human beings. In that case, every person's enjoyment of peace would be enhanced as the enjoyment of peace became available to all. If this were the true "nature" of the order of life in human societies, then what Hobbes expressed as the "laws of nature" might appropriately be conceived as the Will of God. Any mortal human being who would, as a Wolf among the Primates, deny such a possibility would also be a fool.

CHAPTER 8

Artisanship-Artifact Relationships

The languages of parables, metaphors, and narratives are important sources of meaning when learning to orient oneself to that which is problematic. To take a parable, metaphor, or narrative literally in that context is to misunderstand what is being said. A story about Creation and the Source of Creation may be important in addressing creativity in relation to a universe, presuming a unity of knowledge appropriate to the diverse aspects of human experience. Human beings search contexts for meaning that goes beyond the obvious. A "literal" interpretation of a parable about Creation is to view the Source of Creation as a superman. Such an interpretation would be "excellently foolish"—as Hobbes might construe such misunderstanding and/or misuse of language.

As a metaphor, there are important lessons to be associated with a single Source of Creation and with viewing mankind as having been created in God's image—in the image of the Source of Creation. Studying God's Creation is a way of coming to a deeper appreciation of the Source of Creation as a transcendent order and to a deeper appreciation of what it means to work with God's Creation in an expression of human artisanship, craftsmanship, or workmanship. To work in ways that honor the Source of Creation and to use processes inherent in the Creation are appropriate ways to express human creativity in what Eric Voegelin called "the community of being."

Simple instructions to honor God above all else, to love thy neighbor as thyself, and to do unto others as you would have others do unto you are worthy of serious consideration among the Wolves of the Primates, whose potentials lay in the use of language to constitute their conditions of life. The simple instructions derived from the great teachers in human civilizations need to be considered in relation to the harvest of consequences that flow from acting in accordance with those teachings as they bear on peace, creativity, well-being, beauty, liberty, justice, and other fundamental values that can be treated as universal public goods. Moral teachings have their place in the harvest of consequences so long as those teachings are used to inform choices that bias patterns of order in selective ways, even when the source of the precept may reach to that cause of which there is no further cause and which is presumed to be eternal. The cautionary note offered by Hobbes was to seek peace but be prepared to defend oneself. That one needs to seek and be prepared to resist implies standards of selection, which also need to be defended. The ground for an appropriate defense lies in the presupposition that universal public goods are complementary to one another as attributes of a coherent whole.

Human relationships are integrally bound together through artisanship and the artifactual character of human creations that are constitutive of cultures, societies, and civilizations as aggregate patterns of order. The more complex the civilization and the more specialized technical languages become, the more important it is to recognize underlying commonalities and similarities. This is why Orwell's reference to "the function of Science as a habit of mind, or a method of thought, irrespective of its particular branches" ([1949] 1983, 254) is an important complement to the different vocabularies composed entirely of scientific and technical terms. By beginning with basic foundations and fundamental elements, others can acquire the common knowledge and shared communities of understanding necessary for them to work in complementary ways and still act intelligibly with regard to basic principles revealing commonalities in human artisanship and the artifactual creations that are constitutive of cultures, societies, and civilizations. A self-governing society would presumably turn on a universality of artisanship in which each person first becomes one's own governor—one's own master—and then, in the course of coping with problems that inevitably arise in interdependent patterns of artisanship-artifact relationships, becomes capable of working out associated arrangements with others. Using basic orientations and general principles applied to specificities in contextualities is the way to accrue the common knowledge, shared communities of understanding, social accountability, and trust that are constitutive of mutually productive ways of life.

In pursuing this inquiry, I shall turn to Muhsin Mahdi's commentary on Ibn Khaldûn's theory of culture and shall use that theory to construe other works in order to clarify basic features in artisanship-artifact relationships. I presume that the use of languages in artisanship-artifact relationships to relate ideas to activities and deeds is what "culture" is all about. I shall then draw on these principles to indicate their application to a mode of inquiry for assessing problematic situations and as an effort to construe the meaning of what we observe.

The Place of Culture in the Constitution of Order

In my initial efforts to come to terms with the meaning of culture, I identified human cultures with learning and that which was derived from learning through the uses of languages. In his study entitled *Ibn Khaldûn's Philosophy of History,* Muhsin Mahdi emphasizes that the Arabic root for the word translated as "culture" is a *trilateral* verb that refers to (1) a place that is (2) inhabited, stocked, or cultivated by people and kept in good repair, as contrasted to desolation, waste, or ruin, and to (3) the acts of cultivating, building, instituting, or, broadly, I presume, doing something constructive (1964, 184). Hobbes's reference to the Latin term *cultus* has similar connotations meaning "to cultivate." The emphasis in Mahdi's study is more on the place, the doings, and the deeds and is perhaps somewhat less on the ideas and the conceptions used to guide thought. Drawing on Mahdi's commentary, my sense is that culture is a configuration of relationships that brings together ideas and deeds with places inhabited and cultivated by people and kept in good repair through assorted activities of cultivating, building, instituting, and doing what it is that people seek to achieve.

Existentia refers, then, to places, to material conditions of natural occurrences and artifactual creations, and to patterns of human association implied by the term *society,* without being confined to the boundaries of political jurisdictions. *Sensibilia* refers to both the senses and the expression of feelings and aspirations associated with a "sense" of participation in communities of being such that shared communities of understanding have reference to shared sentiments [shared feelings, esprit de corps] and shared identities [sensibilities]. This is, at least in part, what Lasswell referred to as *miranda. Intelligibilia* refers to the place of ideas in the constitution of thought as thinking enters into what it is that human beings do and get done—the relationship of ideas to deeds.

Mahdi emphasizes the "technical" character of the term *culture* with reference to Ibn Khaldûn's concern with a science of culture. He consistently refers to "the diverse arts and institutions of social life and the modes pertaining to them, beginning from the moment man invents them through the exercise of his rational faculty and throughout the various stages of their development" (ibid., 186), presumably including artisanship in producing, maintaining, using, and keeping in good repair. These circumstances might vary from more primitive conditions of tribal [nomadic] communities associated with "the pleasure of companionship" and the "natural propensity for cooperation" in sustaining a livelihood in one's place [conditions] of habitation (ibid.). Mahdi summarizes the thrust of Khaldûn's science of culture as pertaining to "the social habits" associated with "the diverse arts and institutions," as "the various aspects of social life are differentiated and become more complex." "The culture of a society," then, writes Mahdi, "is these habits, and the objects (e.g., tools, buildings, and sciences) created by, and the institutions (political, economic, urban, and scientific) resulting from, the exercise of these habits" (ibid., 187). Culture refers broadly to activities in human associations. Politics from this perspective, then, would be concerned with using ideas to pool, rearrange, and compromise existing interests while *creating and maintaining* the *working arrangements* [administration, management] of households, settlements, communities, cities, and presumably the larger domains of authority relationships through the matrices of language in accordance with moral principles.

These concepts have their analogue to *ecology* [eco/*oikos*] as the logic of the household and to *economy* as the management, administration, or working of the household. The concept of house or household as the domain of a collectivity bringing together the various contingencies of life in a family can then be extended to other realms. The family household, in some sense, is a miniature polis, where children first learn the norms of sharing and the logics associated with the operation of the household. Common knowledge, shared understanding, patterns of accountability, and the degree of mutual trust are accrued in households and among households. Households of masters and slaves provide the languages for autocracies and aristocracies; they are not proper foundations for democratic republics. A science of culture would then have reference to all of the sciences as they manifest themselves as intellectual creations in semiautonomous cognitive systems. So long as one presumes, as Hobbes did, that human beings continually strive to use present means to obtain some future apparent good and that they persist in doing so throughout life, a minimal postulate is available to be applied to whatever situations confront human beings in the social exigencies of life characteristic of different human societies. We might hope to understand processes of acculturation and socialization as commonalities that apply to all mankind and the basic postulates applicable to human artisanship-artifact relationships as the foundation for a science of culture that can be applied to all human societies.

Ibn Khaldûn's science of culture can also be viewed as a science of human ecology. *Place* and *people* are *mediated* with reference to *culture* as language, knowledge, and what is accomplished in both a material sense and in patterns of associated relationships in ways of life. When viewed from this perspective, Tocqueville's mode of analysis in *Democracy in America* is written as though he were relying on Ibn Khaldûn's science of culture. His introduction posed the problematics of his inquiry. The place was the North American continent. The key idea was associated with a people of a distinct cultural heritage—the Puritans; the Anglo-Americans. Specifiable social conditions applied to the larger community of people who developed characteristic patterns of institutional arrangements that were described and subject to both sympathetic and critical analysis.

The Muqaddimah (Khaldûn 1967), as an "introduction to the study of history," was presented as a way to interpret and to evaluate the work of historians in order to construe the meaning of history and to make explicit the science of culture that informed Ibn Khaldûn's own historical inquiries. Histories are diachronic accounts of human experience. Ethnographies are synchronic accounts of human experience. Both need to be grounded in efforts to build a science of culture. What applies to the conduct of inquiries about the meaning of human experience in the past has an essential relationship to an understanding of the present and to the emergence of events in the future, depending on how ideas inform actions and what can be accomplished in human societies. If Tocqueville's mode of analysis were written as though he were relying on Ibn Khaldûn's science of culture, we might anticipate that Tocqueville was not alone in efforts to draw on analogous conceptions that would help clarify the artisanship-artifact relationships in human cultures, societies, and civilizations. These relationships might serve as the key to understanding the constitution of order in human societies. I shall proceed, then, by reference to miscellaneous sources that have helped me understand the character of artisanship-artifact relationships that might serve as the basis for the sciences of the artifactual (Simon [1969] 1981), which I presume applies to all of the cultural and social sciences.

Artisanship-Artifact Relationships

As noted in earlier discussions, Hobbes's conception of power as the present means to obtain some future apparent good is more broadly conceived than Lasswell's conception of power as the making of decisions taken in circumstances involving recourse to severe sanctions [deprivations]. The possibility of severe sanctions is ever present in human societies. Sanctions need not depend on governmental authorities. Simply withholding a willingness to cooperate in a conjoint effort involves a sanction equal to the opportunities forgone. Rejection of a proposal of marriage, for example, may be viewed by the proponent as a crushing blow—an extreme deprivation. The opportunities forgone will depend on the alternatives available in specific exigencies. Retribution is another form of sanction that human beings impose on one another. Expulsion from participation in some association or community of relationships can be a most severe deprivation.

Ludwig Lachmann, associated with the school of Austrian Economics, uses concepts complementary to Hobbes's concept of power. Hobbes's "present means" are conceptualized by Lachmann to be multiple and heterogeneous. In the early classical conceptions of economics, these included land—implying both location and the resources associated with land—labor as human efforts, and capital as the tools and productive facilities necessary to carry on economic activities. These functioned, in turn, with factors being transformed through processes of production to achieve some set of products, by-products, and residual effects. Lachmann refers to the multiple and heterogenous features of any economic endeavor as representing a *principle of heterogeneity*. Bringing these heterogeneous elements together in knowledgeable and intelligible ways requires reliance on a *principle of complementarity*. This implies not only knowledge and intelligibility in human productive efforts but the acquisition of sensitive skills in creating some "future apparent good." The character of the endeavor is, in Hobbes's terms of reference, a "fiction of the mind" until its feasibility is established by accomplishment.

In my judgment, these principles apply to all human activities based on imagination and conscious thought with reference to the voluntary nervous system and the related use of human motor facilities. My reference in chapter 6 to building a coffee table with a cabinetmaker involved the use of present means to achieve some future apparent good that began as a concept—fiction of the mind—and was worked through using two odd boards cut from black walnut trees. The cut edge of one, a piece of slab wood, became the surface of the table. A konky knot had to be removed and filled with a wedged replacement. Another gnarled and splintered board was used to construct a set of legs. The curves used to shape the legs were later used to construct a lamp from blond-colored gumwood, which is now located in a corner opposite the coffee table. Principles of heterogeneity and complementarity were used to put together pieces of furniture that serve both utilitarian [useful] and aesthetic purposes in the ecology and economy of a household. I presume that such activities are expressive of what Ibn Khaldûn meant by culture; and my reflection on that experience in light of concepts advanced by Hobbes and Lachmann is an effort to use a science of culture to understand how the phenomena inherent in artisanship-artifact relationships might function in democratic self-governing societies.

Lachmann, in his own treatment of capital and its structure, places his emphasis on material forms of capital emphasizing tools and productive facilities. As I have already noted, a concept of social capital can be applied to norms and patterns of rule-ordered relationships in both individual and associated efforts and to what might be called "human capital" as referring to the knowledge, intelligibility, and skills of individual members of language communities. Language becomes the matrix holding networks of relationships together that are constitutive of society and for which different analytical perspectives are only different attributes of the whole. It would be entirely appropriate, then, to refer to the culture of a factory, a family, or other forms of enduring association that might be approached from the perspective of Ibn Khaldûn's science of culture.

The four factors—common knowledge, shared communities of understanding, patterns of accountability, and mutual trust or diffidence—can be viewed as four continua that are tied together as complements to one another rather than being mutually exclusive sets. What we come to regard as common knowledge depends on shared communities of understanding as representing shared standards of judgment—agreement. Shared communities of understanding imply accountability for what is being asserted and its relationship to future performance. The mutual trust or diffidence factor reflects the degree of confidence held about these factors as they complement one another in the maintenance of ways of life in which people keep their promises and strive to be helpful to one another in identifiable patterns of relationships.

The same frame of reference, or framework with working principles, can be used to reflect on the observations of the anonymous California engineer who drafted the *Santa Ana Investigation* report (California Department of Public Works 1928). There are engineering problems associated with violent floods in desert regions. Water, which can be retained from flood flows, might reduce the destructive potential of floods and be made available for use during dry seasons of the year. Various possibilities exist in building surface structures and using underground aquifers. Engineers do not produce water as such. Rather, they modify the regimen and characteristics in the patterns of water stocks and flows. Such engineering possibilities always need to be construed in light of economic opportunities that might accrue from an artifactual modification in the regimen of water flows and in patterns of usage associated with those modified flows.

Different modes of analysis can be mobilized to inform the choices that would need to be made in efforts to consider the necessary conditions applicable to any human endeavor. Questions of technical feasibility at an engineering level turn on a response to a question of whether alternatives can be brought to realization: Can it be done? Technical feasibility, in turn, depends on establishing economic feasibility: Is it worth doing? Another aspect pertains to operational feasibility: Can the necessary resources and efforts be mobilized to bring an endeavor to realization? Such a question might alternatively be posed in monetized computations: Will the anticipated flows of revenues cover costs within reasonable time horizons to pay for the necessary debt in capital funds and to cover future operational and maintenance expenditures? Posed in this way, an operational analysis would need to include reference to financial feasibility.

Another form of analysis to establish the operational feasibility of any endeavor pertains to legal feasibility: What formulations would need to be met to allow for the lawful operation of a proposed endeavor? Conditions of political feasibility would then turn on meeting the standards of legal, financial, and operational feasibility under existing and proposed patterns of rule-ordered relationships and on the capacity to maintain those standards of feasibility through time. Criteria of liberty and justice might be used to determine the legitimacy of the legal and political decisions being taken. If new public and semipublic agencies were required to establish the legal and technical feasibility of utilities having the characteristics of a common-pool, flow system, then the exercise of a power of *eminent domain* may be necessary to acquire rights-of-way across intervening property holdings and to have regular access to such rights-of-way to keep the system in good repair. This is why such utility enterprises are closely associated with political entrepreneurship whether or not the particular utility enterprise is conceptualized as a private, public, or semipublic undertaking in the context of the prevailing constitution of authority relationships. The function of a utility depends on a plant or physical facility organized with regard to rights-of-way affording access to all potential users. Any such utility depends on pooling, rearranging, and compromising interests embedded in property rights to establish its essential legal feasibility as a going concern. Legislation with regard to different jurisdictions may be required to establish legal and political feasibility.

How the aggregate structure of authority relationships gets put together would have a profound effect on the type of analysis an entrepreneur would make and the efforts that would be necessary to the viability of any such utility enterprise. In any case, the engineering of men associated with pooling, rearranging, and compromising existing interests and with constituting the configuration of future interests would be of critical proportions. Taking decisions about pooling, rearranging, and compromising existing interests and constituting the configuration of future interests is what politics is presumably all about. Such considerations lay deeply nested in the matrices of languages and cultures in constituting patterns of order in human societies.

Political entrepreneurs who make it their business to put together slates of candidates to win elections and gain control over legislative, executive, and judicial offices have interests that are complementary to the organizers of great utility enterprises concerned with rail and highway transportation, water, electrical, telecommunication, and gas services. These interests were elements in the structure of incentives that gave rise to the era of machine politics and boss rule represented by the Tammany Ring in New York City, the Philadelphia Gas Ring, and Kearneyism in California, all of which are treated in Bryce's *The American Common-wealth* ([1888] 1995). Access to the use of common-pool, flow resources and services created marketing potentials subject both to monopoly pricing in generating revenue flows and to public rights-of-way and powers of eminent domain to reduce the capital costs in constructing and maintaining technically feasible and economically viable enterprises.

Different structures of incentives are operable in different societies. Where military capabilities have loomed large, as in France, Germany, and Russia during the nineteenth and twentieth centuries, technologies involving metallurgy, transport, electrical energy, and telecommunications were of considerable importance. The organization of such endeavors as either State monopolies or as State franchises closely associated with military capabilities yielded different configurations of associated interests. Priority for military contingencies is likely to yield quite different designs for utility systems than would apply in the absence of such contingencies.

The transitions from some conception to viable plans, to feasibility studies, to workable decisions and viable agreements [the stocks and flows of ideas, information, and understandings], to physical works that offer the potential of modifying the stocks and flows of water suppliers and users in any given situation are merely the beginning of developmental potentials. How the incremental water enterprise is to operate and be managed is itself a matter of considerable significance. If it is managed to maximize producer profits, its relationship to future patterns of development will be quite different than if it were operated as a nonprofit cooperative enterprise in which the net advantage accrues to water users. In the latter circumstance, what might have been profits would accrue as economic returns to present and future property holders. Diverse patterns of association yield important differences in patterns of property holdings and developmental potentials as stocks and flows for different communities of relationships.

Such processes do not just happen. They emerge in light of prior cultural achievements in the way that peoples and places are brought together in pooling, rearranging, and compromising existing interests to realize future apparent goods. Features that have formed the institutional heritage of Californians include concepts pertaining to principles of Roman law, haciendas, missions, pueblos, and presidios from imperial Spain; the irrigation institutions of Mormon communities in the arid intermountain plateaus of the American West; the arrangements developed by miners who rushed to the California goldfields; and the arrangements devised by land developers and settlers in the different regions of California. Engineers and lawyers in the Santa Ana watershed have drawn on this heritage to apply their own innovative efforts in addressing problems related to water and the engineering of men. Military concerns were of a minimal order of importance in contrast to those that preoccupied the imperial struggles of Spain, France, England, Germany, Austria, Russia, and Turkey from the sixteenth century onward.

The shift in perspective from an engineering report anticipating a future pattern of development to a history of what happened in the course of some decades of development reveals how artisanship-artifact relationships can be used to explain prior patterns of development. An aggregation of stones in a landscape can stimulate conjectures about their meaning with regard to prior patterns of human habitation. Certain patterns in a given habitat may indicate the prior existence of terraces or fields. The ruins of aqueducts and other waterworks enable archaeologists to begin to reconstruct patterns of life characteristic of prior civilizations.

In a similar way, when I see rice paddies terraced on the slopes of mountains, I attempt to understand how those paddies and terraces are constructed, cultivated, and maintained. I may conjecture about patterns of property rights and patterns of association among those who cultivate the paddies. My conjectures must be tested in light of the experience of those who construct, cultivate, and maintain those terraces. Some combination of individual and joint rights to land and water would likely exist. From paying attention to observables, many other questions would follow, establishing an agenda for further inquiries. Other observations about artifactual creations, including neighborhoods that have been reduced to rubble, can be used as points of departure in exploring research agendas for construing the meaning of human experience.

Plenary Authority and Constitutional Prerogatives

An important issue in the sharing and pooling of authority relationships has to do with the reserved authority to deal with unknown future contingencies. The language of jurisprudence refers to *plenary* authority, implying full or complete authority. The term *plenitude* also suggests a fullness or completeness of authority. How societies make arrangements for the exercise of such a system of reserved authority affects everyone in the relevant jurisdictions. The concept of a single center of Supreme Authority could thus be conceived as "autocephalous," meaning single-headed—a form of rulership having reference to a single center of Supreme Authority. The pooling has the character of a monopoly over the exercise of authority relationships. Such a system of order applies to anyone within the relevant domain, in which a fullness and completeness of authority cannot be limited. In addition to the definitional character of such a concept, a monopoly of authority associated with fullness and completeness carries other implications and puzzles. Who are principals? Who are agents? What is the general character of property relationships? How are the instruments of coercion used in a society? The reserved structure of authority relationships, like the character of vernacular languages, establishes the common "fates," "fortunes," and "commonwealths" of human populations.

A basic question, then, is whether people can learn to use the language and theory of authority relationships to undertake the pooling, rearranging, and compromising of existing interests in crafting authority relationships for working out engineering solutions not only to water problems but to diverse forms of artisanship-artifact relationships existing in human societies, including the craft of designing institutional arrangements as authority structures. If such conditions were attainable, we could appropriately imagine self-governing democratic societies to be feasible. The language of authority relationships might then be used to conceptualize and design the set of rule-ordered relationships appropriate to the governance, operation, and management of common-pool, flow resource systems as would be appropriate to modified regimes of the Santa Ana watershed. The design principles in Elinor Ostrom's *Governing the Commons* (1990) could then be applied in working out microconstitutional arrangements among local communities seeking some joint advantage to be realized in their particular circumstance. When worked out as patterns of authority relationships among the residents of the Santa Ana watershed and any adjoining community of users, incidental by-products of such an endeavor would be the stocks of common knowledge, shared communities of understanding, patterns of social accountability, and mutual trust or diffidence that were derivative of that experience.

Existing entities having juridical standing have uniquely identifiable proper names. Establishing entities implies boundary conditions for some specified domain and a scope of activities and services that apply to functional relationships among discrete populations as communities of people. Working out territorial jurisdiction and the functional scope of authority relationships needs to take account of those features that are necessary to the constitution of an enterprise. The rules for a water conservation district would differ from those that apply to a municipal water distribution system. Any system of conjoint activities has its own system of governance both for dealing with its "internal" affairs and for exercising its authority as it relates to others spanning its boundaries and as it pertains to extraterritorial jurisdictions. Alternatives become available by how the different configurations of relationships get put together in the exercise of internal authority and in the exercise of external authority jointly with others, including ways of processing conflicts and achieving conflict resolution. Systems can be built from the bottom up through coordinated boundary-spanning patterns of relationships, as well as from the top down by reference to command and control from some single center of Supreme Authority.

From the perspective of those who might be assigned plenary authority, the constitution of what is presumed to be a democratic society presents an anomaly of extraordinary proportions. The issue cannot be decided simply on the basis of the form of government. In the case of Parliamentary Supremacy, people might elect their own "representatives." The condition of election and representation can be altered, modified, and limited. Other conditions of governance can also be altered, modified, and limited by those who exercise reserved [plenary] authority. If Parliament is Supreme, Parliament exercises residual authority, not the People. If representatives acting on the basis of majority rule exercise plenary authority, those representatives act only in the name of the People—a legal and political fiction contradicted by presumptions of sovereignty being vested in a single Supreme Authority. This is why Madison considered Majority Tyranny to be the most difficult of republican diseases in a system of democratic [popular] government.

Article III of the French *Declaration of the Rights of Man and of the Citizen* (1789), for example, asserts that "The source of all sovereignty lies essentially in the Nation" and that "*No corporate body, no individual* may exercise *any* authority that does not expressly emanate from it" (my emphasis). The body assigned authority to act on behalf of the Nation is the Supreme Authority, and no individual can exercise an authority not derived from that source. Individuals and elites who presume to speak for the French *Nation* and who win the support of an electoral franchise or referendum thus have substantial latitude to exercise plenary authority on behalf of the French Nation. Under such circumstances, governments and constitutions may come and go in rapid successions. Tocqueville refers to ten changes in the constitutional order in the six or seven decades after 1789. Some ninety-nine changes of "government" occurred in the Third Republic during the approximately seventy years of its existence. Governments may only be passing fancies. Who speaks on behalf of the French Nation may be quite ambiguous. People live and cope with life as best they can.

Consistent with a general theory of limited constitutions, the Tenth Amendment to the *Constitution of the United States* provides that "the powers not delegated to the United States by the Constitution, nor prohibited by it to the States, are reserved to the States respectively, or to the people." These are, however, words in a document to be interpreted and construed by human agents who occupy positions of political authority and who may see their opportunities in different ways.

What began as a complementarity of interests between political entrepreneurs organizing slates to gain dominance over diverse decision structures became collusive coalitions in a system of machine politics and boss rule. Americans responded, in Woodrow Wilson's terms, by "tinkering" with constitutions. Constitutional specifications were established limiting the authority of state legislatures to charter corporations by special legislative enactment, requiring instead general incorporation laws, including the registration of corporate bylaws formulated by those participating in incorporation proceedings. Such corporations became self-organizing and self-governing. Provisions were also made for extending similar principles to municipal corporations and public corporations, including, in the case of municipalities, the option for boards of freeholders to formulate municipal charters. State constitutions also extended general authority for municipalities to organize and conduct utility enterprises as functions of municipal corporations. A great variety of other provisions were adopted through constitutional revisions of state constitutions. These included the registration of voters, the conduct of elections, the printing of official ballots, and the conduct of primary elections in which any party member could challenge any candidate offered by slate-makers for nomination as a candidate in the general election. How the prerogatives of constitutional choice are exercised determines who has plenary authority.

The reforms in the late nineteenth and early twentieth centuries significantly modified the pooling of authority relationships to increase local authority for dealing with the technological innovations of the nineteenth century that reached far beyond township governments, which had been the focus of important inquiries and commentaries in Tocqueville's *Democracy in America.* People, by the exercise of plenary constitutional authority with regard to the government of the American states, rearranged the pooling of authority relationships to enable people to organize diverse types of enterprises and the constitution of different sets of communities of relationships relying on the self-organizing capabilities of people in their diverse circumstances. Tinkering with constitutions was of fundamental importance.

The costs of decision making associated with the Progressive Reform Movement to reform the patterns of governance known as machine politics and boss rule were immense. I cannot realistically attempt to compute those costs in monetized terms. The costs in lives and destruction characteristic of revolutionary and counterrevolutionary struggles in Europe associated with Napoleon in France, Bismarck in Germany, and Nicholas I in Russia might, however, suggest that the costs of constitutional revisions in the United States were much smaller in magnitude. Those costs would need to be arrayed as against the benefits that accrued to people, in their diverse exigencies, by being able to work out authority relationships coincidentally with patterns of development. Working out engineering solutions for potential economic developments often proceeded step-by-step in creating appropriate institutional arrangements associated with pooling, rearranging, and compromising existing interests to constitute systems of authority relationships commensurate with the joint and separable opportunities to be realized. The presumption was that those taking entrepreneurial initiatives were prepared to work with engineers, lawyers, and civic leaders in open public realms being monitored by those whose individual and joint interests were being affected. Through such processes common knowledge, shared communities of understanding, patterns of accountability, and mutual trust are worked out and accrue as forms of social capital—stock resources associated with commonwealths. The processes themselves involve the flows of communication, information, analyses, and expressions of judgment, agreement, and disagreement that are constitutive of order in human relationships.

The Anomalies of Strategic Considerations

In considering artisanship-artifact relationships, methods of thought and habits of mind are creatively applied to the relationships of ideas and deeds. As we have seen with regard to utility enterprises that operate common-pool, flow systems, opportunities arise for strategic considerations that offer selective advantage to some set of interests to manipulate other interdependent interests. Conserving flood waters creates potential advantages for water users during periods of deficient water supplies. If such benefits were to become generally available to all potential users, strategic advantage might accrue to some users to refuse to cooperate and take advantage of any opportunities that were freely available. This circumstance is identified with the commons dilemma in which a free-rider strategy may gain an advantage for those who refuse to cooperate and may threaten the viability of joint efforts as more individuals observe the advantage gained by free riders who function as holdouts.

When free-rider strategies are foreclosed by proceedings in eminent domain or inclusion in public instrumentalities authorized to exercise powers of eminent domain, levy taxes, and enforce regulatory measures, opportunities arise from strategic considerations applicable to those who can dominate collective decisions. Monopoly pricing enables those controlling pricing and/or taxing decisions to impose costs on others. They can also dominate policies and impose regulatory burdens on others. Shareholders, land developers, or other stakeholders may accrue advantages that place burdens on others. Particular configurations of institutional arrangements will give strategic advantages to some to exploit others. No human institution exists that does not offer selective advantage to some at the cost of others under some circumstances. The Faustian bargain inherent in rule-ordered relationships can be used by some to manipulate others. Democratic societies are especially vulnerable to majority tyranny and to the machinations of boss rule.

The magnitude of these anomalies can be illustrated when strategic considerations are applied to the basic problem raised by Alexander Hamilton of "whether societies of men are really capable or not of establishing good government from reflection and choice, or whether they are forever destined to depend for their political constitutions on accident and force" (Hamilton, Jay, and Madison [1778] n.d., 3). I presume that the term *good government* might apply to a popular or democratic government in which considerations of peace, liberty, justice, and well-being can be sought and in which each of these considerations would be advantaged if the opportunity to pursue such aspirations were available to all. The basic organizing principle conceived to be essential to such a system of government is using power to check power through the structuring of opposite and rival interests, which might be extended to the whole system of human affairs, including the distribution of the supreme powers of the State.

For many persons, such a form of government would be strongly counterintuitive. They might presume that any such formulas would be an invitation to stalemate and could tear a society apart. That is possible. The viability of any such system would not turn on the form of government as the only necessary condition. A complementary system of beliefs about human problem-solving capabilities in the presence of limited knowledge and uncertainty and about how different decision structures might be organized in accordance with procedures designed to elucidate information, clarify alternative formulations, and stimulate innovations are also necessary conditions. People who hold such beliefs would view conflict as both a challenge and an opportunity to use human skills and intelligibility to realize creative potentials.

Constituting a system of government as a social experiment requires that the necessary conditions are met and that those who engage in the experiment know what they are doing. As actors behave strategically to gain dominance over others, the validity of the experiment is placed at risk. The method of the experimental sciences requires knowledgeable experimenters concerned with the integrity of the experiment rather than with the rewards to be derived from occupying positions of authority. We face the great irony that the strategies pursued by "realists" in their quest for dominance can only achieve systems of order constituted by "accident and force." The same implications follow from those who proceed in accordance with the idea that politics is getting what you want and making other people like it. Actors so motivated are incapable of determining whether societies of men are really capable or not of establishing good government from reflection and choice.

Relying on accident and force in some combination remains an alternative way for constituting systems of governance. Even assuming that a people, at some point in time, had been willing to undertake an experiment to establish a system of government by reflection and choice, strategic opportunism would still be available. Some of the people may calculate the possibility of putting together winning coalitions to gain dominance over decision structures within any particular unit of government. They could then form coalitions with those people who had gained dominance over multiple units of government. Indeed, the pursuit of such strategic opportunities is the rationale for the organization of political parties. When key decisions pertaining to the potential use of force in international affairs are subject to secrecy as a strategic consideration and when control over the instruments of coercion are themselves subject to strict secrecy, conditions for open public inquiry and contestation among rivals are seriously compromised. Democracies become more vulnerable to corruption, coups d'état, and revolutionary struggles.

We are now in the presence of a serious paradox confronting the diverse political sciences. If the art and science of politics is confined to a science of strategic possibilities, dominant strategists have incentives to gain their own rewards. Such strategic considerations are likely to be inversely related to how societies of men would constitute "good government" by reflection and choice. Where the few govern the many, we would expect the few, as rational actors, to pursue the opportunities that become available to them. Frequent elections and changes of government would place greater emphasis on short-term opportunities for gain in contrast to long-term contingencies.

Professional strategists depend on organizing viable enterprises that bring together resources to enhance their prospects for success. Financial resources, surveys of voter preferences, and analyses of alignments of interests with regard to prospective issues are needed on a continuing basis that takes account of prospects in future elections rather than past promises. Further, ideas are grist for the mill of skillful manipulators of sonorous phrases and glittering generalities. If truth in advertising is a problem, it reaches its most serious proportions in political rhetoric, where ideas can be dismissed as ideologies, and where the possibility of political science gives way to intellectual corruption.

Professional strategists, whether monarchists, Leninist revolutionaries who have gained control over the coercive instrumentalities of State power, or professional politicians in "democracies," have incentives to centralize authority over all instrumentalities of government as a way of reducing transaction costs to themselves. The correlative doctrine advanced by social scientists and publicists is to view stalemate, fragmentation of authority, and overlapping jurisdictions as sources of evil. The integration of authority structures under a single center of Supreme Authority is presumed to be the way to create Responsible Government. These create potentials for both Tyranny of the Majority and Democratic Despotism. The potentials for democratic self-governing societies are eroded as the sciences bearing on strategies of dominance are put to use. These possibilities were rather fully appreciated by Tocqueville in his *Democracy in America, The Old Regime and the French Revolution,* and *Recollections* ([1893] 1959). If strategic conditions prevail in struggles for dominance, the quest for democracy will become, as Robert Michels asserted, a "cruel game" that "will continue without end" ([1911] 1966, 371), as those in leadership positions betray their positions of trust for the intoxication of presuming to exercise power over others.

Does Orwell's reference to science as a method of thought and habit of mind viewed as broadly applicable to artisanship-artifact relationships offer an alternative way? If applied only to specialized sciences and technologies, considerations bearing primarily on specialized preoccupations narrowly construed would be seen as resources that might be used by those pursuing strategies of dominance. There remains the possibility, however, that the view of "strategic opportunities" might be more broadly construed to focus on the general tasks of problem solving without being limited to specialized fields of inquiry within fixed limits. Science as a method of thought and habit of mind might then become applicable to all inquiries devoted to problematic situations. The innovative potential of science as a method of thought and habit of mind is an immense source of possibilities for combating the vulnerability of democracies to strategic opportunism.

The foundation for science broadly construed is not the State exercising tutelage over Society but modes of inquiry and artisanship broadly applicable to all human endeavors. Such modes of inquiry and patterns of artisanship bring together different specialized vocabularies in collegial relationships to focus on variable types of problematic situations. Chemist Brian E. McCarry, in a paper entitled "Organic Contaminants in Hamilton Harbor Sediments" (1993/94), contrasted the "value of an interdisciplinary approach to ecosystem research" to "the traditional approach that academic chemists have attempted to follow to solve problems in chemistry" (59–60). The traditional approach moves toward increasingly narrow specialization reminiscent of Ortega y Gassett's "learned ignoramus." McCarry suggests that strategic success of an interdisciplinary approach has been demonstrated in the pharmaceutical and polymer industries. An ecosystem approach to organic contaminants in Hamilton harbor sediments required that researchers in organic analytical chemistry and genetic toxicology be brought together in one research group that drew on other disciplines—inorganic analytical chemistry, geochemistry, sedimentology, geophysics, atmospheric chemistry, biology, and biochemistry—and that this group, other research groups, policy analysts, and concerned citizens work together with the Hamilton Harbor Ecosystem to establish a Remedial Action Program. Biologist Ralph D. Morris, in reporting on the ecology of gull and tern populations in the Great Lakes, comments that such an ecosystem research effort requires "the interaction and cooperation among investigators from a number of different disciplines." "This means," explains Morris, "that each participant has the opportunity of talking with and listening to colleagues from across the academic spectrum." In turn, the students associated with such ventures acquire a competence "that may well form the basis of some of the best funded studies in coming years" (1993/94, 45).

Among the various sciences, professions, crafts, and skills operable in human communities everywhere are problem-solving capabilities that can be drawn on to conduct inquiries that reach beyond any given limits imposed by the status quo. These potentials are opened through literate vernacular languages not confined to the boundaries of Nation-States and not subject to the dominant leadership and tutelage of State authorities. The realms of science and artisanship afford methods of thought and habits of mind conducive to the exercise of problem-solving capabilities subject to criteria of choice compatible with critical scrutiny in open public realms and consistent with requirements of social accountability and reciprocity. Lasswell's consideration of self-responsibility, voluntarization, impartiality, dispersal of authority, contestability, and balance as attributes of democracy are equally applicable to the realms of "Science," as Orwell used that term.

Anyone who has lived and worked in university communities is fully aware that democratic decision processes make available strategic opportunities for some people to form dominant coalitions to pursue their own advantage to the detriment of others. When strongly competing coalitions struggle for dominance, productive scholarship takes a subordinate place. Universities become corrupt as strategic opportunists struggle to acquire the advantages associated with authority positions. Fortunately, in many university communities, other standards of value than gaining dominance over authority positions prevail. Curiosity, as "love of the knowledge of causes" (Hobbes [1651] 1960, 68), still has its place. Contestation among opposite and rival interests pertaining to achievements other than dominance over authority positions is well established. Innovations enhancing problem-solving capabilities offer their rewards. Politics narrowly construed can, nevertheless, be immensely destructive in university communities and in other communities of relationships in human societies. Participants in partisan politics have strong incentives to pursue strategies that place democracies at risk. Those risks are so great that they exceed the costs of occasional stalemate.

The problem remains whether human beings can develop a culture of inquiry compatible with methods of thought and habits of mind characteristic of science as a general mode of inquiry that might apply alike to affairs of everyday life and to rule-ordered relationships. The potential exists of learning how to process conflict and achieve conflict resolution by means of contestation among people who use methods of thought and habits of mind characteristic of the scientific method broadly construed. An awareness of strategic considerations is important in learning how to assess potential dangers and create complementary remedies. Habits of mind need not function as subconscious blinders; they might be formed as thoroughly habituated skills allowing for interpretive explorations of meaning as new frontiers of inquiries and new forms of artisanship are explored.

For addressing problems that arise in human societies, the method of science broadly construed provides an alternative to the method of politics narrowly construed. Politics narrowly construed can destroy democratic societies and human civilizations. Civic education broadly construed is concerned with developing a culture of inquiry. Conflicts serve as potential indicators of troubles, requiring the mobilization of problem-solving capabilities to find ways of achieving complementarities that offer greater joint advantage in unfolding patterns of relationships. The scarcity conditions of nature pose serious limits; but the universal public-good character of knowledge, peace, justice, liberty, and well-being suggests that the more such qualities are universally enjoyed, the better off everyone will be. Considerations of self-responsibility, voluntarization, impartiality, dispersal of authority, contestability, and balance need to be applied in human relationships. Standards of technical, economic, financial, legal, and political feasibility still need to be met under whatever conditions of "reality" prevail.

The place of conflict and conflict resolution as an essential adjunct of the methods of thought and habits of mind associated with science broadly construed provide opportunities to find ways of compensating for prior errors and achieving coherence in patterns of development. Such efforts require knowledge, skill, and intelligibility in understanding how artifactual creations work in their ecological contexts. Using power to check power as a way of mediating conflict and achieving conflict resolution has immense creative potentials. Manipulation and muddling through are not adequate foundations for incremental change. Nor is synoptic planning an adequate foundation for constituting whole new systems of social order.

Human understanding requires the application of general principles to the variability of ecological conditions existing in particular time and place exigencies. Habits of mind and methods of thought, whatever they may be, have consequences; and these are amenable to inquiry and critical reflections. The moral significance of selective strategies to gain dominance over others can be established when the basis for making interpersonal comparisons is explicitly formulated and taken into account in the choices that are made as people relate to one another. All opportunities for choice in human societies are confronted by the moral hazards inherent in strategic opportunism. These become apparent as people learn to work with one another in enduring patterns of relationships.

The Place of Artisanship in the Cultivation of Life

I consider the artisanship-artifact relationship to be a key to understanding human experience. To reflect critically about that relationship requires us to consider the meaning of the artifactual. James Bryce's efforts to get at the "Facts" ([1921] 1931, 1:12) and Woodrow Wilson's effort to "escape from theories and attach himself to facts" ([1885] 1956, 30) neglected the place of ideas in the conception and design of what human beings attempt to do in efforts to understand what was accomplished or what failed to be accomplished. Every aspect of life in human societies is affected by the relationship of ideas to deeds in whatever it is that human beings attempt to accomplish in the ecological circumstances in which lives are lived.

The artisanship-artifact relationship imposes a burden on human beings to reflect on what we observe from the critical perspective that the states of affairs being observed are likely to be artifactual in character. We need to understand how the human response to rule-ordered relationships reflects incentives and structures actions that, in interactive patterns of relationships, yield consequences. The pursuit of strategic opportunities cloaked in deception and self-deception yields interactive consequences. We need to learn to read the signs of strategism implicit in the march of events, while presuming that the states of affairs being observed are artifactual in character. Artifactual states of affairs in these circumstances would include the unanticipated consequences of confused thinking and opportunistic strategies being pursued by some people to the disadvantage of others. Careful attention needs to be given to the relationship of ideas to deeds in establishing the warrantability of the conceptions being *enacted* not by putting words on paper but by deeds. Expedient opportunism and duplicity can *destroy* the integrity of any experimental effort. Misconceived ideas *cannot* be successfully *implemented* to realize desired consequences.

Mexican Privatization under Scrutiny

At the start of the 1990s, former Mexican president Carlos Salinas de Gortari was a hero, his ambitious privatization program held up as an example to the rest of Latin America. The region embraced neoliberalism with zeal. . . .

. . . .

The government may not want to delve too deeply into privatization deals because many current politicians and businessmen may be involved in shady agreements. . . .

. . . .

Like many who acquired state firms, the men became multimillionaires almost overnight. . . .

. . . .

But with political pressure fierce and scandalous new details emerging almost daily, there is no guarantee that what they say today will bear any relation to what they say tomorrow.

(Andrew Downie, *The Globe and Mail,* July 31, 1996)

Further, the scope and domain of the relevant field of effects need to be given careful attention in attempting to understand the patterns of interaction flowing from the way that incentives affect the choices of strategies. Efforts to modify the costs associated with risks will necessarily change structures of incentives and patterns of interaction operable in human relationships. This is why all insurance schemes are apt to involve "moral hazards." Modifying costs associated with risks will alter the way that incentives affect the choice of strategies. *Pooling risks* through *funds* used to *share burdens* creates new *commonses* vulnerable to predation by strategic opportunists. The world of finance enables assets to be transformed into debts and debts into assets that offer extraordinary rewards to financiers who can manipulate accounts and accounting systems. Opportunities for some to exploit others by transforming fiscal arrangements pertaining to losses and gains inevitably modify patterns of interaction. Financial manipulation alters the structure of operational enterprises—relationships among entrepreneurs, shareholders, workers, and consumers, each of whom has interactive ties with families, neighborhoods, and communities. Nominal financial advantages may come at substantial social costs.

There comes a point where efforts to devise political and legal remedies to every social ill is likely to create burdens that exceed the advantage to be gained. The concept of subsidiarity, for example, has been advanced as articulating a principle that decisions should be taken in the context of the smallest unit capable of addressing problematic situations. That principle is sound for constituting self-governing societies; but we are required to consider what legal remedy or remedies would be appropriate. I can imagine a principle of nullification as an alternative or as a complement to constitutional review. There comes a point, however, where costs of such a remedy may well outweigh the benefits. Such circumstances are likely to be compounded when opportunistic strategies come to dominate the legal profession's quest for winning cases at the sacrifice of jurisprudential understanding. Similar perversities can apply among journalists, public administrators, scholars, and teachers. When political and legal remedies become substitutes for moral, epistemological, and ontological considerations, democratic societies are no longer viable.

Reflection about the meaning of the artifactual and the place of human artisanship in the constitution of order in human societies requires serious consideration of the place of artisanship in the cultivation of life. At that point, we are again concerned with (1) a place that is (2) inhabited, stocked, or cultivated by people and kept in good repair and with (3) the acts of cultivating, building, and instituting. We have come full circle in our quest for peace, knowledge, liberty, justice, and well-being. Each of us faces the burden of using resources in the cultivation of life that require us to be honest with ourselves and with others, if we are to avoid being the sources of our own deceptions and contributing to the deception of others. As we reflect on the place of knowledge in the cultivation of life, we have potentials for using what we learn and derive from the learning of others to cultivate the life we live in association with others.

Ashby's law of requisite variety, Hobbes's concept of power, Lachmann's principles of capital formation, and Ibn Khaldûn's conception of a science of culture provide us with complementary efforts, artisanship-artifact relationships, and the artifactual character of human affairs. We face the challenge of bringing together heterogenous factors in complementary ways without losing the capacity to keep essential values within limits. It takes variety to respond to variety while attempting to realize those values that have the potential for being universal public goods. These conditions, in turn, must be met in societies that have those attributes specified by Lasswell as including self-responsibility, voluntarization, impartiality, dispersal of authority, contestability, and balance. We are beginning to appreciate what the cultivation of life means in a democratic society. A passion for "good government," which would relieve people of the cares of thinking and the troubles of living, is a threat to the viability of democratic civilizations.

PART 4

The Cultural Foundations of
Creative Civilizations

Democratic societies, I presume, depend on self-organizing and self-governing capabilities. Where do we turn to explore potentials for the emergence of self-organizing and self-governing capabilities and the development of creative potentials in crafting mutually productive ways of life? The burdens of poverty are not only borne by individuals; cultures can be or become impoverished. Impoverished cultures entrap people in perverse patterns of existence. We need to consider the cultural foundation of creative civilizations if people are to avoid becoming "a sacrifice to ills of which they are ignorant" (Tocqueville [1835–40] 1945, 1:231).

Only two circumstances are explored in this section. One is why such disparate patterns of development have accrued in Africa and Western Europe, both of which border on the Mediterranean Sea. The only factor explored is the place of language in the constitution of order, and that factor reveals potentials of sufficient significance to offer an explanation for the overwhelming failure of multilateral and international assistance programs to contribute constructively to the development of African societies.

The second circumstance is an inquiry about the place of Confucian and Western civilizations in emerging patterns of global relationships. The search is for commonalities that can be drawn on and that, in turn, can be used to appreciate fundamental differences that may enable the peoples among these civilizations to learn from each other.

These two inquiries are only illustrative. The method of analysis I employ might be used to focus on any of the features that are constitutive of patterns of order and development in human societies. A search for commonalities establishes grounds for commensurabilities in human affairs; a search for variants allows for assessments of what can be learned from others in cultivating meaningful lives.

CHAPTER 9

Comparing African and European Experience

Homo sapiens as a species of the biosphere has developed extraordinary capabilities for shaping the physical, economic, political, social, and cultural conditions of life. All human beings everywhere share a genetic endowment that allows for the manifestation of these extraordinary capabilities. Knowledge is the most fundamental source of human capabilities—a foundation on which all other productive potentials are built. All *Homo sapiens* have access to much the same biological potentials. Why, then, do such great disparities exist among the potentials that human beings actually achieve?

It has been argued, for example, that the last stone-ax makers among the Kim-Yal of New Guinea "are anatomically modern humans possessed of language systems and cultures as complex as anyone else's today" and that "one could easily teach [these] modern hunter-gatherers how to fly and land a Boeing 747 airliner" (Toth, Clark, and Ligabue 1992, 93). I presume, to the contrary, that languages and their relationships to human cultures run very deep, that the human uses of human languages are of varying complexities, and that *adults* learn how to draw on the resources of multiple language systems only with great difficulties. The problem of dealing with these complexities presents a radical challenge for creating cultures of inquiry where life itself requires the acquisition of skills for addressing problematic situations of ambiguous or unknown types.

The development of languages in which alphabets are used to articulate vernacular languages in written and printed forms permits studying and working with common languages in ways that cannot be achieved by relying only on the spoken word. By the use of sagas, some nonliterate cultures gained remarkable achievements through generations of chroniclers who laid important foundations for the development of literatures. Written languages, however, permit careful study and careful craftsmanship that opens new potentials for human achievement.

The development of literate vernacular languages is a problem that has not yet been formulated in an adequate framework for clarifying patterns of development in human societies. I presume that the advancement of human civilizations is ultimately grounded in the relationships of speech and of written vernacular languages to the acquisition, use, and transmission of knowledge and that these relationships emerge in ways that create the most profound tensions and conflicts in human societies. One part of the problem resides in the constitution of rule-ordered relationships in human societies. Some aspects of rule-ordered relationships derive from the way that peoples of diverse linguistic and cultural traditions relate to one another. Still other problems arise from basic presuppositions and structures of incentives that apply to how ways of life in human societies are constituted and from the consequences that emerge from those patterns of order.

My efforts to explore problems associated with the cultural conditions of advancing civilizations will be highly conjectural. What I shall refer to as an African heritage has been marked by successive imperial ventures, all of which have, to a large degree, failed. The efforts to create African States, following the European conception of Nation-States, have also been marked by substantial failure (Davidson 1992; Sawyer 1992; Wunsch and Olowu [1990] 1995). If it is necessary, then, to "return to the source," as suggested by Amilcar Cabral (1973), are there conjectures that can be drawn from African, European, and American experiences that may enable us to reflect critically on the human condition and achieve some increasing potential to cope more effectively with our realities?

The Common Heritage

The roots of Western civilization were nurtured where the African continent and the Eurasian landmass converge. The ancient empires of Egypt and Persia; the strange odyssey of the Israelites and the Prophets that established the foundations for Judaism, Christianity, and Islam; the interlude of Greek and Roman city-states and empires; the burst of Islam across North Africa to Spain and to the headwaters of the Danube; the intrusions of the Norse and the Mongols; the emergence of the Catholic monarchies of Spain and Portugal; and the later imperial thrusts of the Dutch and French Republics, the British Empire, and the American and Soviet power blocs—all these cultural influences have been a part of both the European and the African heritages.

The late imperial thrusts, during the last five centuries, have all derived their missions from adherence to teachings associated with the God of Abraham. That heritage is reflected in the Islamic prayer to be offered at the place of Abraham:

Say ye: "We believe
In Allah, and the revelation
Given to us, and to Abraham,
Ismā'īl, Isaac, Jacob,
And the Tribes, and that given
To Moses and Jesus, and that given
To (all) Prophets from their Lord:
We make no diffrence
Between one and another of them:
And we submit to Allah.

                    (Koran, chap. 2, V 136)

A common intellectual heritage associated with the teachings of the books of the Judaic, Christian, and Islamic lawgivers and prophets has roots in the Hebrew, Arabic, Greek, and Latin languages. These languages have their kinship to diverse Romance and Germanic languages through the Latin script and to the Slavic languages through the Latin, Greek, and Cyrillic scripts. In the African experience, the intrusion of diverse imperial thrusts has brought close association with Arabic, French, Portuguese, Spanish, English, German, and Dutch language traditions.

Why have we had such different responses to common cultural sources? I shall search for explanations in the pragmatics of languages, on the assumption that languages and the uses of languages are the distinguishing features of *Homo sapiens*. Rather than presuming that languages and cultures are of the same complexities, I shall presume that different types of language systems offer varying opportunities for and limits on human achievement. The limits characteristic of the human condition present hazards for all human societies. What I presume to be universal among *Homo sapiens* is a common genetic endowment. This implies that the cognitive characteristics and motor facilities available to individual members of the human species impose limits on human capabilities to use the resources inherent in language systems, to organize knowledge with reference to language, and to pursue artisanship that accrues from the use of language, knowledge, and other tools of artisanship derived from languages. You and I gain access to such potentials by learning how to use our own resources as human beings to attempt to understand others.

The European heritage has long been accessible to many of the diverse peoples of sub-Saharan Africa. The failure of European imperial thrusts in the world at large requires as much attention as the failure of African societies to achieve developments comparable to those achieved in Europe. Both have implications for the relationship of ideas to achievements in the contemporary world. In the African context, the two have interacted with one another. How do we explain the differences? If we take the fifteenth century as a crude point of departure, we have a period of five or six centuries that has been marked by significant contrasts. I shall turn first to Africa and then to Europe to contrast patterns of cultural development. I shall then turn to some reflections about the patterns of interaction between the two. Finally, I shall attempt to draw conclusions about the opportunities that may be available to the emergence of human civilization in Africa as this century comes to a close. I do so in appreciation for what I have learned from my African colleagues and out of a concern for the overwhelming tragedies that afflict African peoples today.

Europe and the Americas are not immune to these same types of tragedies that we have observed working their ways among the South Slavs [Yugoslavs] in the early 1990s. Yugoslavia was viewed as a great experiment that offered an alternative to the great experiment that had occurred in the Soviet Union. Both no longer exist among the systems of political orderings. I observe the signs and anticipate comparable patterns in the making elsewhere in Europe and the Americas.

The African Heritage

By the end of the fifteenth century, I presume the existence of African cultures in which most African peoples relied primarily on nonliterate, vernacular modes of communication. The Islamic culture, grounded in the Arabic language community, was the major exception. Earlier traditions existed in the millennia of the dynasties of the kingdoms of Egypt, among some of the Nilotic peoples, and among the descendants of Abraham who lived to proclaim their covenant with God in the traditions of Israel [Jacob], Moses, Jesus, and Muhammad. The waterways of the Nile and of the Rift valley and the caravan routes across the Sudan [Sahel] to the Atlantic coast and across the Sahara to the Sudan provided access to communication. I cannot imagine that those traditions were without significance for the vernacular cultures of sub-Saharan Africa. The covenantal theology of the Nuer, for example, has strong parallels to the covenantal theology of the Israelites.

Most of the indigenous cultures in sub-Saharan Africa were associated, to some significant degree, with a sedentary agriculture and with some significant range of domesticated animals nurtured on the grasslands of the great expanses of the Sudan and on the higher plateau regions of eastern and southern Africa. The tsetse fly and other sources of parasitic afflictions, however, imposed limits in using "beasts of burden," with correlative necessities for people to bear equivalent burdens. Most of these cultures had achieved skills in working with wood, fibers, textiles, stone, pottery, and metals, including iron. These cultural achievements were and are reflected in an array of diverse skills marked by significant divisions of labor requiring a substantial self-consciousness in the development of language and the explicit transmission of knowledge on an intergenerational basis across age-sets. These divisions of labor imply shared communities of understanding accompanied by patterns of identification associated with specialization in complementary skills in complex patterns of social relationships.

A critical issue is whether people who share common languages and cultural traditions are able to achieve a sufficient level of self-consciousness about their identities and ways of life so as to maintain their continuity on an intergenerational basis. Islam and the Catholic monarchies of Portugal and Spain posed serious challenges. The possibility of peace was presumed in the Islamic, Portuguese, and Spanish traditions to be dependent on a shared community of understanding among those who adhered to a common religious faith. Both the Catholic monarchies and Islam, however, viewed warriors as being in the vanguard of the faith. Submission to spiritual tutelage was an essential condition for "lawful" relationships. The relationship of imperial cultures, led by crusading warriors, to indigenous cultures was and continues to be a most serious source of tension. The Spanish *Requirement* presumed that soldiers were the vanguard in the conquest of the Americas and demanded submission to the tutelage of the Church and the authority of the Catholic monarchy as an alternative to warring on peoples to the point of enslavement and genocide (Todorov 1984). Strong parallels have existed in Islam.

There is among any people a speech community that applies to the organization of the ordinary routines of life and to an intergenerational cycle of life. To the extent that these are strongly reinforced in autonomous communities of relationships, the patterns of indigenous communities can be effectively transformed only from within. Where these relationships are not strongly reinforced, individuals may achieve a successful transition to a new culture. The processes can only be expected to work their way out, however, on an intergenerational basis. The deeper the roots and the stronger the identification with the old, the slower the process will be. The loss of the old and the failure to identify with the new is likely to yield cognitive disorientation and despair for discrete individuals and a loss of cultural identity within speech communities. We confront processes, then, where *adult* Stone Age hunter-gatherers living in some isolated ecological niche in the world are not likely to find the transition from making and using stone tools to flying Boeing 747s to be feasible within a single generation, even though their genetic endowments pose no biological obstacles to learning the skills of a pilot. A child begins to be nurtured in the presence of speech no later than the time of its birth. Flying Boeing 747s is not compatible with the ordinary routines of livelihood and the intergenerational cycles of life among hunter-gatherers working with tools shaped from stone.

Immigrants who cross substantial cultural thresholds often depend on patterns of adaptation that transcend multiple generations. Languages, habits of thought, skills, orientations, identifications, and aspirations are such that they are not infinitely open to the acquisition of radically different cultural heritages. Different forms of learning get stacked on one another in habituated ways that are not easily undone and reordered to meet any and all exigencies in life, in any society, anywhere. Acquiring and maintaining the skills of an accomplished ballet dancer, for example, must necessarily foreclose the pursuit of other opportunities requiring comparable investments in the acquisition of the relevant knowledge and skills. The children of serfs selected to become ballet dancers on princely estates in imperial Russia before the liberation of serfs no longer served as field hands. I would not expect Boeing 747 pilots, or university professors, to be successful enough in achieving the adaptive skills of hunter-gatherers to survive, for example, in the Kalahari Desert.

The languages, the bodies of knowledge, and the narratives and rituals that infuse meaning in life are worked out in identifiable communities of relationships that establish patterns of regularities, accountabilities, and trust in human relationships. These identities can only be raised to levels of consciousness with difficulty and require substantial effort to be communicated to others who are willing to make the efforts to learn. Such processes go on in the intergenerational cycle of life. Any such process is at the margin open to the acquisition of new learning and to processes of transformation influenced by the way that intergenerational cycles of life open opportunities for making choices about how to cope with problems of livelihood that accrue in the daily and seasonal cycles of life. We cannot expect human societies, despite fantasies that presume otherwise, to achieve a radical revolutionary transformation in ways of life from one day to the next or even from one generation to the next. Potentials for learning are substantial; but the cyclicity of the ordinary routines of daily life are deeply embedded in the intergenerational cycles of life that are critical to that which is cumulative for human psychological and cultural development.

What is proposed or initiated depends on the complementarity of consonant activities on the part of others for the achievement of its publicness. Rulers may propose and may even command, direct, and punish, but this does not mean that edicts are acknowledged as the basis for action in establishing acceptable ways of life. The exercise of "will" on the part of "rulers" is as vulnerable to intergenerational cyclicities as the innovations that anyone else may initiate and contribute to human cultural achievements. Those who exercise prerogatives of collective choice depend on the actions taken by others before any potential increment to human culture becomes an accepted feature that is constitutive of ways of life. The constitution of political orders needs, then, to be viewed in an intergenerational context in which important changes are possible but in which the effectiveness of proposed initiatives always depends on the response of others. It is a gross illusion to presume that rulers rule other human beings as ever-obedient and submissive subjects. Human intelligibility implies that each individual acts in light of some array of alternative possibilities, which cannot be foreclosed by the commands of rulers.

I presume that African societies have been marked by a great variety of indigenous cultures that continue to be constitutive of kinship structures and other structures of associated relationships worked out in patterns of villages and communities of relationships. These indigenous cultures reach out to more extended patterns of communications, mutual understandings, and commerce with one another. The covenantal traditions of the Nuer, their conceptions of right and wrong, their ties with kin and with cattle in association with land and water, the constitution of their villages and cattle camps, their expression of conflict, their ways of mediating conflict and achieving conflict resolution, and their ways of defending themselves get expressed in the diverse exigencies of life in the intergenerational cycles of life and are vastly different than the conceptions and ways of life among the Mande peoples (Duany 1992; Magassa 1992). Similar presumptions can be expected to hold for the Ashanti, the Hausa, the Ibo, the Kofyar, the Maasai, the Tiv, the Tureg, the Yuroba, and the many other peoples of Africa. Many of these African peoples have populations larger than the modern European Nation-States Albania, Austria, Belgium, Croatia, Denmark, Estonia, Finland, Ireland, Latvia, Lithuania, the Netherlands, Norway, Portugal, Slovakia, Slovenia, Sweden, and Switzerland. The rise and fall of indigenous African empires marked by successes and failures in warfare were accommodated to patterns of organization that build in mutual accommodations, counteracting tendencies, and restraints that enable diverse communities of people to come to terms with one another in the cycles of life (Ayittey 1991; Davidson 1992). Many of these patterns have persisted and have survived the challenges of Islam, the diverse European empires, and the subsequent efforts to create African Nation-States.

Following the collapse of the major European empires in Africa, strong presumptions existed that the creation of independent Nation-

States would be accompanied by the emergence of Modern Societies fashioned by new African elites drawing on modern intellectual traditions in science and technology to create new Nations analogous to European traditions. Indigenous cultures were identified with "tribalism"; and tribalism was viewed as an obstacle to progress to be eradicated. Cultures can be intentionally eradicated by States only through the practice of extreme repression and genocide. Those who become partners in the elimination of tribalism sooner or later find themselves to be partners in genocide.

Those who are likely to take a critical role in the emergence of African civilization will have to build on the achievement of African peoples within the cultural traditions of what works in viable ways of life in indigenous speech communities. It is possible to learn from the experiences of other peoples; and the burden of productive innovations will fall especially on those who are knowledgeable about the achievements of other peoples within other cultures and who can find ways to reconstrue the meaning of African experiences in explanatory narratives that can be transmitted to successive generations. The future of African societies will not be created by Heads of States relying on others to use guns and clubs to fashion Modern Societies coterminous with African States. To explore the type of challenge facing those concerned with the crafting of African civilizations, it is necessary to undertake a critical assessment of European experiences associated with the transformation of European civilizations over the last half millennium.

The European Heritage

From the fifteenth century onward, a sharp contrast between the cultural heritages of sub-Saharan Africa and Western Europe emerged with the development of common literary vernacular languages from the innumerable spoken dialects of European languages. This development is a difficult transition because each dialect could not, I presume, be an adequate basis for the support of literate civilizations. The potential range of societies with literary vernacular languages is, however, very large. Iceland, with a population of about 250,000, is the smallest society with which I am familiar that has its own language and the associated literature, culture, and related features of a relatively autonomous society capable of achieving a high level of civilization. There may be others. The physical insularity of Iceland in the inhospitable reaches of the North Atlantic helped to sustain the autonomy of the Icelandic people. Not every population of 250,000 can maintain its own university, theater, opera, and literature as well as the associated arts and technologies characteristic of modern civilizations. Modern Norwegian is closer to the Danish language than

Old Norse, on which the Icelandic language is based, though modern Norwegian, Danish, and Swedish languages share common roots in Old Norse and other Germanic languages. I am told that Danes, Norwegians, and Swedes can use their own respective vernacular languages and still understand one another at levels of meaningful communication.

What blossomed in the sixteenth and seventeenth centuries had its antecedents in earlier developments in the Peace of God movement in the tenth and eleventh centuries and its efforts to articulate the law of the land [*Landsfriede*] in a vernacular language, as in the *Sachsenspiegel* [the mirror of Saxony] (Berman 1983; see especially his chap. 2, on the origins of the Western legal tradition). These antecedents were, in turn, grounded in aspects of the Christian faith that presumed that God's Law and God's Peace might be extended to peoples other than the kin of Abraham. Basic concepts of Roman law and basic precepts in God's Law—do unto others as you would have others do unto you—could be used to codify the common law of indigenous peoples (Tierney 1982). Fortunately, Dante Alighieri, in the opening decade of the fourteenth century, attempted to conceptualize the principles that applied to the development of a literate vernacular language as extending a "knowledge most necessary to everyone" and "wishing to *illuminate* to some extent the understanding of those who wander like blind men in public places, uncertain of their landmarks, *to be of service to the speech of the common people (with the inspiration of the heavenly Word)*" (1981, 15, my emphasis).

Dante begins with a presupposition that "with any science what matters is not to prove it but to explain its subject." His subject was the development of a literate vernacular language in which the vernacular is defined as "that which children learn from those around them." At a different level than that learned from those who nurture children is, Dante asserts, a secondary language "which the Romans called 'grammar'" (ibid.). A vernacular language—that which children learn from those around them or their mother's language—has a special significance in the development of attachments and identifications and for establishing meaning associated with essential features of the cultural habitat formed in discrete ecological settings. A secondary language—a metalanguage that the Romans called grammar—permitted literary artisans drawing both on a knowledge of the vernacular language and the metalanguages of grammar and linguistics to achieve the skills appropriate to the construction of a literate vernacular language. This "metalanguage" is what Ibn Khaldûn called "secondary *intelligibilia*" (1967). Levels of achievement get stacked on one another. Achievements worthy of emulation set standards of reference for successive generations, reflecting human efforts to understand the patterns of Creation.

For Dante, the normative implications associated with aspirations and achievements worthy of emulation also turn on a logic of language implying usage in an instrumental sense. Dante writes that "language is an instrument as necessary to our thought as a horse is to a knight." The best knight seeks by combinations of nature and nurture to develop the best horse for the opportunities and struggles of knighthood. A vernacular language to be used as a literary language must be appropriate to complementary patterns of expression suitable to meaningful communications, but, as Dante notes, the best language is necessarily associated with "those who possess learning and intelligence" (1981, 38). Knowledge and the intelligible use of knowledge go together with the linguistic articulation of literate vernacular languages.

Dante associates families of languages with "households," distinguishing Germanic languages and Romance languages, with characteristic reference to the term of affirmation, *yes—jo* and *ja* in the Germanic languages and *oui, oc,* and *si,* referring explicitly to langue d'oïl and langue d'oc, in addition to the *si* of Italian and Spanish usages, among the Romance languages. Italy was presumed to have a thousand dialects. Dante's problem, then, was how to select and create a vernacular to serve as the basis for a literary language. He assessed diverse variants among the vernaculars of Italian dialects and reached the conclusion that

> Those which are the *highest standards* of those *actions* which are specifically *Italian,* are not peculiar to any one city of Italy, but *common to all;* and among these can now be counted the vernacular we have been seeking, whose scent is in every city, and its den in none. (Ibid., 34, my emphasis)

Elements of diverse vernacular dialects contain features that are common to all, and the search for sources in creating an Italian vernacular language must be fashioned by drawing on those features common to all.

Dante then identifies those features of the common vernacular that might be constituted as a literate Italian vernacular as being "an illustrious, cardinal, courtly and curial vernacular" (ibid.). These qualifiers— *illustrious, cardinal, courtly,* and *curial*—are criteria or standards of selection [choice]. *Illustrious* relates to the power to illuminate; *cardinal* to ordering, presumably to a rational ordering of thought; *courtly* to the language of the royal palace, presumably a language of respect; and *curial* to the scales for balancing with reference to law and justice. In the absence of a royal palace, Dante refers to "the court" as the common home of the whole kingdom and to the sovereign ruler of all parts of the realm as properly residing in "whatever is common to all," where "no one individual's property should have its being" (ibid., 35). Presumably a commonality that reaches beyond that which is common to diverse dialects was represented for Dante by "the inspiration of the heavenly Word." I presume that if such were to apply to a self-governing democratic society, the language appropriate to covenantal relationships in communities of relationships would be the "courtly" language—a language of respect. Dante, as a master craftsman in literary artisanship, is often identified with the articulation of a literature that was constitutive of the modern Italian language.

Pieter Geyl's two-volume history of the Netherlands during the century between 1550 and 1650 ([1932] 1988, [1936] 1989) is indicative of common patterns associated with the development of the Dutch language, from variants of "low German" dialects that gained articulation in Chambers of Rhetoric and in the celebration of vernacular poetry and drama on the occasion of "land Jubilees," mixed with a humanist tradition associated with Latin and Greek roots, with Anabaptist and Calvinist religious traditions, with biblical and Hebraic roots, and with the use of the vernacular in the law courts of the countryside in contrast to the "royal court" of Stadtholders. The term *Belgium* means netherlands—lowlands—in Latin. The political aspirations of the Dutch gained articulation in a revolt that succeeded in Holland and the associated provinces in the north for what today is called "the Netherlands," in contrast to that which remained under imperial dominance, successively associated with the Spanish and French monarchies. The Walloons became speakers of French [langue d'oïl] and the Flemish became Dutch speaking. The seventeen provinces of the lowlands [netherlands] became two nation-states: Belgium and the Netherlands. Patterns of thought, ways of life, identifications, and aspirations associated with speech communities remain fundamental facts of life among the peoples of the lowlands formed by the delta of the Rhine, Maas, and Schelde Rivers, which flow to the sea in the same area bordering the English Channel.

Still another variant of profound importance in the development of literate vernacular languages is associated with Martin Luther, an Augustinian monk, who was a careful student of the Bible and knowledgeable in Latin, Greek, Hebrew, and the court language of Saxony. Luther drew on earlier traditions in fashioning the language of the law—the *Sachsenspiegel*—used in Saxony. The inspiration embedded in Luther's translation of the Bible, including the New Testament, was a conviction that individuals are responsible for achieving their own salvation and that the teachings of the Bible provided access to that salvation. Luther, as translator of the Bible, had the critical task of crossing the thresholds of diverse cultural traditions, which were themselves embedded in the historical exigencies of diverse peoples. His effort represented a great literary achievement in which the Bible became a literary masterpiece in the German language. The language, in this case, was the "high German" of the Saxon court, in contrast to the "low German" of the Dutch language, but it was illuminating to the readers of a literate vernacular language.

Somewhat comparable patterns occurred in the development of the English language. David Daniell's biography of William Tyndale suggests that Tyndale's translation of the Bible had a comparable place in the development of modern English. Much of the King James Authorized Translation relied on Tyndale's earlier translation. Work in grammar, theology, logic, and rhetoric at Oxford, greatly influenced by Erasmus and Erasmus's translation of the Bible from Greek to Latin, contributed to Tyndale's passion to make a knowledge of the Scripture accessible to "a boy that driveth the plough" (Daniell 1994, 1). Those who had devoted themselves to stepping out of the magic circle of a vernacular dialect to scholarship in Latin, Greek, and Hebrew faced the task of translating the great teaching of ancient civilizations into literate vernacular languages to illuminate the lives of "those who wander like blind men in public places," to use Dante's metaphor.

Every literate vernacular language presumably has its history in the way that it was constituted and used among communities of people. Can we conceptualize the principle that applies to the development of a literate vernacular language as extending a "knowledge most necessary to everyone," as Dante proposed to do? Such developments did not happen *spontaneously* among people, by their acting naturally, like lions, bears, or wolves. High levels of craftsmanship on the part of masters of languages in fashioning masterpieces played critical roles as producers of literate vernacular languages, whether in the instances of Dante in Italy, Tyndale and Shakespeare in England, and Luther and Goethe in Germany, or in the more general craftsmanship of those associated with Chambers of Rhetoric, land Jubilees, learned societies, religious congregations, and courts of law in the Netherlands. Men who used the power of the pen were, in my judgment, far more significant as language and culture producers in the rise of European civilization than those who wielded the power of the sword. High levels of aspiration that go beyond the dialects of ordinary speech communities have come to be identified with literary vernacular languages. People are themselves transformed as they become articulate in literary vernacular languages. The intellectual achievements of human civilizations are reflected in their languages and in the way that those languages give access to knowledge and the intelligible use of knowledge in all that people aspire to do and achieve in human societies, as creative efforts that take their place in God's Creation.

A Critical Assessment of European Experience

Those who associate the development of Western civilization with the rise of Nation-States presume that States rule over Societies and that those who exercise the prerogatives of manning the "ship" of State are the ones who steer Society and control the course of development in human societies. A Sovereign, then, is the principal who mans the State in the sense of occupying the office having to do with the exercise of Supreme Authority over rulership prerogatives. Parliamentary Supremacy presumes that such prerogatives are exercised by a Parliament. From this perspective, Communists aspired to use the powers of the State to transform Society and achieve the Liberation of Mankind. The French Revolution turned on comparable presuppositions that the French Nation as a whole, through a Sovereign Representative, could exercise the powers of the State. The State would then eliminate provincial traditions and customs and achieve a rational system of order through a universal code of law grounded in the *Declaration of the Rights of Man and of the Citizen.* The New Nations of the Free World were to be fashioned in the image of European Nation-States to achieve the transformation of colonial peoples into modern, developed Societies associating New Nations with Developing Societies. These presuppositions can be used as conjectures with reference to European history to consider how European history might be construed.

The rise of the modern Nation-State, in contrast to the imperial aspirations associated with the Holy Roman Empire and the dynastic aspirations associated with ruling families in Europe, is identified with the Treaty of Westphalia ending the Thirty Years' War in 1648. The Thirty Years' War in the Holy Roman Empire was associated with conceptual challenges presented by Luther and other Protestants to the presumptions of autocratic authority by the Roman Catholic Church and its tutelage over Western Christendom. The fundamental challenge turned on the presupposition that individuals within the Christian Community were responsible for their own salvation; and Luther's translation of the Bible fits into that context. This is consistent with Dante's concern with the development of a literate vernacular language that would be constitutive of the "knowledge most necessary to everyone" and "to be of service to the speech of the common people."

The translation of the Bible and a commitment to the achievement of literacy among the common people so that each individual could read the Bible and seek their own enlightenment and salvation had revolutionary implications. The language appropriate to religious conviction and the governance of religious affairs had implications for everyday life and for the governance of secular affairs. Luther chose to limit his challenge to spiritual, not secular, authorities. Others associated with Zwingli, Calvin, and diverse Anabaptist communities carried on their effort to be of service to the common people through the enlightenment afforded by the knowledge of literate languages in ways that applied to both spiritual and secular authority relationships. Religious teachings applied to everyday life and had demanding implications for communities adhering to Anabaptist and Calvinist teachings. If enlightenment were to prevail, people needed not to wander like "blind men in public places," to use Dante's metaphor, or to "fall a sacrifice to ills of which they are ignorant," to use Tocqueville's metaphor ([1835–40] 1945, 1:231).

What constituted the Thirty Years' War in the Holy Roman Empire had been experienced as the Eighty Years' War in the Netherlands and as the Wars of Religion enduring for more than a century in France. The significance of ideas for organizing ways of life had to be defended by the power of the sword. Self-governing communities of people had to learn to defend themselves and to ward off imperial aspirants. A self-governing society required a knowledge of martial arts and of how to defend itself through an armed citizenry functioning in a militia. The Swiss historian Adolph Gasser, in *Geschichte der Volksfreiheit und der Demokratie* [History of freedom and democracy] (1939) views self-armament—the bearing of arms—to be essential to the constitution of democratic societies (see also McPhee [1984] 1991).

The first modern Nation-States recognized by the Treaty of Westphalia were the Netherlands and Switzerland. By that recognition, they became political entities independent from the dynastic claims and ties associated with the Spanish, French, and Austrian monarchies. Both the Spanish and the Austrian monarchies had dynastic ties to the Holy Roman Empire and to the spiritual tutelage of the Roman Catholic Church. The explanations offered for what transpired in the sixteenth century and the first half of the seventeenth century cannot be confined to a theory of State-governed Societies. Something much more profound was occurring in the transformation of European civilization. This had to do more with enlightenment through the extension of the horizons of knowledge than with the exercise of a power of command by men of the State ruling over Society. The appeal of Luther's Bible and the achievements of master artisans working with the literary vernacular languages, giving expression to the teachings of the Bible and to other intellectual traditions through diverse forms of linguistic expressions, were the foundations for the achievements of the peoples using the German vernacular as distinguished from the Dutch vernacular, both of which function in the Germanic family of languages. Similar patterns prevailed in the development of literate vernacular languages among European peoples to establish the identities of Nationalities.

By a strange irony, the appeal of a unitary theory of sovereignty to "explain" rule-ruler-ruled relationships has come to associate the essential characteristic of European Nation-States not with the Netherlands or Switzerland as the first New Nations but with the Absolutism of the French and Prussian monarchies. The language of the royal courts of Louis XIV of France, Frederick II of Prussia, and the Stadtholder of the Netherlands was the langue d'oïl.

The langue d'oïl came to be identified by those who exercised the prerogatives of the State as the language of the French Monarchy, the French Republic, and the French Empire from at least the sixteenth century onward. Yet the langue d'oc and other linguistic traditions persist among the people within the territorial domain of France and the French Empire. How do we "explain" such circumstances? Perhaps Dante's theory for the creation of literate vernacular languages provides us with better grounds for seeking an explanation than the theory of the centralized Sovereign State. If the vernacular is the thoroughly habituated and familiar mode of expression qualified by a search for that which is common among the diverse vernacular dialects in a way that engages the aspirations of members of language communities for enlightenment, rationality, respectfulness, justness, and achievements worthy of emulations, such a language is likely to win the adherence of peoples. It cannot be imposed by force. It will instead become a vehicle of resistance and a badge of honor.

A theory of the centralized State carries with it a corollary of a single, comprehensive, and uniform code of law. Given a diversity of ecological conditions applicable to *place* and cultural diversity among *peoples,* I presume that a single, comprehensive, uniform, and workable code of law is an impossibility. Under such circumstances, conditions conducive to favorable patterns of adaptation in human societies depend on principles of local administration or self-governance that allow for diversity and complementarity rather than uniformity. The Roman law allowed for local variants in municipal affairs. The Prussian monarchy of Frederick II relied on a principle of self-administration in local affairs.

How would knowledgeable and intelligible individuals be expected to respond in a country with as much environmental and cultural diversity as occurs in the territorial domain of France? Tocqueville's account in *The Old Regime and the French Revolution* ([1856] 1955, 67) provides a plausible explanation. According to Tocqueville, the French system of law was one of "rigid rules, but flexibility, not to say laxity, in their application," and administrative officials were prepared to allow "a law to be discreetly *turned* if this made for the smooth running of public affairs" (my emphasis). Such conditions are the source of confidentialities, favors, corruption, and secret conspiracies to avoid legal requirements by some, noted Tocqueville, and of an "outspoken contempt for the laws of his country" by others. An emphasis on a uniform code of law yields corruption, contempt of the legal order, and the loss of trust grounded in standards of morality.

In the course of two centuries, the French *Republic* has been marked by five different republics, two empires, several restored monarchies, and numerous exercises of despotic authority. The average tenure of a "Government" in the Third and Fourth Republics was less than one year. One mode of accommodation by "turning" the law in an "atmosphere of secrecy" is for those subject to the law to communicate in a vernacular that is not the same language used by State officials. Thus, the centralized State, despite its insistence on a single official language, may reinforce linguistic diversity. Under such conditions, communities relying on divergent vernacular languages can be expected to persist. Literate vernacular languages reinforce the viability of indigenous communities. Another mode of accommodation would be for each individual to keep secrets in the conduct of one's own affairs and to attenuate ties in other patterns of associated relationships, yielding a social and cultural impoverishment and difficulties in calling on one's neighbors and colleagues for help and cooperation in joint enterprises.

Viable vernacular communities at variance with the official language of ruling circles depend on configurations of institutional arrangements sufficient to maintain the intergenerational transmission of language, culture, and customary ways of life. Under such circumstances, multiple regimes come into existence—one that represents the ruling circles and others that are constitutive of the life of indigenous communities and that use vernacular languages to reflect variant patterns of rule-ordered relationships that function as ways of life in those communities. Filippo Sabetti, in *Political Authority in a Sicilian Village* (1984), focuses on the character of the regime in a vernacular-language community in contrast to the centralized Italian State. A Mafia—a secret society—is constituted to defend the security of local communities. The atmosphere of secrecy in the constitution of an enlarged and disassociated Mafia has its counterpart in the atmosphere of secrecy pervading the State bureaucracy. The two become the complement of one another in perverse struggles for existence.

The power of the sword is never sufficient to deny knowledgeable and intelligible peoples access to the adaptive potentials of "informal," "extralegal," or "illegal" accommodations. Heaping facts on facts about the theatrics of politicians in the drama of public theater is a diversion obscuring how ordinary peoples cope with problems and participate in the conduct of their affairs of everyday life. The French State exists, but so do associations of urbanites, neighbors, and villagers in all parts of France. We need to understand the diverse ways that patterns of autonomy and interdependence get put together in French societies in varying ecological and cultural contingencies among different speech communities. Dante's langue d'oïl is not the universal and exclusive language of France.

The French Nation as a territorially bounded space is populated by peoples of diverse cultural traditions that have survived as facts of life through several centuries of autocratic rulership. I do not doubt the devotion of the French bureaucracy to a faith in French rationality as its guiding principle for a French way of life. The French schools for advanced study facilitate the creation of well-educated bureaucratic and professional elites. The French have, as a result, achieved a distinguished civilization despite the problems of political instability at the center of Government. However, we need critical assessments of how the French accommodation, expressed variously in space and time, has both evoked creative and adaptive tensions and served as impediments to other productive and enlightened potentials.

Nominally, the British reliance on a common-law tradition in contrast to the code-law tradition of the European Continent might imply that a common-law jurisprudence could avoid the impossibility of a single, comprehensive, and uniform code of law. The critical issue in dealing with the unfolding of the law as it applies to human actions always pertains to future expectations and prospective achievements. Reference to precedents set in the past does not resolve that problem. Who has authority to revise, alter, and modify the rules in use? This question has been increasingly resolved by reference to a doctrine of Parliamentary Supremacy, according to which the leadership in the House of Commons simultaneously exercises the Crown prerogatives of Privy Councillors and participates as authors of Orders-in-Council having the authority of law. The House of Commons as such, under its doctrine of Ministerial Responsibility and the Official Secrets Acts, has deprived itself of authority to inquire into the conduct of Privy Councillors and members of the bureaucratic establishment. The doctrine of ultra vires is construed in a French way so that nothing of a public character can be done without explicit authorization from State authorities. Local "self-government" is conducted by rules set by Parliament and through Orders-in-Council, following the Local Government Reform measures of the nineteenth and twentieth centuries, rather than by municipal charters established by citizens with reference to the governance of their own affairs.

The *English* common-law tradition has historical roots that have had little or no bearing on common-law traditions in Ireland or Wales. Scotland has some degree of local autonomy accruing from settlements reached through the Acts of Settlement in the creation of the United Kingdom. The failure of the British to achieve a resolution of the so-called Irish Problem has persisted for centuries, and a stalemate remains with reference to Northern Ireland. American commentators who write about Parliamentary Responsibility presuming responsible and effective Party government ignore the centuries-long gridlock with reference to Ireland and Northern Ireland in the constitution of Great Britain.

I presume that every European State and every State in the American hemisphere has its anomalies expressed in cultural diversity accompanied by organized resistance to presumptions of Sovereignty residing in Nation-States. The Quebecois culture in Canada and the African American culture in the United States are two obvious examples. Reliance on the power of the sword does not yield resolutions. Yet the exercise of power in Europe with reasonably high levels of achievement through literate vernacular languages is contestable in larger communities of discourse. Patterns of association in religious, intellectual, commercial, and economic affairs crosscut language communities and State boundaries. The few efforts to establish imperial dominance over Europe in the nineteenth and twentieth centuries have failed in surprisingly short periods of time. Societies shaped by linguistic diversities with high levels of literacy seem to have achieved capabilities for enhancing adaptability with regard to diverse problems both within and across the territorial boundaries of political entities capable of wielding the power of the sword. This has not, however, been achieved without warfare—the Thirty Years' War in the Holy Roman Empire, the Eighty Years' War in the Netherlands, and the Wars of Religion in France. Some of Africa's wars may be of comparable magnitudes. Peoples acquire diverse capabilities for defending themselves. Switzerland is a political entity with armed citizens capable of defending themselves in relation to diverse communities of relationships. No conqueror since Napoleon has seen fit to invade Switzerland. John McPhee's *La Place de la Concorde Suisse* ([1984] 1991) is an informative account of the Swiss military establishment—a militia of more than six hundred thousand soldiers, most of whom function most of the time as civilians rather than as citizen-soldiers.

The European experience with State-governed Societies is plagued by ambiguities in construing the meaning of that experience. The association of States with Absolutism as characteristic of centralized and unitary regimes does not stand critical scrutiny with reference to France, Germany, Great Britain, Italy, Poland, Russia, Spain, or Yugoslavia. Each exists in the presence of diverse linguistic communities with their own characteristic patterns of rule-ordered relationships. This is called "tribalism" in an African context. The significance of the emergence of autonomous political communities in Europe is best represented in the context of Switzerland and the lowlands, represented by Belgium and the Netherlands. Switzerland, Belgium, and the Netherlands have continuing problems in achieving complementarities among diversities. We need a political science that enables us to penetrate the world of rule-ordered relationships reflected in the way that peoples cultivate the opportunities available to them and live their lives, rather than one that obscures social realities by fictions of the mind that are alluded to as Sovereign Nation-States.

Reflections about the Contemporary African Situation

The name *Africa* has been assigned to a large continental landmass composed of a great diversity of peoples and language communities. The stereotyping of negritude [blackness] ignores the genetic diversity among the peoples of Africa and the existence of blackness among other peoples of the world. The African landmass is the site of three great river basins and many lesser watersheds. One of these—the Nile Basin—was the site of one of the most ancient and notable civilizations. Africa's north shore is on the Mediterranean—an area of great cultural achievement associated with early Phoenician, Egyptian, Greek, and Roman civilizations; with the civilizations that emerged from the teachings of those associated with the God of Abraham, expressed in early imperial Christianity following Constantine, in Islam, and in the Catholic monarchies of Spain and Portugal; and with the British, Dutch, and French Empires and the American and Soviet power blocs. The Arabic, Portuguese, Spanish, Dutch, French, English, and Russian language traditions and associated ways of thinking and acting have accompanied these imperial thrusts. What has been neglected is the great diversity of languages and cultures that have been indigenous to Africa and how they might emerge in light of what can be learned from the indigenous peoples in European civilizations.

European peoples learned how to defend themselves through the experiences of decades-long and century-long patterns of warfare. In the course of doing so, they came to appreciate the importance of tolerance for other peoples and the importance of striving for achievements worthy of emulation, developing aspirations of what it means to be Europeans and to share elements of a common cultural heritage, and striving to take a more universal role in the emergence of human civilization. The world has been changed as much by the conduct of commerce among merchants and by dialogues about the realm of ideas among intellectuals and scholars in spiritual and secular traditions as by imperial struggles to gain dominance over others. If patterns of order in human societies can be built on self-governing capabilities, systems of political order need not be in conflict with principles of commerce in exchange relationships, principles of dialogue in achieving problem-solving capabilities, and patterns of creativity consistent with a transcendent order of Creation.

The patterns of interaction in imperial systems have too frequently been dominated by those who presume to know what is good for others whether they come as traders, missionaries, agents of imperial authority, or emissaries of goodwill presuming to exercise tutelage over others. The conditions of Africa were assessed by those who presumed to know what was best for Africa without a knowledge of the diverse African environmental exigencies and African languages, achievements, and ways of life. Those who came brought with them mixed blessings of both good and evil. Helge Kjekshus (1977) offers an account of the Brazilian sand flea and the plague that followed in its wake on the part of a people unacquainted with the afflictions created by those parasites on their unknowing victims. People learn; but learning takes time not available to the early victims of such afflictions. The populations of the Americas and of Africa were devastated by the introduction of diseases by Europeans. Mexico experienced an 80 percent decline in human population after the Spanish conquest. Both people and cattle were afflicted in the case of Africa. Of similar perversity were the nature enthusiasts who, by creating great nature reserves, unintentionally provided a favorable habitat for tsetse flies, with destructive consequences for people and for cattle and with tragic implications for pastoral peoples who had learned to control tsetse flies by burning the bush that harbored the fly.

European hegemony over the African countryside was not firmly established until the last two decades of the nineteenth century. Contestation among the European imperial powers themselves meant that their relationships to African peoples were always contestable. Following the collapse of the major European empires after World War II, the policy of the European powers and the United States to rely on State-to-State relationships and on those who man the State apparatus to transform African Societies into Modern Developed Societies has failed. The American system of cryptoimperialism has been no more successful than British, Dutch, and French imperial orders (Copeland 1969; V. Ostrom, Feeny, and Picht [1988] 1993). Wole Soyinka, in his lecture on "Development and Culture," refers to "carbuncles" being "lifted" and then "grafted" (Soyinka and Kawada 1988, 2). This is an appropriate metaphor for a theory of the Absolutist State being extracted from a European context and "transplanted" into an African context.

Human potentials can only be addressed in relation to the productive capabilities of peoples with reference to their access to the knowledge and the diverse capabilities afforded by languages. Whatever is achieved depends on the shared learning accrued by members of language communities as they relate to one another. This applies to the productive potentials of individuals functioning in shared communities of understanding in the exigencies of everyday life. Each individual's participation in the opportunities perceived to be available is shaped by the common knowledge and shared communities of understanding that accrue in the finite conditions of life.

The more repressive the State apparatus, short of confinement and genocide, the more viable indigenous speech communities become. Resistance to oppression depends on secrecy and oppression in return. Viable speech communities depend on the maintenance of some community of relationships in the context of an intergenerational cycle of life. Secret societies complemented by soldier societies capable of defending their "turf" are indicative of counterregimes and shadow governments. When "gangs" prevail in neighborhoods and other communities of relationships, such "facts" are indicative of a political reality that cannot be ignored because of the linguistic formalities that rely on terms such as "informal," "extralegal," and "illegal" (Soto 1989). Efforts to dominate and to resist domination may themselves be sufficiently perverse to be tragic and sufficiently viable to be intractable to reform.

A basic challenge confronting African peoples, then, is the problem of developing literate vernacular languages and building a sufficient confidence in their own cultural achievements to consider the merit of what others have to offer. This can only be done, following Dante's formulation, by master craftsmen in diverse languages who have a deep appreciation for varying dialects in the common "household" of a vernacular language and who give expression to that which is common to the larger vernacular community in capturing the sense of shared identity. An appreciation of the historical tragedies, struggles and achievements, and sentiments of identification are necessary in building a literate vernacular language and the sense of identity associated with emerging language communities. So is an understanding of the literacy and intellectual achievements of other peoples, combined with aspirations reflecting a quest for illumination [illustrious], rationality [cardinality], respectfulness [courtliness], and justness [curiality]. The aspirations associated with illumination, rationality, respectfulness, and justness, if these represent universal human aspirations, are the foundations for the transformation of the patterns of order prevailing among indigenous communities associated with literate vernacular languages. Such levels of master craftsmanship in creating works worthy of emulation as new generations learn to express themselves in the crafts of artisanship are worthy of attention by anyone relying on the written word as the mirror of human civilizations.

The Peace of God movement in Europe was organized by missionaries and the sense of mission shared by the Church in an effort to establish God's Law by working with the common law of indigenous communities and to establish "lawful" rules of war applicable to Christian warriors. These efforts were associated with the imperial weaknesses of the Holy Roman Empire, which someone has characterized as being neither holy, Roman, nor an empire. The work of Dante and others followed the Peace of God movement after several generations, if not centuries. The development of literate vernacular languages among the African peoples can only be undertaken by master craftsmen capable of creating literary masterpieces that express the sentiments and aspirations of African peoples mediated by a quest for illumination, rationality, respectfulness, and justness and expressed in literatures worthy of emulation. African literary achievements worthy of emulation afford other peoples with opportunities to better appreciate African cultures and civilizations. These tasks cannot be discharged by heads of State who presume to rule over Societies, intellectuals who rely on gross abstractions as idols, or sorcerers who intoxicate the spirit by chanting animating phrases.

Wole Soyinka, recipient of the Nobel Prize in literature in 1986, addressed "the fate of Africa's culture producers" as "twice bitten" in successive plagues associated, first, with European imperialism and, second, with the predation of new African States destructive of indigenous cultural achievements. His culture producers are master craftsmen working on the construction of cultural achievements. He expresses the nature of the task confronting culture producers, like himself, in the following way.

> We were saying that culture is not parts. It is not often a sum of parts, but a summation, a synthesis. That is why culture sometimes leaves one dissatisfied in its definition. Can anyone really add up: two oranges, three hoes, four traditional healers, two roadside mechanics and five beaded crowns? The answer, we know, is not sixteen. But their intrinsic and overt productive processes do offer us an insight into the lived culture of a society. Exhuming, for instance, the remnant of those listed items—including the skeletons of the healers and the mechanics, we can deduce, reconstruct a framework of that society's principles of reproducing itself, of sustaining and enhancing life. We obtain from its cultural artifacts and utilitarian products, a cultural residuum which is the cohering expression of its intellectual life, its secular and religious modalities of existence. Nothing is exempted.

Not even the malformations—indeed, especially not the malformations. What we are saying is that, over the years, those objective products and their inter-related activities—activities of producing oranges,
healers, hoes, beaded crowns, etc.—implant aspects of their own con-
temporaneous being in a people's social psyche which sink, progres-
sively, into the very foundation of a people's culture and can only be
eradicated by a drastic, exceptional surgical act, or a cataclysm on an
unprecedented scale. (1988, 2)

Drastic exceptional surgical acts practiced on a people are forms of genocide; and holocausts are cataclysms on unprecedented scales. Both have
been suffered by African peoples at the hands of those who man the instruments of violence available to States that presume to rule over Societies.

People do not just count artifacts like grains of sand or words disassociated from meaning. They come to appreciate the complementarities in
life by working with ideas, learning, achieving what gets accomplished,
and discerning how activities in ways of life work as a part of a "social psyche" based on tacit understandings gained from living in a finite world.
Development, then, is achieved by drawing on the productive potentials of
peoples functioning in language communities to enhance their enlightenment, freedom, and productive capabilities.

Soyinka has chosen to articulate his literary masterpieces in the English language in appreciation of the circumstance that the English language is a necessary medium to tie the diverse cultures and language communities of Nigeria together. This means that further tasks remain to
accomplish Dante's mission in creating literate vernacular languages to
facilitate the work of culture producers in the context of every settlement,
village, and community. The ties with those who nurture children are fundamental to human achievement; and this implies that literate vernacular
languages are necessary to modern civilizations.

The worst tragedy that might afflict the African peoples would be to
presume that ordinary people are incapable of coping with the conditions
of life on the African continent and to accept a dependency on those from
the "North" who come bearing money, arms, and modern technologies.
Conditions of "poverty" need not be demeaning. Early Christians
accepted poverty in the material conditions of life as a virtue in achieving
spiritual freedom. Various Anabaptist sects, including the Amish, Hut-
terites, and Mennonites, have adhered to a simple life that I find difficult
to regard as impoverished. The great tragedy associated with a simple life
of Christian poverty occurs when people accept conditions of dependency while relying on State authorities to meet their welfare requirements throughout life. Relying on foreign aid could transform Africa

into the equivalent of an American "Indian reservation" of continental proportions.

Many Africans are skilled in linguistic craftsmanship and appreciate the magnitude of the problems involved. They invariably confront problems of hostile regimes and are subject to terms in prison [detention] and in exile that Soyinka refers to as an "INTERNAL Brain Drain" (ibid., 8). They need the help of colleagues who have confronted similar problems in other parts of the world. That type of dialogue—a willingness to work with others in recognizing that what happens today is the necessary foundation for potentials that can be achieved tomorrow—is of fundamental importance. But "todays" and "tomorrows" are to be measured in generations that reflect the intergenerational cycle of life and its articulation in the evolution of cultures and in the emergence of civilizations. North-South dialogue among heads of State is a form of ritualized theatrics that avoids problems rather than developing capabilities for resolving problems and achieving cultural productivity as conceptualized by Soyinka.

My sense is that scholars among the faculties of law and public administration in Africa would be well advised to take Amilcar Cabral's advice to return to the source and begin to appreciate the importance of customary law and patterns of village administration for the future development of African societies. Customary law and village administration need not be exclusively associated with ancient ways. They can be modified based on the experience of others who have learned to cope with common problems in everyday life through self-governing arrangements, by learning how to exercise power with others. The intellectual tools represented by common knowledge, shared communities of understanding, workable patterns of social accountability, and mutual trust must be fashioned in the course of deliberations about solving problems and resolving conflicts in mutually productive communities of relationships. These features of life do not just happen; they have to be worked out.

The African peoples may, in turn, provide us with a way of transforming the Prophet's vision contained in the Islamic prayer to be offered at the place of Abraham. *The Second Message of Islam* ([1967] 1987) offered by Mahmoud Mohamed Taha and his effort to establish a Republican Brotherhood in Islam is a step in that direction. Taha was martyred by State authorities in Sudan, but that does not silence Taha's message among those who gain access to literate vernacular languages. The prayer offered by the prophet Muhammad recognized a community of being in the God of Abraham through the teachings of diverse prophets. Islam faces the challenge of applying the teachings of the Prophet to a republican way of life rather than presuming that the autocracies of the early Caliphates are the only ways. Africans face the necessity of achieving a resolution consistent with the

Prophet's prayer, which seems to have eluded many ordinary mortals who profess Christianity, Islam, and Judaism, but which may become accessible to others among "Africa's culture producers."

The power of the spoken and written word and the place of languages in the matrices of life in human societies are the means for crafting ties among the peoples that are constitutive of human societies. We cannot presume that all language systems and cultures are equivalent to one another. Human cultural achievements differ. Those differences are embedded in the matrices of language usages that become accessible to other language users who acquire the skills and knowledge to communicate and function in diverse language communities, to act, and to accomplish what people do as they communicate with and relate to one another. I have attempted to do this in my comparison of African and European experience in this chapter, by drawing on my experience in communicating with African and European scholars who have been and continue to be my colleagues.

CHAPTER 10

East and West

In the twentieth century, we have witnessed the collapse of major empires associated with both Eastern and Western civilizations. The Spanish Empire expired in the nineteenth century. The Chinese, Russian, Turkish, German, and Austro-Hungarian Empires, at least in their traditional forms, collapsed during the first two decades of this century. The Dutch Empire in the seventeenth century and the late British and French Empires in the nineteenth century sought to combine republican traditions with imperial thrusts. These collapsed following their defense against German and Japanese quests for the revival of great empires in World War II.

Revolutionary thrusts in Russia and China to liberate the Oppressed of the World by relying on principles of autocracy took on strong imperial characteristics. The Soviet Union collapsed. The American system of cryptoimperialism has not proved viable (Copeland 1969; V. Ostrom, Feeny, and Picht [1988] 1993). All systems that depend on the leadership of a single, ultimate center of Supreme Authority are governed by theories of dominance. The People's Republic of China now faces a challenge to determine whether a grand autocracy can reform itself. This problem is of critical proportions to Hong Kong, which ends its association with the British Empire and begins its place in the People's Republic of China in July 1997.

The rise of human civilization over the last five thousand years has been strongly associated with imperial thrusts. The decade of the 1990s presents a basic paradigmatic challenge: Can human civilizations maintain themselves and achieve significant degrees of universality without being driven by autocracies and imperial aspirations? To resolve that question requires a critical diagnostic assessment of the viability of large-scale autocratic systems of governance to maintain lawful patterns of relationships in human societies. My conclusion is that large-scale autocracies inevitably fail. Democracies are also at risk. We live in a world whose global character is increasingly becoming a part of everyday life through commerce and electronic communications. Where, then, do we turn in building the foundations for the constitution of order in the decades ahead? My response is that we are required to build on the basic intellectual resources of our respective civilizations. We are required to give priority to building from the bottom up rather than the top down. The aspiration to achieve greater complementarities among the societies of mankind requires us to understand common features in our respective civilizations that might serve as common foundations. At the same time, we need to come to a deeper understanding of the distinguishing features that might enable peoples to advance their respective civilizations by learning from their own and each other's experiences.

The Failure of Autocratic Bureaucracies

Some twenty years ago, in *The Intellectual Crisis in American Public Administration* (V. Ostrom [1973] 1989), drawing on Herbert Simon's critique (1946), Gordon Tullock's theory of bureaucracy (1965), and James Buchanan and Gordon Tullock's work on constitutional choice (1962), I advanced the argument that relying on the concept of unity-of-command in a bureaucratic structure, associated with an autocratically controlled system of government, is vulnerable to serious problems of institutional failure. I also argued that a system of democratic administration associated with the polycentricity of highly federalized systems of governance provided an alternative way for constituting systems of administration. This way is consistent with principles of democratic governance and an open competitive *public economy,* as distinguished from a commercial *market economy.* In the meantime, the degree of autocratic dominance by Presidential government in the American system of public administration has continued to increase with the presumption that the national Government can address and resolve all problems in American society. Instead of resolving problems, the American system of Presidential autocracy is compounding problems. The intellectual crisis has deepened into a serious moral and cultural crisis that places American civilization itself at risk (Crozier 1984; V. Ostrom 1991).

My own inquiries about American public administration need to be critically assessed in relation to human experience elsewhere. Many supporting analyses and commentaries come from numerous areas of the world. Tai-Shuenn Yang, in "Property Rights and Constitutional Order in Imperial China" (1987), indicates long-standing structural problems associated with the rise and decline of dynasties and the ingenuity of the Chinese people to devise institutional arrangements to defend themselves from imperial impositions. John Dardess's *Confucianism and Autocracy* (1983) provides an account of the reflections of the founder of the Ming dynasty [Zhu Yuanzhang] about the exercise of imperial authority. Ming T'ai Tsu, late in his reign, used a metaphor of a fisherman casting a net to reflect on his own experience. If the lines controlling the net were tightly held, Ming T'ai Tsu found himself functioning as a tyrant. If the lines controlling the net were relaxed, corruption prevailed. This metaphor is an accurate reflection of the principal theses being advanced by Antoni Kaminski in his 1992 study of the failure of the Soviet system of public administration. A partisan state dedicated to the transformation of Russian society could sustain its momentum only by relying on terror. When the reign of terror was relaxed, massive corruption prevailed. Kaminski concluded that the Soviet system as such could not achieve reformability without a radical restructuring of the system of governance. Ibn Khaldûn's *Muqaddimah* (1967), written in the fourteenth century, reached a similar conclusion with regard to Arabic civilization. Amos Sawyer's *The Emergence of Autocracy in Liberia* (1992) and James Wunsch and Dele Olowu's *The Failure of the Centralized State* ([1990] 1995) tell the same story for Africa (see also Davidson 1992), as does Brian Loveman's *The Constitution of Tyranny* (1993) for Latin America.

Max Weber, a wide-ranging scholar of human civilizations, considered a "monocratic" system of governance with a bureaucratic system of administration to be the basis for "legal rationality" in Western civilization. Unfortunately, his commentary on the "full development" of his ideal type leaves us with strange anomalies. Individual bureaucrats find themselves "chained" to "an essentially fixed route of march" (Gerth and Mills [1946] 1958, 228). The superior knowledge of the bureaucratic expert has the commensurate effect of leaving his "master," whether a king, a parliament, or a popularly elected president, unable to alter the course of affairs. Such a system presumably could not be reformed within its own frame of reference. The principle of limited span-of-control necessarily means commensurate losses of information and control, as Herbert Simon (1946), Gordon Tullock (1965), and Oliver Williamson (1975) have also demonstrated. The idea of legal rationality posited by Weber leaves us with Jean-Jacques Rousseau's paradox "Man is born free; and everywhere he is in chains" ([1762] 1978, 46).

If we turn to the Confucian *Analects* ([1910] 1937), we might begin to understand how legal rationality in Western bureaucracies leads to servitude rather than freedom. In book 2, chapter 3, we read, "The Master said, 'If you govern the people by laws and keep them in order by penalties, they will avoid the penalties, yet lose their sense of shame.'" Confucius was placing first priority on the character of a moral order and its appeal to human conscience and mutual trust rather than on legalities as such. If public administration is viewed as a system of command and control in which the letter of the law and the threat of penal sanctions are the controlling criteria for administrative rationality, standards of judgment will inevitably clash about the meaning to be assigned to human actions. Standards of justice cannot be confined to legal rationality. Consensus and mutual trust are necessary in assessing the legitimacy of decisions and actions being taken. Factors bearing on intentionality—what is to be done—and the structure of the situation also need to be taken into account in determining the larger issues of meaning and legitimacy. A narrow reliance on legal rationality with regard to penalties can lead, first, to a perverse game of penalty-avoidance by conforming to the letter of the law and searching for exceptions and, then, to a response of trying to close loopholes and tighten prior rules with still more closely binding rules. If everyone were to advance their own causes to the limits of legality, life would become intolerable. We again face Ming T'ai Tsu's dilemma and Rousseau's paradox.

Bureaucratic rationality in a large country governed by a single center of Supreme Authority presumes that a uniform application of each rule is the essential standard of justice. A single, comprehensive, and uniform code of law is presumed, in much of Western jurisprudence, to be an essential characteristic of a rational legal order. That presumption cannot withstand critical scrutiny. People live their lives in discrete ecological niches subject to great variability. Conditions of life among mountains are vastly different from conditions on the floodplains of great river deltas. Mutually productive communities of relationships depend on achieving rule-ordered relationships that reflect both the ecological characteristics of the discrete world in which people live and the cultural ties, capabilities, and aspirations of peoples associated with different ways of life. Universal attributes and principles, characteristic of nature and of all mankind, are subject to time and place variations of great diversity. Under such circumstances, a single, comprehensive, uniform, and enforceable code of law is an *impossibility.*

Chinese civilization has confronted analogous problems. The strong emphasis in Confucian teachings is on standards of morality that rely on rules of propriety. In Western civilization, these rules of propriety are the equivalent to rules of good manners or rules of etiquette. Concepts of etiquette in the West are more associated with "high society" and what might be called "a culture of rococo." Rules of propriety in Confucian civilization are first closely bound up with family and kin relationships. Then they extend to orders and rank that pertain to rulership prerogatives but that are set within the context of an overarching concern for enlightenment, meaning respect for scholarship and the diverse forms of intellectual and artistic achievement. Ritualizing everyday patterns of conduct has meant that rules of propriety reflect strong self-organizing capabilities in a society that conceptualized relationships as being ordered through principles of inequality rather than equality. The expression of rituals associated with rules of propriety was accompanied by the gestures of inferiors to indicate deference to superiors. Conditions of reciprocity then accrued from an acknowledgment by superiors of the essential mutuality of respectful relationships in a larger context of enlightenment in which the Ways of Man were presumed to reflect the Way of Heaven.

A system of law based on rules of propriety as reflected in Confucian teachings placed a strong emphasis on respect for tradition and on the achievement of self-organizing capabilities reflecting the hierarchies of kin relationships, mediated by concern for enlightenment and forms of artisanship associated with achievements worthy of emulation, including those of skills associated with intellectual capabilities. But these rules of propriety and the accompanying presuppositions are always subject to challenge. A refusal to conform to rules of propriety posed a fundamental threat to Confucian civilization. Despite the Confucian emphasis on morality in the proper ordering of human relationships, a competing body of teachings emphasized the problem of legality and the place of enforcement through recourse to coercive sanctions. The rules of propriety reflected in *li* relationships [good manners] came to be accompanied by a complementary set of *fa* relationships [legalities] relying on instruments of coercion.

The *fa* relationships gained expression by rules applying to the conduct of imperial magistrates, specifying the terms and conditions applicable to the exercise of imperial authority with regard to magisterial functions. The emphasis was on the use of coercion to achieve on the part of someone who had flagrantly violated the rules of propriety a sufficient level of "enlightenment" to cause that person to conform to the standards of good manners. The exercise of the *fa* relationships strongly reinforced prior traditions ameliorated by an overarching emphasis on enlightenment; but the "enlightening" character of force posed a serious anomaly. While the patterns of relationships between East and West are quite different, both are plagued by fundamental tensions having to do with standards of legitimacy applicable to the place of legality in a system of law. These fundamental tensions are reflected in the anomalies expressed in Ming T'ai Tsu's dilemma and Rousseau's paradox. These tensions evoke powerful incentives for deception, self-deception, and opportunism.

Demonstrating that autocratic regimes relying on principles of bureaucratic administration are likely to fail poses a difficult analytical problem. I have presumed that major advances in human civilization have been associated with imperial thrusts. This presumption requires me to establish grounds for the maintenance and advancement of human civilizations based on principles of organization other than dominance. In pursuing such an inquiry, I propose to turn to fundamental principles of organization associated with the basic teachings that are constitutive of the self-organizing and self-governing capabilities among Asian and Western civilizations. A *self-organizing* system relies on fixed principles of organization; a *self-governing* system is capable of reforming itself—of instituting changes through time in rule-ordered relationships. The two concepts are not identical to one another. Self-governing systems are more adaptable to change. Both place greater emphasis on a logic of inquiry for achieving problem-solving capabilities in human societies than on a logic of command and control. A diagnostic assessment of the sources of institutional failure must be accompanied by an analysis of alternative possibilities. In this way we can learn from each other's teachings and experiences.

Fundamental Concepts and Basic Principles of Order

The foundations of Confucian civilization have been built on conceptions of filial piety, reciprocity, individual virtues associated with the cycle of life, and what might be called the "nobility" of enlightenment through study and through distinguished achievements worthy of emulation. The concept of filial piety emphasizes family and kin relationships and individual virtues highlighting the intergenerational cycle of life. A strong emphasis on fundamental inequalities in a static context is attenuated by the changing character of life through time. The child, in some sense, is the father of the man who becomes, in time, the father of another child. Such time-dependent patterns of life reach indefinitely into the future. The weak link in a cosmology of filial piety is its relationship to autocratic authority. The principle of autocratic succession relied on an imperial household of the Inner Court, which seriously attenuated filial piety, unlike the relationship of the Outer Court to the people and to the land, which was mediated through an aristocracy of enlightened scholar-administrators.

The core concepts of filial piety, reciprocity, and perfection in artisanship are the source of profoundly important self-organizing capabilities that can be extended to other patterns of human association as "brotherhoods" for maintaining mutual respect and trust in human relationships. Members of the Chinese cultural community everywhere in the world maintain strong self-organizing capabilities and relatively high levels of productivity under adverse political conditions (Landa 1987, 1994). The concept of filial piety is strongly reinforced by the nobility of enlightenment, which has served as a constraint on autocratic authority and has helped to build productive ways of life and the foundations of a great civilization worthy of emulation. Every civilization needs to build on the achievements of the past; and the Confucian virtues that respect filial piety, proprieties [*li*], and enlightenment would be important contributors to stability in any society.

An anomaly in Confucian civilizations is that those who have been cast out of family and kin relationships for their refusal to conform to rules of propriety are themselves capable of forming "brotherhoods," or outlaw societies. Such outlaw societies function as secret societies with their own "rules of propriety" and resort to harsh structures of *fa* relationships. In part, these "brotherhoods" operate in ways characteristic of organized crime and as the equivalent of the early Italian Mafias who performed services of law enforcement in ways that were more readily accessible to ordinary people than could be gained from the officially recognized Government (Sabetti 1984). The place of secret societies in the constitution of order in human societies is necessarily difficult to fathom. Who provides what protection services for whom and at what costs is ambiguous in both the East and the West, as reflected in the Robin Hood narrative.

The basic concepts that form the foundations of Western civilizations have their roots in religious traditions. The Judaic, Christian, and Islamic conception of God has important ontological and philosophical connotations. In that conception, God is identified as the single, ultimate Source of all Creation. Mankind, nature, and the universe are presumed to be a part of God's Creation. Mankind is viewed as having a distinctive quality—of being capable of creativity and of being created in God's image. The term *Israel* is the name that God, as the Source of Creation, is reputed to have given to Jacob, the Jewish Patriarch. The name means "one who struggled with God," carrying the connotation that obedience to command as such is not an appropriate way to express a devotion to the Source of Creation and to the realization of human creative potentials. Instead, "true" enlightenment is reflected in the attainment of creative potentials through a devotion to the Source of Creation and through a quest for understanding the mysteries of Creation. The core teachings in the Israelite tradition can, with gross simplification, be stated as (1) devote yourself to the Source of Creation above all else, (2) love thy neighbor as thyself, and (3) do unto others as you would have others do unto you. The principles of logic, ethics, and aesthetics merge with reference to processes of Creation. Human affairs are mediated by a search for truth, rightness, justice, beauty (Chandrasekhar [1987] 1991), and mutual trust in one another.

We find strong parallels among Confucian scholars. Confucius, when asked by Tsu Kung what *single word* could be adopted as a lifetime rule of conduct, is reported to have replied, "Is not *Sympathy* the word? Do not do to others what you would not like yourself" ([1910] 1937, bk. 15, chap. 23, my emphasis). David Hume (1948) and Adam Smith ([1759] n.d.)

relied on the concept of sympathy to elaborate, respectively, a theory of justice and a theory of moral sentiments. Xun Zi saw the *creativity* of human artisanship as an important complement to the *vagaries* of Nature. He is reported to have said:

> If agriculture is strengthened and its products are economically used, then Nature cannot bring impoverishment. If the people's livelihood is sufficient and their work in keeping with the seasons, then Nature cannot inflict sickness. If propriety [*li*] is always cultivated, then Nature cannot cause misfortune. Therefore flood and drought cannot bring famine; extreme cold or heat cannot cause illness; and evil spirits [passions] cannot do harm. (Cottrell 1988, 75)

From Xun Zi's perspective, human creativity would have an essential role to play in the Judaic concept of God's Creation.

The teachings of Jesus of Nazareth presumed the application of these principles to be associated with belief—or faith—implying intellectual and moral commitments. Leo Tolstoy, in his summary of the Christian gospel, conceived of the Christian faith as "the inward inevitability of conviction that becomes the basis of life" (Patterson 1992, 150). The Christian community is a community of believers rather than one of kin. Christianity and Islam are presumed to be open to all mankind. The Prophet's prayer to be offered at the place of Abraham indicates commonalities in Christian and Islamic teachings (see chap. 9, "The Common Heritage").

The deeper meaning of the Christian teachings has been subject to serious contestation, as though Christians were true Israelites—those willing to struggle with the Source of Creation to reach a deeper understanding of the meaning of Creation and its significance for a creative life. Missionaries among the nomads beyond the Middle World—the Mediterranean—carried the creative thrust of Western civilization among the Angles, Britons, Celts, Franks, Gauls, Goths, Lombards, Norse, Saxons, Slavs, and Ural-Altaic peoples of the West.

The weak link in the ontology of the Israelite-Christian tradition is the conception of rulership prerogatives. The Greek and Russian Orthodox teachings regarded emperors as Vicars of God serving as shepherds or stewards exercising tutelage over their peoples. Whether or not the Donation of Constantine was a fraud, the Western Church came close to recognizing the tutelage of imperial authority. As Tocqueville suggests in *The Old Regime and the French Revolution,* the State "stepped into the place of Divine Providence in France" ([1856] 1955, 70) to exercise tutelage over the French Nation. Karl Marx and Friedrich Engels, writing in *The Com-*

munist Manifesto ([1848] 1967) like Prophets in the Old Testament, proclaimed the Liberation and Salvation of the Oppressed of the world. The
French philosophers drew their inspiration for a rational legal order from
the place of Confucian scholars as a ruling aristocracy in the Outer Court
of the Chinese Empire. Russian and Chinese Marxist revolutionaries drew
their inspiration from the Prophetic vision of Marx, a European of Jewish
heritage, who renounced religion but drew on his own vision for the Salvation of Mankind. Communists dedicated themselves to serve as a Vanguard, presuming to exercise tutelage over peoples while leading them to
Salvation.

Two other political traditions prevailed in the West. One viewed the
Church as the Home [House] for the People of God, independent of imperial and secular authority. The bishop of Rome, using this concept, viewed
himself as the head of the Roman Catholic Church by apostolic succession. Following the Gregorian dictate of 1075, the Roman Catholic
Church presumed to exercise spiritual tutelage with regard to secular
authorities as members of the Church (Berman 1983). The Church as the
Home for the People of God presumed to judge the exercise of secular
authority in accordance with God's law. The Divine Right of the Christian
Community challenged the Divine Right of Kings. The Spanish and Portuguese Empires were, in the same tradition, commissioned by the bishop
of Rome, as Supreme Pontiff, treating the Catholic monarchies of Spain
and Portugal as emissaries of the Church to extend Christianity to Africa,
the Americas, and East Asia by the power of the sword. The Philippines
bear the name of Philipp II, Catholic monarch of Spain.

A third tradition drew on the concept of a covenantal relationship
between God and those who, in a covenant with God, bound themselves to
adhere to God's laws and to govern their relationships with each other by
binding covenants. This third tradition was the conceptual foundation for
constituting the Free Cities of Europe (Berman 1982), the Protestant
Reformation, the Swiss and Dutch Republics (Gasser 1939; Geyl [1932]
1988, [1936] 1989), the Commonwealth of Seventeenth-Century England,
and what became the United States of America (Tocqueville [1835–40]
1945). The Hebraic term *b'rit* and the Latin term *foedus* mean "to
covenant." The concepts associated with both Swiss and American *federalism* have their roots in a covenantal theory of political orders (Elazar
1995; Elazar and Kincaid 1980; V. Ostrom [1971] 1987, 1991). The concept
of constitutionalism, relying on a rule of law to set the terms and conditions of governance, has its roots in the concept of covenant, sometimes
conceptualized as a "contract theory" of State. The great problem, then, is
how to make covenants binding on those who exercise rulership preroga-

tives. That problem cannot be resolved within the confines of an autocratic structure of authority (Hobbes [1651] 1960). The power of the sword prevails too easily over the scales of justice and standards of right.

The resolution of the problem of constitutional law requires us to turn to the self-organizing and self-governing characteristics of Western societies. These characteristics have their roots in religious precepts: to honor God—the Source of Creation—above all else, to love thy neighbor as thyself, and to do unto others as you would have others do unto you. If each participant in patterns of interactive relationships follows these precepts to take account of each other's interests, they can clarify and arrive at communities of understanding, taking account of common knowledge, shared norms and rules of conduct, and what is required to carry on associated relationships in joint enterprises to realize common achievements. Such principles can be used in variable times and places to achieve patterns of mutually productive relationships based on shared rules reinforced by credible commitments, mutual trust, and graduated sanctions (E. Ostrom 1990).

Problematics in the Meeting of East and West

Western societies drawing on these covenantal traditions, however, run serious risks in failing to appreciate the foundations on which their civilizations were constituted. It is much too easy to repudiate religion, to assume that each generation is master of its own fate, and to rely on something called "the Government" to attend to everyone's welfare. The mode of democratic elections means that officials come and go in rapid succession. It is much too easy for those who are elected to presume a popular mandate, ignore prior achievements, and exercise the prerogatives of rulership on behalf of an amorphous allusion to "the People," with an opportunistic regard for the present. Scholars too easily share the passing enthusiasms of the masses and the infatuations of their elected representatives. Few struggle toward achieving a deeper appreciation for the meaning of Creation, offer a critical understanding of political rhetoric, and bear the burdens of human artisanship and the craft of creativity commensurate with the processes of Creation. Each new generation fails to inform itself about the past. Each new set of elected officials neglects the lessons of the past and the burdens of critical reflections, while using glittering generalities and sonorous slogans to win votes and build coalitions, with a view toward enjoying the fruits of victory and winning the next election (Crozier 1984; Jencks 1992; Magnet 1993; Murray 1984; Slater 1991). As long as these circumstances prevail, students and practitioners of public administration run serious risks of confining their attention to public policies that ignore what can be learned from the past while serving political masters who ignore the demands and burdens of creativity and rely primarily on a mandatory legal rationality enforced by threats of penalties.

Under these circumstances, turning to the Government to attend to everyone's welfare is fatal to civilization itself. When the Government becomes the universal foster parent, substituting for fathers in families with dependent children, the bonds of filial piety and covenantal households are destroyed. New generations of the young show a proneness for preying on one another in ways that are far more clever and destructive than that achieved by lions, bears, and wolves. Stalin's struggle with the peasantry of Russia yielded more human casualties than Hitler's war on the Soviet Union. Mao's Cultural Revolution mobilized immature adolescents to destroy the roots of Chinese civilization.

A different set of problematics confronts Confucian civilizations. The rules of propriety associated with Confucian teachings are strongly oriented toward conflict avoidance. The *Analects* reveal levels of discourse among the circle of the learned that were both respectful and challenging. The teachings of Mencius and other Confucian scholars do not reflect obsequious deference to the Master. Yet the principles of a culture of inquiry among the first circle of scholars in Confucian societies was not extended to develop a due process of inquiry related to a due process of law.

The relationship of rules of propriety to the avoidance of conflict has had a dampening effect on the development of innovative potentials and on the application of those innovative potentials to the ordinary exigencies of life in Confucian civilizations. Relying on systems of autocratic authority through revolutionary efforts has not been a successful method for reform. Sun Yat-sen's efforts to draw on Western traditions of thought as reflected in the teachings of John Dewey, for example, were confronted by challenges both from within Chinese society and from without—by the Japanese quest for an Asian empire. Mao Zedong's reliance on the teachings of Marxist-Leninist traditions have been marked by gross failures of monumental proportions, as revealed in Fox Butterfield's *China: Alive in the Bitter Sea* (1983). Achieving reform by drawing on the self-organizing capabilities inherent in Confucian traditions depends, in my judgment, on achieving a broad culture of inquiry as a means of coping with conflict and on achieving conflict resolution through the exercise of problem-solving capabilities in dealing with the ordinary problems of life. The teachings of the great teachers in Confucian civilization are not incompatible with the metaphor of Jacob wrestling with God. God's the Way of Heaven. I presume that a meeting of East and West is possible. But those efforts depend much more on what Wole Soyinka (1988) has referred to as "culture producers" than on heads of State.

Problematics in the meeting of East and West still run very deep. The East is much more concerned with the diachronics in the cycle of life and with how achievements at each stage relate to potentials for achievement in succeeding stages in that cycle. The West, by contrast, attempts to move from the autonomy of the individual to project universals that might apply to all mankind, without regard for the common knowledge, shared understandings, patterns of accountability, and mutual trust that are constitutive of relationships in human societies.

The Kantian categorical imperative to act in a way in which one's rule of action would be regarded as a universal law has its foundation in the basic precepts of biblical teachings but runs the risk of being transformed into a naive globalism. Demands for universal human rights under circumstances where States are mandated to supply all of the requirements of life is a bizarre form of linguistic deception. Under such circumstances, challenge and contestability pursued in a problem-solving mode are necessary conditions for the meeting of East and West.

Some Conclusions

The quest for excellence in the nineties poses a greater challenge than any of us can imagine. I have reached the following conclusions.

1. Autocracies—the energizing features of imperial thrusts over the last several millennia—are not appropriate systems of governance for the future of human civilization.
2. Bureaucratic reliance on a unified system of command and control using standards of legality and mandatory penalties cannot be used to achieve lawful, trustworthy, and mutually productive relationships in human societies.
3. A single, comprehensive, uniform, and enforceable code of law for all mankind, or even for moderately-sized political entities, is an impossibility.
4. The enduring and creative potentials of human civilizations are associated with self-organizing and self-governing patterns of relationships that are crafted with shared communities of understanding taking account of time and place specificities in known ecological and cultural circumstances and that are built on standards of rightness, justice, reciprocity, and mutual trust.

These conclusions reflect deep intellectual tensions in the contemporary world. The global orientation of neo-Kantian ethics reinforces the universalism associated with Jeremy Bentham's Utilitarianism as elaborated in neoclassical economic theory and in the neoclassical theory of the State. Both confront a challenge from an ecological approach to human communities seeking to avoid the tragedy of the commons by crafting institutions appropriate to the governance of great varieties of commonses. The abstract logic of market economies needs to take account of the problems of collective organization in addressing the aspects of political economies associated with the governance and administration of common-pool resources and facilities and of public goods and services associated with communities of relationships that are variable with the ecological niches in which peoples live their lives. We shall be required to come to terms with these problems as reflecting differences between the Western Way and the Asian Way. These analytical problems cannot be adequately addressed in superficial communication among heads of States or their emissaries. Rather, these issues turn on deeper questions about creativity in relation to Creation and about the Ways of Man in relation to the Way of Heaven (Tao 1990).

The Continuing Quest

If we accept these conclusions as a point of departure, a quest for excellence suggests the need to pursue an extended agenda of inquiry into the indefinite future. I would place first priority on understanding the basic social infrastructures afforded by the families, kinships, and other patterns of local associations and communities of relationships. These are the source of both individual and social creativity and the basic source of investment in human and social capital accruing to each new generation (Netting 1993; E. Ostrom 1990). The source of all productive potentials in human societies resides in the knowledge and skills of individuals as these are amplified by the opportunities for people to learn to work with one another in mutually respectful relationships. Students and practitioners of public administration need to know how to work with and build on these creative potentials, rather than viewing themselves as servants who obey the command of autocratic political masters and rely on the coercive power of the cudgel to dominate others.

Those features that are common and those features that are variable across human experience are, in turn, the foundations for building cultural and social sciences that might apply to all mankind. The same principles of inquiry would apply to structures and processes that reach from local to global patterns of relationships. Each needs to be considered on its own merit. Human societies cannot be micromanaged by central authorities operating in macrostructures (Liu 1994).

As we inquire about the contemporary world with a view to future potentials, we cannot afford to neglect the task of critically assessing our own inquiries in light of prior human achievements. What bears the label of "religion" in some contexts and of "philosophy" in other contexts inevitably applies to unknowns with regard to Creation and creativity. Whether we address these issues as metaphysics, ontology, cosmology, and/or epistemology, we are required to recognize that there are basic precepts of fundamental importance about how human beings *orient* themselves toward the conduct of inquiry, the exercise of problem-solving capabilities, and the meaning of life. The Confucian traditions; the Vedic, Brahman, and Buddhist traditions; the Judaic, Christian, and Islamic teachings; Greek philosophy; equity jurisprudence coming from roots in Roman and canon law; modern epistemology, as an effort to build a philosophy of science—all these belief systems offer basic orientations toward the conduct of inquiry and the meaning of life. They are alternatives to that form of legal rationality that relies primarily on the threat of penalties in a system of command and control run from the top down.

A quest for excellence poses a challenge for each of us to do what we can in fashioning a culture of inquiry appropriate to recognizing that creative potentials arise from conflict situations. The presumed anarchy of conflict, as Byron S.J. Weng has said to me, is revealed in the symbolism of Chinese characters that join concepts of danger and opportunity as complements to one another. Learning how to mediate conflict through mutual efforts to clarify the sources of conflict and exploring potentials for conflict resolution, including the use of our imaginations to offer new conceptions that lead to conflict resolution, are essential features in a culture of inquiry. In a culture of inquiry, scholarship merges with the exercise of problem-solving capabilities, and human creativity achieves its place in Creation.

Both peoples and ideas have flowed across the Eurasian landmass and spread to diverse areas of the world. The Mongols of Asia exercised hegemony over most of the Western and Eastern worlds within the last millennium. The Mongols, whose predecessors and successors have been among the Uralic and Altaic peoples, carried Eastern traditions to the West. The Vedas of India, like the Norse sagas, were associated with a Western culture grounded in the Indo-European language community. These patterns were reinforced by merchants and other emissaries on their respective missions between East and West. The covenantal traditions of the Hebrews and the Confucian traditions of filial piety, reciprocity, enlightenment, and distinguished artisanship may better enable us to understand the self-organizing and self-governing capabilities of peoples everywhere. The Ways of Man have their relationship to the Way of Heaven in much the same way that creativity has its relationship to Creation.

Mutual trust is an essential condition for crafting free societies in self-governing civilizations. Relying extensively on legal rationality and the coercive power of the sword places mutual trust at risk. When trust is abandoned, people become diffident and begin to prey on one another until they are all bound by the tethers of legality, which are then torn asunder by violence. The baton of power passes to those who command the use of the cudgel and the sword. We can also build by creating and maintaining bonds of trust rather than patterns of dominance through command and control. The creation and maintenance of common understanding and mutual trust are the bonds that hold human societies together (Gambetta 1988; Williamson 1993). Credible commitments (Williamson 1993) reinforced by graduated sanctions (E. Ostrom 1990) can be used to inform those who are tempted to free ride that colleagues and neighbors are monitoring their performance. This way of building configurations of trust places minimal reliance on mobilizing instruments of evil to do good.

The greatest of all tragedies would be for the universalism of the West to destroy filial piety. The viability of family life—of kinship—in linking the past to the present and in linking the present to prospects for the future is a universal aspect of human experience and is an essential feature of whatever forms of global order now exist and are likely to emerge in the future. The public realm cannot be made to work without arrangements for nurturing the intergenerational cycle of life among human beings everywhere and through all time into the indefinite future. God's Law is an effort to express the Way of Heaven and provide human beings, as Wolves among the Primates, with an image of Peace as the means for achieving ways of life worthy of emulation. The concepts of East and West are not immutable. They are tractable to human artisanship, provided that those who have their roots grounded in Eastern and Western civilizations are willing to work together to find common ground in crafting their futures. Neither the East nor the West has an exclusive claim to the Mandate of Heaven.

PART 5

The Possibility of Progress

The possibility of progress involves continuities in being and becoming. That problem is deeply embedded in the matrices of languages that are constitutive of life in human societies. Yet the possibility of progress reaches beyond the cognitive capabilities of human beings. The future remains unknown. Whatever resolution human beings are able to achieve turns on reflection and choice in the context of artisanship-artifact relationships. In the following chapter, I look back on the course of this inquiry to reach conclusions—about basic anomalies—that will enable us to come to some resolutions about the meaning of democracy. The problem of how to weave the strands of computations in the exercise of choice remains. We must build on the early experiences of childhood that facilitate inquiry in the context of reflection and choice, and we must do so in ways that are consonant with the development of the sciences and arts of association as a science for citizenship. Whatever human beings achieve by reflection and choice can only be done by discussion, reflection, choice, and intelligible action, not by command and control over others. Discussion, reflection, choice, and intelligible action are effectively mobilized as creative efforts, implying a determination and a willingness that is voluntary in character. This creative potential is the key to life in democratic societies and to the possibility of progress.

CHAPTER 11

Toward a Science of Citizenship in Democratic Systems of Order

In this inquiry, I have sought to understand democracy in its most basic considerations rather than to address a multitude of specific problems and their symptoms in particular democratic societies. If people are to rule, members of society should know how to govern themselves. They should not presume that Governments exercise tutelage over Societies and steer and direct those Societies. The future place of democracies in human civilization will not just happen; it will be constructed and will require attentive care. Those concerned with the constitution of democratic societies are required to give critical attention to the development of a science of citizenship and civic enlightenment. That science should not be confined to the education of students in schools. It should be a science of association that is studied and applied by all as we assume responsibility for living our lives and learning how to work with others under variable and changing conditions that reach out to global proportions.

Democratic societies are vulnerable to an unlimited pursuit of strategic opportunism when peoples are spared the cares of thinking and the troubles of living. Such conditions in their aggregation yield societies that defy human understanding and rational considerations. If everyone were bent on the pursuit of strategic opportunities at the cost of everyone else, the cumulative result would be the trampling of civilization underfoot. Problems of deception, self-deception, and strategic pursuits can only be alleviated by extended experience in coping with problems in artisanship-artifact relationships. If individuals can learn to become master artisans capable of working with other master artisans in open artisanship-artifact relationships, they have the potential for becoming self-governing. The challenge in democratic societies is to extend the horizons of knowledge and skills by learning to work with others in ways that enhance error-correcting capabilities, rather than fabricating patterns of deception and self-deception to tranquillize, tease, and terrorize the mind into states of helplessness. We need to look back and pull together the threads of contending ideas about the place of Governments, States, and power relationships as these bear on the meaning of democracy.

Looking Back

I began with a puzzle about the relationship of ideas to deeds in the constitution of the American system of governance. The meaning of that "experiment" was contested. Woodrow Wilson, as a young political scientist, vigorously challenged conceptions that had been used to formulate the design articulated in the *Constitution of the United States* as one of the essential components in the American system of governance. Two foreign observers, Alexis de Tocqueville and James Bryce, provided us with quite different commentaries and analyses, as did two preeminent American scholars: John Dewey, a philosopher, and Harold Lasswell, a political scientist. Key concepts shaped their thinking and what they had to say; but their modes of analysis were not commensurable to one another.

Power Relationships

My way of resolving the contradictions and anomalies that are apparent in these works is to conclude that the concept of power as defined by Lasswell and used by Bryce and Wilson does not enable us to advance very far in coming to terms with the constitution of order in democratic, as contrasted to authoritarian, societies. Wilson emphasized Responsible Party Government in a Parliamentary system rather than the civic responsibility of persons and citizens. Bryce's focus was on the voting multitude—the sovereignty of the masses—rather than on ways of working out patterns of associated relationships in civil societies and in the exercise of prerogatives of constitutional choice with regard to the diverse instrumentalities of governance. Lasswell's concept of power was closer to that of dominance, implying command and control over others. The absence of coercive capabilities was identified with anarchy. Anarchy was viewed as beyond the scope of political science.

I cannot imagine that human societies can exist without the exercise of some coercive capabilities. A question, however, remains of whether, in the presence of common knowledge, shared communities of understanding, and mutual trust, modest coercive capabilities might be sufficiently diffused through a system of social and political order so that a monopoly of rulership prerogatives can be foreclosed. Principles of self-governance might then be applied to the diverse patterns of associated relationships existing in societies. These principles are always threatened by the preemptive moves of those who, acting strategically, can put together either dominating coalitions or blocking alliances. As long as a culture of inquiry can be maintained and open discussions of interrelated interests can be pursued, a way is available to achieve enlightenment and resolution consistent with standards of fairness inherent in methods of normative inquiry implied by the Golden Rule. Achieving conflict resolution through consensus would then be the means of reestablishing common knowledge and shared communities of understanding in the maintenance of basic elements of accountability and trust consistent with the requirements of community. These are the conditions necessary for systems of self-governance to work. Only as long as people in the ordinary exigencies of life learn how to become self-governing and work out mutually productive relationships with others can we expect democracies to function as viable ways of life. Transaction costs cannot be reduced below these minimum levels without placing democratic societies at risk. Capital expenditures cannot be viewed as slack when the task is that of building human and social capital.

A system of rule-ordered relationships is subject to challenge and to inquiry about its implications and meaning by the way that it is modified and affirmed through processes of conflict resolution. The static characteristics of rules at any point in time reveal dynamic characteristics over time by the way that constitutive and authoritative relationships are the essential complements to authorized relationships in giving a dynamic quality to the language of rule-ordered relationships. Dynamics are essential complements to statics as human beings relate themselves in the present as mediating between the past and the future. Rules and the structures and processes for mediating change are essential complements to one another.

The basic attributes that Lasswell associated with democracy—self-responsibility, voluntarization, impartiality, dispersal of authority, challengeability [contestability], and balance—are *not* attributes to be associated with the exercise of *power over* others. They are, by contrast, attributes to be associated with the exercise of *power with* others. The exercise of *power with* others occurs in mutually agreeable patterns of covenantal relationships in which patterns of social accountability are broadly shared among those constituting diverse patterns of association and communities of relationships. The basic precepts applicable to the concept of covenantal relationships in the biblical tradition are consistent with republican traditions conceptualized with reference to *res publica* in the early tradition of the Roman republic and to the polis of the Greek republics. *Power with* relationships apply to how people choose to associate with one another rather than to be governed by others. Imperial Athens and imperial Rome placed the polis, *res publica,* and the spirit of democracy at risk, contributing to their destruction.

Tocqueville acknowledged that while "authority must always exist somewhere," it "may be distributed in several ways" ([1835–40] 1945, 1:70). He equated "the principle of the sovereignty of the people" to a *power with* relationship in which "every individual has an equal share of power and participates equally in the government of the state" (ibid., 1:64), meaning the several American states. Tocqueville asked why such individuals "obey society." He then elaborated:

> Every individual is always supposed to be as well informed, as virtuous, and as strong as any of his fellow citizens. He obeys society, not because he is inferior to those who conduct it or because he is less capable than any other of governing himself, but because he acknowledges the utility [usefulness] of an association with his fellow men and he knows that no such association can exist without a regulating force. He is a subject in all that concerns the duties of citizens to each other; he is free, and responsible to God alone, for all that concerns himself. Hence arises the maxim, that everyone is the best and sole judge of his own private interest, and that society has no right to control a man's actions unless they are prejudicial to the common weal or unless the common weal demands his help. (Ibid., 1:64–65)

Thomas Jefferson articulated a similar conception.

> We (the founders of the new American democracy) believe that man was a rational animal, endowed by nature with rights, and with an innate sense of justice, and that he could be restrained from wrong, and protected in right, by moderate powers, confided to persons of his own choice and held to their duties by dependence on his own will. (Quoted in Huxley [1958] 1965, 30)

Jefferson contrasted this conception to European presuppositions "that men in numerous associations cannot be restrained within the limits of order and justice, except by forces physical and moral wielded over them by authorities independent of their will [choice]" (ibid.). The distinction between *power over* and *power with* relationships is of fundamental significance for the governance of human societies.

If the concept of covenantal relationships was universally held among the members of human societies, they might presume to create and establish patterns of accountability that would manifest a moral significance worthy of public scrutiny. Such circumstances would yield not a single, comprehensive, and uniform code of law but patterns of complementarity among diverse sets of rules built on common foundations. A jurisprudence grounded in principles of equity could be used to conduct proceedings with reference to the basic mode of normative inquiry grounded in the Golden Rule, or its equivalents, to achieve complementarities among diverse patterns of relationships. Bounding every detail of human relationships by universal rules and regulations makes everyone a slave of legalities.

If the core organizing concept of *power over* relationships is marginal to the constitution of democratic societies, we face the problem of reconceptualizing the constitution of patterns of order in democratic societies by relying on concepts of *power with* relationships. Here again we face anomalies. Hobbes's conception of "power" is revealed in the assertion previously quoted: "The POWER *of a man,* to take it universally, is his present means, to obtain some future apparent good" ([1651] 1960, 56, Hobbes's emphasis). This is equivalent to an articulation of the basic artisanship-artifact relationship that might apply to the place of any individual in any human endeavor as purposive activities mediated by the use of one's voluntary nervous system and one's potential for drawing on the help of others.

Hobbes, however, opted for the Supreme Authority of a sole sovereign representative rather than for the sovereignty of those who were being represented. Reliance on the authority of a single sovereign representative as Supreme Authority puts Hobbes's sovereign in the position of violating his seventeenth Law of Nature: that no one is a fit arbitrator of one's own cause in relation to the interest of another. Hobbes's formulation also creates an anomaly of the representative who, as an agent in some ontological sense, becomes the ultimate principal in the exercise of sovereign authority within a commonwealth. A sovereign *representative* presumably *represents* those who are *represented.* A further anomaly exists in Hobbes's theory of sovereignty: a rule of law cannot be applied to sovereigns and to the relationships among sovereign States.

To paraphrase Hobbes's allusion to a sovereign as possessing "the greatest of human powers," it would be possible for the peoples of democratic societies to individually and collectively enjoy the states of affairs in which men are "united by consent" and have "the use of all their [diverse] powers" (ibid.) with which they are associated. The American federalists and Tocqueville, in my judgment, conceptualized the possibility that Hobbes failed to grasp. These elements can be seen in *Leviathan* with regard to the conception of what Hobbes referred to as a "democracy," in which the Supreme Authority would reside in an assembly of all who would come together. The possibility of a democratic assembly of all citizens that would exercise Supreme Authority could only exist in the presence of common knowledge, shared communities of understanding, agreeable patterns of social accountability, and mutual trust in one another sufficient to constitute an assembly.

A host of issues pertaining to who may participate, how proceedings are to be organized, who establishes the agenda and controls the proceedings, and how the agents of an assembly are to be selected and held accountable to an assembly would have to be resolved by the rules of assembly. These issues would require recourse to varying decision rules, rather than presuming that a single rule might apply to different types of decisions to be taken. *Rule by assembly* can only occur when *rules of assembly* are *constitutive* of an assembly as a going concern. These are two sides of the same coin if an assembly is to function as a going concern. If such conditions were made explicit in a working covenant setting the terms and conditions for the proceedings of the assembly, a constitution as a working covenant would exist subject to change through time. Basic organizing principles and limits need articulation, not detailed rules for every contingency.

We immediately confront the constraints of the asymmetries of speaking and listening relationships inherent in large deliberative assemblies. Montesquieu attempted to address and resolve that problem of size by the concept of confederation as a means of crafting a system of *power with* relationships applicable to both small and large republics organized as confederations. The failure of Montesquieu's concept of confederation was the core problem in crafting the design of the *Constitution of the United States,* specifically addressed in *Federalist* Nos. 15 and 16 and elaborated at many other junctures in *The Federalist.*

Tocqueville, in my judgment, came to appreciate the deeper meaning of American federalism in light of the prior intellectual achievements of Montesquieu, Pascal, Rousseau, the Scottish philosophers, and the American federalists and in light of the initial workings of the American experiment. That experiment was of such paradigmatic significance that Tocqueville recognized in his introduction to volume 1 of *Democracy in America* that "a new science of politics is needed for a new world" ([1835–40] 1945, 1:7). Tocqueville refers to this new political science as a "science of association," the practice of which is an "art of association": "[T]he science of association is the mother of science; the progress of all the rest depends upon the progress it has made" (ibid., 2:110); "the art of association then becomes . . . the mother of action, studied and applied by all" (ibid., 2:117). The condition "studied and applied by all" has been seriously neglected. Reading and talking about current events more closely approximates gossip than serious study. Gossip has only a marginal relationship to knowledgeable and intelligible artisanship applied to the construction of associated relationships. Gossip is, however, of some importance in monitoring and assessing performance in light of known persons, positions, and appropriate standards of performance.

The shift in perspective from *power over* relationships emanating from a Supreme Authority to *power with* relationships fundamentally affected the science and art of association. The covenantal character of constitutional law establishes the terms and conditions of governance in which fundamental exercises of authority are subject to limits. Covenantal societies depend on differential assignments of authority relationships in which some exercise specialized agency relationships, but in which no one exercises ultimate, absolute, and indivisible authority beyond the reach of challenge through a due process of law. Such a system of authority depends, however, on habits of the heart and mind of citizens—habits informed by a science of association and practiced in an art of association "studied and applied by all." The cumulative character of such a system of relationships yields a self-governing society rather than a State-governed Society.

The prerogatives for dealing with other peoples might specifically be assigned subject to patterns of accountability in a way that would make agency relationships publicly accountable in the discharge of public trusts. Properly formulated and duly ratified treaties might then be considered as part of "the law of the land." Such treaties would presumably be formulated in accordance with a general theory of limited constitutions vesting authority in persons and citizens subject to appropriate monitoring and adjudicatory arrangements. The authority of persons and citizens need not be limited to Nation-States. Europe is taking steps toward what I would call a "federal union" with covenantal associations among self-governing entities operating in complementary domains and functional relationships. Unfortunately, Europeans, like many Americans, conceptualize a federal system as being equivalent to the Federal Government, presuming a Federal State. Such formulations are incoherent. Democracies cannot be confined to units of government that fail to take account of the cultural features of life that gain expression in ways of life that nurture children, forming the identities, character structures, and attachments of successive generations. Abstract entities like States, Societies, and Markets do not nurture children.

If societies are constituted, as Lasswell argued, from complementary aspects of an identical subject matter [object of study], the appropriate standard for self-conscious understanding of societies is the complement of those analytical perspectives used in the analysis, construction, and maintenance of social relationships. The analytical perspective of an anthropologist is applicable not only to some "primitive" society in some isolated ecological niche in the world but to the events observed as institutional facts and artifactual constructions in any society. These events can be viewed as trilateral constructions, reflected in the work of Ibn Khaldûn, which have reference to *people* and *place* mediated by *culture,* meaning to *cultivate* the various facets of life in the ecological context of some place. People who cultivate transform themselves by becoming and being culti- vators of the place that forms their habitat—that which is cultivated. The same perspectives could apply to administrators, economists, historians, journalists, jurists, legislators, linguists, literary artisans, philosophers, political scientists, sociologists, students, and all others. If a synthesis of these analytical perspectives could be applied to the constitution of order in human societies, people might aspire to a higher level of consciousness about the *cultural,* meaning *cultivating,* characteristics of life in human societies and about their manifestations in ways of life. To administer, then, is to facilitate productive efforts in ways that are constructive in working with others—to engage in entrepreneurship of diverse types.

These problems cannot be resolved by specializations devoid of com- plementarities. Because the condition of human fallibility allows only lim- ited comprehension, greater and greater specialization would yield Ortega y Gasset's "learned ignoramus." Reliance on abstract concepts of Markets and States evokes a bureaucratic consciousness in which a job on a payroll is presumed to be necessary to a "meaningful" life and in which the ratio- nality of bureaucratic methods becomes the characteristic way of life. In these circumstances, market rationality gives way to bureaucratic rational- ity, bureaucratic rationality gives way to corruption, and life gives way to helplessness and despair.

Alternatively, such problems can be addressed by competent artisans in the diverse cultural and social sciences and humanities and in the diverse facets of life who learn how to work with one another in circumstances marked by Lasswell's attributes of democracy to the point of challenging one another about *problems* of unanticipated consequences that arise from conjoint efforts. Unanticipated consequences imply counterintentional and counterintuitive effects, suggesting the need to reformulate the way that ideas work to achieve effects. Scholars concerned with the application of "economic reasoning" to nonmarket decision making, as in the Public- Choice tradition, cannot afford to neglect the epistemic character of their inquiries. These inquiries cannot be met by standards of logical proof alone. Further, scholars must be prepared to address anomalies that arise when assumptions that work reasonably well in competitive market economies do not apply with equal force to patterns of nonmonetized rela- tionships.

Conditions that are likely to be basic factors of substantial significance in nonmarket decision making include knowledge and infor- mation conditions; law and order conditions; production, distribution, and use conditions; and conditions of faith, sympathy, and trust. These conditions cannot appropriately be treated as parameters outside the focus of inquiry. Shifting exogenous parameters to endogenous variables is an important way to extend the frontiers of inquiry in the cultural and social sciences and humanities. New generations of scholars and practitioners need to be exposed to working with others who bring complementary skills to bear on the study of cultural/social phenomena. They may then develop appropriate skills in learning how to challenge patterns of deception, self-deception, and opportunism sufficiently to ameliorate the strong incentives to compound such tendencies.

Limits, Deceptions, and Opportunistic Pursuits

No single criterion of choice is adequate to take account of both monetized and nonmonetized relationships or of both the quantifiable and the nonquantifiable features of life in human societies. If there is a Oneness to the Universe, that Oneness cannot be quantified, except as indicators of qualitative significance. Maximizing utility or minimizing transaction costs does not apply to epistemic choice or constitutional choice in the same way that such calculations might be thought to apply to the choice of substitutable alternatives in one-to-one comparisons of distinguishable but similar items. To rely on a single specifiable criterion of choice, such as Utility, is to treat human societies as one-dimensional realms in which the forest cannot be seen for all of the trees that obstruct one's view. One can only come to appreciate the character of forests by living and working with forests. Forests too need cultivation to realize their potentials.

The covenantal character of constitutional choice in democratic societies suggests that the character of covenants is not purely an intellectual construction. Hobbes imagined that the covenant to generate a commonwealth was an intellectual construction to be expressed as if "every man should say to every man, *I authorize and* **give up my right of governing myself***, to this man, or to this assembly of men, on this condition, that thou give up thy right to him, and authorize all his actions in like manner*" ([1651] 1960, 112, Hobbes's italics, my boldface). Covenants in associated relationships in democratic societies need to be working arrangements specifying the general terms and conditions of governance provided that citizens assume responsibility for governing and defending themselves and for monitoring and enforcing the terms of constitutive charters. All assignments of authority are subject to limits reinforced by veto capabilities giving opportunities for challenge and contestation in diverse arenas having recourse to operational, judicial, legislative, political, and constitutional processes. If essential provisions of working covenants cannot be met, the character of the construction cannot be maintained. The ecology of the forest, so to speak, cannot be maintained if attention is only given to trees.

The complement of other plants and of insects and other forms of life are necessary to forests (Atran and Medin 1996).

Choices made in constituting the rules of a fair game can meet standards of general agreement [consensus] accompanied by presumptions that systems of governance can be conducted in accordance with the rules of fair games. The quest for justice in accordance with standards of fairness as well as decisions in competitive markets and decisions about the warrantability of knowledge might all be grounded in general agreement creating conditions of consensus, informed consent, reciprocity, and trust among communities of self-governing people. Such potentials are, however, always vulnerable to shirking, duplicity, and the quest for special advantage by some at the cost of others and to the use of ideas as partisan weapons to war on others.

The American federalists and Tocqueville were able to conceive how democracy as a form of government could be used to craft the architecture of authority relationships in ways that were constitutive of what could appropriately be conceptualized as self-governing societies (V. Ostrom 1991, chaps. 2 and 3). Such concepts drew on prior experiences in constituting free cities, monastic orders, religious congregations, merchant societies, craft guilds, associations among peasants, markets, and other patterns of human association. A quest for conflict resolution consistent with the reestablishment of communities of associated relationships based again on precepts of covenantal relationships is the way for maintaining the covenantal character of self-governing societies through time and across generations. Such an approach is facilitative of innovations consistent with standards of enlightenment, freedom, justice, reciprocity, and mutual trust in patterns of order in human societies.

If democratic societies place primary emphasis on voting and winning elections, it is possible for politicians and citizens to become obsessed with counting votes. Counting votes before any election occurs, or any decision is taken, to calculate what appeal or deal can be made to modify the outcome can dominate patterns of thought related to entrepreneurship and problem-solving efforts. When the election is over, or a decision is taken, the primary preoccupation can turn on conjectures about how a modification of strategy would have yielded a different result. The assessment of successes and failures applies to *campaign* strategies, whether the *campaign* is to win elections, legislative decisions, or the verdicts of juries.

Campaigns have an analogue to warfare applied to the manipulation of symbols as wars of words rather than using other weapons of violent warfare. Wars of words are thought to be less harmful than wars with other weapons. This may be true in the short run. Wars of words, however, can become so destructive in the long run that they dwarf the casualties of open warfare. Wars of words can destroy civilizations. The place of ideas in human thought, actions, and what gets accomplished is abandoned in such wars to mad displays of chanting and shouting slogans being expressed as ideologies. In wars of words, the sciences and arts of association practiced and studied by all with reference to the meaning of working covenants conducted in light of artisanship-artifact relationships go undeveloped, and a struggle to dominate decisions leads to the neglect of problem-solving capabilities, the loss of the capabilities and skills associated with artisanship-artifact relationships, the corruption of language, and the decline of human civilizations. These circumstances can lead citizens in democratic societies to trample civilizations underfoot.

John Dos Passos, in *Mr. Wilson's War,* refers to a statement made by Woodrow Wilson, as president of the United States, in his proclamation of the draft [conscription] on May 18, 1917. In that statement, President Wilson asserted:

> In the sense in which we have been want to think of armies, there are no armies to this struggle. There are entire nations armed. . . . It is not an army that we must shape and train for war; it is a nation. (Dos Passos 1963, 185)

Training and shaping a nation for war, without long-standing and well-trained militia, inevitably places democracies at risk. Shaping and training a nation for an unanticipated war requires direction by those in command. Paradoxically, the rhetoric of warfare has come to pervade much of American politics in the twentieth century. Franklin Roosevelt thought of himself as leading a "great army of the people, dedicated to a disciplined attack on our common problems," and as calling for "power to wage war against the emergency as . . . if we were in fact invaded by a foreign foe" (quoted in Schaffer 1991). Lyndon Johnson engaged in a War on Poverty. Others have called for "crusades" that are the "moral equivalent of war"—a sonorous phrase of great moral ambiguity. Using the rhetoric of warfare as a substitute for the exercise of analytical capabilities in addressing problems in human societies places human intelligibility at risk. Scholars abandon their commitment to scholarship as they become partisans in the use of ideas as weapons in partisan crusades.

Putting words on paper is *never* sufficient for achieving knowledgeable or lawful relationships in human society. Instead, human actors need to achieve such levels of sympathy, skill, and intelligibility that they know what they are doing in the context of any and all efforts to achieve creative potentials. We must then confront the anomaly that Lasswell and Kaplan, in *Power and Society* (1950), associated Tocqueville's *Democracy in Amer-*

ica with "brute empiricism" without observing how "facts" characteristic of societies are "institutional facts" to be construed in light of relevant theoretical conceptions for constructing institutional arrangements and for what follows in the operation of those institutional arrangements. While I regard Lasswell as the premier American political scientist in the twentieth century, I am forced to conclude that his concept of power associated with patterns of dominance did not allow him to see Tocqueville's commentary and analysis as focusing on *power with* relationships in which a science and art of association, rather than a science of command and control, was viewed as constitutive of democratic societies. This fundamental difference in perspective has radical paradigmatic implications in addressing the question "Who govern?" in the plural rather than "Who governs?" (Dahl 1961) in the singular. A minor distinction in language may have radical implications for theoretical discourse in the same way that a shift in perspective from a revolving sun to a spinning and orbiting earth had profound implications for many different sciences, professions, and technologies.

In light of these considerations, both James Bryce and Woodrow Wilson took the nominal position of being "brute empiricists." In the name of "reality," each proceeded to posit a theoretical conception of Supreme Authority residing in a sovereign representative analogous to the doctrine of Parliamentary Supremacy. These realists, however, ignore the oath of secrecy required of Privy Councillors in the English Constitution and the place of the Official Secrets Acts in establishing a cloak of secrecy associated with ministerial deliberations in the constitution of what is deceptively alluded to as Responsible Party Government. Wilson recognized that a system of Parliamentary Government entailed a constitutional formalization of machine politics and boss rule. The effective boss—the head of Government—was presumably held accountable to Parliament. Bryce was quite explicit about the problem that Will associated with the mandate exercised by the ruling authority in a Parliament was a potential source of deception. Madison called this condition "majority tyranny," while Wilson identified it as "responsible government." The radical divergence in these conceptualizations provides opportunities to test disparate conjectures derived from contrary arguments as competing hypotheses.

These uses of languages are indicative of the Newspeak and Doublethink that have come to pervade the patterns of deception and self-deception characteristic of the language of partisan political discourse in the contemporary world. Talking about political Myths, Doctrines, Ideologies, and Utopias is part of an occult enterprise in which the worship of words becomes a form of idolatry allowing duplicity to reign. Scholars in the social sciences and humanities too often use words as weapons to repudiate one another and become participants in collusive efforts to use instruments of State power to coerce "citizens," who are no more than subjects. One-to-one comparisons, however, cannot be easily made in comparing the United Kingdom with the United States of America as aggregate entities. Careful analysis of particular institutional arrangements in the context of comparable types of human experience should allow for more coherent discourse about human affairs.

Questions about tendencies through the course of history also require consideration. In chapter 1, I quoted the concluding paragraph from Robert Michels's *Political Parties,* in which Michels notes that the successive waves that occur in the democratic currents of history reflect a "cruel game" that "will continue without end" ([1911] 1966, 371). As long as there are substantial incentives toward patterns of deception, self-deception, and strategic opportunism, we can expect such struggles to continue, no matter what parties gain dominance. Such strategic considerations offer an explanation for why democratic modes of government might contribute to the erosion of "social and humane ideals" and to the *eclipse* of the "public" in Dewey's analysis.

We now face the irony that those who led the struggle against Majority Tyranny manifest as machine politics and boss rule would as "rational actors" be expected to advance reforms to strengthen their own hands as leaders occupying positions of executive control in particular units of government. Woodrow Wilson's *Congressional Government* provided him with a rationale for becoming a leading reformer on behalf of "the new leadership of the Executive," substituting "statesmanship for government by mass meeting" ([1885] 1956, 23). Wilson's successors who aspired to leadership in undertaking reform programs were motivated by the same principles. Michels's "gradual transformation" occurs across succeeding generations in which democracies adopt "the aristocratic spirit, and in many cases also the aristocratic forms, against which at the outset they struggled so fiercely" ([1911] 1966, 371). Democracies carry the seeds of their own destruction. Democracies are vulnerable to the neglect of their own citizens, who can destroy democracies as well as reducing buildings to rubble.

We can now understand how Madison's concern about Majority Tyranny gives way to Tocqueville's concern for Democratic Despotism as reformers and their successors restructure the constitution of authority relationships to strengthen their leadership prerogatives. Reformers, like revolutionaries, have rational incentives to enhance the prerogatives of autocratic authority. Individual reformers may be bound by their commitments. Their successors, however, are likely to take advantage of the opportunities made available to them. Democracies are not viable over the long run if they depend on Governments to reform themselves. Democracies are grounded in the covenantal character of constitutional choice governing all patterns of human association, including what had been presumed to be the supreme power of the State. Forgetfulness—the loss of knowledge, moral integrity, skill, and intelligibility among human artisans—is the plague of humanity.

The problems of strategic opportunism pose fundamental challenges of the most serious proportions to the viability of the cultural and social sciences and to the viability of human societies. Unless ideas can be related to deeds in the sense of what is achieved, I can see no prospect for applying the method of "Science," as Orwell used that term, to the vocabularies pertaining to cultural creations. As long as ideas are treated as "ideologies," not worthy of treatment as credible hypotheses, then those ideas cannot plausibly be treated as conjectures to be critically scrutinized. To presume that States exercise guidance and control over Society, that Reasons of State have no essential connection to ideologies being expounded in the political process, and, at the same time, that statesmen are being driven by social forces is incoherent. Such incoherence is grounds neither for scientific discourse nor for rational consideration of public policies.

This problem of coherence is addressed in the experimental sciences, which rely on laboratory methods, by attempting to set the relevant parameters so that key variables can be worked with under isolable conditions, recognizing that the flow characteristics of electrons, for example, can be distinguished from the flow of water. Potentials for isolability in the practical world of human experience with regard to scope, domain, and periodicity of patterns of order in human societies need to be established with regard to whatever human beings attempt to do. To establish canons of measurement presuming commensurable units in mutually exclusive and exhaustive sets with regard to a domain identified with the boundaries of Nation-States and to be characteristic of Societies as a Whole is, I presume, absurd, foolhardy, and conducive both to deception and self-deception. Exercising a blind faith in knowledge is not an appropriate way to resolve the problem of knowledge among the dwellers of Plato's Cave.

Where to Turn?

The vulnerability of democratic societies to Majority Tyranny and to Democratic Despotism when combined as complements to one another creates immensely destructive potentials that cannot be readily addressed. At stake are not only institutional features of societies but "the whole moral and intellectual condition of a people" that constitutes "their character of mind" (Tocqueville [1835–40] 1945, 1:299). Political crises are compounded by cultural crises. These are conditions that require critical reflection and inquiry about the more general course of human affairs. The paradigmatic shifts undertaken by Marx, Engels, Lenin, and Stalin and by Wilson, Roosevelt, and Nixon only offer us different versions of Newspeak and Doublethink. Both versions assume that the State is the unique association for the common good of all rather than a Faustian bargain with instruments of evil. We are addressing the most difficult problems that challenge the limits of human cognition.

Constitutional Choice

Critical points of leverage exist in the context of constitutional choice. Those potentials are little more than illusions if confined to a single constitution somehow presuming a contract between the Sovereign and the People. Such a concept is, in my judgment, a pure fiction of the mind that cannot meet standards of empirical warrantability and public reproducibility. Tocqueville's reference to the art and science of association would, by contrast, imply that principles of constitutional choice might be applied to all enduring patterns of human relationships. Agreements about enduring human relationships are not simple exchange relationships but open-ended commitments best characterized as covenantal in nature. Perhaps it is more appropriate to refer to the arts and sciences of association in the plural. Assignments of authority would then always imply both distinguishable and complementary features fit in a more general configuration of associated relationships. A separation of powers always implies a sharing of powers. The exercise of veto capabilities is essential to the preservation of the autonomous standing of any position, including those of persons and citizens. The exercise of veto capabilities also poses a threat of stalemate unless conflicts, as signs of trouble, can be mediated through processes of conflict resolution.

Processes of conflict resolution place priority on the search for just and equitable solutions that yield consensus and informed consent among adversaries seeking to reestablish shared communities of understanding among those who associate together. Thus, the core of the law needs to be concerned with principles of equity jurisprudence rather than criminal jurisprudence, fully recognizing that criminal jurisprudence has an essential but presumably marginal place in the constitution of order in democratic societies. For this reason, I would presume that the requirements of criminal jurisprudence are quite different than a search for equitable solutions. Yet fairness has a place in all forms of due process, whether applied to the due process of law in rule-ordered relationships or to a due process of inquiry applicable to any problematic situation.

There are inevitable limits beyond which problems cannot be resolved within present and intermediate time horizons. Such circumstances presumably exist in exaggerated form in numerous regions of the world, including the Middle East, the Caucasus, the Balkans, and Central Europe. Such problems also prevail in the British Isles, North America, France, and Spain. Conquest by a dominant power and dominance by long-standing majority factions inevitably meet resistance. The English conquered Ireland and dominated it by political authority and military force; but the Irish continued to resist. People who are subject to dominance will find capabilities for resistance. If they are driven "underground," conspiracies of silence will be accompanied by the creation of secret societies. Patterns of corruption inevitably prevail with secret accommodations; and such societies may become sufficiently corrupt to be impervious to reform. Under such circumstances, "democratic" societies are likely to become corrupt democracies vulnerable to coups d'état and popular crusades that, without access to constitutional change, inevitably blossom and die. If citizens cannot be trusted with the right to bear arms, they are unlikely to appreciate the limits that must necessarily apply both to the proper exercise of authority and to the appropriate exercise of resistance to the abuse of public authority. No form of government can cope with deep disagreements. Such issues can only be resolved by inquiry and discourse at the most fundamental levels. Patched-up deals inevitably unravel.

The Construction of Associated Relationships

If we presume that each individual is first his or her own governor, all patterns of human relationships involve potentials for both opportunities and dangers. To assume responsibility for the decisions one makes in relation to others requires a considerable accumulation of personal and local knowledge about the time and place exigencies in which and with whom one lives and works. Every child can learn what it means to play games. To appreciate what it means to play the game of life in accordance with rules and to meet standards of fairness, individuals must appreciate that all exigencies of life fit into patterns of relationships that are constitutive of order in human societies. While customs, norms, and rules can be presumed to exist as features or attributes of a community, they also exist in each individual's mind and become habituated in the ways that people relate to one another. Whatever you and I do is always intermediate between what has been and what might be. We take habituated routines for granted without thought, but habits of the heart and mind are always grounded in the moral and intellectual traditions of peoples unless those are forgotten. The forgotten is lost to consciousness.

Whatever we propose to do in relation to others requires communication. By the very language we use as we craft present means to achieve some future apparent good—to use Hobbes's concept of power—we bring together a background of common knowledge that we use as a resource to realize some possibility. The more demanding concept of common knowledge presumes that you know what I know and vice versa to the extent that what each of us knows is subject to a high level of mutual awareness. But the proportioning of present means to some future apparent good always involves elements of futurity that require us to draw on and build common knowledge as associated relationships unfold. Further, that repertoire of common knowledge, which is in the process of being made, reinforced, or challenged, must also be accompanied by a mutual understanding in a sense of agreement, concurrence, or consensus.

An exercise of *power with* others implies both responsibility and a willingness to take account of the interest of others in what can be called "patterns of social accountability." How our associated efforts are worked out is the basis for mutual feelings about one another, the degree of mutual trust that emerges from our association with one another, and our faith in the basic presuppositions—the inner convictions—that lay at the foundation of human rationality and become the basis of life. These contingencies apply to all patterns of human relationships. The rudiments of what I consider to be a democratic society get built as mutual understandings grounded in common knowledge, agreeable patterns of accountability, and mutual trust functioning in a context of work with others as autonomous lawful equals in patterns of associated relationships. When trust is broken, trustworthy relationships cannot be maintained—a tautology that is too frequently neglected. An acknowledgment of wrongdoing—repentance—is necessary to the reestablishment of trust.

In many ways, we differ from one another. We choose to craft relationships to draw on each other's diverse capabilities. In the course of doing whatever we seek to achieve, we also engage in a process of building common knowledge, shared communities of understanding, patterns of accountability, and mutual trust as essential residuals. These efforts are constitutive in character. They reflect the application of principles of constitutional choice to ordinary interpersonal relationships. A naive commitment to minimize transaction costs would neglect the importance of taking the time to explain, to understand, and to build trust in the pursuit of problem-solving efforts. If building human and social capital is confused with the concept of transaction costs, minimizing transaction costs has immense destructive potentials.

Alternatively, we might attempt to command, conceal our intentions, create false impressions, play others for suckers, destabilize the circumstances of others, and engender suspicion, distrust, and hostility. Systems of relationships based on command and control over others endanger consensual associated relationships. In a society in which every indiscretion of speech runs the risk of being treated as a high crime subject to summary punishment, including a bullet in the back of the head, the character of mind is not conducive to self-governing arrangements except in the formation of conspiratorial alliances with their own enforcers. Secretive and closed societies are not open to public problem-solving modes of inquiry. Efforts to achieve reform in secretive, closed societies are unlikely to succeed until conditions of mutual trust can be established.

The condition of freedom requires the courage to assume responsibility for one's own actions and for the way that one makes use of relevant knowledge, skill, and intelligibility to relate to others in mutually productive ways. Hapless victims are not free and cannot achieve collegiality in any undertaking unless they are willing to assume responsibility for their own actions. These conditions are necessary for making democratic societies work as one learns to live and work with others in the practice of human artisanship. Self-governing democratic societies can only exist under conditions in which individuals become their own masters and become capable of governing their own affairs and working with others in mutually productive working relationships.

Pathways among the Matrices of Human Artisanship

If human societies are viewed as matrices reflecting the diverse ways that languages are put to use by human beings, these matrices are likely to form networks of relationships in which societies are structured and restructured by those who are both the "matter" and the "artificers" of societies and whose "pacts" and "covenants" form diverse patterns of association. These patterns of association in their aggregations become commonwealths that need not be confined to the commonwealths of Nation-States. We might, following such an image, search for the pathways that fallible creatures can pursue in artisanship-artifact relationships that become constitutive of human societies. As we do so, we should recognize many of the signs with which we have become familiar in the course of these conjectures about patterns of order in human societies.

Problematics, I presume, always turn on the way that some pattern of relationships might be transformed to create a new reality envisaged by the use of the imagination. What is imagined is some future apparent possibility. If that future apparent possibility is to be brought to realization, one must have recourse to some present means to transform the matrices of some existing state of affairs in the world, represented by one's image of that state of affairs, into some artifactual state anticipated by the imagination. What is called "induction" is, in my experience, nothing more than the use of the imagination to array what-if conjectures with if-then inferences. Whether present means can be acted on in a way to realize some future apparent possibility has great significance for human potentials in the exercise of choice. Artisanship is the fundamental relationship constitutive of human societies, cultures, and civilizations. It is the key to the relationship of ideas to deeds.

All human endeavors reach into multiple facets of relationships that tie the world of material conditions and technologies to patterns of human relationships in whatever is achieved and put to use. We come back to the reflections of the anonymous engineer in the investigation of flood control in the Santa Ana watershed (California Department of Public Works 1928). Floods exist in arid regions. What appears to be a seamless web of nature can be modified to put flood flows into storage and increase the percolation of water on spreading grounds located on gravel cones where mountain streams discharge onto the sediments of the valley floor. An engineer who knows geology, hydrology, and other relevant fields of universal principles can, in light of a knowledge of the local situation, begin to imagine alternative possibilities. Those possibilities simultaneously bear on economic opportunities that can be brought to realization by modifying the natural regimen of floods and droughts to create an *artifactual regimen* for storing water and arranging water flows in ways to better serve those engaged in the pursuit of diverse opportunities. A "problem" associated with floods has implications for wide-ranging "problematics," involving both dangers and opportunities that impinge on diverse facets of life.

The task of inquiry about problematic situations is how to realize opportunities while being sensitive to ways of limiting dangers in constituting patterns of development. What-if conjectures need to be related to if-then inferences. To constrain inquiry only to intellectual specialties imposes arbitrary constraints on the range of inquiry associated with what-if conjectures and locks one into the constraining character of logical inference. Those what-if conjectures are as essential to human rationality as are if-then inferences. The course of deductive reasoning cannot reach beyond the initial stipulation of the "if" conditions. The larger bounds of human rationality need to take account of what-if conjectures to allow for innovative potentials. The what-if conjectures and if-then inferences are essential complements—not binary opposites—that allow human beings to gain some basic leverage for tying the past as memory to the future as creations of the mind in processes of being and becoming. The great problem is in learning how to relate ideas to deeds by the way thinking is related to acting and by the way acting is related to what gets accomplished.

Today, the regimen of water stocks and flows in the southern California metropolitan region reaches from the Colorado Basin, the Mono Basin and Owens Valley, and the Central Valley of California to complement the modified stocks and flows of all of the waterways and groundwater basins in the southern California coastal region. Water flows through networks of aqueducts and pipes, controlled by valves at every outlet, supplying water to each and every water user. Most outlets discharge into receptacles that, in turn, discharge into sewerage systems carrying waste waters to reclamation facilities to be used for irrigation or limited industrial purposes, recycled into groundwater basins for general use, and eventually discharged into the Pacific Ocean. The whole system is an artifactual construction built into the material conditions of a natural habitat and is a place of human habitation where choices are exercised through diverse patterns of rule-ordered relationships accompanied by pricing and taxing "mechanisms." All of these patterns of relationships are mediated through the matrices of language-ordered technologies. Money, for example, is a medium of exchange and a unit of account routinely expressed as symbols printed on paper.

The patterning of authority relationships represents the stocks and flows of knowledge, communications, thoughts, choices, understandings, and activities, which are articulated in structures and processes that have stock and flow characteristics that need to be understood and worked with in the same way that the stock and flow characteristics of water are worked with. Such potentials depend on the use of ideas in pooling, rearranging, and compromising existing interests by restructuring the patterns of authority relationships to constitute the emerging patterns of relationships among all of those who are affected by modifications in the regimen of water flows.

These were the patterns of relationships of concern to John Dewey in *The Public and Its Problems* (1927). All of the people who are affected by a modified regimen of water stocks and flows and by the consequences that emerge would constitute Dewey's inchoate public—those who are affected. How an *inchoate public* is brought to the *consciousness* of a *shared community of understanding* depends on the existence of *decision-making arrangements* in an *open public realm* and on a willingness to explore how to pool, rearrange, and compromise existing interests and to provide for the constitution of new and altered patterns of relationships. By raising "The Public" to a level of abstraction capable of addressing the problems of Graham Wallas's Great Society, Dewey engaged in a search for discovery of "the state" as a way of achieving the Great Community. The State as an effort to articulate the Great Community could never evoke a conscious understanding of the problematics of floods and droughts in the

Santa Ana Basin. In the Santa Ana investigation, the public was confined to those living in and adjacent to the Santa Ana watershed. Drawing boundaries for a flood control or water conservation "district" and working through the stocks and flows of knowledge, information, and shared understandings that are constitutive of such a public enterprise is a vastly different task than discovery of the State. If Dewey had been a careful student of *The Federalist* and *Democracy in America,* he might have addressed himself, as I indicated earlier, to "The Public*s* and Their Problem*s.*" Such a conception would have been more closely related to his philosophy of pragmatism and education, concerned with learning by doing. Great Societies are not organized by some single center of Supreme Authority exercising tutelage over Society. Knowledgeable, skillful, and intelligible persons build great societies by working with one another and mediating conflicts to achieve conflict resolution in forming coherent patterns of relationships with one another.

Human beings can achieve the skills needed to become self-governing by gaining a mastery of artisanship-artifact relationships that can be applied to diverse facets of life, including those of conflict and conflict resolution. They can acquire the habits of heart and mind characteristic of artisanship. Any master artisan can learn to work with other master artisans in pooling their resources for whatever problematics they may confront. These are the conditions for the emergence of cultures of inquiry in which conflict can be viewed as an opportunity to elucidate information, array arguments, and draw on innovative potentials for achieving problem-solving capabilities to resolve conflicts. In the course of such efforts to struggle with one another's formulations, those who participate in such discussions are simultaneously crafting elements of common knowledge, shared communities of understanding, agreeable patterns of accountability, and mutual trust that are constitutive of patterns of order in human societies.

The conditions applicable to the quest for and the use of knowledge are met under conditions of general agreement among skilled artisans. The conditions of trade in an open exchange economy are also met by mutual agreement among informed participants. Constituting the rules for a fair game are met by general agreement among informed players of a game who view the essential condition of a game as being played in accordance with agreeable rules. The conditions of community are met when consensus prevails about the common knowledge, shared communities of understanding, and patterns of accountability to such a degree that mutual trust prevails among those participating in such communities of relationships. These are the "stocks" necessary to complement the "flows" of information and activities characteristic of ways of life in human societies. Dimitry

Morgachev, a Russian peasant with three years of schooling, in a memoir entitled "My Life," recognized basic essentials when he observed:

> . . . order in life, not only within the family but also in society, can exist only when people are sincere, when they have one thing in common, a good and reasonable understanding of life, when they have a religion [faith, inner conviction] in common. Then everything that is so difficult, even impossible, to settle just settles itself. [W]e are living in an age when people have no philosophy in common. The old one has been outlived and no longer has any power, but no new one has yet taken shape. And from this comes all of the suffering, the chaos in life, that we see all over the world. (Edgerton 1993, 179)

Those who are preoccupied with ideas have serious work to do in establishing the commonalities that apply to the corpus [stock] of knowledge. Such inquiry requires a critical awareness of how universals relate to particulars in constituting within human societies patterns of order appropriate to the ecological circumstances in which people live. Fashioning a philosophy appropriate to a culture of inquiry in self-governing societies can accrue only by learning to work with others to resolve problems in constructive ways. Philosophy is not confined to words on paper. Working out the conceptual ingredients for creating ways of life is how *public philosophies* are constructed (Lippmann 1955).

Opportunities will always exist for some to prey on others. Under conditions of unanimity, some have incentives to hold out for special advantages. Whenever it becomes expedient to relax the conditions of general agreement for other decision rules, including majority-vote rules, opportunities are created for some to take advantage of such circumstances to prey on and exploit others. Instead of maintaining standards of consensus that are constitutive of self-governing communities of relationships, it is easy to be lulled into believing that others are responsible for one's fate. One can then find that the structure of covenantal relationships has been replaced by a system of command and control. An overemphasis on legality can transform the conditions of life into a quest for exceptions and favors that eventually lead to the corruption of life, to the abandonment of morality, and to conditions of servitude in which everyone is bound by the tethers of legality and the loss of self-governing ways of life.

The pathway to Peace, as an alternative to War, in self-governing societies involves quite different opportunities, burdens, and risks than does obedience to a Sovereign exercising tutelage and wielding the power of the sword over subjects. That pathway to Peace always entails requirements to take time out to reflect critically on the diverse facets of life and to explore the implications associated with the different patterns of choice that exist and might be made available in networks of human relationships. All human societies are networks of epistemic relationships, economic relationships, and political relationships. These relationships are interconnected with sentiments and feelings of identity [affective, esprit de corps relationships] and are bound together by the norms of a moral order, which are constitutive of communities of relationships in human societies. A sharing of authority requires a dispersal of authority. The condition of self-responsibility turns on contestability when one's standing [autonomy, integrity] is threatened. Systems of checks and balances are necessary to contestability. Contestability is necessary to the elucidation of information, the clarification of argumentation, and the quest for innovations to achieve conflict resolution.

My critique of Lasswell's conception of power, as the focus of inquiry in political science, is that such a conception cuts one off from essential considerations that apply to democratic societies. The focus of citizens in democratic societies needs to be broader, concerned more with the constitution of social orders than with political orders narrowly defined. The same problem applies to the use of economic reasoning narrowly construed to nonmarket decision making. The concept of self-interest associated with maximizing Utility ignores the problem of normative inquiry as fundamental to the constitution of rule-ordered relationships. Hobbes's conception of the power of a man as being his present means to obtain some future apparent good offers a more general analytical focus that takes account of complementary aspects of any problematic situation.

Exercising *power with* others in consensual relationships occurs as each citizen functions amid "republics" of science, "republics" of commerce, and "republics" of rule-ordered relationships as complementary facets of associated relationships. The pathway to peace in self-governing societies requires as much attention in reflecting on where one has been and on narratives about where others have gone before as on the course to take in further steps along the way. We as human beings can never know an ultimate destination. We need to learn to be at home [eco/*oikos*] with others in the pursuit of that which is worth doing in diverse communities and patterns of associated relationships. The universal, public-good characteristics of justice and well-being leave opportunities for each of us to contribute to the common good in our association with others. We need to understand how to configure the ideational, relational, and material aspects of life to realize such potentials.

A Science of Citizenship

I conclude then that Tocqueville's "new science of politics" needed for a "new world" is a science of association that is appropriate to an art of association to be exercised by citizens in self-governing societies. Such a science and art of association would be compatible with the exercise of authority relationships in a system of governance marked by Lasswell's attributes of self-responsibility, impartiality, dispersal of authority, challengeability, voluntarization of relationships, and balance. I also presume that such a science of association is consistent with Dewey's concern for the creation of coherent communities of relationships among inchoate publics in their search for becoming self-conscious, articulate identities. I further presume that such a science and art of association is a way of resolving Bryce's reference to the fallacies associated with the "Will of the People" without resorting to the habit of conceiving the People as One. I know of no way to penetrate the fogs of deception, self-deception, and strategic opportunism and their association with fantasies about heroes, angels, supermen, monsters, and devils except by challengeability and contestability among those bound together in covenantal relationships. These bounds need to be assessed by those who scrutinize the course of events in light of long-term reflections about the past and commitments for the future. I cannot imagine how democratic societies can be sustained without checks and balances in systems of dispersed authority.

We can now understand why Montesquieu viewed using power to check power as essential to lawful republics and why such republics, in using power to check power, depend on the virtues of moral communities that seek to use the opportunities associated with conflict as a means of achieving conflict resolution. We can then understand why Madison proposed that a principle of opposite and rival interests could apply to the constitution of order through the whole system of human affairs, including the supreme powers of the State. These powers can only work with the development of a culture of inquiry in which conflict can be addressed in a problem-solving mode of inquiry rather than in a way that provokes fight-sets where threats and counterthreats easily escalate into violent confrontations. Rhetoric about rage and outrage is the language of violent confrontation, which is not an appropriate prelude to inquiry and the exercise of problem-solving capabilities.

Once we begin to see that the "facts" that we observe in human societies are manifestations of "institutional facts" and "artifacts" constitutive of patterns of order in human societies and all human creations, the whole world in which we function as participants in communities of being begins to take on different potentialities. We begin to understand how such systems can be made to work in building patterns of associated relationships for each of us as we work together in accomplishing achievements worthy of our efforts. These relationships are the grounds for mutual respect, affection, honor, and trust. They are steps that can be taken on a pathway that is open to the possibility of continuing progress. With an appropriate awareness of our own limitations as dwellers in Plato's Cave, we have the potentials for cultivating the Tree of Knowledge in ways that enable us to appreciate that the choices we make always affect the potentials that can be realized and the dangers to be given due consideration. Those who fantasize that they can command others by relying on the power of the cudgel or the sword must sooner or later come to realize that these weapons are tools of destruction. The sanctions appropriate to the basic rudiments of learning can only be exercised by those who are bound together by ties of respect, affection, honor, and trust for one another. People who cannot achieve such relationships cannot become self-governing. They can only tell narratives about their visions and the adventures of others. Many fictions of the mind only achieve the status of false illusions and never become a part of human "reality."

Relying on "brute empiricism" fails to distinguish between any perversity and achievements worthy of emulations. Perverse events construed as "brute empiricism" are likely to evoke a form of razzle-dazzle that sells newspapers, attracts viewers, stimulates notoriety among those seeking to attract attention, and destabilizes human relationships. Giving notoriety to those seeking to attract attention and being tolerant of the intolerable are not compatible with serious inquiry, self-responsibility, impartiality, and the mobilization of problem-solving capabilities. Given the patterns of strategic opportunism that pervade American society and the contemporary world, the first order of priority requires critical reflection on what it means to be a human being struggling to understand, rather than "surfing" through turbulent waves in endless seas of razzle-dazzle. A tap on a button gives another image on the television tube, which allows the viewer to surf from one image to another as though he or she were on a magic carpet with nothing to do but stimulate nerve cells in the brain in much the same way that drugs might be used to stimulate fantasies and induce forms of addiction that poison and stupefy the mind. The tube is as addictive as any drug.

If the "street" is a "jungle" where children fend for themselves, we may be observing patterns of order analogous to Hobbes's State of Nature. Instead of each individual warring on each other individual, we are likely to find patterns of association emerging in which associations struggle to establish control over their turf, war on one another, and offer protection for tribute in their respective turfs as imperial domains.

It is surprising how easy and how early the iron law of oligarchy can come to prevail in street "cultures" and how irrelevant the sonorous slogans and the fighting words of aspiring politicians are in coping with crime in the streets.

What transpires in family, kin, and neighborhood relationships in the first decade of life is apt to be critical in establishing patterns of candor, security, and trust, or their variants, mediated by rudiments of common knowledge, shared communities of understanding, and patterns of identity and accountability. If insecurity, hostility, and distrust begin to prevail as the acquisition of language is accompanied with the basic orientation of oneself to others, the foundations for the "culture" of the "street" are being formed. The fighting words of aspiring politicians merely reinforce the "law of the jungle." Somehow the Way to Peace needs to be recognized as an alternative to War.

The first step on the way to becoming self-governing is to presume that each individual is first one's own governor rather than that one gives up one's right to govern oneself to some sovereign representative as Supreme Authority. One gains one's right to be self-governing by appreciating that human creativity illuminates the larger meaning of Creator and Creation for the dwellers in Plato's Cave. The principles of equal rights and equal liberties would then imply that each citizen reserves to oneself only such authority that one would extend to every other citizen and acknowledges commensurate obligations expressed as duties and exposures.

For such presumptions to become realities depends on the development of a self-conscious awareness that language and the proper uses of language turn on the acquisition of a discriminating judgment of what is appropriate to diverse types of situations. These skills begin to accrue in the early years of childhood. Basic norms expressed in phrases like "take turns," "draw straws," "share and share alike," and "first come, first served" are allocational principles that children learn to apply in appropriate situations. Other principles learned in early childhood include distinguishing between "what is mine" and "what is thine"; understanding what it means to lend, borrow, or trade; discerning how to be helpful to others; discovering how to accomplish a task, or get a job done; and determining how to acquire a skill and how to express oneself in ways that earn the respect and trust of others. These principles need to be taught and learned among those who nurture children, wherever one is at home [eco/oikos] in accruing common knowledge, shared communities of understanding, patterns of social accountability, and mutual trust in one another. It is surprising how early the rudiments can and must be learned for how to become self-governing.

Jean Piaget, in *The Moral Judgment of the Child* ([1932] 1969), viewed the processes for developing standards of moral judgment as being derived from children learning how to play games. His object of study was to observe and reflect on children playing marbles. The first step is to acquire the physical skill in learning how to shoot marbles. The next step is to learn the rules of the game and what it means to play a game in accordance with rules. At this stage, rules are presumed to have an external reality that can be arbitrated by older persons. Another stage is reached in which children learn to modify the rules of a game and to resolve conflict by reference to rules of their own making and by exercising their own standards of judgment. Playing marbles can become an experience in self-governance in the villages of Switzerland or anywhere else in the world. I have observed children in Buenos Aires playing "marbles" with bottle caps and doing so with a skill and companionship worthy of emulation.

I presume that by ten or twelve years of age, children have acquired a sufficiently diverse experience in playing the different games of childhood that they could benefit from a course in the science of citizenship. Such a course could be devised to exemplify each of the rules in Hobbes's Laws of Nature (table 4.1), with the rules viewed as ways to constitute patterns of order in human societies. Objects of inquiry could include how to organize teamwork in playing games involving teams, the place of officials in monitoring games and rendering judgments that meet standards of fairness, the place of leagues and conferences in organizing tournaments, and methods of monitoring, enforcing, and revising rules.

I see no reason why the rudiments in the mathematics of game theory cannot be introduced as early as the introduction to algebra and geometry, to enable students to understand the puzzles associated with social dilemmas, moral hazards, struggles for dominance, the intergenerational loss of memory and continuities, and other basic anomalies that occur in the constitution of order in human societies. The logic of choice in economic contingencies, the logic of choice in establishing the rules of correct reasoning and the warrantability of knowledge, and the logic of choice applicable to both hypothetical and normative contingencies bearing on patterns of rule-ordered relationships appear to me to be no more difficult than the logic of grammar in developing and acquiring knowledgeable standards of literacy in the composition of various forms of literary expression.

How to begin to make the choices pertaining to investments in learning the skills of artisanship appropriate to a meaningful and productive life is a difficult problem that can begin to be resolved in light of the achievements and aspirations of parents, kin, friends, neighbors, and other members in one's own community. The "home," associated with family, neighborhood, and community, has all of those manifestations of the trilateral contingencies that bring together people and place in all that is associated with human creativity, by which I mean the creation, institution, and constitution of patterns of order, marked by efforts to cultivate and to accomplish whatever gets done. Neither children nor adults are just blank pages; all people should always be viewed as participants in communities of being that reflect both genetic and cultural achievements and that combine both potentials and limitations together with the dangers, threats, risks, and burdens that accompany whatever opportunities are pursued.

Family, neighborhood, and community bring together all essential elements in constituting all the diverse aspects of language usages that are constitutive of the matrices of society and contingencies of culture. Life at home, in a neighborhood, and in a community bring together all of those facets that are the focus of concern among the diverse cultural and social sciences and humanities. How *well* the diverse aspects of language usage constitute the matrices of society and contingencies of culture are the critical considerations. A response to the question "How well?" implies reference to multiple criteria pertaining to well-being, not confined to selective measures of success as expressed by the size of bank accounts or of some account identified as "gross national product." Circumstances in which, as Adam Smith asserted, "progress of the division of labour" might yield a condition where "the far greater part of those who live by labour, that is, of the great body of the people . . . , generally becomes as stupid and ignorant as it is possible for a human creature to become" ([1776] n.d., 734) are not compatible with well-functioning societies. Ideational and relational contingencies imply that human and social capital are as important as land, labor, and capital in the political economy of human societies.

The problem of "we" and "they" is embedded in forming teams to play games involving teams. Members of the "we" team have an identity in contrast to those who form the other team: "they." The rules of a fair game apply to both teams. To serve as referee requires the capacity to deal impartially and equally in judging the actions of the players on each team. "We" and "they," in such circumstances, are friends, neighbors, and colleagues in larger sets of relationships, which can be addressed in ways that ameliorate the inconveniences that neighborhood brings and realize the mutual advantage that can accrue in communities of associated relationships. The universality inherent in the human condition can be used to take mutual advantage of whatever opportunities accrue to people in their particular situation, as long as the basic principles applicable to covenantal relationships can be used in a problem-solving mode appropriate to sharing *power with* others, presuming that both "we" and "they" acquire *our* sense of being in relation to a Transcending Other.

I cannot understand how human beings can construct democratic self-governing societies without drawing on the essential experiences of first living in the small traditions of family, neighborhood, and community as places to be cultivated [cultured] as worthy of emulation. Speaking in face-to-face relationships is fundamental to building reciprocity and potentials for trust. Literate vernacular languages open the culture of indigenous communities to a universe that gives immortality to the soul and reaches to an appreciation that Creation and the Source of Creation bring God, man, world, and society into communities of being that can be understood by participants. In such circumstances, the relationships of ideas to deeds acquire meaning. Reform in the sense of modifying systems of authority relationships to secure adaptive potentials is possible under such circumstances. Revolution in the sense of constituting a whole new way of life as a form of Salvation to be undertaken by States relying on a single center of Supreme Authority to exercise command and control over Society is not possible. Human beings are much too clever for that possibility to be realized.

Unfortunately, literate vernacular languages can also run the risk of moving to levels of abstraction in which "affordable housing" has no relationship to keeping a house in working order, being "employed" has no relationship to knowing how to get a job done, "gender" has no relationship to the reproduction of life, and "child care" has no relationship to mammary functions. How we understand ourselves becomes a matter of fantasy. Happiness is associated with the bliss of being spectators watching spectacles without having to think. Such societies cannot successfully reproduce themselves into the indefinite future.

Each person in each generation confronts the deep puzzle posed by Anatol Rapoport when he observed that "to understand something means to see it as a special instance of a general principle, one already known" ([1964] 1969, 210). Rapoport further observes that "understanding a baffling event can come from two sources: (1) discovery of hitherto hidden circumstances which, when revealed, make the event appear expected instead of unexpected and (2) enlargement of one's range of experiences, that is, the range of what is expected." He further asserts, "Once events have been explained, they fit into a *framework* of explanation" (ibid.). Chinua Achebe (1988) might express these relationships by stating that *people create explanations create people.* Or is it the other way around—*explanations create people create explanations?* The human condition is caught up in this rondo of life, with its biological and cultural characteristics played out in Plato's Cave.

I construe Rapoport's comments to mean that one must achieve some significant level of habituation and mastery of knowledge and information to exercise problem-solving capabilities. A substantial effort devoted to education and continued learning is required of citizens if they are to participate effectively in maintaining the viability of democratic civilization. Democratic societies cannot rely on principles of command and control by central authorities as a way of ordering choices. Instead, the structures for processing conflict and achieving conflict resolution are essential to building, modifying, and maintaining democratic ways of life. These structures must be applied to every aspect of life, not confined to something called "politics" narrowly construed.

According to Chinua Achebe's rondo of life—combining people and stories, stories and people—the cycle of life through time involves visions, deeds, and realities. Efforts worthy of emulation had their antecedents in some conception that became the basis for joint efforts and cooperative endeavors. Standards of epistemic, economic, legal, political, and moral judgment enter into feasibility considerations. These considerations always need to be worked out with regard to visions, concepts, designs, and plans within the discrete context of the cultural and ecological circumstances in which efforts worthy of emulation achieve their fit. Knowledge, skill, and intelligibility are required for whatever human beings choose to do.

All of the stories and explanations about all of the diverse "games" [endeavors] of life are of such gigantic proportions that they are reminiscent of Michel Foucault's archaeology of knowledge buried layer upon layer in mammoth accumulations of artifactual remains ([1972] 1982). How to bring these into proportions that can be mastered by each member of each succeeding generation is an immense challenge that can never be adequately resolved. This is why forgetfulness is both the plague and the necessary condition of humanity. Both symbols and their referents need to be well enough known so that thought can be skillfully articulated in actions and in what gets accomplished. This process never ends. Thus, the practice and development of the sciences of citizenship never end. The felicity that we enjoy turns on our successes in continual striving. The adventure has its own rewards. Success in the adventure depends on the mastery of artisanship-artifact relationships, accompanied by a sense of modesty about what can be accomplished by acting alone and a sense of respect for others who contribute so much to what we are able to accomplish with the help of others.

The networks of human relationships extend beyond the horizons of the small traditions of family, neighborhood, and community to other communities of relationships, reaching to global proportions. I can imagine how citizens deeply aware of the essential configurations of relationships in artisanship-artifact relationships might learn to work with others under conditions of common knowledge, shared communities of understanding, agreeable patterns of social accountability, and mutual trust in federated patterns of relationships. They can begin to evolve conditions compatible with a covenantal way of life that reaches to patterns of global proportions. These conditions cannot be achieved by parliamentarians, kings, emperors, or presidents who presume to exercise command and control over others. Enlightened leadership is possible; but an indefinite succession of enlightened leaders among those who struggle to gain positions of preeminence and dominance is not possible.

As a "learned ignoramus," in Ortega y Gassett's terminology, I cannot anticipate when efforts to seek strategic advantage through deception and self-deception in the normal course of political affairs may provoke people to take time out to engage in the level of critical reflection appropriate to reconstituting their lives. Hope is nurtured when people seek to discern the sources of their troubles and seek remedies by constructing communities of relationships consistent with the normative standards to do unto others as you would have others do unto you, to love thy neighbor as thyself, and to honor God above all else. Dangers arise when people place blame on some abstract "they" and lose themselves in spasms of violence while aspiring to do the impossible.

Life as it has emerged on this planet is most improbable. To aspire to the impossible is to presume that people are gods. The creation and maintenance of democratic societies is highly improbable, but not impossible. These circumstances enable people to become self-governing. The power of the sword cannot be abandoned; but it can be cautiously exercised by a due process based on common standards of moral judgment applicable to mutual respect, the warrantability of knowledge, and measures of liberty and justice consistent with standards of fairness. These norms function in choice-making processes among participants in communities of relationships, and these processes are the means for realizing the common knowledge, shared communities of understanding, agreeable patterns of social accountability, and mutual trust that save us from isolation and helplessness.

The cycles of life occur in the relationships of ideas to deeds in ways of life that have potentials for continuity, adaptability, and change. Means-ends relationships are not confined to linear relationships; they reach to cyclical configurations of relationships fit into complex patterns of order that have the potentials for cohering in multiple networks and clusters of relationships. As fallible creatures, we go to heroic efforts to create isolable systems to enable us to reconstitute cyclical networks of relationships; but we are still caught up in rich networks of interactive relationships that we must attempt to understand, appreciate, and cultivate.

Such is the life of dwellers in Plato's Cave. The sciences and arts of association are worthy of being carefully studied and applied by all.

Perhaps, Searle's concluding sentence in *Speech Acts* deserves to be quoted here.

> But the retreat from the committed use of words ultimately must involve a retreat from language itself, for speaking a language . . . consists of performing speech acts according to rules, and there is no separating those speech acts from the commitments that form essential parts of them. (1969, 198)

Commitments to achieving coherence with regard to the relationships of ideas and deeds must be acknowledged and adhered to if we are to understand the meaning of democracy. We have responsibilities in carefully using the purely human creations like languages, knowledge, and just patterns of rule-ordered relationships unencumbered by the constraints of nature. Each of us is required to cope with the constraints of nature common to each of us as the Wolves of the Primates as well as with the burden of making appropriate uses of languages in the social matrices of the ways of life we constitute in whatever we do and achieve. The world as such is not free or just; freedom and justice are human creations that can only be constituted and maintained by learning how to be both free and just. Coping with the vulnerability of democracies among those engaged in the art of manipulation is essential to understanding the meaning of democracy.

Bibliography

Achebe, Chinua. 1988. *Hopes and Impediments: Selected Essays.* New York: Doubleday.

Advisory Commission on Intergovernmental Relations [Ronald J. Oakerson]. 1987. *The Organization of Local Public Economies.* Washington, D.C.: Advisory Commission on Intergovernmental Relations.

———. [Ronald J. Oakerson, Roger B. Parks, and Henry A. Bell]. 1988. *Metropolitan Organization: The St. Louis Case.* Washington, D.C.: Advisory Commission on Intergovernmental Relations.

———. [Roger B. Parks and Ronald J. Oakerson]. 1992. *Metropolitan Organization: The Allegheny County Case.* Washington, D.C.: Advisory Commission on Intergovernmental Relations.

Albert, Hans. 1984. "Modell-Denken und historische Wirklichkeit." In *Oekonomisches Denken und sociale Ordnung,* ed. Hans Albert. Tübingen: J. C. B. Mohr (Paul Siebeck).

Arendt, Hannah. 1965. *On Revolution.* New York: Viking, Compass Books.

Aristotle. 1942. *Politics.* Trans. Benjamin Jowett. New York: Modern Library.

Ashby, W. Ross. 1956. *An Introduction to Cybernetics.* New York: John Wiley.

Atran, Scott, and Douglas L. Medin. 1996. "Knowledge and Action: Cultural Models of Nature and Resource Management in Mesoamerica." Guatemala: Bio-Itzaj Reserve, San Jose-Peten.

Ayittey, George B. N. 1991. *Indigenous African Institutions.* Ardsley-on-Hudson, N.Y.: Transnational Publishers.

Bagehot, Walter. 1908. *Physics and Politics.* New York: D. Appleton and Company.

———. [1865] 1964. *The English Constitution.* Ed. R. H. S. Crossman. London: C. A. Watts.

Bain, Joe S., Richard E. Caves, and Julius Margolis. 1966. *Northern California's Water Industry: The Comparative Efficiency of Public Enterprise in Developing a Scarce Natural Resource.* Baltimore: Johns Hopkins University Press.

Barry, Brian, and Russell Hardin, eds. 1982. *Rational Man and Irrational Society?: An Introduction and Sourcebook.* Beverly Hills: Sage.

Beaumont, Gustave de. [1835] 1958a. "Note on the Social and Political Conditions of the Negro Slaves and of Free People of Color." Appendix A in *Marie, or Slavery in the United States: A Novel of Jacksonian America.* Trans. from the French by Barbara Chapman. Intro. Alvis L. Tinnin, 189–216. Stanford: Stanford University Press.

———. [1835] 1958b. *Marie, or Slavery in the United States: A Novel of Jacksonian America.* Trans. from the French by Barbara Chapman. Intro. Alvis L. Tinnin. Stanford: Stanford University Press.

Bentham, Jeremy. [1823] 1948. *An Introduction to the Principles of Morals and Legislation.* New York: Hafner. The 1823 edition was corrected by the author from the original 1780 publication.

Berman, Harold. 1983. *Law and Revolution: The Formation of the Western Legal Tradition.* Cambridge: Harvard University Press.

Bish, Robert L. 1971. *The Public Economy of Metropolitan Areas.* Chicago: Markham.

Blomquist, William. 1992. *Dividing the Waters: Governing Groundwater in Southern California.* San Francisco: Institute for Contemporary Studies Press.

Bonner, John Tyler. 1980. *The Evolution of Culture in Animals.* Princeton: Princeton University Press.

Boulding, Kenneth E. 1963. "Toward a Pure Theory of Threat Systems." *American Economic Review* 53 (May): 424–34.

Bryce, James. [1888] 1995. *The American Commonwealth.* 2 vols. Indianapolis: Liberty Fund, Liberty Classics.

———. [1921] 1931. *Modern Democracies.* 2 vols. New York: Macmillan.

Buchanan, James M. 1979a. "Natural and Artifactual Man." In *What Should Economists Do?* 93–112. Indianapolis: Liberty.

———. 1979b. *What Should Economists Do?* Indianapolis: Liberty.

Buchanan, James M., and Gordon Tullock. 1962. *The Calculus of Consent: Logical Foundations of Constitutional Democracy.* Ann Arbor: University of Michigan Press.

Butterfield, Fox. 1983. *China: Alive in the Bitter Sea.* London: Coronet.

Cabral, Amilcar. 1973. *Return to the Source: Selected Speeches.* New York: Monthly Review Press.

California Department of Public Works. 1928. *Santa Ana Investigation, Flood Control and Conservation.* Bulletin No. 19. Sacramento: Division of Engineering and Irrigation.

Campbell, Donald T. 1969. "Reforms as Experiments." *American Psychologist* 24, no. 4 (April): 409–29.

Cassirer, Ernst. [1946] 1953. *Language and Myth.* Trans. Susanne K. Langer. New York: Dover.

Chandrasekhar, S. [1987] 1991. *Truth and Beauty: Aesthetics and Motivations in Science.* New Delhi: Penguin.

Chomsky, Noam. 1968. *Language and Mind.* New York: Harcourt, Brace, and World.

Coleman, James S. 1990. *The Foundations of Social Theory.* Cambridge: Harvard University Press.

Commons, John R. [1924] 1968. *Legal Foundations of Capitalism.* Madison: University of Wisconsin Press.

Confucius. [1910] 1937. *The Analects or the Conversations of Confucius with His Disciples and Certain Others.* Trans. William Edward Soothill. London: Oxford University Press, World Classics.

Copeland, Miles. 1969. *The Game of Nations.* London: Weidenfeld and Nicolson.

Cottrell, Arthur. 1988. *China: A Cultural History.* New York: New American Library.

Crawford, Sue E. S., and Elinor Ostrom. 1995. "A Grammar of Institutions." *American Political Science Review* 89, no. 3 (September): 582–600.

Crozier, Michel. 1984. *The Trouble with America: Why the System is Breaking Down.* Berkeley and Los Angeles: University of California Press.

Custine, Marquis de. [1839] 1989. *Empire of the Czar: A Journey through Eternal Russia.* New York: Doubleday.

Dahl, Robert. 1961. *Who Governs? Democracy and Power in an American City.* New Haven: Yale University Press.

Daniell, David. 1994. *William Tyndale: A Biography.* New Haven: Yale University Press.

Dante Alighieri. 1981. *Literature in the Vernacular.* Trans. Sally Purcell. Manchester: Carcanet New Press. Originally written in 1304.

Dardess, John W. 1983. *Confucianism and Autocracy: Professional Elites in the Founding of the Ming Dynasty.* Berkeley and Los Angeles: University of California Press.

Darwin, Charles. [1839] 1958. *The Voyage of the Beagle.* New York: Bantam.

Davidson, Basil. 1992. *The Black Man's Burden: Africa and the Curse of the Nation-State.* New York: Times Books.

Dewey, John. 1927. *The Public and Its Problems.* New York: Holt.

———. 1938. *Logic: The Theory of Inquiry.* New York: Holt.

———. 1946. *The Problems of Men.* New York: Philosophical Library.

Djilas, Milovan. 1957. *The New Class: An Analysis of the Communist System.* New York: Praeger.

———. 1962. *Conversations With Stalin.* New York: Harcourt, Brace, and World.

———. 1969. *The Unperfect Society: Beyond the New Class.* Trans. Dorian Cooke. New York: Harcourt, Brace, and World.

Dos Passos, John. 1963. *Mr. Wilson's War.* London: Hamish Hamilton.

Dosi, Giovanni. 1984. *Technical Change and Industrial Transformation.* New York: St. Martin's.

Duany, Wal. 1992. "Neither Palaces nor Prisons: The Constitution of Order Among the Nuer." Ph.D. diss., Indiana University, Bloomington.

Edgerton, William, ed. 1993. *Memoirs of Peasant Tolstoyans in Soviet Russia.* Bloomington: Indiana University Press.

Elazar, Daniel. 1995. *Covenant and Polity in Biblical Israel.* New Brunswick, N.J.: Transaction.

Elazar, Daniel J., and John Kincaid. 1980. "Covenant, Polity, and Constitutionalism." *Publius* 10, no. 4 (fall), 3–30.

Encyclopaedia Britannica. 1967. Volume XI.

Eucken, Walter. [1940] 1951. *The Foundations of Economics.* Chicago: University of Chicago Press.

Fathy, Hassan. 1973. *Architecture for the Poor: An Experiment in Rural Egypt.* Chicago: University of Chicago Press.

Fodor, Jerry F. 1987. *Psychosemantics: The Problem of Meaning in the Philosophy of Mind.* Cambridge: MIT Press.

Follett, Mary Parker. [1924] 1951. *Creative Experience.* New York: Peter Smith.

Foucault, Michel. [1972] 1982. *The Archaeology of Knowledge and the Discourse on Language.* Trans. A. M. Sheridan Smith. New York: Pantheon.

Freyre, Gilberto. 1946. *The Masters and the Slaves: A Study in the Development of Brazilian Civilization.* New York: Alfred A. Knopf.

———. 1963. *The Mansions and the Shanties: The Making of Modern Brazil.* New York: Alfred A. Knopf.

———. 1970. *Order and Progress: Brazil from Monarchy to Republic.* New York: Alfred A. Knopf.

Fromm, Erich. 1947. *Man for Himself: An Inquiry into the Psychology of Ethics.* New York: Rinehart and Company.

Gambetta, Diego. 1988. *Trust: Making and Breaking Cooperative Relations.* Oxford: Basil Blackwell.

Gasser, Adolph. 1939. *Geschichte der Volksfreiheit und der Demokratie.* Aarau, Switzerland: Verlag H. R. Sauerlaender.

Gerth, H. H., and C. Wright Mills, eds. [1946] 1958. *From Max Weber: Essays in Sociology.* New York: Oxford University Press, Galaxy Books.

Geyl, Pieter. [1932] 1988. *The Revolt of the Netherlands, 1555–1609.* London: Cassell.

———. [1936] 1989. *The Netherlands in the Seventeenth Century, 1609–1648.* London: Cassell.

Grossi, Paolo. [1977] 1981. *An Alternative to Private Property: Collective Property in the Juridical Consciousness of the Nineteenth Century.* Trans. Lydia G. Cochrane. Chicago: University of Chicago Press.

Hamilton, Alexander, John Jay, and James Madison. [1788] n.d. *The Federalist.* Ed. Edward M. Earle. New York: Modern Library.

Harsanyi, John C. 1977. "Rule Utilitarianism and Decision Theory." *Erkenntnis* 11, no. 1 (May): 25–53.

Hayek, Friedrich A. von. 1944. *The Road to Serfdom.* With a foreword by John Chamberlain. Chicago: University of Chicago Press.

———. 1945. "The Use of Knowledge in Society." *American Economic Review* 35 (September): 519–30.

———. 1973. *Rules and Order.* Vol. 1 of *Law, Legislation and Liberty: A New Statement of the Liberal Principles of Justice and Political Economy.* Chicago: University of Chicago Press.

Head, John G. 1962. "Public Goods and Public Policy." *Public Finance* 17, no. 3: 197–219.

Heller, Joseph. 1955. *Catch-22.* New York: Dell.

Hesse, Hermann. [1927] 1963. *Steppenwolf.* Trans. Basil Creighton. New York: Modern Library.

Hobbes, Thomas. [1651] 1960. *Leviathan or the Matter, Forme and Power of a Commonwealth Ecclesiasticall and Civil.* Ed. Michael Oakeshott. Oxford: Basil Blackwell.

Hohfeld, Wesley N. 1964. *Fundamental Legal Conceptions.* Ed. W. W. Cook. New Haven: Yale University Press.

Hume, David. 1948. *Hume's Moral and Political Philosophy.* Ed. Henry D. Aiken. New York: Hafner.

Huxley, Aldous. [1952] 1959. *The Devils of Loudun.* New York: Harper and Brothers, Harper Torchbooks.

———. [1958] 1965. *Brave New World Revisited.* New York: Harper and Row, Perennial Library.

Jencks, Christopher. 1992. *Rethinking Social Policy: Race, Poverty, and the Underclass.* Cambridge: Harvard University Press.

Jillson, Calvin, and Rick K. Wilson. 1994. *Congressional Dynamics: Structure, Coordination, and Choice in the First American Congress, 1774–1789.* Stanford.: Stanford University Press.

Kaminski, Antoni Z. 1992. *An Institutional Theory of Communist Regimes: Design, Function, and Breakdown.* San Francisco: Institute for Contemporary Studies Press.

———. 1996. "The New Polish Regime and the Specter of Economic Corruption." Paper presented at the Woodrow Wilson International Center for Scholars, Smithsonian Institution, Washington, D.C., April 3.

Keller, Helen. [1902] 1965. *The Story of My Life.* New York: Dell.

Keohane, Robert, Michael McGinnis, and Elinor Ostrom. 1993. *Linking Local and Global Commons.* Bloomington: Indiana University, Workshop in Political Theory and Policy Analysis.

Keohane, Robert O., and Elinor Ostrom, eds. 1995. *Local Commons and Global Interdependence: Heterogeneity and Cooperation in Two Domains.* London: Sage.

Khaldûn, Ibn. 1967. *The Muqaddimah: An Introduction to History.* Trans. Franz Rosenthal. Abridged ed. Princeton: Princeton University Press. Originally written, in Arabic, in 1377.

King, Martin Luther. 1967. "Letter from Birmingham Jail." In *Politics in the Metropolis,* eds. Thomas R. Dye and Brett W. Hawkins. Columbus, Ohio: Charles E. Merrill.

Kirzner, Israel M. 1973. *Competition and Entrepreneurship.* Chicago: University of Chicago Press.

Kiser, Larry L., and Elinor Ostrom. 1982. "The Three Worlds of Action: A Metatheoretical Synthesis of Institutional Approaches." In *Strategies of Political Inquiry,* ed. Elinor Ostrom, 179–222. Beverly Hills: Sage.

Kjekshus, Helge. 1977. *Ecology Control and Economic Development in East African History: The Case of Tanganyika 1850–1950.* Berkeley and Los Angeles: University of California Press.

Knight, Frank H. [1921] 1971. *Risk, Uncertainty, and Profit.* With an introduction by George J. Stigler. Chicago: University of Chicago Press.

Koestler, Arthur. 1959. *The Sleepwalkers: A History of Man's Changing Vision of the Universe.* New York: Macmillan.

[*Koran*] *The Holy Qur-ān. English translation of the meanings and Commentary.*

n.d. Rev. and ed. by the Presidency of Islamic Researches, IFTA, Call and Guidance. Al-Madinah Al-Munawarah: King Fahd Holy Qur-ān Printing Complex.

Kropotkin, Peter. [1902] 1972. *Mutual Aid: A Factor of Evolution.* Ed. Paul Avrich. New York: New York University Press.

Lachmann, Ludwig M. 1978. *Capital and Its Structure.* Kansas City, Mo.: Sheed Andrews and McMeel.

Landa, Janet Tai. 1987. "The Economics of Trust, Ethnicity, and Identity: Beyond Markets and Hierarchies." Paper presented at the annual meeting of the Public Choice Society, Tucson, Ariz., March 27–28.

———. 1994. *Trust, Ethnicity, and Identity: Beyond the New Institutional Economics of Ethnic Trading Networks, Contract Law, and Gift-Exchange.* Ann Arbor: University of Michigan Press.

Langer, Susanne K. 1972. *Mind: An Essay on Human Feeling.* Vol. 1. Baltimore: Johns Hopkins University Press.

Lasswell, Harold D., and Abraham Kaplan. 1950. *Power and Society: A Framework for Political Inquiry.* New Haven: Yale University Press.

Lenin, V. I. [1902] 1932. *What Is to Be Done?* New York: International Publishers.

Lilienthal, David E. 1945. *TVA: Democracy on the March.* New York: Pocket.

Lippmann, Walter. 1955. *The Public Philosophy.* New York: New American Library, Mentor Books.

Liu, Yichang. 1994. "The Development Trends in the Public Administration in China in the 1990s." Paper presented at the international conference "Quest for Excellence: Public Administration in the Nineties," Hong Kong, February 25–26.

Loveman, Brian. 1976. *Struggle in the Countryside: Politics and Rural Labor in Chile, 1919–1973.* Bloomington: Indiana University Press.

———. 1993. *The Constitution of Tyranny: Regimes of Exception in Spanish America.* Pittsburgh: University of Pittsburgh Press.

Machiavelli, Niccolò. 1940. *The Prince and The Discourses.* Trans. Luigi Ricci. Revised by E. R. P. Vincent. With an introduction by Max Lerner. New York: Modern Library. Originally written, in Italian, in 1513.

Machlup, Fritz. 1962. *The Production and Distribution of Knowledge in the United States.* Princeton: Princeton University Press.

Magassa, Hamidou. 1992. "Bambara-Mandingo Islamization through the Western Sudan Empires and Kingdoms (Religion and Cultures Relationships)." Paper presented at the miniconference of the Workshop in Political Theory and Policy Analysis, Indiana University, Bloomington, May 2 and 4.

Magnet, Myron. 1993. *The Dream and the Nightmare: The Sixties' Legacy to the Underclass.* New York: William Morrow and Company.

Mahdi, Muhsin. 1964. *Ibn Khaldûn's Philosophy of History: A Study in the Philosophic Foundation of the Science of Culture.* Chicago: University of Chicago Press.

Maine, Henry Sumner. [1861] 1864. *Ancient Law: Its Connection with the Early History of Society, and Its Relation to Modern Ideas.* New York: Henry Holt & Company.

Mannheim, Karl. 1936. *Ideology and Utopia: An Introduction to the Sociology of Knowledge.* Trans. Louis Wirth and Edward Shils. New York: Harcourt, Brace.

Marais, Eugène. 1969. *The Soul of the Ape.* With an introduction by Robert Ardrey. New York: Atheneum.

Marvick, Dwaine, ed. 1977. *Harold D. Lasswell on Political Sociology.* Chicago: University of Chicago Press.

Marx, Karl, and Friedrich Engels. [1848] 1967. *The Communist Manifesto.* With an introduction by A. J. P. Taylor. Harmondsworth, England: Penguin.

McCarry, Brian E. 1993/94. "Organic Contaminants in Hamilton Harbour Sediments." In *The Ecowise Seminar Series,* 54–60. Hamilton, Ontario: McMaster University, McMaster Eco-Research Program for Hamilton Harbour.

McPhee, John. [1984] 1991. *La Place de la Concorde Suisse.* New York: Noonday.

Michels, Robert. [1911] 1966. *Political Parties: A Sociological Study of the Oligarchical Tendencies of Modern Democracy.* Ed. S. M. Lipset. New York: Free Press.

Montesquieu, Charles Louis de Secondat. [1748] 1966. *The Spirit of the Laws.* New York: Hafner.

Morris, Ralph D. 1993/94. "Gulls and Terns on the Great Lakes: How Important are the Hamilton Harbour Colonies?" In *The Ecowise Seminar Series,* 42–53. Hamilton, Ontario: McMaster University, McMaster Eco-Research Program for Hamilton Harbour.

Murray, Charles A. 1984. *Losing Ground: American Social Policy, 1950–1980.* New York: Basic.

Netting, Robert McC. 1993. *Smallholders, Householders: Farm Families and the Ecology of Intensive, Sustainable Agriculture.* Stanford: Stanford University Press.

North, Douglass C. 1990. *Institutions, Institutional Change, and Economic Performance.* New York: Cambridge University Press.

Oakerson, Ronald J. 1992. "Analyzing the Commons: A Framework." In *Making the Commons Work: Theory, Practice, and Policy,* ed. Daniel W. Bromley et al., 41–59. San Francisco: Institute for Contemporary Studies Press.

O'Brien, David J. 1975. *Neighborhood Organization and Interest-Group Processes.* Princeton: Princeton University Press.

Olson, Mancur. 1965. *The Logic of Collective Action: Public Goods and the Theory of Groups.* Cambridge: Harvard University Press.

Ortega y Gasset, José. [1932] 1957. *The Revolt of the Masses.* Twenty-fifth anniversary ed. New York: Norton.

Orwell, George. [1949] 1983. *1984.* New York: Penguin, Signet Classics.

Ostrogorski, Moisei. [1902] 1964. *Democracy and the Organization of Political Parties.* 2 vols. Edited and abridged by S. M. Lipset. Garden City, N.Y.: Doubleday, Anchor Books.

Ostrom, Elinor. 1989. "Microconstitutional Change in Multiconstitutional Political Systems." *Rationality and Society* 1, no. 1 (July): 11–50.

———. 1990. *Governing the Commons: The Evolution of Institutions for Collective Action.* New York: Cambridge University Press.

————. 1992. *Crafting Institutions for Self-Governing Irrigation Systems.* San Francisco: Institute for Contemporary Studies Press.

Ostrom, Elinor, Roy Gardner, and James Walker. 1994. *Rules, Games, and Common-Pool Resources.* Ann Arbor: University of Michigan Press.

Ostrom, Vincent. 1953. *Water and Politics: A Study of Water Policies and Administration in the Development of Los Angeles.* Los Angeles: Haynes Foundation.

————. 1968. "Water Resource Development: Some Problems in Economic Political Analysis of Public Policy." In *Political Science and Public Policy,* ed. Austin Ranney, 123–50. Chicago: Markham.

————. 1971. *Institutional Arrangements for Water Resource Development—With Special Reference to the California Water Industry.* Springfield, Va.: National Technical Information Service.

————. [1971] 1987. *The Political Theory of a Compound Republic: Designing the American Experiment.* 2d ed., rev. and enlarged. San Francisco: Institute for Contemporary Studies Press.

————. [1973] 1989. *The Intellectual Crisis in American Public Administration.* 2d ed. Tuscaloosa: University of Alabama Press.

————. 1991. *The Meaning of American Federalism: Constituting a Self-Governing Society.* San Francisco: Institute for Contemporary Studies Press.

————. [1988] 1993. "Cryptoimperialism, Predatory States, and Self-Governance." In *Rethinking Institutional Analysis and Development: Issues, Alternatives, and Choices,* ed. Vincent Ostrom, David Feeny, and Hartmut Picht, 43–68. San Francisco: Institute for Contemporary Studies Press.

Ostrom, Vincent, David Feeny, and Hartmut Picht, eds. [1988] 1993. *Rethinking Institutional Analysis and Development: Issues, Alternatives, and Choices.* 2d ed. San Francisco: Institute for Contemporary Studies Press.

Ostrom, Vincent, and Elinor Ostrom. 1977. "Public Goods and Public Choices." In *Alternatives for Delivering Public Services: Toward Improved Performance,* ed. E. S. Savas, 7–49. Boulder, Colo.: Westview.

Ostrom, Vincent, Charles M. Tiebout, and Robert Warren. 1961. "The Organization of Government in Metropolitan Areas: A Theoretical Inquiry." *American Political Science Review* 55 (December): 831–42.

Palmer, R. R., ed. 1987. *The Two Tocquevilles: Father and Son.* Princeton: Princeton University Press.

Patterson, David, ed. 1992. *The Gospel According to Tolstoy.* Trans. D. Patterson. Tuscaloosa: University of Alabama Press.

Peter of Mladonovice. [1451] 1965. *John Hus at the Council of Constance.* Trans. and intro. Matthew Spinka. New York: Columbia University Press.

Piaget, Jean. [1932] 1969. *The Moral Judgment of the Child.* New York: Free Press.

Pipes, Richard. 1974. *Russia under the Old Regime.* New York: Charles Scribner's Sons.

Polanyi, Michael. 1962. *Personal Knowledge: Toward a Post-Critical Philosophy.* Chicago: University of Chicago Press.

Popkin, Samuel. 1979. *The Rational Peasant.* Berkeley and Los Angeles: University of California Press.

Popper, Karl R. [1945] 1963. *The Open Society and Its Enemies.* 2 vols. New York: Harper and Row.

———. 1967. "Rationality and the Status of the Rationality Principle." In *Le fondements philosophiques des systèms économiques: Textes de Jacques Rueff et essais rédigés en son honneur,* ed. E. M. Classen, 145–50. Paris: Payot.

———. 1972. *Objective Knowledge: An Evolutionary Approach.* Oxford: Clarendon.

Proudhon, Pierre-Joseph. [1863] 1979. *The Principle of Federation.* Trans. with intro. Richard Vernon. Toronto: University of Toronto Press.

Pylkkänen, Paavo, ed. 1989. *The Search for Meaning: The New Spirit in Science and Philosophy.* Northamptonshire, England: Crucible.

Rapoport, Anatol. [1964] 1969. *Strategy and Conscience.* New York: Schocken.

Rheinstein, Max. 1967. *Max Weber on Law in Economy and Society.* New York: Simon and Schuster, Clarion Books.

Riker, William H. 1986. *The Art of Manipulation.* New Haven: Yale University Press.

Rousseau, Jean-Jacques. [1762] 1978. *On the Social Contract.* Trans. R. D. and J. R. Masters. Ed. Roger D. Masters. New York: St. Martin's.

Sabetti, Filippo. 1984. *Political Authority in a Sicilian Village.* New Brunswick: Rutgers University Press.

Samuelson, Paul A. 1954. "The Pure Theory of Public Expenditure." *Review of Economics and Statistics* 36:387–9.

Samuelson, Robert J. 1995. *The Good Life and Its Discontents: The American Dream in the Age of Entitlement, 1945–1995.* New York: Times Books.

Sawyer, Amos. 1992. *The Emergence of Autocracy in Liberia: Tragedy and Challenge.* San Francisco: Institute for Contemporary Studies Press.

Schaffer, Ronald. 1991. *America in the Great War: The Rise of the War Welfare State.* New York: Oxford University Press.

Schlager, Edella, and Elinor Ostrom. 1992. "Property-Rights Regimes and Natural Resources: A Conceptual Analysis." *Land Economics* 68, no. 3 (August): 249–62.

Schultz, Theodore W. 1961. "Education and Economic Growth." In *Social Forces Influencing American Education,* ed. Nelson B. Henry, 46–88. Chicago: University of Chicago Press.

Scott, James C. 1976. *The Moral Economy of the Peasant: Rebellion and Subsistence in Southeast Asia.* New Haven: Yale University Press.

Searle, John R. 1969. *Speech Acts: An Essay in the Philosophy of Language.* New York: Cambridge University Press.

Selten, Reinhard. 1986. "Institutional Utilitarianism." In *Guidance, Control, and Evaluation in the Public Sector,* ed. F. X. Kaufmann, G. Majone, and V. Ostrom, 251–63. Berlin and New York: Walter de Gruyter.

Sen, A. K. 1977. "Rational Fools: A Critique of the Behavioral Foundations of Economic Theory." *Philosophy and Public Affairs* 6 (summer): 317–44.

Siedentopf, Larry. 1994. *Tocqueville.* Oxford and New York: Oxford University Press.

Simon, Herbert A. 1946. "The Proverbs of Administration." *Public Administration Review* 6 (winter): 53–67.

———. [1969] 1981. *The Sciences of the Artificial.* 2d ed. Cambridge: MIT Press.

Slater, Philip. 1991. *A Dream Deferred: America's Discontent and the Search for a New Democratic Ideal.* Boston: Beacon.

Smith, Adam. [1759] n.d. *The Theory of Moral Sentiments.* Indianapolis: Liberty.

———. [1776] n.d. *The Wealth of Nations.* London: Ward, Lock, and Tyler.

Smith, Vernon. 1991. "Rational Choice: The Contrast between Economics and Psychology." *Journal of Political Economy* 99, no. 4: 877–97.

Solzhenitsyn, Aleksandr I. 1979. *The Gulag Archipelago, 1918–1956: An Experiment in Literary Investigation.* 3 vols. New York: Harper and Row, Perennial Library.

Soto, Hernando de. 1989. *The Other Path: The Invisible Revolution in the Third World.* New York: Harper and Row.

Soyinka, Wole. 1988. "Twice Bitten: The Fate of Africa's Culture Producers." In *Development and Culture,* by Wole Soyinka and Junzo Kawada, 1–24. New York: Africa Leadership Forum.

Soyinka, Wole, and Junzo Kawada. 1988. *Development and Culture.* Discussions of the Inaugural Programme of the Africa Leadership Forum held in Ota, Nigeria, October 24–November 1. New York: Africa Leadership Forum.

Sproule-Jones, Mark. 1993. *Governments at Work: Canadian Parliamentary Federalism and Its Public Policy Effects.* Toronto: University of Toronto Press.

Stein, Robert. 1990. *Urban Alternatives: Public and Private Markets in the Provision of Local Services.* Pittsburgh: University of Pittsburgh Press.

Sundquist, James L. 1969. *Making Federalism Work: A Study of Program Coordination at the Local Level.* Washington, D.C.: Brookings Institution.

Taha, Mahmoud Mohamed. [1967] 1987. *The Second Message of Islam.* Trans. Abdullahi Ahmed An-Na'im. New York: Syracuse University Press.

Tang, Shui Yan. 1992. *Institutions and Collective Action: Self-Governance in Irrigation.* San Francisco: Institute for Contemporary Studies Press.

Tao, Julia. 1990. "The Chinese Moral Ethos and the Concept of Individual Rights." *Journal of Applied Philosophy* 7, no. 2: 119–27.

Teilhard de Chardin, Pierre. [1955] 1965. *The Phenomenon of Man.* New York: Harper and Row, Harper Torchbooks.

Thomson, James T. 1992. *A Framework for Analyzing Institutional Incentives in Community Forestry.* Rome: Food and Agriculture Organization of the United Nations.

Tierney, Brian. 1982. *Religion, Law, and the Growth of Constitutional Thought, 1150–1650.* Cambridge: Cambridge University Press.

Tocqueville, Alexis de. [1835–40] 1945. *Democracy in America.* 2 vols. Ed. Phillips Bradley. New York: Alfred A. Knopf.

———. [1856] 1955. *The Old Regime and the French Revolution.* Trans. Stuart Gilbert. Garden City, N.Y.: Doubleday, Anchor Books.

———. [1893] 1959. *The Recollections of Alexis de Tocqueville.* Trans. Alexander Teixeira de Mattos. Ed. and intro. J. P. Mayer. New York: Meridian Books.

Todorov, Tzvetan. 1982. *Theories of the Symbol*. Trans. Catherine Porter. Ithaca, N.Y.: Cornell University Press.

———. 1984. *The Conquest of America: The Question of the Other*. Trans. from the French by Richard Howard. New York: Harper and Row, Colophon Books.

Toth, Nicholas, Desmond Clark, and Giancarlo Ligabue. 1992. "The Last Stone Ax Makers." *Scientific American* 267, no. 1 (July): 88–93.

Tucker, Robert C., ed. [1972] 1978. *The Marx-Engels Reader*. 2d ed. New York: Norton.

Tullock, Gordon. 1965. *The Politics of Bureaucracy*. Washington, D.C.: Public Affairs Press.

Turchin, V. F. 1977. *The Phenomenon of Science*. New York: Columbia University Press.

Turgenev, Ivan S. [1861] 1939. *Fathers and Sons*. New York: Bantam.

Voegelin, Eric. 1952. *The New Science of Politics: An Introduction*. Chicago: University of Chicago Press.

———. 1956. *Israel and Revelation*. Vol. 1, *Order and History*. Baton Rouge: Louisiana State University Press.

———. 1957. *The World of the Polis*. Vol. 2, *Order and History*. Baton Rouge: Louisiana State University Press.

———. 1975. *From Enlightenment to Revolution*. Ed. John H. Hallowell. Durham, N.C.: Duke University Press.

Waal, Frans B. M. de. 1996. *Good Natured: The Origins of Right and Wrong in Humans and Other Animals*. Cambridge: Harvard University Press.

Wallas, Graham. 1914. *The Great Society: A Psychological Analysis*. New York: Macmillan.

Williamson, Oliver. 1975. *Markets and Hierarchies: Analysis and Antitrust Implications*. New York: Free Press.

———. 1993. "Calculativeness, Trust, and Economic Organization." Part 2. *Journal of Law and Economics* 36, no. 1 (April): 453–86.

Wilson, Woodrow. 1887. "The Study of Administration." *Political Science Quarterly* 2 (June): 197–220.

———. [1885] 1956. *Congressional Government: A Study in American Politics*. New York: Meridian.

Wright, Georg Henrik von. 1951. "Deontic Logic." *Mind* 60:48–74.

———. 1963. *Norms and Action. A Logical Enquiry*. London: Routledge and Kegan Paul.

Wunsch, James S., and Dele Olowu, eds. [1990] 1995. *The Failure of the Centralized State: Institutions and Self-Governance in Africa*. 2d ed. San Francisco: Institute for Contemporary Studies Press.

Yang, Tai-Shuenn. 1987. "Property Rights and Constitutional Order in Imperial China." Ph.D. diss., Indiana University, Bloomington.

Zweig, Stefan. 1933. *Marie Antoinette: The Portrait of an Average Woman*. Trans. Eden Paul and Cedar Paul. New York: Viking.

Index